Integrated Curriculum for Young Children

Early Childhood Education

Virginia Harmelink

Early Childhood Faculty and Education Department Head
Pima Community College
Tucson, Arizona

Publisher
The Goodheart-Willcox Company, Inc.
Tinley Park, IL
www.g-w.com

Copyright © 2025
by
The Goodheart-Willcox Company, Inc.

All rights reserved. No part of this work may be reproduced, stored, or transmitted in any form or by any electronic or mechanical means, including information storage and retrieval systems, except as permitted by U.S. copyright law, without the prior written permission of The Goodheart-Willcox Company, Inc.

ISBN 978-1-63776-751-1

1 2 3 4 5 6 7 8 9 – 25– 27 26 25 24 23

The Goodheart-Willcox Company, Inc. Brand Disclaimer: Brand names, company names, and illustrations for products and services included in this text are provided for educational purposes only and do not represent or imply endorsement or recommendation by the author or the publisher.

The Goodheart-Willcox Company, Inc. Safety Notice: The reader is expressly advised to carefully read, understand, and apply all safety precautions and warnings described in this book or that might also be indicated in undertaking the activities and exercises described herein to minimize risk of personal injury or injury to others. Common sense and good judgment should also be exercised and applied to help avoid all potential hazards. The reader should always refer to the appropriate manufacturer's technical information, directions, and recommendations; then proceed with care to follow specific equipment operating instructions. The reader should understand these notices and cautions are not exhaustive.

The publisher makes no warranty or representation whatsoever, either expressed or implied, including but not limited to equipment, procedures, and applications described or referred to herein, their quality, performance, merchantability, or fitness for a particular purpose. The publisher assumes no responsibility for any changes, errors, or omissions in this book. The publisher specifically disclaims any liability whatsoever, including any direct, indirect, incidental, consequential, special, or exemplary damages resulting, in whole or in part, from the reader's use of or reliance upon the information, instructions, procedures, warnings, cautions, applications, or other matter contained in this book. The publisher assumes no responsibility for the activities of the reader.

The Goodheart-Willcox Company, Inc. Internet Disclaimer: The Internet resources and listings in this Goodheart-Willcox Publisher product are provided solely as a convenience to you. These resources and listings were reviewed at the time of publication to provide you with accurate, safe, and appropriate information. Goodheart-Willcox Publisher has no control over the referenced websites and, due to the dynamic nature of the Internet, is not responsible or liable for the content, products, or performance of links to other websites or resources. Goodheart-Willcox Publisher makes no representation, either expressed or implied, regarding the content of these websites, and such references do not constitute an endorsement or recommendation of the information or content presented. It is your responsibility to take all protective measures to guard against inappropriate content, viruses, or other destructive elements.

Image Credits. Front cover (clockwise from top left): MartinPrescott/E+ via Getty Images, Avalon_Studio/E+ via Getty Images, SDI Productions/E+ via Getty Images, FatCamera/E+ via Getty Images; Back cover: BraunS/Royalty-Free/Getty Images +

Printed in Canada

PREFACE

Integrated Curriculum for Young Children is more than a book about curriculum development. It is a comprehensive focus on creating engaging experiences using backward design that includes daily learning plans, connections to state early learning standards, and authentic assessment.

Integrated Curriculum for Young Children is written for future and beginning educators, and it is also useful for veteran teachers who teach children 0–8 years of age. For the beginning educator, this text will provide guidance on integrating the academic disciplines that can be applied using a variety of approaches while applying the foundations of age-, individually-, and culturally-appropriate teaching and learning. For the veteran teacher, this text will encourage exploration of differentiated instruction and integration of core learning experiences and approaches, drawing upon their current practices.

This text is an invitation to explore the richness and diversity that builds on developmentally appropriate practice (DAP) in the early childhood years via an integrated curriculum. Individual academic areas are taught in a spirit of combining or integrating two or more subject areas into one experience that aligns to authentic assessment and standards. Learning from across the world is sprinkled throughout the text to show theory-to-practice applications and reflect different approaches and choices that are available for teachers of young children.

Where there are challenges, there are opportunities to innovate. Integration of academic subject matter takes additional time to plan and is dynamic, as young learners arrive at different places based on their prior experiences. This requires teachers to be flexible and creative. However, as you become more aware of the advantages of integrating academic subjects, the connections between learning outcomes, standards, and integrated subjects become increasingly clear and achievable. An integrated curriculum allows children to pursue learning in a holistic way, without the restrictions often imposed by subject or standards boundaries.

This text provides authentic examples that illustrate a variety of early childhood practices and reflect on how teachers can implement true integration of materials throughout the learning areas (also known as learning centers or learning spaces). The early chapters focus on theory, DAP, creating community, and engaging the family. Examples provide tools to help with planning, then move to create strong outcomes that integrating academic subjects, form authentic assessment, and align to standards. Part 2 provides students with an opportunity to reflect on what they have learned. The inclusion of the academic content areas across the 0–8 years is the focus of Part 3. I hope you enjoy the book!

For the Children,

Ginny Harmelink

ABOUT THE AUTHOR

Ginny Harmelink has spent her life working with children and families. She is currently an early childhood faculty and department head at Pima Community College in Tucson, Arizona.

Ginny grew up in Wyoming, where she went on to operate the first nationally accredited home childcare program in the state for 17 years. She was also the director of professional development at the statewide resource and referral agency for five years while working on a graduate degree in early childhood education from the University of Wyoming.

Shortly after accepting a faculty position in Arizona, Ginny led the college's pursuit for achieving national accreditation at the college level. She also spent a semester on sabbatical in Israel, where she studied critical thinking and early literacy.

Creating positive learning experiences has always been Ginny's goal, and she continues to embed this value into the coursework she creates for college students pursuing early childhood degrees. Pulling from many theories of development and learning, Ginny believes that the integration of subjects and intentional focus on assessment provide evidence that supports the child in being the driver of their own learning.

This text features a solid foundation of DAP, play, community, and theory as the basis for planning curriculum using a framework called backward design. Images used throughout the text include early childhood classrooms from across the world and are meant to inspire future teachers who also believe that children are the spirit of the community.

REVIEWERS

The author and publisher wish to thank the following industry and teaching professionals for their valuable input into the development of *Integrated Curriculum for Young Children*.

Joanne Baham
Hill College
Cleburne, Texas

Ginger Harris Bartholomew
Central Carolina Community College
Sanford, North Carolina

Beverly Bennett-Roberts
University of the District of Columbia
Washington, DC

Terry Bridger
College of Southern Maryland
La Plata, Maryland

Katie Champlin
Des Moines Area Community College
Ankeny, Iowa

Channell Cook
Lee College
Baytown, Texas

Dr. Lisa Taylor Cook
Tarleton State University
Stephenville, Texas

Dawn Cross
Flordia Gateway College
Lake City, Florida

Amanda Deliman, PhD
Utah State University
Logan, Utah

Heather Donoho
Iowa State University
Ames, Iowa

Jannice Ellen
Community College of Vermont
Winooski, Vermont

Jennifer Forker
Hutchinson Community College
Hutchinson, Kansas

Jill E. Gelomino
St. Joseph's College
New York, New York

April M. Grace
Madisonville Community College
Madisonville, Kentucky

Amy Huebner
St. Philip's College
San Antonio, Texas

Jamileth Jarquin
Miami Dade College
Miami, Florida

Wendy Koile
Central Ohio Technical College
Newark, Ohio

Laura Kujo
Borough of Manhattan Community College
New York, New York

Christine A.B. Maier
Dean College
Franklin, Massachusetts

Annmarie Malchenson
Harrisburg Area Community College
Harrisburg, Pennsylvania

Amanda McPherson
Pima Community College
Tucson, Arizona

Kerry Belknap Morris
River Valley Community College
Claremont, New Hampshire

Dawn S. Munson
Elgin Community College
Elgin, Illinois

Martha J. Page
Elizabethtown Community and Technical College
Elizabethtown, Kentucky

Kristen Pickering
Ivy Tech Community College
East Chicago, Indiana

Jennifer Roberts
Gwinnet Technical College
Gwinnett County, Georgia

Ardythe Rodriguez
Riverside Community College District
Riverside, California

Rita Rzezuski
Bunker Hill Community College
Boston, Massachusetts

Tammy Schrickel
Washburn University Institute of Technology
Topeka, Kansas

Clover Simms Wright
California University of Pennsylvania
California, Pennsylvania

Heidi Broad Smith
Northern Maine Community College
Presque Isle, Maine

Jacque Taylor
Greenville Technical College
Greenville, South Carolina

Catherine Twyman
Daytona State College
Daytona Beach, Florida

Seungyoun Ward
Troy University
Troy, Alabama

Laurie Westcott
Manchester Community College
Manchester, New Hampshire

Lisa White
Athens Technical College
Athens, Georgia

Dr. Brenda K. Williamson
Durham Technical Community College
Durham, North Carolina

ACKNOWLEDGMENTS

The author and publisher would like to thank the following companies, organizations, and individuals for their contribution of resource material, images, or other support in the development of *Integrated Curriculum for Young Children*.

Lisa Atkinson, Martongate Primary School, Yorkshire, United Kingdom
The Bluebird Class, Mis Manos Montessori, Tucson, AZ
Child-Parent Centers; Prince Head Start, Tucson, AZ
City Kids, Tel Aviv, Israel
Creer School, Guadalajara, Mexico
Danielle Dittmer, Evan Yehuda, Israel
Julia Eastes, Casper, WY
Adriana Franklin, The Sandbox, Fortaleza, Brazil
Laura Hintze, Little Cherub's Preschool, Spring Arbor, MI
Jennifer Hook, Creation Preschool, Vail, AZ
Holly Karlsen, Next Generation Learning Center, Manistee, MI
Deb Lawrence, Delaware County Community College, Media, PA
Kim Lewis, Tucson Waldorf School, Tucson, AZ
Patty Meritt, University of Alaska Early Childhood Lab School, Fairbanks, AK
Shelby Miskimins, Foundations Early Care and Education, Casper, WY
Lisa Morley, Westshore Community College, Scottville, MI
Debra Riordan, Southlake Montessori, Southlake, TX
Lauren Ryan, Childspace, Wellington, New Zealand
Robin Stirling, Sandbox Early Learning Center, Tucson, AZ
R. Taylor, Chemeketa Community College Child Development Laboratory, Salem, OR
Audrey and Don Wood, Hilo, HI
Kate Yeomans, Merrohawke Nature School, Boxford, MA

TOOLS FOR STUDENT AND INSTRUCTOR SUCCESS

Student Tools

Student Text

Integrated Curriculum for Young Children highlights how two or more subject areas can be integrated into one experience that aligns to authentic assessment and standards. This comprehensive text walks students through the fundamentals of an integrated curriculum while correlating to NAEYC's developmentally appropriate practices for learners ages 0–8. The author explores how several existing programs implement integrated curriculum, then offers real-world advice on how future and current teachers can put these methods to practice in the classroom.

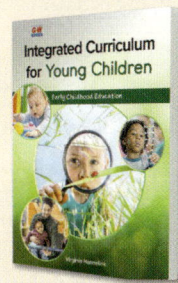

The text periodically showcases learning examples and images from around the world to show theory-to-practice applications and to reflect different approaches and choices that are available for teachers of young children. The initial section lays the important foundations necessary when creating curriculum; the middle section walks students through writing daily learning plans that include backward design; the final section focuses on state standards for students to concentrate on when writing curriculum.

G-W Digital Companion

- E-flash cards and vocabulary exercises allow interaction with content to create opportunities to increase achievement.

Video Library

- Videos assets enrich learning by capturing authentic examples of physical, cognitive, and social-emotional development of children. The videos were created in a developmentally appropriate learning environment and are rich in examples of childcare best practices and effective classroom design. Videos are accompanied by assignable quiz questions that challenge students to identify the skill, stage of development, or best-practice endeavor that is being displayed in the video and think critically about the content.

Instructor Tools

LMS Integration

Integrate Goodheart-Willcox content within your Learning Management System for a seamless user experience for both you and your students. EduHub LMS–ready content in Common Cartridge® format facilitates single sign-on integration and gives you control of student enrollment and data. With a Common Cartridge integration, you can access the LMS features and tools you are accustomed to using and G-W course resources in one convenient location—your LMS.

G-W Common Cartridge provides a complete learning package for you and your students. The included digital resources help your students remain engaged and learn effectively:

- **Digital Textbook**
- **Videos**
- **Drill and Practice** vocabulary activities

When you incorporate G-W content into your courses via Common Cartridge, you have the flexibility to customize and structure the content to meet the educational needs of your students. You may also choose to add your own content to the course.

For instructors, the Common Cartridge includes the Online Instructor Resources. QTI® question banks are available within the Online Instructor Resources for import into your LMS. These prebuilt assessments help you measure student knowledge and track results in your LMS gradebook. Questions and tests can be customized to meet your assessment needs.

Online Instructor Resources

- The **Instructor Resources** provide instructors with time-saving preparation tools such as answer keys, editable lesson plans, and other teaching aids.
- **Instructor's Presentations for PowerPoint®** are fully customizable, richly illustrated slides that help you teach and visually reinforce the key concepts from each chapter.
- Administer and manage assessments to meet your classroom needs using **Assessment Software with Question Banks**, which include hundreds of matching, completion, multiple choice, and short answer questions to assess student knowledge of the content in each chapter.

See https://www.g-w.com/integrated-curriculum-for-young-children-2025 for a list of all available resources.

Professional Development

- Expert content specialists
- Research-based pedagogy and instructional practices
- Options for virtual and in-person Professional Development

FEATURES OF THE TEXTBOOK

The instructional design of this textbook includes student-focused learning tools to help you succeed. This visual guide highlights these features.

Chapter-Opening Materials

Each chapter opener contains a list of learning outcomes, a list of key terms, a scenario-based "Snapshot" feature, and an introduction. The **Learning Outcomes** clearly identify the knowledge and skills to be gained when the chapter is completed. **Key Terms** list the key words to be learned in the chapter. **Snapshot Features** introduce students to real-life challenges that teachers face and provide critical-thinking questions that encourage students to brainstorm solutions. The **Introduction** provides an overview and preview of the chapter content.

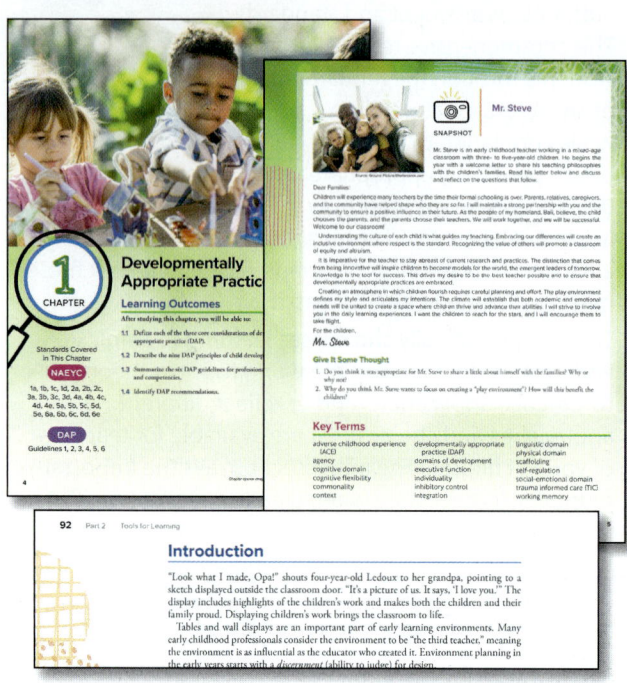

Additional Features

Additional features are used throughout the body of each chapter to further learning and knowledge. **Checkpoints** support reflection and knowledge after major chapter sections. **The Teacher's Lens** provides advice and guidance that is especially applicable for on-the-job situations. **Stop and Think** highlights critical thinking questions that are designed to spark classroom discussions. **Real-World Classroom** introduces content and photographs that describe practical application of educational theories in classrooms all around the world.

Illustrations

Illustrations have been designed to communicate the specific topic clearly and simply. Photographic images have been selected to reflect the diversity of children, families, communities, and classrooms.

Expanding Your Learning

Give It Some Thought questions appear within **Snapshot** features to develop higher-order thinking and problem-solving skills.

End-of-Chapter Content

End-of-chapter material provides an opportunity for review and application of concepts. A concise **Summary** provides an additional review tool and reinforces key learning objectives. An expanded summary matches the content to the learning outcomes for section-by-section review. This helps you focus on important concepts presented in the text. **For Further Reflection** questions enable students to demonstrate knowledge, identification, and comprehension of chapter material. **Recall and Application** questions extend learning and develop your abilities to break down material into its component parts.

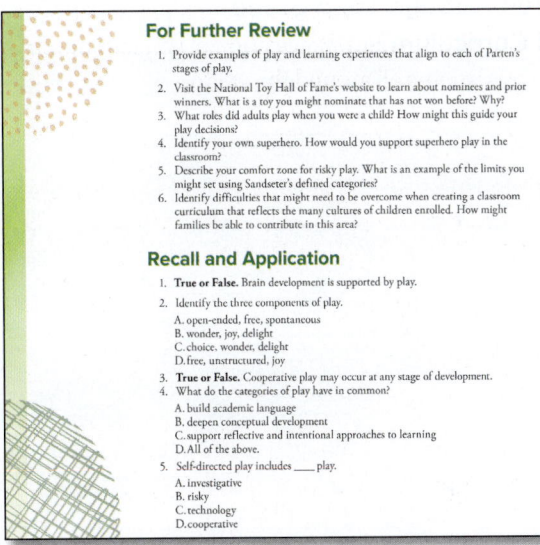

BRIEF CONTENTS

PART 1 The Learning Foundation

- **CHAPTER 1** Developmentally Appropriate Practice (DAP) 4
- **CHAPTER 2** Play 26
- **CHAPTER 3** Theories of Curricula and Approaches 44
- **CHAPTER 4** Creating a Community of Learners 70

PART 2 Tools for Learning

- **CHAPTER 5** Environment 90
- **CHAPTER 6** The Written Curriculum 122
- **CHAPTER 7** Assessment, Collaboration, Modification, and Accommodation 140
- **CHAPTER 8** The Implementation Phase 164

PART 3 Integrating the Learning

- **CHAPTER 9** Academic Disciplines 192
- **CHAPTER 10** Infant-Toddler Integrated Curriculum 218
- **CHAPTER 11** Preschool Integrated Curriculum 248
- **CHAPTER 12** Kindergarten Through Third Grade Integrated Curriculum 264

CONTENTS

PART 1 — The Learning Foundation

CHAPTER 1 — Developmentally Appropriate Practice (DAP) 4
- Section 1.1 Core Considerations 6
- Section 1.2 Principles of Child Development and Learning 9
- Section 1.3 Child Development Knowledge and Learning in Context 16
- Section 1.4 Recommendations for Developmentally Appropriate Practice 20

CHAPTER 2 — Play 26
- Section 2.1 The Developing Brain and Play Pedagogy 28
- Section 2.2 Stages and Categories of Play 30
- Section 2.3 Self-Directed Play 31
- Section 2.4 Guided Play 34
- Section 2.5 Teacher-Led Play 34
- Section 2.6 Technology and Play 36
- Section 2.7 Cultural Differences in Play 38

CHAPTER 3 — Theories of Curricula and Approaches 44
- Section 3.1 Tools of the Mind Curriculum 46
- Section 3.2 HighScope Curriculum 50
- Section 3.3 Montessori Curriculum 54
- Section 3.4 Waldorf Curriculum 56
- Section 3.5 Thematic Curriculum 59
- Section 3.6 Project Approach 61
- Section 3.7 Reggio Emilia Approach 63

CHAPTER 4 — Creating a Community of Learners 70
- Section 4.1 Ecological Systems Theory 72
- Section 4.2 Creating a Community 73
- Section 4.3 Engaging with Children 75
- Section 4.4 Engaging with Families 77
- Section 4.5 Engaging with Colleagues and Community 82

PART 2 — Tools for Learning

CHAPTER 5 — The Environment 90
- Section 5.1 Designing Early Learning Environments 92
- Section 5.2 Labeling 96
- Section 5.3 Culture 97
- Section 5.4 Setting the Stage 98
- Section 5.5 Learning Areas 101

CHAPTER 6 — The Written Curriculum 122
- Section 6.1 Standards and Learning Outcomes 124
- Section 6.2 Planning Strategies 127
- Section 6.3 The Daily Learning Plan and Catalytic Event 132
- Section 6.4 Topic of Interest and the Focus Topic 134

CHAPTER 7 — Assessment, Collaboration, Modification, and Accommodation 140
- Section 7.1 Assessment, Assessment Bias, and Ethical Connections 142
- Section 7.2 Authentic Assessment 144
- Section 7.3 Formal Assessment 150
- Section 7.4 Portfolios 153
- Section 7.5 Differentiation, Modification, and Accommodation 155

CHAPTER 8 — Implementation Phase 164
- Section 8.1 Characteristics of the Learner 166
- Section 8.2 Schedules 168
- Section 8.3 Instructional Strategies 170
- Section 8.4 Circle Time 173
- Section 8.5 Elements of the Implementation Phase 178
- Section 8.6 Components and Strategies of a Completed Daily Learning Plan 180

PART 3 Integrating the Learning

CHAPTER 9 Academic Disciplines 192
- Section 9.1 Disciplines 194
- Section 9.2 Language and Literacy Discipline 196
- Section 9.3 Science-Technology-Engineering-Mathematics (STEM) Discipline 198
- Section 9.4 Social Studies Discipline 204
- Section 9.5 Creative Arts Discipline 207
- Section 9.6 Physical Education: Health Discipline 213

CHAPTER 10 Toddler-Infant Integrated Curriculum 218
- Section 10.1 Infant-Toddler Curriculum 220
- Section 10.2 Curriculum Across Domains and State Lines 224
- Section 10.3 Infant-Toddler Resources 244

CHAPTER 11 Preschool Integrated Curriculum 248
- Section 11.1 Components of a Learning Plan 250
- Section 11.2 Putting Together a Learning Plan 251
- Section 11.3 Aligning the Learning Plan Components 255
- Section 11.4 Evaluating Teacher Resources 259

CHAPTER 12 Kindergarten Through Third Grade Integrated Curriculum 264
- Section 12.1 Kindergarten–Third Grade Curriculum Standards 267
- Section 12.2 Integration Strategies across Grades and Discipline Subjects 275
- Section 12.3 Credible Academic Subject Resources 287

GLOSSARY 290
INDEX 295
REFERENCE LIST 300

FEATURE CONTENTS

SNAPSHOT
4, 27, 45, 71, 91, 123, 141, 165, 193, 219, 249, 265

THE TEACHER'S LENS
8, 35, 47, 51, 56, 60, 76, 96, 98, 133, 180, 184, 196

STOP AND THINK
8, 13, 16, 28, 30, 32, 36, 39, 49, 52, 57, 61, 73, 77, 83, 95, 100, 125, 135, 143, 147, 150, 166, 175, 197, 220, 223, 230, 234, 238, 243, 268, 269, 274, 280, 284, 286

REAL-WORLD CLASSROOM
37, 53, 80, 84, 103, 109, 110, 212

INTRODUCTION

Integrated Curriculum for Young Children is the first book of its kind. As of this writing, there isn't another comprehensive text about integrated curriculum that is solely focused on the unique needs of young learners. In this book, you will learn not only about how to integrate topics of interest amongst the different academic subject areas, but how to create an early learning program that is child-led and where all learning experiences are built using backward design.

Children need play in a way that is similar to the way they need air and water. Play is their natural state, and the catalyst to all learning. When a child is bringing a plastic basket of faux groceries to a toy cash register, they are learning. When two children are arguing over which outfit a doll should wear, they are learning. When a baby releases their grip on a sippy cup and watches it fall to the floor, they are learning. An early learning program that is not play-based is robbing children of the cognitive, physical, and social-emotional experiences they need in order to grow and develop healthfully. This book will show you how to facilitate play in a way that is constructive and meaningful for children. You will also learn how to build and maintain a learning environment that encourages fruitful play experiences and maximizes opportunities for positive social interactions and authentic learning.

Borrowing from our education colleagues, this text applies a framework called backward design to assure students connect with their state's early learning standards, followed by learning to write measurable learning outcomes that use authentic assessment to measure the outcome and finally creating rich and engaging learning experiences.

Another unique feature of this text is its international lens. You will learn about various child-led early education programs around the world and see images that feature children and educators engaged in learning in a way you may not have seen before. Early childhood education is an ever-changing field, constantly evolving to meet the needs of children in an ever-changing world. It is important for educators to be lifelong learners and to keep a broad focus when it comes to classroom development and innovation. At the end of the day, every teacher wants to believe that they did the very best they could for the children.

For the Children,

Ginny Harmelink

The Learning Foundation

PART 1

Chapter 1 Developmentally Appropriate Practice (DAP)
Chapter 2 Play
Chapter 3 Theories of Curricula and Approaches
Chapter 4 Creating a Community of Learners

CHAPTER 1

Developmentally Appropriate Practice (DAP)

Learning Outcomes

After studying this chapter, you will be able to:

1.1 Define each of the three core considerations of developmentally appropriate practice (DAP).

1.2 Describe the nine DAP principles of child development and learning.

1.3 Summarize the six DAP guidelines for professional standards and competencies.

1.4 Identify DAP recommendations.

Standards Covered in This Chapter

NAEYC

1a, 1b, 1c, 1d, 2a, 2b, 2c, 3a, 3b, 3c, 3d, 4a, 4b, 4c, 4d, 4e, 5a, 5b, 5c, 5d, 5e, 6a, 6b, 6c, 6d, 6e

DAP

Guidelines 1, 2, 3, 4, 5, 6

Image credit: Kali9/E+ via Getty Images

Mr. Steve

SNAPSHOT

Ground Picture/Shutterstock.com

Mr. Steve is an early childhood teacher working in a mixed-age classroom with three- to five-year-old children. He begins the year with a welcome letter to share his teaching philosophies with the children's families. Read his letter below and discuss and reflect on the questions that follow.

Dear Families:

Children will experience many teachers by the time their formal schooling is over. Parents, relatives, caregivers, and the community have helped shape who they are so far. I will maintain a strong partnership with you and the community to ensure a positive influence in their future. As the people of my homeland, Bali, believe, the child chooses the parents, and the parents choose their teachers. We will work together, and we will be successful. Welcome to our classroom!

Understanding the culture of each child is what guides my teaching. Embracing our differences will create an inclusive environment where respect is the standard. Recognizing the value of others will promote a classroom of equity and altruism.

It is imperative for the teacher to stay abreast of current research and practices. The distinction that comes from being innovative will inspire children to become models for the world, the emergent leaders of tomorrow. Knowledge is the tool for success. This drives my desire to be the best teacher possible and to ensure that developmentally appropriate practices are embraced.

Creating an atmosphere in which children flourish requires careful planning and effort. The play environment defines my style and articulates my intentions. The climate will establish that both academic and emotional needs will be united to create a space where children thrive and advance their abilities. I will strive to involve you in the daily learning experiences. I want the children to reach for the stars, and I will encourage them to take flight.

For the children,

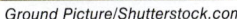

Mr. Steve

Give It Some Thought

1. Do you think it was appropriate for Mr. Steve to share a little about himself with the families? Why or why not?
2. Why do you think Mr. Steve wants to focus on creating a "play environment"? How will this benefit the children?

Key Terms

adverse childhood experience (ACE)
agency
cognitive domain
cognitive flexibility
commonality
context

developmentally appropriate practice (DAP)
domains of development
executive function
individuality
inhibitory control
integration

linguistic domain
physical domain
scaffolding
self-regulation
social-emotional domain
trauma informed care (TIC)
working memory

Introduction

Integrated curriculum combines content from all subject areas into thematic lessons. It ensures that all domains of development are present to build on the child's understanding in a holistic manner. Founded on constructivist theory, integrated curriculum encourages children to be the leader in their own learning via meaningful and interactive experiences. This approach also promotes critical thinking, experiential learning, and instruction that can be tailored to the unique needs of individual students. It can be said that adopting an integrated curriculum creates a classroom in which learning is unlimited. Consider this textbook a roadmap for first understanding, and then implementing, integrated curriculum in early learning environments.

Developmentally appropriate practices (DAP) are "methods that promote each child's optimal development and learning through a strengths-based, play-based approach to joyful, engaged learning" (NAEYC, *DAP*, 2020). DAP provides a framework for early childhood professionals to use not only when building integrated curriculum, but any time they are making decisions that impact the growth and development of children. It also provides a route to reimagining education in our time (Hirsh-Pasek 2020). Early childhood educators must strive to create learning experiences that will nurture each child's social, emotional, physical, and cognitive development (NAEYC, Power to the Profession 2020). Integrated curriculum in early childhood programs focuses on the interrelatedness of developmental and academic areas to help children gain basic learning tools.

Integrated curriculum supports children's learning by taking one concept or learning target and implementing it into all academic subject areas. The curriculum also promotes healthy relationships between educators and the families in the community (Nebraska Department of Education).

Chapter 1 employs the structure of National Association for the Education of Young Children's (NAEYC) *Developmentally Appropriate Practice in Early Childhood Programs* (2020) as the foundation of learning, as well as the foundation of upcoming chapters. Beginning with the core considerations, followed by the principles and guidelines, then ending with recommendations that align to the professional standards and competencies for early childhood educators, this textbook explores high quality learning experiences as they connect to curriculum.

1.1 Core Considerations

DAP requires early childhood educators to have a solid foundation in (and seek continuing education related to) understanding the following three areas when planning their curriculum (NAEYC, *DAP*, 2020):

- The commonality in children's development and learning
- The individuality of a child's unique characteristics and experiences
- The context of where a child's development and learning happen

Common threads run through developmentally appropriate practices. The goals are teaching children that differences are strengths versus deficits, understanding and addressing bias, and considering that there are many best practices when working with young children. These principles are woven throughout the text, as they are meant to be incorporated throughout the concepts of integrated curriculum. **Figure 1.1** reflects developmentally appropriate practice in action.

Commonality

The first DAP core consideration is ***commonality***, defined as "current research and understandings of processes of child development and learning that apply to all children." This includes the understanding that all development and learning occur within specific social, cultural, linguistic, and historical contexts (NAEYC, *DAP*, 2020).

The foundational knowledge of how children grow and develop, paired with an ongoing awareness of the latest field research, should support teaching decisions. Teachers should consider each child's culture, abilities, and experiences to promote optimum learning in the classroom through all the ***domains of development***:

- Social-emotional
- Cognitive
- Linguistic
- Physical

Much of the prior research around commonalities was based on a westernized image (white, middle-class, monolingual English-speaking) when considering a child's development. Child-rearing practices, attachment norms, reactions to different environments, and child behavior were expected to develop in accordance with that one western model. Today's research embraces the many differences between children and their families that should be valued, embedded into practice, and considered a positive factor in early learning environments. The salad bowl metaphor that celebrates retaining one's culture has replaced the melting pot theory, which, in earlier decades, emphasized abandoning home culture toward becoming one culture: American.

Families around the world value their children and try to do the best for them, but practices vary from one culture to another. The commonalities of children's development and learning can take distinctive forms because they also reflect the social and cultural frameworks in which they occur. Teachers' recognition of their own cultural beliefs and biases and the application of the many elements of commonality is part of what creates a high-quality environment. Social and cultural well-being provide the framework for all development and learning.

Dmitry Naumov/Shutterstock.com

Figure 1.1 Painting with the hands is a developmentally appropriate activity for the toddler age group. Would the same activity be appropriate for a six-month-old infant? Why or why not?

Individuality

The second DAP core consideration is ***individuality***, which NAEYC defines as "the characteristics and experiences unique to each child, within the context of their family and community, which have implications for how best to support their development and learning" (NAEYC, *DAP*, 2020). Making strong connections with a child's family is crucial when supporting the young child.

Early childhood educators include each family in classroom events and reach out to them in a variety of ways, including face-to-face communication, social media, newsletters, and phone calls. Involving the family in daily learning experiences is an important part of DAP.

Individuality includes the differences of children's skill levels and knowledge. Each child has their own unique personality and set of interests. Individuality is also affected by a child's family and cultural experiences. Children's learning needs vary greatly: Some children learn in accordance with the expected benchmarks and timelines, while others may need extra supports or an accelerated learning program. It is the educator's responsibility to identify these learning needs and advocate for children when necessary (NAEYC, *DAP*, 2020).

Educators must understand that diversity in the classroom provides rich learning experiences for children. Children can learn and grow together as unique individuals and learn to respect and celebrate their differences.

THE TEACHER'S LENS

In his classroom, Mr. Steve is tasked with providing learning experiences that support *all* of the children and their families. His mixed-age classroom includes children from three to five years old who have various abilities and experiences.

Jonah is new to America and does not speak or understand English. Mykala has been identified as having special needs. Some of the children have had previous early learning experiences, while others are attending preschool for the first time. The children's families' structures also vary widely.

Developmentally appropriate practices will influence Mr. Steve and provide needed support to reach all of the children, no matter where they are in their development. Making a difference in the lives of his students today will frame their tomorrows.

Context

The third DAP core consideration, **context**, is defined as "everything discernible about the social and cultural contexts for each child, each educator, and the program as a whole" (NAEYC, *DAP*, 2020). This includes personal *cultural context*, meaning the complex influences, traditions, and values reflected by a child's family and other caregivers. Context includes broader and intersecting cultural elements, such as the social, racial, economic, historic, and political aspects of a person's environment. Context is dynamic, both shaping and shaped by individuals and all the other factors they encounter.

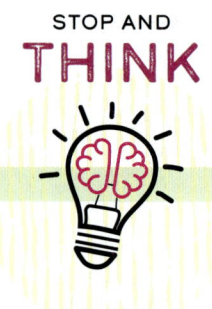

STOP AND THINK

Consider differences to be strengths, and apply this to your work with young children. This mindset values unique perspectives and challenges those around you to do the same. Be a role model for others. How can you support children who have strong feelings different from your own? Share an example.

Early childhood teachers and programs are also shaped by these same intersecting contexts. Awareness is of particular importance when educators do not share the same cultural context as the children in the classrooms. Early childhood educators must be careful to not interject their own values and beliefs, but instead respect and honor the values and beliefs of the children and their families. Every teacher has their own opinions and biases and must work hard to avoid letting those interfere when supporting each child's learning. It can be challenging to not share one's own cultural contexts with that of the children. Being mindful, understanding implicit biases, and learning anti-bias strategies can help educators use best context practices. Even when educators have the same or similar cultural contexts as children, a lack of understanding can occur (Adair et al. 2012).

✓ Checkpoint

☐ What are the three core considerations of DAP? Why is each important in early learning environments?

☐ Describe the "salad bowl metaphor" and the "melting pot theory." Which is a healthier approach for early childhood educators when working with children and their families?

1.2 Principles of Child Development and Learning

Empowered with the three DAP core considerations, the teacher can make connections to the principles that comprise all of child development and learning. NAEYC published guidelines and recommendations for DAP that are based on nine core principles for early childhood education professional practice. Each of the following principles are intertwined with the others, and together they represent the foundation of the guidelines for early childhood teachers (NASEM 2015). **Figure 1.2** provides a map of these principles.

Principle 1: Development and Learning

It is important for early childhood educators to understand child development and to be devoted to nurturing the whole child. The in-depth back and forth between the child's unique characteristics and the world around the child contribute to all domains of growing and learning. Principle 1 focuses on the following:

- Insights regarding children's brain development and the long-term consequences on development and learning
- Interplay between biology and the environment from birth through third grade and the implications for children who experience adversity

The rate of brain growth that starts before birth and continues into early childhood is staggering. The brain continues to develop well into adulthood; however, the first eight years of brain development are foundational for a child's future learning, health, and success (CDC.gov).

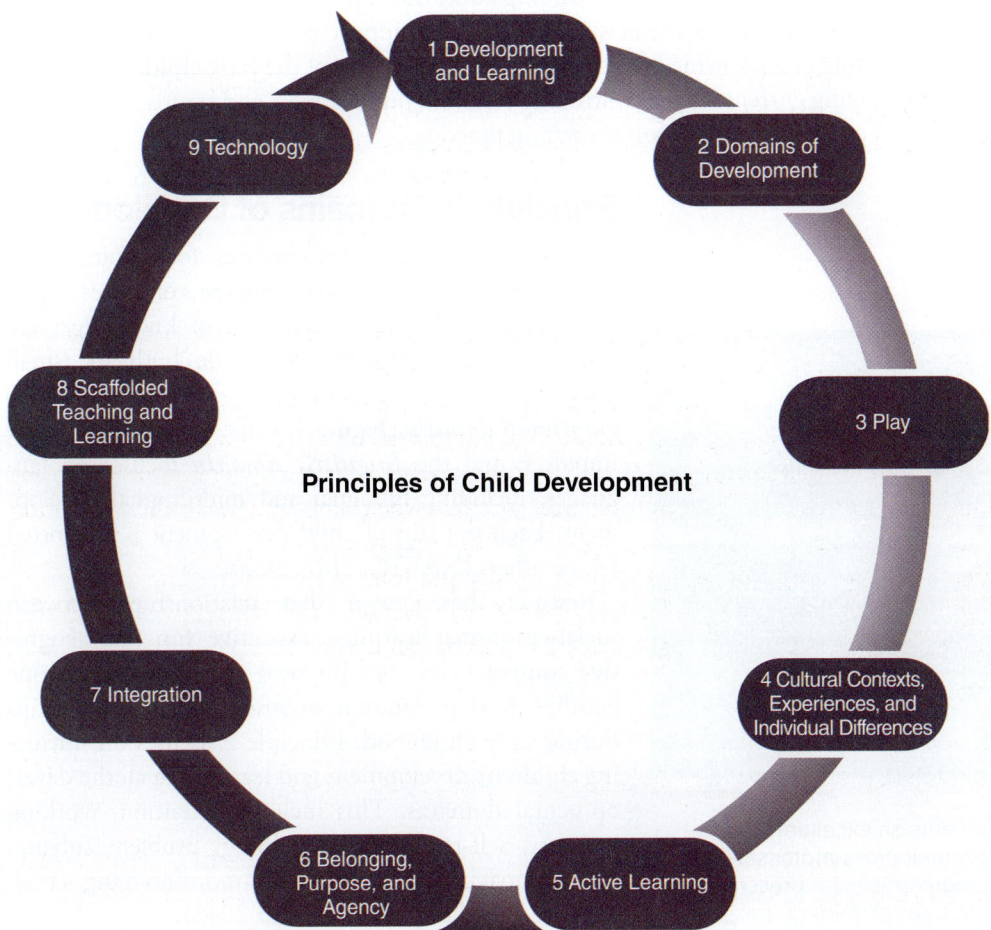

Figure 1.2 The nine DAP principles of child development and learning. Can you see how the nine principles overlap one another? Share an example.

Children are affected by their surroundings. A child's development is profoundly impacted by the surrounding environment during their earliest years. Neurological functioning is established in early childhood through neural connections in the brain (NSCDC 2004).

Adverse Childhood Experiences

The US Centers for Disease Control and Prevention (CDC) defines *adverse childhood experiences (ACEs)* as potentially traumatic events that occur in childhood, including violence, abuse, neglect, death of a loved one, and growing up in a family with mental health or substance abuse problems. ACEs can create toxic stress, which can disrupt healthy brain development and increase a child's likeliness to develop serious mental and physical health problems later in life.

It is critical for educators to understand the impact an ACE can have on a child. However, with the right tools and supports, children who have experienced ACEs can prove resilient to adversity. By providing consistent and responsive care, early childhood educators can be instrumental in helping traumatized children achieve positive outcomes (Center on the Developing Child 2010).

Trauma-Informed Care

Trauma-informed care (TIC) is a treatment framework that requires understanding, recognizing, and responding to the effects of all types of trauma. *Trauma* is an emotional response to an adverse experience that can have long-term implications for health (Immordino-Yang et al. 2018).

Schools and programs that commit to practicing TIC make a commitment to inclusive support. TIC includes a review of policies and practices and a plan to establish and empower a trauma workgroup. Continuing education and online seminars that focus on ACEs and trauma can provide new information to support all children in the classroom. Understanding and knowing how to implement TIC is part of the early childhood teacher skill set. Staying current on the continuing research, publications, and trends around early childhood can continually inform teaching practice.

Principle 2: Domains of Development

The second principle encompasses four domains of development. The *cognitive domain* comprises a person's mental skills and acquisition of knowledge; the *physical domain* (**Figure 1.3**) includes both fine (small muscle) and gross (large muscle) development; the *social-emotional domain* (**Figure 1.4**) focuses on feelings and impulses; and the *linguistic domain* focuses on languages, including bilingual and multilingual development. Each domain of child development is supported by the others (NAEYC, *DAP*, 2020).

Research has shown that relationships between social-emotional learning, executive function, cognitive competencies, and physical activity reinforce one another. It is paramount to foster these relationships during early childhood. Principle 2 focuses on nurturing children's development and learning in all the developmental domains. This includes attention, working memory, self-regulation, reasoning, problem solving, and approaches to learning (Immordino-Yang et al. 2018; Council on School Health 2013).

zlikovec/Shutterstock.com

Figure 1.3 A play tunnel presents an excellent opportunity for a toddler to use their gross motor skills. Identify different gross motor experiences for preschoolers and for children in kindergarten through third grade.

Executive Function

Understanding general learning competencies and executive function skills for the developing child is essential. ***Executive function*** comprises the mental skills, including the working memory, cognitive flexibility, and self-regulation that support intentionally controlling attention in order to accomplish a goal (Diamond & Ling 2015). See **Figure 1.5** for the three areas of executive function.

When the components of executive functioning come together to determine behavior, they are called ***self-regulation***. Self-regulation, a crucial element of early development, is the ability to stop, think, and then make a choice before acting. Self-regulation is another major element of Principle 2 (Tominey 2016).

Working Memory

Working memory is one of the brain's executive functions. It is a skill that allows people to work with information and keep track of what they are doing. Working memory includes two life skills: communicating and making connections. *Communicating* takes practice, and use of language is driven by development stages. This skill requires that children understand what they want and can express it correctly. Encouraging children to communicate during the day provides strength-based opportunities and supports all life skills. *Making connections* is learning how to discern and figure out what is the same and what is different, then sorting the elements into categories. Making unusual connections moves children beyond repeating facts to using information creatively (MITM 2020). Ways to increase making connections include:

- Open-ended questions (to spark new ideas)
- Guessing games
- Sorting games
- Charades
- Closing your eyes and imagining

Cognitive Flexibility

Cognitive flexibility involves being able to think about something in a new way. Cognitive flexibility includes three life skills: perspective, critical thinking, and responding to challenges. *Perspective* involves ways of regarding a situation and understanding what others think and feel. Gaining perspective is foundational for children's understanding of the intentions of parents, teachers, and friends. As they develop an improved perspective, children are less likely to be drawn into conflicts. For children younger than three years old who have not yet developed theory of mind, the early childhood teacher must be careful to not set unrealistic limits.

Theory of mind is a cognitive skill that reflects a child's ability to separate their thoughts from those of another. Three-year-old children in the classroom may not yet be able to fully understand the actions of others, and teacher expectations for them should be different than for the older children. Providing many ideas to support learning perspectives that include role play, pretend play, and a persona doll are strong classroom practices.

Creatas/Royalty-Free/Getty Images Plus

Figure 1.4 Playing with baby dolls is one way for children to practice care skills and develop empathy. Consider different ways to support social-emotional development in a young child.

Executive Function Cognitive Competencies	
Executive Function	**What Is It?**
Working memory	Ability to keep information in mind and use it
Cognitive flexibility	Ability to think about something in a new way
Inhibitory control	Ability to ignore distractions and resist temptations

Goodheart-Willcox Publisher

Figure 1.5 Promoting executive function skills is a goal in all early learning programs. How do each of these three executive functions benefit children in group settings?

Critical thinking (problem-solving, reasoning) helps children reflect on differing possibilities to direct their thoughts, decisions, and actions. Children need to practice critical thinking to problem-solve as well as to make sense of the world around them. A foundational element of critical thinking is that the questions do not have right or wrong answers, so all children can be successful when answering them. Asking an open-ended question every morning is a way to promote critical thinking in the classroom.

Responding to challenges encourages children to invent strategies to solve problems. Emergent leadership skills arise from allowing children to take risks. Children also learn to manage their emotions and try again when one strategy does not work out.

Inhibitory Control

Inhibitory control includes two of the life skills: focus and self-control and self-directed and engaged learning. *Focus and self-control* include the ability to pay attention, remember rules, and make decisions. Teaching students self-control of their behaviors and actions is a primary goal for kindergarten teachers. Mr. Steve from the opening Snapshot has developed a list (**Figure 1.6**) that reminds him and his assistant to support children in this life skill and help prepare them for kindergarten.

Self-directed and engaged learning includes setting goals and evaluating what works and what does not. By creating a classroom that instills trust, the teacher supports the children to become a community of learners who can depend on one another and on themselves.

There are considerable overlaps and interactions across the developmental domains and competencies. Changes within one domain often influence other areas of development and learning. For this reason, integrating all domains when possible creates multiple learning experiences that connect to play and academic subjects. Principle 2 defines the importance of a comprehensive curriculum along with the interrelatedness of the developmental domains for all young children's well-being and success (NAEYC, *DAP*, 2020).

Principle 3: Play

Supporting play leads to positive learning experiences that promote self-regulation, language, and cognitive, physical, and social competencies, as well as content knowledge across disciplines. Play is imperative for all children, birth through age eight" (NAEYC, *DAP*, 2020).

Play embodies the qualities of effective development and learning and is Principle 3, as shown in **Figure 1.7**. Play is synonymous with work for the child, and total engagement is the outcome of a play-based curriculum. As described in Chapter 2, "Play", there are three main categories of play that range from one end of an interactive continuum to the other. Play is universal, a basic and vital part of growing up, and during times of crisis, playing is one way a child copes.

Principle 4: Cultural Contexts, Experiences, and Individual Differences

A central understanding in child development and learning is that although general progressions of child development are widely recognized, cultural contexts and experiences, as well as

Figure 1.6 Mr. Steve created this chart as a way to keep himself on-track and focused as a teacher. What are some things you would add to your chart?

Mr. Steve's Self-Control and Focus Reminder Chart

- Create an environment in which children can focus by incorporating low shelves and attractive learning areas, and by rotating interest items to support engagement.
- Reflect on my teaching styles: Do they match children's temperaments? Reminder: what works for one child may not work for another child.
- Be aware of emotional needs and be responsive.
- Provide a structure and a schedule so children know what to expect.
- Involve the children in setting classroom rules.

individual differences, are variables that impact progress. Despite foreseeable changes across all domains, cultural and linguistic contexts influence the demonstration of changes and the meaning attached to them (NAEYC, *DAP*, 2020).

Principle 4's focus on cultural contexts includes those that impact the teacher's efforts when creating a sense of belonging for all children. In some cultures, children are encouraged to actively explore, while in others, the child is taught to ask questions first within an environment that is structured by adults (Rogoff 2003). In some cultures, adults encourage one-on-one interactions with children using a variety of methods, including eye contact. In others, children are socialized to avoid looking directly into an adult's eyes as a sign of respect. Methods of greetings also vary among cultures and individuals. Many teachers ask what kind of greeting the child would like when they arrive for the day: for example, hug, fist bump, high five, or just a verbal greeting. Knowing which approach to take in acknowledging the children and their families is important in honoring their values.

Ermolaev Alexander/Shutterstock.com

Figure 1.7 By learning how to hold a wand and blow bubbles, children are practicing fine motor skills. Revisit your early years. What form of play do you recall?

Providing strength-based language strategies for bilingual and multilingual children is important. Social interactions help children learn language, but individual needs differ for monolingual, bilingual, and multilingual children (NASEM 2017).

A child who consistently is not understood or able to understand others may begin to depend on context, verbal cues, and/or hand gestures to assist with communication. This may result in improved development of theory of mind and comprehension of pragmatics (Yow & Markman 2014). *Pragmatics* describes how words or actions can be used in a social setting. Examples include how children greet others or have a conversation with one another.

Children should be exposed to elements of their culture and home language in the early classroom setting. Incorporating each child's culture promotes a community of learning as experiences and supports social identities in positive ways. Teachers should recognize language differences as strengths, not deficits, and support them appropriately (NAEYC, *DAP*, 2020). Children who feel represented culturally are more ready to be part of a classroom.

STOP AND THINK

What are different ways to represent the value of cultural similarities in the classroom? How might the families be involved in your idea?

Principle 5: Active Learning

NAEYC's fifth principle states, "Children are active learners from birth, constantly taking in and organizing information to create meaning through their relationships, their interactions with their environment, and their overall experiences" (NAEYC, *DAP*, 2020). Even babies can have complex thoughts and understand that they can learn from adults. This underscores the importance of quality caregiving that allows children to form healthy relationships as children come to recognize patterns, make predictions, and apply what is learned to new situations (NASEM 2015).

Early childhood is a time for rapid learning and for exploring the world via healthy, strong relationships with caregivers and peers. Principle 5, *active learning*, encourages early childhood educators to develop a stimulating, play-based learning environment that fosters child development in all domains (NAEYC, *DAP*, 2020).

Children need teachers who are committed to helping them reach their potential. Principle 5 is clear on including all children of all abilities and specifies that some children are socialized to learn quietly on their own, while others are socialized to learn through direct and frequent interaction with adults (NAEYC, *DAP*, 2020).

A major emphasis of this principle is creating positive learning environments in which children are supported in forming social identities—environments that do not favor one group over another. Understanding how *implicit bias*—a form of bias that occurs unintentionally but nevertheless affects judgments, decisions, and behaviors—can influence interactions with children of all social backgrounds and being aware of how nonverbal signals may impact children's attitudes toward their peers is equally important. Children perceive that a classmate who receives more positive nonverbal signals from a teacher is superior to a classmate who receives fewer positive signals (Brey 2018).

Principle 6: Belonging, Purpose, and Agency

Principle 6 draws from the National Academies of Science, Engineering, and Medicine's *How People Learn II*. It asserts that a nurturing, developmentally appropriate learning environment will motivate a child to learn. A child's strengths will be fostered if the child is supported not only in their learning environment, but in their home and their community (NAEYC, *DAP*, 2020).

Providing safe experiences for children while creating intentional connections with the child's home and the community is valuable (**Figure 1.8**). *Cultural representation* is important for children. They need to see people who look like them and speak like them in positions of authority and in media and popular culture (Ladson-Billings 2022). This will help children develop both emotionally and linguistically and provide them with a sense of psychological safety and security.

It is equally important to encourage each child's decision-making confidence. **Agency** is the ability to choose which experiences one will engage in and decide how those experiences will proceed. A child's motivation is a personal decision based on their own determination of meaningfulness, interest, and engagement. Classroom learning experiences need to be achievable yet challenging and should be differentiated to meet the various ability levels within the classroom.

Children's feelings of belonging, purpose, and agency help them develop higher-order thinking skills. An educator who encourages a child-led learning environment will take note of children's natural interests and foster them through conversation and responsive curriculum. This helps young children develop self-confidence and understand that their thoughts and actions can influence their environment (NAEYC, *DAP*, 2020).

Rawpixel.com/Shutterstock.com

Figure 1.8 These children are playing a game together that requires them to clasp hands and look at one another. Identify other ways to create a sense of belonging for children.

Principle 7: Integration

When considering curriculum, **integration** is the process of combining multiple learning experiences that include multiple subjects. Integration allows children to learn in a holistic way, versus separating subjects to be taught in isolation, one subject at a time.

Principle 7 states that children "learn in an integrated fashion that cuts across academic disciplines or subject areas. Because the foundations of subject area knowledge are established in early childhood, educators need subject-area knowledge, an understanding of the learning progressions within each subject area, and pedagogical knowledge about teaching each subject area's content effectively" (NAEYC, *DAP*, 2020).

The interdisciplinary approach to academics is more meaningful than teaching content areas separately. Just as domains of development overlap and influence each other, the same is true for academic areas. Teachers need to have a strong understanding of the core structures (concepts and language) of different academic subject areas in order to teach them appropriately to children. The early childhood teacher must include meaningful connections between domains and subject areas when planning curriculum to explore the different subject core concepts, procedures, and structures. For example, counting when playing hopscotch connects the physical domain when teaching math. Pairing children to sing harmony in music connects the social-emotional domain to music.

Teachers should encourage children to explore their environments and reflect on their surroundings. This helps children build their knowledge base and build their vocabularies (NAEYC, *DAP*, 2020). Most importantly, the teacher should present each subject in ways that are meaningful. Teaching young children academic subject matters is a tenet of developmentally appropriate practice.

Principle 8: Scaffolded Teaching and Learning

Scaffolding refers to teachers "providing the support or assistance that allows the child to succeed at a task that is just beyond their current level of skill or understanding" (NAEYC, *DAP*, 2020). "This includes emotional support, as well as strategies such as pointing out important details or providing other cues that can help children make connections to previous knowledge and experiences" (NASEM 2015). A curriculum that supports all learners will provide breadth and depth with recurring opportunities to revisit concepts and experiences based on the children's interests. Offering opportunities to practice and integrate new skills and concepts is essential (NAEYC, *DAP*, 2020).

To determine how much scaffolding a child needs, an early childhood educator needs base knowledge of child development and the fundamentals of how children learn. This includes understanding the typical timelines that children follow as they learn and acquire new skills. It is also imperative for teachers to take the time to get to know each child and their families, then use that knowledge to inform their curriculum and teaching style in a way that will best benefit that child (NAEYC, *DAP*, 2020).

Other important components of Principle 8 are *learning outcomes* that reflect early learning standards and are measured by *authentic assessment*. The approaches to learning include identifying children who are at risk and would benefit from additional support, then collaborating with special educators as needed. These are pinnacles of the high-quality early childhood classroom.

Principle 9: Technology

If used "responsibly and intentionally, technology and interactive media can be valuable tools for supporting children's development and learning" (NAEYC, *DAP*, 2020). The inclusion of technology can work in today's early childhood classroom when guidance and limitations are implemented. Principle 9 cautions that for children under age two, there is no evidence that development is enhanced with the use of digital devices or media. However, there is value in including digital media in some situations with older children if developmentally appropriate practices are in place (American Academy of Pediatrics 2019).

Mr. Steve's communication plan began with a welcome letter to the families. He plans to stay connected using a private social media space where he can upload images during the week. Using technology, he plans to create electronic portfolios to house the many authentic assessments he collects through the year to measure proficiency in learning outcomes and early learning standards.

Mr. Steve plans to communicate with families using an electronic bimonthly classroom newsletter that will feature a 'Kids' column created by different pairs of children. The children will learn to work as a team, interview peers, and place images they photograph in a newsletter layout, in addition to beginning identification of letters.

A variety of assistive technology aids will be available for children who may need additional support in the learning environment. Mr. Steve sees value in using live cameras to support increased engagement around the curriculum. When learning about bees, for example, a virtual visit to a live hive will engage children further. When appropriately integrated into the curriculum, technology enhances the focus of the lesson or activity. The focus should never be on the technology itself (NAEYC/Fred Rogers Center 2012).

Use of technology enables children to participate in class remotely if they are unable to be present for a variety of reasons. When children engage with technology and media, the most effective uses will be active, direct, and empowering (Donahue 2017). Technology never replaces opportunities for direct experiences, but it can be used as a tool when learning something new.

"Given the rapid changes in the types and uses of new media, the research on the effects on children's development and learning continues to grow and shift. Emerging evidence suggests a number of cautions, including concerns about negative associations between excessive screen time and childhood obesity, as well as negative impacts on toddlers' performance on measures of fine motor, communication, and social skills" (American Academy of Pediatrics 2019).

Checkpoint

☐ What are examples of theory of mind?

☐ How does agency support high-order thinking skills?

STOP AND THINK | The teacher takes on many roles: assessor, facilitator, guide, model, mediator, and cheerleader, to name a few. How does a teacher decide which role is appropriate at any given time?

1.3 Child Development Knowledge and Learning in Context

Based on the three core considerations and the nine principles previously covered, the following guidelines consider decisions that early childhood professionals must make in six areas of practices that support children, their families, and the community. Educators adhere to these guidelines (see **Figure 1.9**) and use them to advocate for young children and their families. Standard 6 of the *Professional Standards and Competencies for Early Childhood Educators* provides distinct guidelines for early childhood professionals (NAEYC, *DAP*, 2020).

Figure 1.9 NAEYC guidelines. Why is each of these guidelines important for an early childhood educator to know?

NAEYC GUIDELINES
• Creating a Caring, Equity Community of Learners
• Engaging in Reciprocal Relationships with Families and Fostering Community Connections
• Observing, Documenting, and Assessing Children's Development and Learning
• Teaching to Enhance Each Child's Development and Learning
• Planning and Implementing an Engaging Curriculum to Achieve Meaningful Goals
• Demonstrating Professionalism as an Early Childhood Educator

Goodheart-Willcox Publisher

The tables in **Figure 1.10** through **Figure 1.15** show how NAEYC guidelines are interconnected, and how they are integrated within the textbook. The guidelines listed are embedded into future chapters as the foundation of integrated curriculum and noted with each criterion below as a reference. The textbook chapters that align with each of the guidelines are listed for reference.

Guideline 1: Creating a Caring, Equitable Community of Learners
Each member of the community is valued by the others and is recognized for the strengths they bring. (See Chapters 1, 2, 4, and 8.)
Relationships are nurtured with each child, and educators facilitate the development of positive relationships among children. (See Chapters 4 and 8.)
Each member of the community respects and is accountable to the others to behave in a way that is conducive to the learning and well-being of all. (See Chapters 1 and 4.)
The physical environment protects the health and safety of the learning community members, and it specifically supports young children's physiological needs for play, activity, sensory stimulation, fresh air, rest, and nourishment. (See Chapters 1, 2, 4, and 5.)
Every effort is made to help each and every member of the community feel psychologically safe and able to focus on being and learning. The overall social and emotional climate is welcoming and positive. (See Chapters 4, 5, 6, and 8.)

Goodheart-Willcox Publisher

Figure 1.10 NAEYC Guideline 1

Guideline 2: Engaging in Reciprocal Partnerships with Families and Fostering Community Connections
Educators take responsibility for establishing respectful, reciprocal relationships with and among families. (See Chapters 1 and 4.)
Educators work in collaborative partnerships with families, seeking and maintaining regular, frequent, two-way communication with them and recognizing that the forms of communication may differ for each family. (See Chapters 1, 4, and 8.)
Educators welcome family members in the setting and create multiple opportunities for family participation. (See Chapters 1 and 4.)
Educators take care to learn about the community in which they work, and they use the community as a resource across all aspects of program delivery. (See Chapters 4 and 8.)
Educators acknowledge a family's choices and goals for their child and respond with sensitivity and respect to those preferences and concerns. (See Chapters 1, 4, and 8.)
Educators and the family share with each other their knowledge of the particular child and understanding of child development and learning as part of day-to-day and other forms of communication (e.g., family get-togethers, meetings, support groups). (See Chapters 1, 4, and 8.)
Educators involve families as a source of information about the child (before program entry and on an ongoing basis). (See Chapters 1, 4, and 8.)

Goodheart-Willcox Publisher

Figure 1.11 NAEYC Guideline 2

Figure 1.12 NAEYC Guideline 3

Guideline 3: Observing, Documenting, and Assessing Children's Development and Learning

Observation, documentation, and assessment of young children's progress and achievements is ongoing, strategic, reflective, and purposeful. (See Chapter 7.)

Assessment focuses on children's progress toward developmental and educational goals (See Chapter 7.)

A system is in place to collect, make sense of, and use observations, documentation, and assessment information to guide what goes on in the early learning setting. (See Chapter 7.)

The methods of assessment are responsive to the current developmental accomplishments, language(s), and experiences of young children. They recognize individual variation in learners and allow children to demonstrate their competencies in different ways. (See Chapter 7.)

Assessments are used only for the populations and purposes for which they have been demonstrated to produce reliable, valid information. (See Chapters 1 and 7.)

Decisions that have a major impact on children, such as enrollment or placement, are made in consultation with families. (See Chapters 4 and 7.)

When a screening assessment identifies a child who may have a disability or individualized learning or developmental needs, there is appropriate follow-up, evaluation, and, if needed, referral. (See Chapter 7.)

Goodheart-Willcox Publisher

Figure 1.13 NAEYC Guideline 4

Guideline 4: Teaching to Enhance Each Child's Development and Learning

Educators demonstrate and model their commitment to a caring learning community through their actions, attitudes, and curiosity. (See Chapters 4 and 7.)

Educators use their knowledge of each child and family to make learning experiences meaningful, accessible, and responsive to each and every child. (See Chapters 1, 4, 5, and 8.)

Educators effectively implement a comprehensive curriculum so that each child attains individualized goals across all domains (physical, social, emotional, cognitive, linguistic, and general learning competencies) and across all subject areas (language and literacy, including second language acquisition, mathematics, social studies, science, art, music, physical education, and health). (See Chapters 1, 2, 5, 6, 7, 8, 9, 10, 11, and 12.)

Educators know how and when to strategically use the various learning formats and contexts. (See Chapters 1, 3, and 8.)

Educators plan the environment, schedule, and daily activities to promote each child's development and learning. (See Chapters 5, 6, 7, and 8.)

Educators differentiate instructional approaches to match each child's interests, knowledge, and skills. (See Chapter 3.)

Educators possess and build on an extensive repertoire of skills and teaching strategies (See Chapters 1, 2, 3, 4, 5, 6, 7, 8, 9, 10, 11, and 12.)

Educators know how and when to scaffold children's learning. (See Chapters 1, 3, 7, and 8.)

Goodheart-Willcox Publisher

Figure 1.14 NAEYC Guideline 5

Guideline 5: Planning and Implementing an Engaging Curriculum to Achieve Meaningful Goals
Desired goals that are important for young children's development and learning in general and culturally and linguistically responsive to children in particular have been identified and clearly articulated. (See Chapters 1, 6, 7, and 8.)
Educators make meaningful connections a priority in the learning experiences they provide each child. (See Chapters 5, 6, and 8.)
Educators collaborate with those teaching in the preceding and subsequent age groups or grade levels, sharing information about children and working to increase continuity and coherence across ages and grades. (See Chapter 8.)
Although it will vary across the age span, a planned and written curriculum is in place for all age groups. (See Chapters 5, 6, 7, 8, 9, 10, 11, and 12.)
The program has a comprehensive, effective curriculum that targets the identified goals across all domains of development and subject areas. (See Chapters 5, 6, 7, and 8.)
Educators use the curriculum framework in their planning to make sure there is ample attention to important learning goals and to enhance the coherence of the overall experience for children. (See Chapters 2, 3, 5, 6, 7 and 8.)

Goodheart-Willcox Publisher

Figure 1.15 NAEYC Guideline 6

Guideline 6: Demonstrating Professionalism as an Early Childhood Educator
Identify and involve oneself with the early childhood field and serve as an informed advocate for young children, families and the profession. (See Chapter 1.)
Know about and uphold ethical and other early childhood professional guidelines. (See Chapter 7.)
Use professional communication skills, including technology- mediated strategies, to effectively support young children's learning and development and work with families and colleagues. (See Chapter 11.)
Engage in continuous, collaborative learning to inform practice (See Chapters 4 and 8.)
Develop and sustain the habit of reflective and intentional practice in their daily practice with young children and as members of the early childhood profession. (See Chapter 8.)

Goodheart-Willcox Publisher

Creating and implementing developmentally appropriate curriculum is a priority for all early childhood educators. These best practices strengthen the profession and provide the best possible start for young children (NAEYC, *DAP*, 2020).

Checkpoint

- How do the six DAP guidelines support the early childhood professional? Are any of the guidelines more important than others?
- In what ways are the guidelines different from the core considerations and principles? Share an example.

1.4 Recommendations for Developmentally Appropriate Practice

Read each of the NAEYC recommendation practices in **Figure 1.16** through **Figure 1.19** to ensure your understanding of what is needed to build a stronger workforce and inform advocacy efforts. These are valuable sources for early childhood professionals and, as such, are included in the DAP position document.

Figure 1.16 NAEYC recommendations for schools, family childcare homes, and other program settings

Recommendations for Schools, Family Childcare Homes, and Other Program Settings
Support educators' access to higher education and professional development opportunities that allow them to build the knowledge, skills, and dispositions identified in the Professional Standards and Competencies for Early Childhood Educators, and ensure they are prepared to carry out each of these guidelines.
Support and incentivize professional development for administrators, supervisors, and those responsible for assessment and evaluation of early childhood educators to ensure they understand the principles and guidelines of developmentally appropriate practice and use them to inform decisions regarding program implementation.
Strive to ensure that program policies facilitate and support strong, continuous relationships between teaching staff and children by offering working conditions and compensation (wages and benefits) that attract and retain a diverse and qualified staff.
Seek and maintain early learning program accreditation based on systems that are built to support developmentally appropriate practice.
Strive to ensure that the school or program provides equitable learning opportunities to all children to help them achieve their full potential and avoids the use of suspension or expulsion.
Ensure that the curriculum promotes all domains of development while providing a coherent and flexible framework that supports educators in making adaptations to meet the unique interests and needs of the children they are serving.
Provide mentoring and coaching for educators and administrators to encourage reflection and continuous learning about the children, families, and communities served.
Actively engage family members and the broader community in all aspects of program planning and implementation, recognizing and considering the systemic inequities that can make it difficult for members of traditionally marginalized groups to participate.
Cultivate relationships with community resources, including local libraries, museums, public parks, physical and mental health consultants, and government services that can support the program and families as well as strengthen civic connections.

Goodheart-Willcox Publisher

Recommendations for Higher Education and Adult Development

Adopt and align coursework to the Professional Standards and Competencies for Early Childhood Educators, with the appropriate leveling and with emphasis on equity and diversity, as part of the overall implementation of the Unifying Framework for Early Childhood Education Profession.

Prepare current and prospective early childhood educators to understand and implement all components of developmentally appropriate practice and to provide equitable learning opportunities for all young children

Ensure that practicums, internships, and apprenticeships for prospective educators provide experiences working in various settings (including schools, centers, and family childcare homes) that serve racially, linguistically, culturally, and economically diverse groups of children across all age groups, including children with and without disabilities.

Ensure that faculty in higher education programs reflect the diversity of children and families and that they understand and embrace the principles and guidelines of developmentally appropriate practices.

Goodheart-Willcox Publisher

Figure 1.17 NAEYC recommendations for higher education and adult development

Recommendations for Policymakers

Ensure that all those working directly with children in early childhood settings, from birth through age 8, have equitable, affordable access to high-quality professional preparation required to meet the standards and competencies at all professional designations.

Provide adequate funding to ensure all children have equitable access to high-quality early childhood programs that meet these guidelines and follow other guidelines established by the profession, including small class/group sizes and sufficient numbers of well-prepared and well-compensated teaching staff to provide the individualized attention needed to implement these guidelines effectively (and as stipulated in the *NAEYC Early Learning Program Standards*).

Recognize the limitations of accountability systems that narrowly focus on skill-based assessments and revise policies accordingly.

Provide more equitable learning opportunities for all young children, recognizing the need for comprehensive services for families.

Goodheart-Willcox Publisher

Figure 1.18 NAEYC recommendations for policymakers

Figure 1.19 NAEYC recommendations for research

Recommendations for Research
Identify which instructional strategies (and other characteristics of early childhood programs) work most effectively for which children under which circumstances. (See Chapter 3.)
Identify strategies by which educators can recognize and effectively address their implicit biases to provide more equitable learning opportunities for all children. (See Chapters 1 and 7.)
Develop assessment methodologies that fully capture the complexity and diversity of children's development and learning in authentic, reliable, and valid ways that consider multiple aspects of children's identities and reflect various cultural ways of learning. (See Chapter 7.)
Continue to explore various dimensions of young children's development and learning, teaching quality, dimensions of effective teaching, and the ways in which these play out in different social and cultural contexts. (See all chapters.)
Identify areas of further knowledge needed to help monolingual and multilingual teachers understand how and why to adapt strategies and environments to meet the needs of children who are learning more than one language. (See Chapters 1 and 5.)

Goodheart-Willcox Publisher

Checkpoint

- ☐ Identify ways to engage the family in program planning across all languages. Provide ideas to encourage inclusivity for all.
- ☐ Considering your own area, what are ways to connect with the community to support the children's learning while supporting local businesses?

Chapter 1 Review and Assessment

Summary

1.1 Define each of the three core considerations of developmentally appropriate practice (DAP).

- *Commonality* refers to the practice of keeping up with the current research and best practices in the child development field.
- *Individuality* refers to respecting each child's uniqueness. To understand a child's uniqueness, an educator must make strong connections with the child's family and other caregivers.
- *Context* involves seeing a child as part of their social and cultural communities. To achieve this, educators must understand and overcome their own implicit biases.

1.2 Describe the nine DAP principles of child development and learning.

- *Development and Learning* is focused on insights regarding early brain development and the long-term implications on development and learning that include connections between biology and the environment.
- *Domains of Development* includes all domains of child development—cognitive, physical, social-emotional, and linguistic development (including bilingual or multilingual development) as well as approaches to learning.
- *Play* promotes joyful learning across all domains of development. Play is essential for learning and is synonymous with work for the child.
- *Cultural Contexts, Experiences, and Individual Differences* focuses on how each child develops at an uneven rate that can vary from one day to the next, based on many variables.
- *Active Learning* is focused on teachers appreciating the importance of their role in creating a rich, play-based learning environment that encourages the development of knowledge (including vocabulary) and skills across all domains.
- *Belonging, Purpose, and Agency* includes creating an environment that is welcoming to each child, assuring children see people who look like them across levels of authority, they hear languages they are familiar with and they are supported in making their own decisions.
- *Integration* refers to teachers having a strong understanding of the core structures (concepts and language) for all the academic subject areas to be able to support children holistically in ways that are appropriate.
- *Scaffolded Teaching and Learning* includes matching curriculum with the typical paths and sequences that children follow regarding specific skills, concepts, and abilities, as well as practicing teaching skills that will challenge each child in appropriate ways.
- *Technology* includes effective uses of technology and media by children that is active, hands-on, engaging, and empowering with guidance.

1.3 Summarize the six DAP guidelines for professional standards and competencies.

- *Creating a Caring, Equity Community of Learners.* Each member of the learning community is valued and respected. The physical environment protects the health and safety of the learning community members.
- *Engaging in Reciprocal Relationships with Families and Fostering Community Connections.* Educators partner with families to promote the healthy development of each child.
- *Observing, Documenting, and Assessing Children's Development and Learning.* This is an ongoing, strategic, and purposeful process. The methods of assessment are responsive to the current developmental accomplishments. Major decisions that affect the child are made in consultation with the family.

- *Teaching to Enhance Each Child's Development and Learning.* Committed teachers use their knowledge of each child and family to implement a comprehensive and strategic curriculum.
- *Planning and Implementing an Engaging Curriculum to Achieve Meaningful Goals.* Educators collaborate with colleagues to set goals that are important for young children's development. Goals are implemented through a developmentally appropriate curriculum.
- *Demonstrating Professionalism as an Early Childhood Educator.* Early childhood educators should act as advocates for young children and uphold professional and ethical standards at all times.

1.4 Identify DAP recommendations.
- *Recommendations for Schools, Family Childcare Homes, and Other Program Settings*
- *Recommendations for Higher Education and Adult Development*
- *Recommendations for Policymakers*
- *Recommendations for Research*

For Further Review

1. Reflecting on Mr. Steve's welcome letter in the chapter introduction, what would you identify as its strengths? Weaknesses?
2. Compose a sample one-page letter to share with a family that includes your emphasis when teaching their child. What are the three most important elements you will include?
3. Make a list of your top three values. How might you include a lesson around values in the early childhood classroom?
4. Summarize the differences between a consideration, a principle, and a guideline.
5. What professional development opportunities do you find supportive in creating a high-quality classroom?
6. What is the difference between best practice and high quality?
7. How might you advocate for early learners to local policymakers in your area? How would you use the DAP recommendations to support your efforts?

Recall and Application

1. Identify the three core considerations of DAP.
   A. uniqueness, value, diversity
   B. context, commonality, individuality
   C. culture, individuality, curriculum
   D. commonality, appropriateness, culture

2. **True or False.** Making connections to families is important when teaching children.

3. What is TIC an acronym for?
   A. Teaching Infant Care
   B. Technology of Infant Cognition
   C. Trauma Informed Care
   D. Trauma Influenced Cognition

4. What is cognitive flexibility?
   A. ability to ignore distractions and resist temptations
   B. ability to keep information in mind and use it
   C. ability to think about something in a new way
   D. ability to pass IQ tests

5. **True or False.** The NAEYC's six guidelines provide a framework around which teachers can create schedules.

6. How do the six guidelines support teachers and learners?
   A. advance the creation of state standards that impact development of curriculum
   B. a framework for teachers to conduct themselves as members of the profession
   C. list the supplies they need in the classroom
   D. helps them understand when scaffolding is needed

7. **True or False.** The NAEYC recommendations are guidelines that support best practices in early childhood education.

8. Identifying recommendations provides the ability to increase knowledge to _____.
   A. policymakers, parents, and educators
   B. children and teens
   C. the community
   D. the media

2 CHAPTER

Play

Learning Outcomes

After studying this chapter, you will be able to:

2.1 Describe play connections to brain development and the pedagogy of play.

2.2 Identify Mildred Parten's five stages of play.

2.3 Summarize types of self-directed play.

2.4 Summarize types of guided play.

2.5 Describe teacher-led play.

2.6 Explain connections between technology and play.

2.7 Identify ways to support cultural diversity in play.

Standards Covered in This Chapter

NAEYC

1a, 1b, 1c, 1d, 4b, 5b, 6d

DAP

Guideline 4; Principle 4

Image credit: BraunS/Royalty-Free/Getty Images Plus

FatCamera/Royalty-Free/Getty Images Plus

SNAPSHOT

Mayra

Teacher Mayra is aware of the importance of play and has been asked many times by family members what their children are learning in her preschool class if they are *only* playing. Mayra understands the importance of open communication with families and has created many strategies to support play in the classroom. Signs are posted at the different learning areas that list the benefits of play when the child has chosen that space. Another strategy that she has adopted in the classroom is a monthly play date for families to attend and practice their own play skills. Mayra feels that introducing families to the different theories of play and the benefits derived from play is an effective way to support her curriculum.

Give It Some Thought

1. Do you think Mayra is right to base the curriculum of her preschool class on play? Why or why not?
2. Do you agree with Mayra's decision to include families in play activities once a month? Do you agree that the playdates are an effective way to support the curriculum? Explain your answer.

Key Terms

classism	nature play	screen time
cooperative play	pedagogy	self-directed play
culture	pedagogy of play	sequential neurodevelopment
executive functions	play	superhero play
guided play	pretend play	teacher-led play
investigative play	risky play	technology

Introduction

"What are my children learning if they are only playing all day?" This is a question parents commonly ask the teacher in early learning classrooms. What some parents do not realize is that play is deservedly one of the most important facets of early childhood education. A fundamental tenet of early childhood education is that engaging in play is one of the most effective ways for young children to learn. Observing how a child embraces play provides knowledge and educates families on the critical importance of this natural phenomena in the early years. Play enhances the child's developing brain structure and function, and it promotes the process of learning (Yogman et al. 2018).

The focus of Chapter 2 is the importance of play when developing curriculum for the young child. The stages of play, current research, the teacher's role, and the impact of culture and intentional practices to support the value of play are explored to help teachers develop intentional learning experiences.

2.1 The Developing Brain and Play Pedagogy

Play promotes happy learning experiences, self-regulation, language, cognitive and social competencies, and knowledge. Play is important for all young children, ages birth through age eight. In order for a child to develop successfully, they must have regular access to play opportunities. When children play, they develop confidence, intrinsic motivation, and a sense of freedom.

Children at play display happiness, referred to as *positive affects* (Nell et al. 2013). A positive affect relates to expressions of positive emotions such as excitement, energy, and pride. When children are playing, they are able to discover higher-level skills and begin to think symbolically; for example, imagining a block is a cup for drinking or a cape has magical powers. At play, children are able to concentrate on the process at hand.

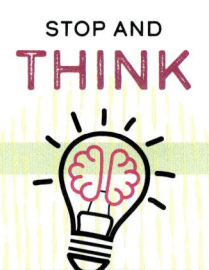

STOP AND THINK | The experiences babies have during play help strengthen and expand networks of connections in their developing brains (Bales 2018). How might you use this information to inform your practice?

Brain power requires energy to support abstract thought. Understanding that our brains follow a sequential order when developing is essential to understanding child development. The brain relies on neurons to release neurotransmitters, which generate a wave to thousands of other neurons, leading to the formation of thoughts. Present in all cultures, play is universal, though play may take different forms in different social and cultural contexts. When children play, they are making sense of the world around them (Gosso & Carvalho 2013).

Experts in the area of brain science call this ***sequential neurodevelopment***. An infant's brain growth occurs in a sequence, from the brainstem, the most basic area, progressing to the more complicated areas.

Brain Activity and Play

The brainstem (**Figure 2.1**) is essential to bodily functions. For example, it controls temperature, heart rate, sleep, and blood pressure. Tactile play or games such as peekaboo engage this part of the brain. The midbrain, a part of the brainstem, regulates motor skills (movement). The midbrain supports development of both fine motor skills (use of small muscles) and gross motor skills (use of large muscles), while also helping the integration of complex sensory input. Playing a musical instrument and dancing are examples of beneficial motor skills.

The limbic area of the brain controls emotions such as belonging. As the limbic area develops, children are increasingly able to understand social relationships. When a child is ready, learning to share and taking turns are supported by the limbic level of the brain.

The cortical area (neocortex) is the most complex area of the brain and supports abstract thoughts, humor, and language. This area promotes playing games, laughing at jokes, and thinking out scenarios in play.

The human brain grows swiftly during childhood. To support this growth, teachers and primary caregivers must encourage children to follow their curiosities and develop skills (Murray et al 2016). The experiences provided in early childhood have the longest lasting effects on a person's brain. The power of play helps the brain develop in optimal ways. When play is central and each child's culture is supported, valued, visible, and celebrated, providing intentional play is not only a best practice, it is a critical practice.

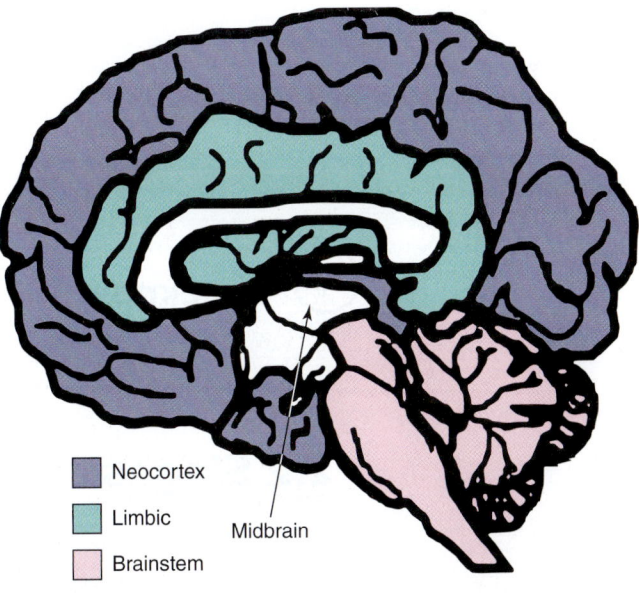

Goodheart-Willcox Publisher

Figure 2.1 The main sections of the brain. Name three bodily functions that are regulated by the brainstem.

Pedagogy of Play

Pedagogy is a synonym for *teaching*, be it an academic subject or a theoretical concept. The **pedagogy of play** is broken into three key components: choice, wonder, and delight.

Choice reflects not only the child's decision to engage in play, but also decisions about what form and direction that play will take. Experiences, materials, and interactions provided to children support engagement of learning through play.

Wonder is reflected in the child's continued engagement in play. A child with wonder will use their imagination and push boundaries. Wonder also helps children practice new skills.

Delight refers to the child's laughter and feelings of happiness as they engage in play. Discoveries and achievements are very joyful occasions for children (Zosh et al. 2017). Play experiences that are developmentally appropriate support children across all developmental domains (Yogman et al. 2018).

Empty boxes or a mound of sand are open-ended materials that support choice, wonder, and delight (**Figure 2.2**). These classic items will enthrall any child, at little or no cost to the teacher, while providing hours of uninterrupted play and learning, if supported. Another example of supporting choice, wonder, and delight is building forts using sheets, blankets, pillows, and play clothes.

Danielle Dittmer

Figure 2.2 Young children experiencing mud at their school in Accra, Ghana, Africa. How does this activity support the pedagogy of play?

STOP AND THINK | As you have learned, play and learning can be synonymous. What were your favorite play spaces as a child? How might you incorporate your childhood play ideas into your classroom?

 **Checkpoint**

- How does play support brain development? Provide an example.
- Make connections to the pedagogy of play and explain how it will inform your practice.

2.2 Stages and Categories of Play

Mildred Parten defined the stages of play based on ages of children. Parten was a graduate from the University of Minnesota, where she studied the effects of play on children's behavior. Parten's early studies connected a child's development of social skills to the way the child plays.

Parten's Stages of Play

Parten's five play stages include unoccupied, solitary or independent, onlooker, parallel, associative, and cooperative play (**Figure 2.3**). An additional initial stage was termed *unoccupied play*, when a child may be only watching others and not playing. First published in 1932, these stages span the years of early child development and are still widely accepted in the field today. Each stage provides resources for teachers to inform instruction and to educate families about their children's development. For example, if parents are concerned that their toddler is not interacting with other children at play, it reassures them to know that their child is in the onlooker or parallel play stage, and that their behavior is on-track developmentally.

Parten's Stages of Play		
Stage of Play	**Indicators**	**Commonly Occurs**
Solitary or independent play	During the first two years of life, babies learn to entertain themselves as they explore, learn cause and effect, and experiment with the world around them.	0–2 years
Onlooker play	Observing others in play; this stage supports the young learner in many ways, as watching others teaches new ways of doing things.	2 years
Parallel play	During parallel play, children play by themselves, but they may do so beside other children using the same toys. Having two of the more popular toys is a best practice, if possible.	2+ years
Associative play	At age three, many children have acquired *theory of mind*, which is the ability to understand the feelings of others. During this play, children interact and engage with their peers as their sense of imagination soars.	3–4 years
Cooperative play	This stage of play includes groups with many opportunities to interact and interject a child's own interests. This stage includes games with rules with winners and losers, which is often hard to accept until 6 years and older.	4+ years

Goodheart-Willcox Publisher

Figure 2.3 Mildred Parten stages of play. How can you support each of these stages in your classroom?

Categories of Play

As **Figure 2.4** shows, types of play can be divided into three categories: self-directed (free play), guided, and teacher-led; self-directed play is at one end of the continuum, and teacher-led play is at the other. Neither end of the continuum is effective by itself in creating a high-quality early childhood program. When skillfully supported by the teacher, the three categories in combination support language development, cognitive function, and conceptual learning (NAEYC, *DAP*, 2020).

It is crucial for teachers to understand that simply letting children play is not enough. Teachers must create developmentally appropriate learning environments that promote healthy development and afford opportunities for children to explore and acquire new skills (NAEYC, *DAP*, 2020). When creating learning experiences, understanding different play types is important, both indoors and outdoors. Play is the main teaching device that supports a young child's development and learning, and the categories can be interspersed across the curriculum.

Figure 2.4 Types of play organized into three categories. Why is it important to provide different types of play experiences for children?

 **Checkpoint**

☐ Parten's work focused on the importance of play in early learning environments. What are some play activities that might be beneficial?

☐ Why should all the categories of play be visible in the early childhood classroom?

2.3 Self-Directed Play

Self-directed play, or free play, involves both child-led and adult-led experiences. This includes risky, outdoor, nature, and pretend play. In self-directed play, the teacher's direct role is lessened. Teachers provide the play opportunities and materials, but strive to remain on the sidelines and interrupt the play as little as possible (Cooper 2014; Pyle & Danniels 2017). Research shows that this type of play builds executive functions. *Executive functions* are the mental processes that regulate thought and action in support of goal-directed behavior.

Studies around executive functions are especially applicable to the early years when the cognitive functions of the brain have the most dramatic growth potential. Executive function is a higher-level cognitive process that includes planning, decision making, and completing tasks with little or no support from adults (Barker et al. 2014).

Self-directed play is often practiced during risky play, nature play, and outdoor play. One of the defining characteristics of self-directed play is that it is directed by the children or players themselves, thus *self*-directed.

Risky Play

Risky play is a form of unstructured, thrilling play that children engage in when they assess their physical limits (**Figure 2.5**). In risky play, children fearlessly challenge their comfort zones. Factors that influence children's opportunities for risky play include cultural differences in rules

Figure 2.5 This child is involved in risky play. Do you think this illustrates an appropriate level of risk? Why or why not?

and regulations for playground design, being held accountable for children's injuries, and the risk of litigation (Spiegal et al. 2014). Risky play encourages children to become autonomous and competent decision makers.

Norwegian researcher Ellen Sandseter identified eight categories of risky play by observing children engaged in unstructured outdoor play. She wanted to make sense of the thrill-seeking component in their activities (**Figure 2.6**) (Sandseter & Kleppe 2019).

Risky play is a relatively new area of study, but researchers have seen the benefits risky play can have for children (Lavrysen et al. 2015). Some people believe that risky play makes children safer overall because through these activities, they gain some lived experience on which to base their future choices (Jelleyman et al. 2019). Risky play often occurs outdoors, but it can also appear inside the classroom. Using real tools to prepare a snack, playing disappearing games such as hide-and-seek, or creating sturdy structures to climb on are some examples.

STOP AND THINK

One daily recess period of 15 minutes or more in length was associated with better teacher's rating of class behavior scores for children in grade school. A study by R.M. Barros et al. (2009) suggests that schoolchildren in this age group should be provided with daily recess. How would you advocate for daily planned recesses?

Eight Categories of Risky Play	
Type of Play	**Risk Factors**
Play with great heights	Danger of injury from falling, including all forms of climbing, jumping, hanging/dangling, or balancing from heights
Play with high speed	Uncontrolled speed and pace that can lead to a collision with something (or someone); for instance bicycling at high speeds, sledging (winter), sliding, and running (uncontrollably)
Play with dangerous tools	Can lead to injuries; for instance axe, saw, knife, hammer, or ropes
Play near dangerous elements	Children can fall into or from something, such as water or a fire pit
Rough-and-tumble play	Children can harm each other; for instance, wrestling, fighting, fencing with sticks
Play where children go exploring alone	Exploring without supervision where there are no fences, such as in the woods
Play with impact	Crashing into something repeatedly just for fun
Vicarious play	Experiencing thrill by watching other (most often older) children engaging in risk

Goodheart-Willcox Publisher

Figure 2.6 Categories of risky play. *How can you encourage risky play while still exercising caution in your classroom?*

Outdoor Play

Another form of unstructured play that is crucial for child development is *outdoor play*. Recess is a form of outdoor play. The Centers for Disease Control and Prevention (CDC) defines *recess* as "regularly scheduled periods within a school day for unstructured physical activity and play." Outdoor experiences are a daily expectation in early learning environments. Because outdoor play meets several of children's fundamental needs, educators should never withhold recess as a punishment (NAEYC, *DAP*, 2020).

Nature play is unstructured play time in nature. It is important for children to have free play time during which they can explore the natural world. Some programs have taken incorporated nature play into social studies and science experiences, such as planting and maintaining community gardens (**Figure 2.7**).

Rawpixel.com/Shutterstock.com

Figure 2.7 A teacher and a student working together in a school garden. What can children learn in a school garden?

Pretend Play

Pretend play is known by many names, including *fantasy*, *make-believe*, or *dress-up*. Pretend play provides opportunities to try out social skills, develop language, and role play, and is connected to self-directed and guided play. Pretend play is a type of play in which a child is able to impersonate another person or have an experience in a safe way. This type of play is divided into two categories: *self-directed* and *guided*. In pretend play, "a child sometimes needs to express pretend emotions, if these are associated with a particular role and imaginary situation" (Bodrova & Leong 2019), such as when a child needs to play the role of an unhappy customer in one scenario or a hungry baby in another. By expressing their emotions, children are showing emotional awareness and taking steps toward learning self-control. An example of guided play would be the teacher suggesting that two children play "dinner" with toy foods. In self-directed play, the children would begin to play "dinner" themselves without prompting from an adult.

Superhero Play

Superhero play is a form of pretend play. It is amazing how a cape (even a pillowcase used as a makeshift cape) thrown across a child's shoulders can transform the child into a true superhero. Role models are important for young children. Support superheroes play if the play exhibits qualities that are worth respecting, such as honesty, courage, being able to do extraordinary feats for the good of all. Examples include Superman and Wonder Woman.

The innate good qualities of superheroes inspire children and help them focus on positive characteristics. Superheroes influence children through play by (**Figure 2.8**) (Gongala 2023):

- building self-confidence in children who need a boost in their self-esteem.
- instilling compassion because a superhero protects the needy and innocent.
- helping children understand the concepts of right and wrong and learn new words such as *ethical*.
- helping children feel empowered because superheroes usually have a life apart from their superhero persona.

Superhero play is a popular form of play in the early years and should be supported by caregiver conversations exploring concepts of good versus bad.

Checkpoint

- How do risky, pretend, and outdoor play support executive function? Provide an example for each.
- Which types of self-directed play also fall into the guided play category? Identify what those might look like.

2.4 Guided Play

In the middle of the play continuum is guided play. In *guided play*, teachers may provide materials and resources to support play choices. Guided play is common during pretend, investigative, and cooperative play. Guided play promotes language development across subject areas and is more effective than rote vocabulary exercises (Riley-Ayers & Figueras-Daniel 2019).

RichVintage/E+ via Getty Images

Figure 2.8 Two young children dressed as superheroes play outside. What are the benefits of superhero play?

Investigative Play

Investigative play provides time to tinker, explore, and experiment. Giving children autonomy and *agency* (the child's ability to make and act upon choices) helps them learn how to solve problems and improve their executive functioning (Barker et al. 2014). Teachers should provide time for investigative play every day. During this time, children should be free to explore their environment, interact with their peers, and play. They also *tinker*, or take things apart, put things together, figure out how things work, and attempt to make new creations (Heroman 2017).

Examples of investigative play can be found across the classroom in the science, woodworking, and math areas, or in a special area called a tinkering lab. Tinkering is also an integral component of a STEM-specific (science, technology, engineering, math) focus.

Cooperative Play

Cooperative play is defined as play in which children work together to solve a problem or complete a task (**Figure 2.9**). This type of play can take many forms. Groupings vary from pairs to small groups. This play is usually guided by the teacher, who presents challenges and often decides how children will be grouped. Examples of cooperative play include playing games such as Candy Land® or red-light-green-light; working to solve a teacher-created mystery; or playing different roles as part of a pretend scenario. Cooperative play serves an important place in children's learning.

Claudia Paulussen/Shutterstock.com

Figure 2.9 Cooperative play in action. Do you think these children would benefit from adult guidance in this moment? Why or why not?

Checkpoint

- How does "tinkering" support the development of agency?
- Identify ways in which cooperative play can be incorporated into a family's routine at home. How might you share these ideas with families?

2.5 Teacher-Led Play

Teacher-led play can occur in any of the types of play. Teacher-led play involves a high level of adult decision-making about the play experience. Epstein (2014) defined this type of play as "engaged with a high level of adult control." An example is children following step-by-step directions to build a craft. Teachers decide how much to insert themselves into the play experiences based on the learning target for that activity and on the children's scaffolding needs (Weisberg et al. 2013).

Planning for Play

With limited time in a day, teachers must plan play experiences carefully. Providing materials to support each child's knowledge and interests will engage children in their own learning (**Figure 2.10**). Well-planned play experiences allow children to be spontaneous and use their decision-making and executive function skills.

THE TEACHER'S LENS

Mrs. Bill is writing her daily learning plan and will include a learning outcome for counting out loud, which is one of the state math standards for four-year-olds. There are many possible experiences through which her students demonstrate understanding, including examples of guided, self-directed, and teacher-directed play. Below is an example of each.

1. Guided play: Experiments with and uses numbers in play (dramatic play area restaurant includes cash register and menus with numerals).
2. Self-directed play: Counts numbers in outdoor play from chalk-drawn hopscotch game.
3. Teacher-directed play: Participates in counting activity.

Knowing that the children have different interests, Mrs. Bill is confident that many will be able to demonstrate the learning outcome in one way or another. Offering many ways to assess a learning outcome is a best practice.

When planning for children's play, teachers identify the learning target while individualizing for children of all ability levels. This means the teacher must have a strong base of knowledge about each child, including cultural background. A teacher who has a goal of increasing the amount of receptive language a child uses throughout the day may invite the child to the dramatic play area with another child who is more verbal to engage in a play scenario. The teacher might ask open-ended questions such as "Why is the baby crying?" or "How do you think the daddy can help the baby?". Open-ended questions provide the child with an opportunity to use expressive language and to think and formulate an answer.

Children need to be seen as capable. The freedom to play and interact with other children helps them build confidence. Play becomes a springboard for "investigating play materials, art materials, the ideas of peers, and the world beyond the classroom".

Implementing Play

When teachers carefully plan developmentally appropriate play experiences, the benefits to the children are

Robin Stirling

Figure 2.10 These children have buckets of blocks that their teacher gave them to wear outside. How do these buckets encourage the children to interact with one another?

STOP AND THINK

Parents in the United States provide dolls, toys, and other objects in their children's private play areas (**Figure 2.11**). This is typical of cultures that emphasize independence. In Japan, however, the same dolls, toys, and other objects are seen as tools to enhance peer social play. This is typical of cultures that emphasize interdependence (Schulz & Bonawitz 2007). This remains true today. Which of these types of play do you most connect with?

Marko Poplasen/Shutterstock.com

Figure 2.11 This child is engaged in doll play. Do you think doll play is valuable for young children? Why or why not?

maximized (Rice 2017). The interventions a teacher makes during play include assisting with conflict resolution, providing ideas or problems to expand a play scenario, and helping with learning as needed. It may also be important to model play skills for children who are struggling with a play experience (**Figure 2.12**).

Effective teachers offer play experiences in areas children are familiar with and plan curriculum based on the child's prior knowledge and experiences. It is amazing how easy it is to support play and imagination with few to no supplies. The novel is often the most fascinating. In contrast, teachers today must decide how and when to use technology in the classroom. This question is the focus of the next section.

✓ Checkpoint

- Compare two examples of teacher-led play. What are the differences? What are the similarities?
- What are the benefits of teacher-led play? What are the possible consequences?

2.6 Technology and Play

Technology in an early learning environment can be used as a tool of teacher-directed play. NAEYC defines **technology** as any human-made device that is used to solve a problem or fulfill a desire. Technology can be an object, a system, or a process that results in the modification of the natural world to meet human needs and wants. Additionally, technology includes digital tools such as computers, tablets, apps, e-readers, smartphones, televisions, music players, handheld games, cameras, digital microscopes, interactive whiteboards, electronic toys, non-screen-based tangible technology, and robots. Familiar analog tools are also found in early childhood classrooms

Mario Arango/E+ via Getty Images

Figure 2.12 Facilitating play requires observation to support children in their attempts. How do you think this teacher is supporting this child?

and include audio recorders, headphones, crayons, pencils, scissors, rulers, blocks, and magnifying glasses (NAEYC, *DAP*, 2020).

Digital Media

Screen time is the term for use of digital media. In an early learning environment, screen time should be limited. The more time children spend watching screens, the fewer opportunities they have for play and interaction with other children and caring adults, both of which are critical to healthy development and learning. Many states' regulations restrict or limit the hours an early childhood program can spend sharing screens with young children.

The internet is commonplace today, but there is still no way to ensure that it is absolutely safe for children. Supervision is crucial, and technology play should always be considered a teacher-directed activity. However, despite the many concerns, multiple elements provided by technology can enrich play. It is hands-on, engaging, empowering, and provides adaptive scaffolds to help each child progress in skill development at their individual pace.

Three examples of digital technology that are developmentally appropriate for children are digital cameras (to engage with photography), live cams (to explore different parts of

REAL-WORLD CLASSROOM

Consider this example of the proper way to use technology in the classroom. Megan and Diego are enrolled in classrooms that value the use of technology. Their families see this as an opportunity to provide experiences that they will be able to build on for future learning opportunities. Their teacher oversees these learning experiences, which are rich play activities.

This week, four-year-old Diego is the reporter for his classroom's weekly newsletter (**Figure 2.13**). Putting himself in the reporter role, he scans the room and decides to interview two classmates who are playing with blocks. He writes his story with invented spelling and sketches an image to go with it. The teacher will sit down with Diego later to transcribe the story, then show him how to scan his image for the weekly *Kid Zone* article.

Megan is six years old and is interested in writing a book about her family pet. The teacher begins by teaching Megan the word *edit* and explains that Megan will use the computer to write several *drafts* of her writing before going to print. Megan is also the illustrator and spends many weeks working on her book before sitting down at the computer to type it. There she learns about *fonts*, how to make spaces between words, and how to manipulate a mouse, all with teacher supervision.

Taking on the role of class reporter and contributing to the class newsletter, authoring one's own storybook, and creating a digital image are all examples of being a producer of technology rather than a passive consumer. This example shows how technology can be part of pretend play as well as an important element in literacy.

SDI Productions/E+ via Getty Images

Figure 2.13 Diego's teacher is helping him with his story. *Do you think she should let Diego practice inventive spelling or tell him how to spell each word? Explain your answer.*

the world), and listening to voice recordings (to assist with literacy activities). Technology also provides children with an opportunity to develop *digital literacy*, or the ability to find, evaluate, create, and communicate using digital platforms. In appropriate moderation, technology can be a useful learning tool for young children.

Cautions About Children and Digital Technology

The COVID-19 pandemic required technology to be part of all learning experiences across the world, and it certainly served a purpose as a conduit of information. However, it is important for early childhood educators to ensure that technology does not replace active play. Technology and interactive media can expand children's access to content and skills, but it is not a replacement for hands-on experiences (Donohue & Schomburg 2017).

Research indicates that screen time has a negative impact on young children's developing cognitive and self-regulation capacities (Canadian Paediatric Society 2018). As academic expectations for younger children expand, an increased focus on skills and content knowledge means there is less time for play in early childhood classrooms. A focus on teaching academic concepts rather than lifelong skills such as listening to directions, practicing problem-solving, or applying critical thinking strategies can have negative results (Yogman et al. 2018). The American Academy of Pediatrics (AAP) calls for no screen time at all for children until 18 to 24 months, except for video chatting, and says children ages 2 to 5 should get an hour or less of screen time per day.

For teachers, these guidelines can have many classroom implications. Teachers should carefully consider which technologies are developmentally appropriate. Also, it is important that teachers provide a balance. Technology and media can be valuable and useful tools, but should not replace other critical hands-on and creative learning opportunities (NAEYC and Fred Rogers 2012).

 **Checkpoint**

- ☐ How do you see technology being used in the classroom? What are DAP considerations to be aware of?
- ☐ Identify positive uses of digital literacy and how it can be applied in the classroom.

2.7 Cultural Differences in Play

The focus of this final section is ensuring that all children are provided with the same opportunities. Diverse and equitable learning experiences should include *all* children.

Play reflects and transmits cultural values. **Culture** is defined as patterns of beliefs, practices, and traditions associated with a particular group of people. Culture is increasingly understood as inseparable from development (Reid et al. 2017).

Children's preferences around play reflect the culture and values they are raised with, regardless of where they came from. Understanding different ways in which families raise their children is important to inform a teacher's instruction. Some children prefer to spend time alone, while others choose to spend time doing competitive activities. Some children may be motivated by individual achievement and do well in smaller groups, whereas other children may prefer to play within larger groups and are less interested in competition (Sosik & Jung 2002).

Cultures differ in the level and quality of expressiveness that is permitted or encouraged. In some cultures, emotional restraint is emphasized. In other cultures, self-expression is encouraged.

A parent from one culture may view a classroom as disorderly or aggressive, while a parent from another culture will see the classroom as boisterous and highly spirited. Teachers must understand families' customs and attitudes when planning learning experiences.

There are many pathways and practices that symbolize quality play, and some are better suited to particular cultures than others. For instance, in Guatemala, play is not considered important, and the adults find the suggestion of playing with young children amusing. Such beliefs are in stark contrast to the very close attention some US parents pay to their children's experiences (Roopnarine & Davidson 2015). In New Guinea, children learn through a combination of work and play. Examples include hunting (making traps), collecting insects, fishing, playing house, and creating accessories (making eyeglasses out of vines) (Roopnarine & Davidson 2015) (**Figure 2.14**).

Mike Workman/Shutterstock.com

Figure 2.14 In New Guinea, children are taught to fish for survival from a very young age. How is this different from what young children are taught in your culture?

STOP AND THINK

There is no argument that access to technology is an inevitable necessity for school-age children and teens. But is it an advantage or disadvantage for preschoolers? Through play, a child learns how to deal with real-life situations in a safe environment. How can technology be used to build life skills through play?

Whatever form it takes, play should have a central role in early childhood education programs. The core tenets of play should be valued (**Figure 2.15**). When children are told frequently "select another center" or "it is time to move on to something else," they are not allowed to engage with the materials long enough to develop problem solving skills. *Persistence* is a firm or obstinate continuance in a course of action in spite of difficulty or opposition. It is important that teachers realize that persistence is a universal character strength, required in order to overcome obstacles and build resilience, and that it takes time. Learning through play can provide these lifelong values.

Teachers must provide diverse play materials and change classroom props frequently to relate to children's real-life interests and experiences. Books and music that reflect different cultures should be accessible in the classroom. The dramatic play area should include clothing and pretend foods from various cultures. Hanging diverse family photos on the walls is a great way to help children feel seen and to understand that not all families look exactly like their families.

Educators are driven by developmentally appropriate practice and culture in the early childhood classroom. Unfortunately, not all children have access to the same types and quality of play experiences. Black and Latino children are the highest risk group (NAEYC, *DAP*, 2020). The restriction and sometimes loss of this central tool of learning is a major equity issue of classism. ***Classism*** is any attitude, action, or practice that gives one group of people greater opportunities or resources or preferential treatment based on economic means. Children often learn classist ideas from the curriculum at school, which may emphasize the work of people in professional careers with

Core Tenets of Play

taking risks
making mistakes
exploring new ideas
supporting imagination
experiencing joy

Goodheart-Willcox Publisher

Figure 2.15 The core tenets of play. Why is it important for children to be afforded play opportunities?

middle- to higher-income jobs (Edwards & Derman-Sparks 2020). For example, children's books often depict families shopping at grocery stores and living in houses or apartments. Families who depend on a community food bank or live in a homeless shelter are rarely depicted.

There are many ways to be inclusive and respectful when planning learning experiences. Curriculum themes such as community helpers provide an opportunity to focus on roles such as bus drivers, janitors, and mechanics versus only doctors, firefighters, and police officers. Inviting both low-income and high-income guest speakers to share their work on career day will encourage awareness of different economic situations.

Another way teachers can help children understand different lifestyles is to create scenarios in the dramatic play area in which children try to solve a conflict involving money or social status. Consider a restaurant scenario in which a customer who may be unhoused does not have enough money to pay for a food order. The cook prepares the food, and the server delivers it. These are valuable play and learning opportunities that will benefit all children regardless of their backgrounds.

Play as an integral component of curriculum is sometimes seen as being at odds with the demands of formal schooling, and this may be of particular concern for children growing up in under-resourced communities (McCoy et al. 2017). The early childhood teacher who embraces the multifaceted approaches of inclusivity will be part of making a difference for the next generation of leaders.

Checkpoint

- Define the character trait "persistence" and provide examples of how this can be supported in the classroom.
- How does classism affect teaching practices today? Identify two examples.

Chapter 2 Review and Assessment

Summary

2.1 Describe play connections to brain development and the pedagogy of play.
- Tactile play or games such as peekaboo engage the brainstem, which supports all body functioning.
- The midbrain supports development of both fine motor skills (use of small muscles) and gross motor skills (use of large muscles), while also helping to integrate complex sensory input.
- The limbic area of the brain controls emotions, such as belonging. As the limbic area develops, children are increasingly able to understand social relationships. When a child is ready, learning to share and taking turns are supported by the limbic level of the brain.
- The cortical area (neocortex) is the most complex area of the brain and supports abstract thoughts, humor, and language. This area promotes playing games, laughing at jokes, and thinking out scenarios in play.
- Pedagogy of play comprises three key components: choice, wonder, and delight.
- Choice reflects the child's decisions to engage in play.
- Wonder is reflected in the child's continued engagement as they explore, gather information, test hypotheses, and make meaning.
- Delight is seen in the child's joy and laughter associated with the pleasure of the activity, making discoveries, and achieving new things.

2.2 Identify Mildred Parten's five stages of play.
- Parten's stages of play are solitary, onlooker, parallel, associative, and cooperative play. They are organized according to age to provide guidance for teachers who are planning curriculum.
- Three categories represent the different types of play: self-directed (free play), guided, and teacher-led; self-directed play is at one end of the continuum, and teacher-led play is at the other.
- Play is the central teaching practice that supports a young child's development and learning. The categories can be interspersed across the curriculum.

2.3 Summarize types of self-directed play.
- The five types of self-directed play are risky play, outdoor play, pretend play, and superhero play.
- Self-directed play limits the teacher's role to providing resources for play and supporting without taking over or interrupting the play.
- Research shows that self-directed play builds executive functions, or the mental processes that regulate thought and action in support of goal-directed behavior.

2.4 Summarize types of guided play.
- The two types of guided play are investigative and cooperative play. Each involves the teacher at some level to support the child in exploring and learning with others.

2.5 Describe teacher-led play.
- Teacher-led learning experiences are present in the classroom daily.
- Most play types can be teacher-led in addition to being self-directed or guided.
- The two steps of teacher-led play are planning for play and implementing play.

2.6 Explain connections between technology and play.
- Technology is a valuable teacher-led element in the classroom today.
- Many states' regulations restrict or limit the hours an early childhood program can spend sharing screens with young children.
- Technology and interactive media should not replace other beneficial learning activities such as creative play, outdoor experiences, and social interactions with peers and adults in early childhood settings.

2.7 Identify ways to support cultural diversity in play.
- Supporting cultural diversity in play explores the specific cultural differences and important classroom practices that support, honor, and respect all children and families when creating curriculum.
- Teachers must understand families' customs and attitudes when planning learning experiences.

For Further Review

1. Provide examples of play and learning experiences that align to each of Parten's stages of play.
2. Visit the National Toy Hall of Fame's website to learn about nominees and prior winners. What is a toy you might nominate that has not won before? Why?
3. What roles did adults play when you were a child? How might this guide your play decisions?
4. Identify your own superhero. How would you support superhero play in the classroom?
5. Describe your comfort zone for risky play. What is an example of the limits you might set using Sandseter's defined categories?
6. Identify difficulties that might need to be overcome when creating a classroom curriculum that reflects the many cultures of children enrolled. How might families be able to contribute in this area?

Recall and Application

1. **True or False.** Brain development is supported by play.
2. Identify the three components of play.
   A. open-ended, free, spontaneous
   B. wonder, joy, delight
   C. choice, wonder, delight
   D. free, unstructured, joy
3. **True or False.** Cooperative play may occur at any stage of development.
4. What do the categories of play have in common?
   A. build academic language
   B. deepen conceptual development
   C. support reflective and intentional approaches to learning
   D. All of the above.
5. Self-directed play includes ____ play.
   A. investigative
   B. risky
   C. technology
   D. cooperative

6. **True or False.** Self-directed play builds executive functions.
7. **True or False.** Cooperative play requires children to work alone, while investigative play is often done with others.
8. **True or False.** The benefits of play are maximized when teachers facilitate play.
9. **True or False.** Digital literacy is the practice of listening to audio books.
10. Classism is an "ism" that ____.
    A. creates a sense of unity
    B. gives preferential treatment to certain groups
    C. provides a sense of balance
    D. is no longer present in society
11. **True or False.** Persistence is a firm or obstinate continuance in a course of action in spite of difficulty or opposition.

Theories of Curricula and Approaches

CHAPTER 3

Standards Covered in This Chapter

NAEYC
4b, 4c, 5a, 5b, 5c. 6d, 6e

DAP
Guideline 5; Principle 7

Learning Outcomes

After studying this chapter, you will be able to:

3.1 Summarize the theory and framework of the Tools of the Mind curriculum.

3.2 Identify HighScope curriculum goals in the early childhood classroom.

3.3 List Montessori curriculum components.

3.4 Describe how anthroposophy is integral to the Waldorf curriculum.

3.5 Explain the concept behind thematic curriculum.

3.6 Apply Project Approach strategies in the early childhood classroom.

3.7 Identify Reggio Emilia Approach influences in the early childhood classroom.

Image credit: FatCamera/E+ via Getty Images

Lin

SNAPSHOT

DGLimages/iStock via Getty Images Plus

Lin was interviewing for his first teaching position when the director of the school asked, "What is your favorite type of curriculum?" Having studied curriculum development in college, Lin had a ready answer. He knew about the major theorists and their approaches to curriculum and was eager to share why he supported his choice. Lin had done his research and knew that the program where he was interviewing shared his preference of child development curriculum.

Lin had studied many different curricula and approaches and selected the program he was interviewing for based on what was a good fit for his preferred curriculum type. His solid understanding of child development and milestones supported his views, and he did not want to begin work and develop relationships with families and their children that were not long term.

Lin was aware of how important it is to create strong relationships in the early years. Strong relationships develop trust and constitute one element of the foundation of developing self-regulation. His dream of making a difference in the lives of young children will be shared during the interview as a factor of why he is the best choice for the school's job opening.

Give It Some Thought

1. Lin has done research on a possible place for employment. What are the benefits for children? For the employer? For Lin?
2. Do you think Lin should share additional information with the prospective employer? If so, what would you include?

Key Terms

anthroposophy
atelierista
co-construction of learning
dynamic assessment
emergent curriculum
key developmental indicator (KDI)

looping
manipulatives
mediators
plan-do-review process
prepared environment
private speech
Project Approach

scaffold
self-regulation
shared learning
thematic curriculum
written speech
zone of proximal development (ZPD)

Introduction

The world *curriculum* has at least 83 definitions and more than 72 different curricula are currently practiced in early childhood education across the world (Wiggins 2015). Chapter 3 provides an overview of the major early childhood development theorists and their approaches to curriculum, including overviews of the two major approaches. Each section of the chapter provides a broad introduction to topics that will be further explored in later chapters, in keeping with the concept of integration and interconnectedness of subjects throughout child development. With so many varying definitions of curriculum, it is important to examine the concept in broad terms. Throughout this textbook, *The Teacher's Lens* features provide insights into the specific types of education or training required to teach each curriculum.

The broad definition of *curriculum* is "a course of study taught in school." At each curriculum's core is a framework derived from a certain theoretical perspective about how children learn. However, an early childhood program may use its own invented curriculum that borrows from many different frameworks and theorists.

Approaches to curriculum address how education should be designed to work best with children. Approaches are also connected to different theoretical principles and work hand-in-hand with curriculum. Curricula and approaches embrace a philosophy shared by the people responsible for developing them. This chapter starts with Lev Vygotsky and the curriculum that has embraced his work, Tools of the Mind.

3.1 Tools of the Mind Curriculum

Psychologist Lev Vygotsky (1896–1934) was born in Russia and spent his life primarily focused on the relationship between language and thinking. He believed that social interaction plays a pivotal role in the development of thinking (Vygotsky 1986).

The world did not know of Vygotsky's research until the late 1950s when the Soviet Union allowed sharing of information. Today, Vygotsky's research is embodied in the *Tools of the Mind (ToM) curriculum* and is evident in other different curricula and approaches in one way or another. ToM was first introduced in 1993 by Dr. Elena Bodrova and Dr. Deborah Leong to children at the Metropolitan State College of Denver's laboratory school.

Tools of the Mind Curriculum Structure

ToM stems from Vygotsky's belief that people can use mental tools to extend mental abilities in the same way they use physical tools, such as ladders and hammers, to extend their physical abilities. Applying this concept to early childhood education helps children achieve success in the classroom and in life. The ToM curriculum focuses on self-regulation, understanding, and applying scaffolding within a child's *zone of proximal development*, paired with a variety of tactics to support a child's development. The **zone of proximal development (ZPD)** describes what a child can do with maximum assistance and what the child can do alone. The boundaries of a child's ZPD are measured by two levels of performance:

- The lower zone specifies what the child can do alone. For example, with no help from anyone, first-grader Liam is able to put together a seven-piece puzzle.
- The upper zone specifies what the child can do with maximum assistance. For example, Liam can put together a 50-piece puzzle with his teacher sitting next to him showing where each piece goes.

For the most effective instruction, the ToM teacher aims inside the child's current ZPD. Knowing that each child's ZPD is always updating as the child gains new information, the ToM teacher continually challenges the child to perform at higher levels (**Figure 3.1**).

THE TEACHER'S LENS

Miss Miles has completed an in-depth two-year study of ToM, and the school has purchased the ToM curriculum for teachers to use. Knowing that every child in the classroom has a different ZPD in different areas of development, Miss Miles will scaffold using the provided supports to ensure that sequential activities individualize learning.

The central focus of the ToM curriculum is the development of cognitive and social-emotional self-regulation alongside academic skills. By using a variety of strategies and tools in a variety of areas in the classroom, in particular through play, children are taught approaches that expand their mental abilities. See **Figure 3.2** for an example of a ToM sample schedule.

Understanding the role of self-regulation is a major goal of the ToM classroom. ***Self-regulation*** is the ability to keep emotions in check and control physical behavior. The development of self-regulation impacts social interactions and supports a person's ability to pay attention when learning across all levels of development.

According to Vygotsky, "until children learn to use mental tools, their learning is largely controlled by the environment; they attend only to the things that are brightest or loudest, and they can remember something only if has been repeated many times." Once children master those mental tools, Vygotsky claimed, they can take charge of their own learning and build self-regulation to support staying on task, ignoring distractions, and remembering on purpose. They will also become capable of holding two strategies in mind at one time and developing self-discipline (toolsofthemind.org) (Leong, n.d.).

Three types of interactions are important when learning self-regulation skills. Bodrova and Leong (2017) stress that children begin developing self-regulation by absorbing a teacher's rules, but to fully develop self-regulation children must participate in the following interactions:

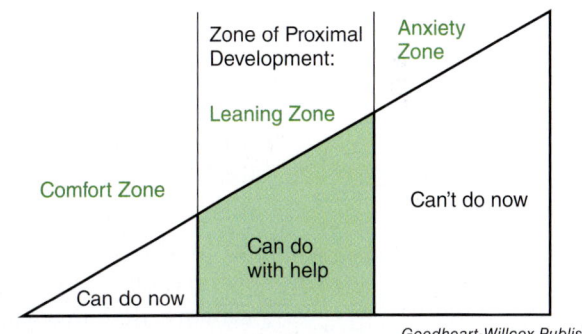

Goodheart-Willcox Publisher

Figure 3.1 The zone of proximal development (ZPD) represents what a child can do unsupported and with assistance. What is an example of something a toddler needs assistance with?

Sample Tools of the Mind Schedule		
Time	Activity	Learning Experience
9:00 a.m.–9:15 a.m.	Opening Group	Active self-regulation activities, large group sharing, share the news, message of the day
9:15 a.m.–10:30 a.m.	Play Block	Play planning, play in learning areas/centers
10:35 a.m.–10:50 a.m.	Large Group	Story-time, writing practice
10:55 a.m.–11:55 a.m.	Outside Play	Open choices
12:00 p.m.–12:30 p.m.	Lunch	
12:35 p.m.–1:45 p.m.	Rest or Quiet Time	
1:50 p.m.–2:10 p.m.	Small Groups	Science and math or literacy
2:15 p.m.–2:45 p.m.	Outside Play	
2:45 p.m.–3:00 p.m.	Closing Group	Wrap-up meeting

Goodheart-Willcox Publisher

Figure 3.2 This is an example of a ToM daily schedule. Do you think this schedule is appropriate for young children? Why or why not?

1. **Being regulated by someone else (teacher, parent, or peer).** Another person teaches the foundation of self-regulation.
2. **Regulating someone else.** Children need to internalize rules. For example, if "wash your hands" is a classroom rule, it applies whether the teacher says it, another child says it, or the child says it. The ability of children to use their knowledge to regulate others constitutes a big step in being able to internalize rules for themselves.
3. **Regulating yourself.** For true self-regulation to emerge, children have to inhibit their behavior because they want to.

Instructional Strategies

The ToM teacher *scaffolds* (provides hints to support the child) inside the child's ZPD, while encouraging independent performance as needed. Though Vygotsky did not coin the term "scaffold," it is often associated with teachings based on his theory.

"Teacher interactions are used in the course of formal or informal instruction to help a child move from being assisted by an adult or by a more competent peer to being able to perform this and similar tasks independently" (Bodrova & Leong 2018). ToM teachers individualize instruction in math, science, and literacy to fit each child's developmental path. They use scaffolds connected to all learning activities and utilize three tactics to support children's developing mental abilities: mediators, language, and shared learning.

Mediators

Mediators are external, tangible tools to support children's learning, such as cards with pictures. Mediators positively impact all domains of development (cognitive, physical, and social-emotional). Effective mediators help children become masters of their own behavior (toolsofthemind.org).

In a ToM classroom, mediators are designed to help children internalize their thinking and actions. Tangible mediators include pictures that indicate various actions. For example, a picture of an eye to 'watch' or an ear to 'listen' might be shown to help children focus their attention. With practice, children internalize the rules with support from the pictorial cards. Visible mediators can include labels in the different learning areas or a class schedule that includes pictures of the activities performed at various times of the day. Examples of mental mediators include counting to five to control an action or singing the same song when it is time to transition to another classroom activity. These mediators support a child's memory and assist with social interactions with their peers. **Figure 3.3** illustrates an example of mediator that can be shown to children to encourage listening skills.

Mediators support development and the child's shift from assisted to independent performance. Mediators are meant to be internalized so children will eventually no longer need them. For example, a child's name tag is a mediator to support learning to write the letters of the child's name. This mediator is removed once the child has mastered the skill.

Hiranmay Baidya/iStock/Getty Images Plus

Figure 3.3 Visual images called mediators help children make connections to what is needed. An ear represents 'listen.' *What other mediators might be helpful in an early learning environment?*

Language

Vygotsky believed that *language* plays a central role in learning and development (Bodrova & Leong 2018). The ToM teacher supports language in two ways: private speech and written speech. ***Private speech*** is self-regulatory speech. We use it to tell ourselves what to do or what *not* to do, and it strengthens the influence of mediators. ***Written speech*** is more than oral speech on paper; written speech reflects capacities for higher-level thinking. To assist with the process of unfolding verbal thinking, the ToM classroom teacher asks children to articulate their thought process, to think while talking to others, and to use written words and drawings to express their understanding.

Talking to yourself is a form of private speech, and one that many adults utilize when trying to solve a complex problem. Young children use private speech often, as they are not yet able to internalize thought processes in their head. Supporting children in verbalizing their actions is a common element in the ToM classroom. Vygotsky (1987) proposed that a child's social environment affects their use of private speech. This claim is supported by the fact that high positive correlations between rates of social interaction and private speech in children.

The ToM curriculum captures written speech through the use of scaffolded writing, which is found to have a profound influence on development. *Scaffolded writing* is a strategy that:

- makes thinking more explicit (allows you to look at your thoughts)
- makes thinking and the use of symbols more deliberate (only what is on paper communicates)
- makes the child aware of the elements of language (words make up sentences)

Vygotsky believed that young children's drawings are a precursor to later writing skills. He noted that the way children learn to say their first words is similar in many ways to the way they first learn to draw. The ToM classroom integrates drawing into the classroom to increase a child's awareness of their own thinking. and they understand the purpose of written speech prior to learning to write (toolsofthemind.org).

Shared Learning

Shared learning is the third Vygotsky tactic. Shared learning in the ToM is a way to scaffold learning and connect to the idea of a **co-construction of learning**. Vygotsky believed that what people learn *while* learning is a shared state between people: the expert and the novice. Working cooperatively, the expert and the novice arrive at a shared conclusion or outcome. In true Vygotsky form, the learning does not imply that only the teacher is the expert. Children can learn from their peers while supporting one another.

> **STOP AND THINK**
> The number one challenge kindergarten teachers face is children who are not able to control their own behavior and focus on learning in the classroom (Scholastic Parents Staff n.d.). Identify ways in which children can be supported in their learning.

Imaginative Play

ToM recognizes that imaginative mature make-believe play supports cognitive, emotional, and social development. Imaginative play has three elements in the ToM classroom (toolsofthemind.org):

1. Children create an imaginary situation.
2. Children take on and act out roles.
3. Children follow a set of rules determined by specific roles.

Mature make-believe play helps children develop imagination, symbolic function, and self-regulation while also integrating emotions and thinking. To define where play starts, begin with a play plan. Mature make-believe play involves children having a role (baby, daddy, mommy, restaurant chef, etc.), not simply playing with toys in an open-ended manner.

ToM teachers engage children in mature make-believe play practice. They act out different characters and scenarios first, then let children have a try (Bodrova & Leong 2018).

Children are assigned specific roles to play in the ToM dramatic play group and the teacher intentionally pairs children together to ensure that:

- children engage in other regulation.
- learning is meaningful.
- deeper reflection of thinking is encouraged.

Children in ToM programs create their own play plans each morning (**Figure 3.4**). Drawing what they plan to do each day helps children develop cognitive self-regulation and higher-level play skills. The play plan helps children identify roles, actions, and scenarios and play these out in the dramatic play area. This is critical for developing self-regulation. The play plan also provides a basis to alter one's plan if changes are needed so the children learn to regulate one another.

By using oral and written speech as methods for remembering, each child's drawing and scaffolded writing records a plan, while developing emergent literacy skills and phonemic awareness as depicted in Figure 3.4 reflects a child created play plan. The TOM teacher receives specific training to support emergent literacy skills in the curriculum in regards to the teaching and how to conduct dynamic assessment.

Ginny Harmelink

Figure 3.4 Tools of the Mind students create their own play plans. What are the benefits for the child of creating their own plans?

Dynamic Assessment

The ToM teacher receives specific training to support emergent literacy skills in the curriculum, including how to conduct dynamic assessment.

Dynamic assessment is a practice that is unique to the ToM curriculum. Dynamic assessment often occurs during a group activity when additional reflection is needed for some children. Teachers consider the ZPD of each child to guide decisions about when and to whom to offer scaffolding. This unique form of assessment focuses on awareness of what the child is able to do independently and using that knowledge to probe what skills they are on the verge of grasping with and without scaffolding. This is much different than most assessments, which typically only consider what the child is currently able to do.

 **Checkpoint**

☐ Describe a learning experience to which a teacher might apply the principles of the ZPD.

☐ Provide examples of private speech and written speech.

☐ Compare dynamic assessment to another form of assessment when observing children. What are the similarities? the differences?

3.2 HighScope Curriculum

HighScope teachers use intentional arrangements of the classroom and predictable daily routines to cultivate children's sense of competence, to encourage social interactions, and to build a secure community. This approach evolved from a federal longitudinal study called the *Perry Preschool Project*, which started in 1962. The project studied the impact of high-quality early childhood education on children with risk factors for failing at school. The study found that children who were exposed to the HighScope "active participatory learning" approach were more likely to graduate from high school than adults who did not have any preschool. They committed fewer crimes, were more likely to be employed, and reported higher financial earnings (HighScope.org). David Weikart established the HighScope curriculum in 1970 and it remains popular today.

THE TEACHER'S LENS

Miss Lisa is a lead HighScope teacher, having completed the appropriate training that included demonstrating knowledge of the COR Advantage. She has taught the HighScope curriculum for seven years and works at a program that is HighScope accredited in both the infant-toddler and the preschool curriculum endorsement, both setting a high bar of learning.

HighScope Curriculum Structure

HighScope curriculum is an open-framework approach that encourages teachers to follow children's interests. The context for learning is implemented and supported by four elements: active learning, classroom arrangement, the daily schedule, and the content or curriculum. See **Figure 3.5** for an example of a HighScope daily routine.

This curriculum has roots in Piagetian cognitive theory. The idea is that if the teacher follows the child's lead, the development of self will occur naturally. This curriculum focuses on similarities rather than differences and stresses the positive elements people can learn from one another as depicted in the Wheel of Active Learning (**Figure 3.6**), which reflects the components that make up the active learning framework. The HighScope approach affords children the freedom to explore, make their own choices, manipulate materials, and interact with adults and peers in a supportive, nurturing environment.

HighScope's *key developmental indicators (KDIs)* describe how children develop and guide adults in supporting development during active learning time. KDIs are behaviors that reflect the child's developing mental, emotional, physical, and social abilities. As children follow their self-directed goals, they engage with the curriculum's content, as measured by the KDIs.

HighScope acknowledges that young children need to master a wide range of specific knowledge and thinking skills (Epstein & Hohmann 2012). Allowing academic subjects to flow right into the HighScope curriculum is part of the learning experience. Various subjects are intentionally woven throughout the different learning areas. In the HighScope curriculum, the content of children's learning is organized into the following eight major divisions made up of 58 KDIs (highscope.org):

HighScope Daily Routine

Activity	Learning Experience
Small Group Time	In small groups, children actively participate in teacher-introduced activities that may include cooking, art, movement, motor, or cognitive skills.
Large Group Time	Children participate in songs, stories, flannel board activities, and movement activities.
Planning	Children choose an activity in one of the areas of the classroom to participate in during Choice Time.
Do	Children conduct their plans by building, painting, counting, dressing up, and so on. Teachers function as facilitators by becoming part of the child's play and enhancing and extending the child's skills through play, exploration, and language.
Cleanup Time	Children restore order to the classroom by returning items to their proper places, using labels as guides.
Review	Children actively review what they have done during Choice Time.

Goodheart-Willcox Publisher

Figure 3.5 The HighScope active learning circle represents hands-on involvement with individuals, events, ideas, and materials. *What role does teamwork play in this environment?*

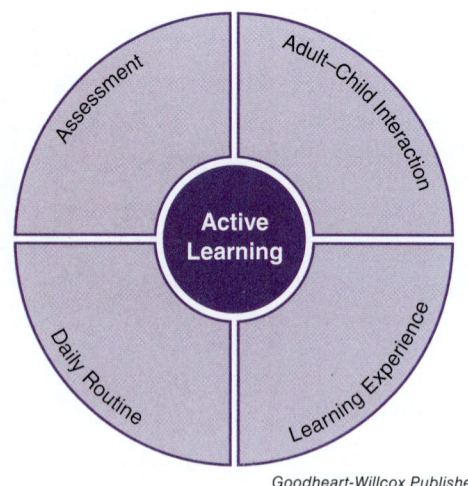

- Approach to learning
- Social and emotional development
- Physical development and health
- Language, literacy, and communication
- Mathematics
- Creative arts
- Science and technology
- Social studies

The specific KDIs found in the science and technology division are shown in **Figure 3.7** to provide perspective on the scope of the curriculum.

The learning focus of the HighScope curriculum is called a *study* and can last five minutes or multiple weeks based on child interest. The teacher creates the opportunity for individual children to achieve the standards they are working toward, but the children are not forced to participate. The HighScope classroom includes the following elements:

Figure 3.6 This is the Wheel of Active Learning. What is the value of teamwork in this model?

STOP AND THINK | Based on HighScope practices, children are not expected to be able to recognize their name until they are interested in print. For this reason, they use symbols. What would your HighScope symbol be? Why?

- **Language.** A HighScope classroom is ripe with language whenever and wherever possible. Teachers read books to children and encourage them to give verbal feedback. Another common practice among HighScope teachers is asking children to tell them a story, then writing it down for them. This helps children see the power of their words in written form.
- **Room arrangement.** All HighScope classrooms have four basic areas: art area, block area, house area, and quiet area. Other areas that may be included are sand and water area, construction area, computer area, nature and science area, and music and movement area. All materials to be used by the children are available to them on low, open shelves.

Figure 3.7 Science and technology key developmental indicators (KDIs) reflect the focus of learning supported in these two areas. How are these indicators beneficial in a classroom setting?

Science and Technology Key Developmental Indicators (KDI)	
45. Observing	Children observe the materials and processes in their environment.
46. Classifying	Children classify materials, actions, people, and events.
47. Experimenting	Children experiment to test their ideas.
48. Predicting	Children predict what they expect will happen.
49. Drawing conclusions	Children draw conclusions based on their experiences and observations.
50. Communicating ideas	Children communicate their ideas about the characteristics of things and how they work.
51. Natural and physical world	Children gather knowledge about the natural and physical world.
52. Tools and technology	Children explore and use tools and technology.

- **Labels.** Labeling almost everything in the classroom helps children with matching, color and shape recognition, seriation by size, and classification. Labels also help children and teachers keep the classroom neat and orderly.
- **Symbols.** HighScope school do not expect 3- and 4-year-old children to be able to recognize and read their written name. Instead, each child selects a symbol to represent themselves. This symbol is then placed on the child's chair, coat hook, cubby, supply box, etc. Providing children with personal symbols helps them achieve a sense of control and independence in their learning environment (highscope.org).

HighScope Unit of Study: Transportation

There are several suspension bridges in the area of the West Shore Community College early childhood program, which employs a HighScope curriculum. **Figure 3.8** shows a child's creation of a suspension bridge, integrating art, science, math, and social studies. A poster-map of the local area shows bridges drawn by children to identify locations, another strong example of integrating curriculum.

Lisa Morley, Westshore Community College

Figure 3.8 This is a student-created suspension bridge. How are hands-on projects like these beneficial to children?

Assessment in HighScope

The *plan-do-review process* is the most important part of the daily routine and a trademark of the HighScope curriculum. Children are allowed to make choices about what they will do during certain designated times of the day. They are then given the opportunity to reflect upon their activities and experiences with adults and their peers. The HighScope plan-do-review is a valued element of the daily routine that has withstood decades of practice and supports child-initiated experiences. Plan-do-review is considered a foundation for children's future success in life (highscope.com).

The HighScope teacher pulls together daily anecdotal notes, planning materials, and child assessment, then adjusts teaching based on the findings. The *COR Advantage* is a criterion-referenced, evidence-based online tool that assesses children's development and achievements. A whiteboard reflects the eight COR Advantage categories and KDIs for a HighScope informational session (**Figure 3.9**) delivered to families and the community.

HighScope curriculum is an example of a three-component evaluative cycle that many consider a complete curriculum for early childhood education. With the support of their teachers, the children have agency over their own learning experiences and develop executive functioning skills.

☐ Describe an example of the plan-do-review process.

☐ How does a study support individual children's interests in the HighScope curriculum?

3.3 Montessori Curriculum

Dr. Maria Montessori (1870–1952) (**Figure 3.10**), an Italian educator, physician, and scientist, opened the first Montessori school in 1907 in Rome, Italy, where she designed unique learning materials and created a classroom environment that fostered children's natural desire to learn (American Montessori Society). Montessori's influence is seen in most classrooms today. For example, she is responsible for the child-sized furniture and natural wooden materials used in many programs. This approach to learning is hands-on, inviting direct and active exploration and participation. Montessori believed (and modern science has confirmed) that children must move, physically, in order to learn. In a Montessori classroom, children work with special toys and manipulatives materials that promote exploration and high levels of engagement (montessori.org).

Montessori Classroom Structure

Montessori considered the classroom a *prepared environment* for specific age groups, depending on a continuum of abilities. The focus for each age group is independence, social skills, and awareness of surroundings. The environment includes materials that are precise, simple, and inviting to support the children's learning and channel the information surrounding them. Montessori materials are designed to be *self-correcting*. These simple and inviting materials provide feedback for children on their performance without requiring the teacher's presence (**Figure 3.11**). Examples include shape sorters, flip cards, matching cards, and puzzles. If a piece does not fit or is left over, the child is easily able to correct independently.

Montessori believed that material and information are best retained when they are introduced with as many senses as possible and with a fun attribute (Montessori 1995). In a Montessori program, children learn about a variety of topics including weather, animals, habitats, chemistry, and much more. **Figure 3.12** provides an example of a Montessori schedule.

Lisa Morely, Westshore Community College

Figure 3.9 A whiteboard created for informational purposes reflects the eight COR Advantage categories and KDIs. Is there anything on this board you would change? Why?

Wikimedia Common

Figure 3.10 This is Dr. Maria Montessori (1870–1952). How do self-correcting materials support children's development in a Montessori curriculum?

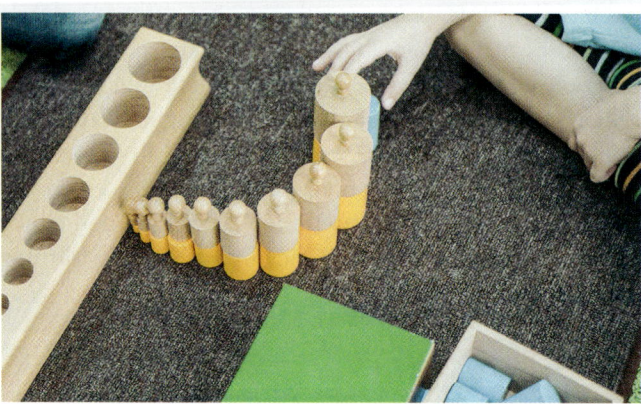

Aleksandra Nigmatulina/iStock/Getty Images

Figure 3.11 Many Montessori toys are self-correcting. Does this toy qualify as self-correcting? Why or why not?

Sample Montessori Schedule	
8:45 a.m.–9:00 a.m.	Outside play time
9:00 a.m.–11:30 a.m.	Montessori work time. In a fully equipped Montessori environment designed to meet both the learning and social needs of children ages 2 1/2 to 6, each child chooses activities of specific interest. Areas of the classroom include Practical Life, Art, Sensorial, Math, Language, Geography/Botany, and Special Units of Study. Each child moves at his/her own pace and develops self-responsibility and care for others. (Each morning includes 2 1/2 hours of individual choice of activity and 20 to 30 minutes of group activity. This includes foreign language, creative dramatics, story-telling, music and movement, science study, and show and tell.)
11:30 a.m.–1:00 p.m.	Lunch time and free play Play outdoors in beautifully equipped play areas.
1:00 p.m.–2:40 p.m.	Nap time for nappers
1:00 p.m.–2:45 p.m.	Circle time and Montessori work time for non-nappers
2:45 p.m.–3:00 p.m.	Cleanup Montessori work is put away, nappers are awakened, and the children gather for a short circle time before "second lunch," a time to finish any uneaten lunch food.
3:00 p.m.–3:15 p.m.	Additional foreign language lesson or story time

Goodheart-Willcox Publisher

Figure 3.12 This is a typical Montessori schedule. How is this schedule similar to the HighScope schedule? How is it different?

Teacher Role

Vocabulary is often introduced with objects rather than pictures. Interacting with others to voice opinions and desires is exercised in all areas of the Montessori prepared environment. Some areas, such as the blocks or sensory areas, might require minimal adult supervision, while others may require some adult assistance based on steps needed to complete. An example requiring adult supervision may be following a recipe to create food that needs baked in the oven. Regardless, all areas are enhanced when the teacher acts as the *guide*. This means that teachers prepare the environment and make suggestions to extend learning experiences but insert themselves into the actual play activities as little as possible. Guides encourage the children to follow their own curiosity at their own pace, taking the time they need to fully understand each concept and meet individualized learning goals.

Checkpoint

- ☐ Demonstrate understanding of self-correcting learning materials. How do these support the individual child?
- ☐ What are examples of Montessori materials used in many classrooms today?

THE TEACHER'S LENS

After completing a bachelor's degree, Miss Kim completed a Waldorf one-year teacher training at a Waldorf-accredited school to gain the credentials required to teach. Extensive practice in the arts, including singing, music, painting, clay, drawing, puppetry, and learning handcrafts such as sewing, knitting, doll and puppet making, woodworking, and metalworking were part of the program of studies.

The importance of understanding and embracing child development and theory as Steiner did, as well as growing through meditation, art, and working in collaboration with the staff and families and community comprised Miss Kim's studies. A willingness to work in the spiritual realm overtly is the foundation of a Waldorf teacher. Miss Kim is able to apply to a Waldorf-accredited school anywhere in the world.

3.4 Waldorf Curriculum

The Waldorf School was founded in 1919 in Stuttgart, Germany, for the children of employees in the Waldorf-Astoria Cigarette Factory, under the supervision of Emil Molt. Molt brought spiritual philosopher Rudolf Steiner in to offer lectures for the new teachers. These lectures are used today in Waldorf/Steiner teachers trainings all over the world. Today Waldorf schools are found in over 70 countries.

Anthroposophy is Steiner's spiritual philosophy. He believed that humans have the intellectual capacity to understand the truths of the universe and the spiritual world. Using this belief as a basis for early childhood education, Waldorf schools create a humane and nurturing environment to foster the development of the whole child. Steiner believed that an individual grows spiritually by developing clear thinking and a truthful perception of the world. The International Association of Steiner/Waldorf Early Childhood Education (IASWECE) oversees this international early childhood movement (Koetzch & Riegel 2020).

Waldorf Curriculum Structure

The Waldorf learning process involves engaging the head, heart, and hand. Waldorf teachers work to nurture and engage each child through a curriculum and methodology that integrates academics, arts, and practical skills.

Waldorf teachers tell children many stories throughout their studies: fairy tales, folk tales, fables, myths, legends, biographies, and stories from history. From first grade on, academic subjects include math, science, history, art, and handwork. Prior to first grade, subjects are introduced through storytelling, with emphasis placed on play and enjoying the outdoors. In an ideal Waldorf school, aesthetics of the internal and external environment are consciously designed to support children's development.

The teacher creates a daily schedule, referred to as a rhythm, to provide children with the comfort and security of knowing exactly what to expect each day. Once they know what to expect, children have the freedom to focus their time and energy on more important work, such as social learning, emotional development, and both gross and fine motor skills (waldorfeducation.org).

The weekly rhythm of each classroom changes from year to year, and sometimes from season to season. A typical daily rhythm is depicted in **Figure 3.13**. Notice that the weekly rhythm involves the children's active participation in making snacks each day, depending on ability, in mixed preschool/kindergarten rooms where six-year-olds are learning alongside their younger peers. Snacks are homemade, using high-quality, wholesome ingredients, and are often prepared by the children (Harbor Waldorf School).

Sample Waldorf Rhythm	
8:20 a.m.	Door opens
8:30 a.m.	Arrival, indoor play-activities
9:30 a.m.	Cleanup
9:40 a.m.	Circle time/storytime
10:00 a.m.	Morning snack
10:20 a.m.	Outdoor play/gardening
11:30 a.m.	Cleanup/wash-up
11:50 a.m.	Lunch
12:15 a.m.	Pickup time
12:30 a.m.	Nap time begins
2:45 a.m.	Wake up from nap/snack/outdoor play
4:00 a.m.	Pickup time

Goodheart-Willcox Publisher

Figure 3.13 An example of a daily Waldorf rhythm. How does this rhythm consider the needs of the whole child?

Another key principle of Waldorf education, ***looping*** refers to children remaining with the same teacher and the same classmates for many years. Most Waldorf schools try to keep young children in the same class with the same teacher as long as possible. Children may be in the same class for many years, regardless of their academic interests and capabilities. When questioned, former Waldorf students cited their strong classroom communities as a significant influence on their development (Rawson 2020).

Festivals

Festivals play an essential role in the Waldorf school and bring a sense of rhythm and anticipation, particularly for young children. Waldorf schools consider these festivals to be an important part of children's development and find that honoring festivals together is a way of keeping time and tradition. Throughout history, festivals have been interwoven with life and the cycles of nature. Each year, a Waldorf school celebrates a festival they already enjoy or discover one from a culture that is not well-known to their students. This might be the Japanese Children's Day or Sweden's Waffle Day or Mexico's Cinco de Mayo, for example.

STOP AND THINK

If asked to create a festival that is special to you, what would you celebrate? Drawing on your imagination, identify that a Waldorf teacher might consider around the following elements. Hint: Start by naming your festival.
- The mood (is the light dwindling like winter is now?)
- The elements (maybe a golden silk cloth on a table with a lantern with little battery candles and some squash from the farmer's market if it is autumn?)
- A story
- A song or a verse
- Any special food
- Any special game
- Any special craft
- What day/time
- How long

Share your own festival and how it connects to your own personal experiences.

The Waldorf curriculum is a strong fit for many children, and it is actively taught across the world. The next section describes the strengths and challenges of implementing thematic curriculum and explores how it embraces many different practices.

REAL-WORLD CLASSROOM

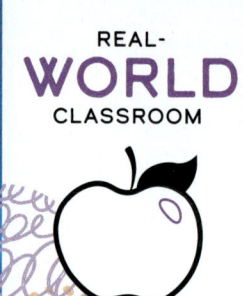

At the Tucson Waldorf school in Arizona multiple festivals are planned in the autumn. It is a lot of work for teachers, with parent engagement playing an important part. "It sometimes feels as if we are going from festival to festival, and it wears the teachers out, so we try to be selective. If it's a whole community festival, each teacher only works on one per year" (Kimberly Lewis, Tucson Waldorf teacher). It is a project of the imagination, but all incorporate several Waldorf philosophies.

Martinmas Lantern Walk

Martinmas, celebrated annually on November 11, is known as the festival of inner light. Waldorf programs celebrate Martinmas with many activities and traditions. (**Figure 3.14**).

Irina Wilhauk/Shutterstock.com

Figure 3.14

The idea behind Martinmas celebrations is that everyone has an inner light that they should share with others. The legend of St. Martin is from fourth century Rome. St. Martin was a soldier who, one cold winter's night, met a homeless man who was freezing to death. St. Martin cut his own cloak in two and gave half to the man to keep him warm. Later, St. Martin had a dream that the homeless man was really the representative of all humanity. St. Martin was inspired to live a life of service to others.

At Waldorf Martinmas celebrations, the children sing songs and read the legend of St. Martin. To represent their own inner light, each child creates their own lantern to carry into the woods at night. To honor St. Martin's charitable work, Waldorf families collect winter blankets and clothing to donate to local homeless shelters (Tucson Waldorf n.d.).

Harvest Festival

The Harvest Festival is a joyous event for Waldorf children and their families. Everyone gathers around a crackling fire for a feast of homemade bread and soup. Many children and adults make their own costumes and dance to live music. Prior to the event, teachers and families decorate areas of the school to represent two paths: The Protected Path for the young ones and the Quest Path for children in second grade and older. The children read fairy tales and then explore the paths, which are made to look like the settings in the stories (Tucson Waldorf n.d.) (see **Figure 3.15**).

Marina Tikhonova/iStock/Getty Images Plus

Figure 3.15

Continued

Michaelmas

Many Waldorf schools around the world celebrate the festival of Michaelmas, known as the "festival of courage," on September 29. Michaelmas was inspired by the story of St. George and the Dragon. According to the legend, the soldier St. George slayed a dragon that was terrorizing the villagers. To honor this courageous act, the children at Waldorf schools perform a pageant for the community that reenacts St. George's story (**Figure 3.16**). After the pageant they enjoy a field day filled with various athletic events and activities (Tucson Waldorf n.d.).

Imgorthand/E+ via Getty Images

Figure 3.16

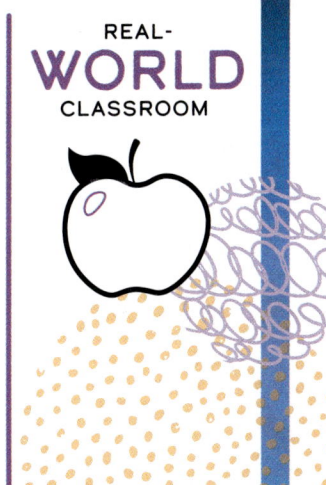

REAL-WORLD CLASSROOM

 Checkpoint

- ☐ How does looping support the developing child? What are the benefits to this practice? Are there areas of concern?
- ☐ Celebrating different events across the year is integral to the Waldorf curriculum. How might this support learning?

3.5 Thematic Curriculum

Thematic curriculum borrows components from various curriculum frameworks. Thematic curriculum can be considered an emergent curriculum when it is child-led and teacher-framed. *Emergent curriculum* refers to a process in which teachers plan the activities and projects based on the children in their classroom, considering the children's skills, needs, and interests. The main difference between thematic and emergent approaches is that an emergent curriculum is always child-led, whereas thematic curriculum can be child- or teacher-led. There are no specific schools accredited by a thematic curriculum. Often, thematic curricula are purchased from various sources and are easily modified by the teacher.

Theme Selection

Many early childhood classrooms today attempt to base themes on the interests of the majority of children while blending multiple curricula. This approach is sometimes called *eclectic*, which means deriving ideas, style, or taste from a broad and diverse range of sources. Just as a person may tend to wear unique outfits that may not match but look impressive when paired, the teacher is able to do something similar when putting together elements from different sources to create an individual teaching style.

Using *themes*, the teacher may predetermine the topics. Because many teachers choose themes based on the children's interests, this somewhat structured approach assumes that all children will be interested in learning the same things at the same time (Bonnay 2022). A typical daily schedule is depicted in **Figure 3.17**.

THE TEACHER'S LENS

Teacher Jackson is excited to begin a new school year and will be working in the "Dragon Room" with 4-year-old children. The curriculum will be a blending of many different curriculum elements with children of different abilities using information gained from many sources. A teacher biography has been posted on the classroom website and a beginning topic of interest shared. Teacher Jackson is excited for a brand-new group of children to learn along with.

Sample Thematic Curriculum Schedule		
7:30 a.m.–9:00 a.m.	Open Choice	Early arrival with open choices of learning experiences inside and outside available as children arrive, routines—some programs offer children breakfast
	Transition	
9:00 a.m.–9:20 a.m.	Large Group	Circle time
	Transition	
9:25 a.m.–11:30 a.m.	Small Group	Active learning, open snack; choices inside and outside
	Transition	
11:40 a.m.–11:55 a.m.	Large Group	Closing circle time
	Transition	
12:00 p.m.–12:45 p.m.	All	Lunch
	Transition	
12:50 p.m.–2:30 p.m.	All	Storytime followed by quiet time or quiet activities (Allowing children to have a picture book helps some children settle down. Many programs allow children who do not fall asleep within 40 minutes to play quietly in a different location.) Some states limit rest time—check those regulations!
	Transition	
2:30 p.m.–4:00 p.m.	Open Choice	Afternoon active learning, snacks, and stories

Goodheart-Willcox Publisher

Figure 3.17 This is a sample thematic curriculum schedule. Do you think it is important for children to choose some of their activities?

Thematic Curriculum Structure

Thematic curriculum often begins with identifying a concept around which to learn, then creating learning experiences on that concept in a variety of areas. One concept might be pets, which is usually well received by the children. The teacher begins planning the thematic curriculum by researching the many ways to teach using pets to focus learning. They integrate this theme into different academic disciplines.

The thematic-eclectic style has many possibilities, and although many concepts can enrich the curriculum, it should be noted that the concepts themselves are only a small part of the true curriculum for which each was designed. Consider the following focuses of the thematic classroom using a pets theme:

- To teach math quantities, the teacher may use animal *manipulatives* (small handheld items) to count.
- To teach social skills, the teacher may set up a pet store or veterinarian office in the dramatic play area. This dramatic play scenario can integrate literacy (writing prescriptions), math (paying the cashier), and/or art (creating signage for the area).
- To teach science, the teacher may bring in different foods that birds eat and set up a window observatory. The children can monitor which birds each which food. Integrating math skills to look at quantity and amounts is a natural combination.
- To teach language arts, the teacher can provide a dozen different nonfiction and fiction books about pets to extend learning.
- To teach art, the teacher may introduce clay and encourage children to sculpt a pet.
- To engage with the community, the teacher might invite a local veterinarian or pet store owner to speak to the children about their profession. After the visit, the children can practice literacy by writing thank-you notes.

Recall that approaches consist of how things should be done, created, and designed, whereas curriculum is a framework derived from a certain perspective about how children learn. In thematic education, the chosen theme of the day/week/month sets the foundation of all learning for children in any given classroom, while the *Project Approach* usually involves a small group of children who have displayed a common interest. The next section will focus on the Project Approach and how to implement it into a curriculum.

STOP AND THINK

Are there concerns with implementing many different curriculum tools together, or is this a strength? What are the pros and cons of this practice?

 **Checkpoint**

- ☐ Thematic curriculum is a common teaching strategy. How does this curriculum support all children?
- ☐ Describe a concept that can be taught using thematic curriculum. Identify some of the ways to integrate different subjects around the same concept.

3.6 Project Approach

The *Project Approach* refers to a set of strategies that enables teachers to guide children through in-depth studies of real-world topics. Projects typically do not constitute the whole educational program; instead, teachers use this approach alongside systematic instruction and as a means of achieving curricular goals (ProjectApproach.org).

A project-based framework was influenced by the work of British educators in the early 1900s. The focus on early learning was supported by John Dewey during the Progressive era in American history. The Project Approach we know today is attributed to early childhood education researchers and the work of authors Lillian Katz and Sylvia Chard.

This approach promotes the "whole child." The concept of the whole child involves support from caring adults that promotes the health of children in all areas: physical, social, emotional, and cognitive. They must be challenged in realistic ways and provided with learning experiences that are engaging and interesting. By using the Project Approach in all curriculum areas, teachers can promote the whole child (Schuler 2000).

Project Approach Curriculum Structure

Hands-on investigations are a trademark of the Project Approach, making strong connections between academic and project-based learning. Children can choose topics that appeal to them, and the teacher will plan a curriculum that weaves that topics through all subject areas. Children are encouraged to ask questions and to be researchers in their own quest for learning.

A project reflects the experiences and cultures of the children who are enrolled and can last for weeks or months. The teacher who supports the interests of the child will create a richer project experience in which all will be invested. The topic and direction are guided by the child, not the teacher or the calendar.

Helms described keyways to check if you plan to follow the Project Approach (Helm & Katz 2016):

- Did the topic come from the child based on their own interests?
- Were there meaningful questions asked?
- What happened as a result of the questions?
- How did the children's learning shape their actions and representations?

An authentic Project Approach includes child initiation, child decision making, and child engagement as the investigation begins and ends. Investigation is a common term in the Project Approach and refers to the learning that is happening.

When planning a Project Approach, teachers should ask themselves five questions. These questions are based on Katz's five principles (Katz 2017):

- Does it strengthen children's understanding of their own experience?
- Does it provide the children with a direct, firsthand experience?
- Is the process interactive, rather than passive?
- Does the learning have horizontal, versus vertical, relevance?
- Is the children's understanding of experiences and events strengthened by the project?

Phases of the Project Approach

Phase 1 of the Project Approach is a planning stage. This stage can last many days as the teacher seeks the children's interest in a topic. Phase 1 is full of inquiry and discussion. Often, but not always, the topic is connected to an event that provoked a child's interest. The Project Approach calls this a *catalyst* (an event that stimulates deeper interest). The teacher and the children work together to identify the topic and explore what is currently known about it. Ample time is spent discussing various aspects of the topic and finding out what they want to learn more about.

Phase 2 is the investigation stage. This is when the collection of information occurs (taking notes, making sketches, counting, measuring, and creating) during field experiences. Guest speaker presentations occur, and research is done with the family and in the classroom.

Phase 3 is the culmination of the project, in which the children demonstrate their learning and share project creations with families, peers, school, and community members. State standards that were met through the content of the project or the processes of investigation are defined, and the completion reveals what the children have learned. This is the time to showcase their learning.

Checkpoint

☐ Define and demonstrate what a catalyst is.

☐ How does Phase 1 differ from Phase 2 in the Project Approach.

☐ What are some ways to culminate a project during Phase 3?

3.7 Reggio Emilia Approach

Reggio Emilia is an educational philosophy that guides the decisions of teachers in how they approach education, and as such it does not have an accrediting organization (as High-Scope, Waldorf, and Montessori do). Loris Malaguzzi (1920-1994) founded the Reggio Emilia approach, which takes its name from the town in Italy where a school was founded that embraced a distinctive and innovative set of philosophical assumptions and design for the environment. Fostering children's intellectual development through symbolic representation is a hallmark of Reggio. "A major lesson from Reggio Emilia is the way preprimary school children can use what they call graphic languages include children's ideas, observations, memories, feelings, and so forth," (Rinaldi 1991). Graphic languages refer to children's drawings or art creations (**Figure 3.18**). Reggio is known for deep connections to supporting children's creative abilities and considering the child's first language.

Many US teachers prefer to introduce topics in hopes of exciting the children's interests, assuming that everyday experiences would not be interesting. However, the Reggio Emilia approach focuses on becoming familiar with everyday objects and events that can be deeply interesting and meaningful to a child. Being aware of nature is meaningful to the Reggio Emilia approach. The value of project work for a child is knowing a topic in depth and feeling proficiency as part of the learning process. "Such early experiences of feelings can be highly rewarding for young children. Feelings of proficiency may also lay the foundation of a lifelong disposition to seek in-depth understandings of topics worthy of their attention" (Katz 1994).

Reggio Emilia Approach Structure

The Reggio Emilia Approach follows a project-based framework, much like the Project Approach, but the framework is less formal. Reggio Emilia supports learning from the particular interests of children with topics derived from talking with children and their families, as well as from things that are known to be interesting to children. The fundamental principles of Reggio Emilia are best represented by Cadwell (1997) and include the following views.

Child as Protagonist

A *protagonist* is the leading character in the story, an active participant, and major influencer of what occurs in a setting. Children are strong, rich, and capable learners who combine their potential and curiosity, with an interest in forming their own learning and navigating everything in their environment.

Child as Collaborator

Working together is a lifelong skill and is recognized as such. Working together to solve problems, creating dialogue with one another, and practicing different team building roles promote a sense of community. Supporting each child's own voice creates a foundation of important interpersonal skills.

Southlake Montessori School at Grapevine, TX

Figure 3.18 This child is engaged in an art activity. Why is art important in integrated curriculum?

Child as Communicator

Reggio focuses on symbolic representation allowing the child to use any materials to discover and communicate. The Reggio Emilia approach supports new ideas and concepts to be learned and represented in multiple forms, for example in mediums such as art, clay, drama, music, paint, print, puppetry, wire and so on.

The Environment Is the Third Teacher

The environment is the third teacher that utilizes every space to support the child. The Reggio inspired classroom environment if evident by the lighting (table lamps), plants, real dishware, rugs, and other aesthetics that reflect beauty. The Reggio classroom is designed to produce a homey feeling versus an academic classroom and influence exploration of the materials provided.

The Teacher as a Partner and Facilitator

The teacher functions as a partner and facilitator to support the child's lead and exploration on short and long-term projects with knowledge of how to plan and use observation to inform practice. Teachers help children decide the direction they are interested in researching and provide the materials most suited to their project; materials that will help represent their learning.

The Teacher as Researcher

Working in pairs, teachers research and create documentation with the children, whom they also consider researchers (Gandini 1993) not for the children. The Reggio teacher actively supports projects and documents learning as part of a team approach that includes the child as well as colleagues. The projects intentionally involve the families and members of the community and can span a week to an entire year if there is interest.

The Parent as Partner

Communication with and involvement by the family as well as staying engaged in conversations with the child are important factors that stimulates learning in many appropriate ways. The family is considered an active partner in the child's learning, and strategies to support their involvement are shared and communicated with them.

The Documentation as Communication

Reggio documentation reflects both the learning as well as the growth of the children. Teachers capture photos of children at work and play, along with dictations of the many learning experiences. The documentation panels help teachers and parents learn more about what does and does not work for a child and are displayed at the child's eye level. Documentation panels become a chronicle of events that portray the learning that occurred over time. They are displayed at the child's eye level and are revisited many times over the school year by the children and classroom visitors. These panels are a unique part of the Reggio Emilia Approach. (To see how the Reggio Emilia compares to other approaches and curricula, see **Figure 3.19**.)

Teacher Role

Reggio Emilia teachers see themselves as *provocateurs*, meaning they present challenges or problems to be solved by children as central to their learning experiences. Reggio learning environments rely on learning provocations or invitations to learn as a technique to inspire engagement and thinking in the children. When conflict occurs, the Italian cultural approach is to have conversations; these are teachable moments for children, or ideas to build on. Reggio Emilia teachers see their role as one who understands that children must learn to be producers rather than solely consumers. Reggio teachers teach nothing to children except what children can learn by themselves (Edwards 1993).

Comparison Chart of the Major Curricula and Approaches

Curriculum/Approach	Notable People	Teacher Role(s)	Learning Focus	Noteworthy Contributions
Tools of the Mind reggiochildren.it/en/reggio-emilia-approach/	Lev Vygotsky Deborah Leong Elena Bodrova	Supporter	Imaginative Play Literacy-Language Mathematics Science	Self-regulation focus, ZPD, private speech, scaffolded writing, play plans, dynamic \ assessment
High Scope highscope.org/our-practice/preschool-curriculum/	Jean Piaget David Weikart	Facilitator	Study: Social and emotional development, Physical development and health, Language, literacy and communication, Mathematics, Creative arts, Science and technology, Social studies	Plan, do, review, COR advantage
Montessori montessori.org/	Maria Montessori	Guide	Practical Life, Sensorial, Culture, Language, Mathematics	Sensitive periods, child-size furniture; self-correcting materials
Waldorf waldorfeducation.org/	Rudolph Steiner	Model Observer	Story Telling, Head-Heart-Hand	Anthroposophy looping rhythm
Thematic	Varies	Varies	Varies	Varies
Project Approach projectapproach.org/	Lilian Katz Sylvia Chard	Facilitator	Investigations	Projects, open-ended learning, phases
Reggio Emilia Approach reggiochildren.it/en/reggio-emilia-approach/	Loris Malaguzzi Leila Gandini Carlos Rinaldi	Guide-Provocateur Atelierista	Adventures	Process art, documentation, beautiful spaces, protagonist, environment-3rd teacher, parent as partner

Goodheart-Willcox Publisher

Figure 3.19 Comparison chart showing the major curriculums and approaches in use today. Do you think these approaches have more in common or more differences? Explain your answer.

The atelierista is another teaching role. An *atelierista* is a studio teacher with a background in education and art. Atelieristas work with classroom teachers and children, devising and facilitating learning experiences that link to curricular learning. The atelierista documents child communications, identifying topics of interest in order to connect ideas with active expressions of creativity in a variety of mediums and materials (**Figure 3.20**). The atelierista oversees the *atelier*, a large art studio that is considered a core of the Reggio Emilia Approach (Fiore 2013). The atelierista also provides ongoing documentation of children's learning.

Reggio Emilia is an inspiring and highly effective method of expanding children's minds—one adventure at a time.

Figure 3.20 This is a recognizable symbol for Reggio-Emilia-inspired practices. How does this image represent the concepts that Reggio Emilia embraces?

REAL-WORLD CLASSROOM

In Ginny's Preschool in Casper, Wyoming, children engaged in a rich conversation about a frozen fish that reflects their fascination, inquisitive questioning and wondering.

A poster or documentation panel captures the exchange that occurred around the table when some trout was taken from the freezer to use for an art print. The four children are fascinated with the frozen fish, and the teacher records the conversation verbatim. These types of dynamic elements on a Reggio Emilia documentation panel bring learning to life.

- Graham (4 years old): "Is he alive?"
- Hadley (4 years old): "Can I touch it?"
- Graham: "Why is that fish not alive, Ginny? What is this fish not alive?"
- Ginny: (Teacher) "What kind of fish is this?"
- Willy (3 years old): "A big one!"
- Shawn (3 years old): "I want to see that fish!"
- Graham: "Why's he not alive?"
- Willy: "I like this fish so much."
- Graham: "Is this fish dead or alive? Is he alive or what? Is this guy dead? Is this guy dead or freezed?"
- Bryce (co-teacher): "Do you think he is freezed?"
- Graham: "He has ice on him. When you take him out of the water, did he freezed?"
- Bryce: "He got freezed in the freezer!"

 **Checkpoint**

☐ Identify different examples of graphic language.

☐ Share your understanding of the role of documentation in a Reggio-inspired classroom.

☐ What is the role of the parent in a Reggio-inspired classroom.

Chapter 3 Review and Assessment

Chapter Summary

3.1 Summarize the theory and framework of the Tools of the Mind curriculum.
- The Tools of the Mind (ToM) curriculum brings the tenets of Lev Vygotsky's theory to life with a focus on the development of skills that include academics, self-regulation, working memory, dramatic play, and learning to play and learn together.
- ToM includes a focus on developing executive function skills to promote learning.
- The ToM curriculum includes the use of visual reminders known as mediators. Writing and literacy are integrated as children draw what they plan to do for the day and are introduced to invented writing to make connections to letters that form words.
- Scaffolding during learning is a key element of the ToM curriculum that provides hints to support the child within their zone of proximal development (ZPD).
- A focus on the importance of language includes private and written speech.
- The ToM classroom uses dynamic assessment, which is very different than common assessments that focus on what the child is currently able to do.

3.2 Identify HighScope curriculum goals in the early childhood classroom.
- HighScope curriculum provides methods to support children built on the Piagetian theory of development. It includes five basic principles: active learning, positive adult-child interactions, a child-friendly environment, a consistent daily schedule, and team-based assessment.
- The HighScope curriculum includes key developmental indicators (KDI) that are organized under eight content areas. The HighScope learning focus is called a study and can be brief or last many weeks or more.
- HighScope includes a plan-do-review process. This sequence supports each child in planning an action for the day, carrying it out, and then reviewing what occurred or did not at the end of the learning day.
- The COR Advantage is the HighScope assessment and covers elements that will best prepare children for school success.

3.3 List Montessori curriculum components.
- The Montessori curriculum is a unique combination of practical life skills woven with academics, following the child's lead.
- Self-correcting materials are attributed to Montessori. These materials allow children to correct themselves and support independent problem solving.
- Virtually every early childhood classroom has Montessori influences, such as the child-size furnishings and wood toys attributed to Dr. Montessori.
- Montessori teachers are called *guides* because their role is one of helping each child identify their own strengths and abilities through engaging lessons and self-correcting materials.

3.4 Describe how anthroposophy is integral to the Waldorf curriculum.
- The Waldorf curriculum is built around spiritual teachings termed anthroposophy.
- The Waldorf daily schedule is referred to as a rhythm.
- Waldorf embeds oral storytelling and folk tales that include messages with strong moral and character development themes.
- Looping is a practice in which children remain with the same teacher and classmates for many years. This practice creates a strong community of learners.
- A variety of festivals that embody the spirit of anthroposophy are celebrated each year.

3.5 Explain the concept behind thematic curriculum.
- Thematic curriculum embodies concepts from many of the different curricula.
- Emergent curriculum refers to a process that is teacher led based on the children's skills, needs, and interests.
- Focusing on different topics or themes around which to build the curriculum provides multiple opportunities to explore a variety of learning opportunities.

3.6 Apply Project Approach strategies in the early childhood classroom.
- The Project Approach is structured, building learning with the child as the lead while intentionally involving the family and community with learning.
- Using phases (stages) of learning, the teacher guides the curriculum based on children's interests and prior experiences.

3.7 Identify Reggio Emilia Approach influences in the early childhood classroom.
- Reggio teachers see themselves as provocateurs and work with a teacher educated in the arts called the *atelierista*.
- The Reggio Emilia Approach integrates documentation of children's learning as a key element and considers the environment to be the "third teacher."
- Reggio makes strong connections between the classroom and community.
- Elements of a beautiful classroom are often evident in Reggio-inspired early childhood classrooms.

For Further Reflection

1. The number of early childhood programs has grown nationwide. How many different curricula are practiced in your area/state?
2. How does the HighScope daily routine differ from other curricula?
3. The Tools of the Mind curriculum integrates mediators to support children. What additional uses of mediators might be employed in a classroom of learners?
4. Montessori weaves separate strands such as math, science, history, geography, and language through an integrated approach. What are the strengths of this type of curriculum?
5. Waldorf includes festivals as part of the curriculum. Based on your location and culture, what would an event look like?
6. Thematic curriculum is eclectic and borrows elements from many different curricula and approaches. What are the benefits and weaknesses of this practice?
7. Approaches are practiced as part of many curricula. Considering the Project Approach and the Reggio Emilia Approach, which elements would you embrace and why?
8. How can teachers modify or revise a curriculum that ensures all children's interests, culture, and prior learning experiences are celebrated and part of the curriculum?

Recall and Application

1. What is the central focus of the Tools of the Mind curriculum?
   A. learning to read
   B. teaching artistic skills
   C. self-regulation skills
   D. physical strength

Chapter 3 Theories of Curricula and Approaches 69

2. What are mediators?
   A. picture cards designed to help children internalize their thinking and actions
   B. picture cards designed to show children how to perfect their art skills
   C. picture cards designed to provide fun activities during instructional time
   D. None of the above.
3. What does ZPD stand for?
   A. zone of personal dimension
   B. zone of practical domain
   C. zone of proximal development
   D. zone of promising development
4. Which of the following activities are included in the HighScope daily routine?
   A. purpose, learn, evaluate
   B. pretend, dream, revise
   C. play, draw, review
   D. plan, do, review
5. What is the learning focus called in a HighScope curriculum?
   A. study
   B. project
   C. focus
   D. plan
6. A Montessori teacher is known as a(n) ____.
   A. leader
   B. guide
   C. instructor
   D. facilitator
7. **True or False.** The focus of each age group in a Montessori classroom includes independence, social skills, and awareness of surroundings.
8. **True or False.** The Waldorf process includes engaging the head, heart, and hand.
9. What is looping?
   A. a practice to revisit work not understood
   B. remaining with the same teacher many years
   C. a game played during festival time
   D. the art of weaving during craft time
10. What is emergent curriculum?
    A. any curriculum that is new to the field.
    B. a curriculum that is child-led and teacher-framed.
    C. a curriculum that is initiated in the early years.
    D. a curriculum that provides only family experiences.
11. What is an example of a thematic topic of interest?
    A. shoes
    B. the ocean
    C. my family
    D. All of the above
12. Identify the phases practiced in the Project Approach.
    A. implementing, discussing, revising
    B. creating, discovering, evaluating
    C. learning, exploring, studying
    D. planning, investigating, culmination
13. **True or False.** The Reggio Emilia Approach follows a project-based framework, much like the Project Approach, but it is much more formal.

Copyright Goodheart-Willcox Co., Inc.

Creating a Community of Learners

CHAPTER 4

Learning Outcomes

After studying this chapter, you will be able to:

4.1 Explain how the ecological systems theory supports community and family engagement.

4.2 Summarize practices that create communities in the classroom.

4.3 Describe methods to engage children to become part of the classroom community.

4.4 Discuss the variety of communication practices to support family engagement.

4.5 Describe strategies to engage colleagues and the broader community.

Standards Covered in This Chapter

NAEYC

1a, 1b, 1c, 2a, 2b, 3a, 3b, 3c, 4a, 4b, 4c, 4d, 4e, 5a, 5b, 5c, 5d, 5e

DAP

Guidelines 1, 2, 3, 4, 5, 6

Image credit: kali9/E+ via Getty Images

FatCamera/E+ via Getty Images

SNAPSHOT Mrs. K

Mrs. K spent months before the first day of school preparing to welcome each child and their family into her classroom. She believes that building a classroom community is a key element to success and that it all begins with communication that is inclusive, respectful, and open. Using what she had learned in her program of studies, she reached out to each family and shared a little about herself and her philosophy of early childhood education. In return, each family was asked to share a little about their child's characteristics and provide a photo that would be made visible in the classroom.

Understanding and accepting each child where they are is an important element in developing a classroom community. Mrs. K knows that no two children come to school with the same experiences and knowledge. Having insight into the children's special attributes helps Mrs. K create an environment that is safe and welcoming. She knows if she creates learning plans that are developmentally appropriate, she will make connections to each child where they are in their learning.

Mrs. K has created exclusive spaces for each child to store their belongings and treasures in the classroom. Also, she created the first two weeks of learning plans around the topic of "community." Involving families will be an on-going practice, as will creating opportunities for the community at large to become familiar with their youngest citizens. Mrs. K is ready to begin school.

Give It Some Thought

1. What should Mrs. K consider when she is planning family meetings or sending welcome letters to the families?
2. Identify different roles the family can assume in their child's classroom. What are the challenges and opportunities when families are involved?
3. How can Mrs. K intentionally involve the families in her beginning topic of interest: "community"?

Key Terms

chronosystem
collaborations
cooperative learning
critical thinking

digital application (app)
ecological systems theory
exosystem

macrosystem
mesosystem
microsystem

Introduction

All eyes are on the teacher: 15 smiling three-, four-, and five-year-olds are ready to learn. It is the beginning of the school year, and the teacher wants to create a classroom that says, "All are welcome here." The children are the spirit of the neighborhood, the spirit of the community, and of course the spirit of tomorrow. But what is a community of learners, and why is this important to understand when creating curriculum? Chapter 4 uncovers the value and benefits of adopting a classroom community mentality to strengthen learning and connections.

The chapter begins with Urie Bronfenbrenner's ecological systems theory, which explores how the social development of a child is affected by their environment. It is important for the teacher to understand outside influences when writing curriculum. The early childhood classroom is often one of the first communities of influence outside of the child's home.

4.1 Ecological Systems Theory

Urie Bronfenbrenner devised the *ecological systems theory*, which supports curriculum that builds communities of caring and strong social relationships. Bronfenbrenner's theory explains how a child's growth and development is affected by everything in their environment. Entire programs of studies are built on the foundations of Bronfenbrenner's work. It is a valuable resource for teachers in early childhood environments.

The ecological systems theory is represented by circles (**Figure 4.1**). Beginning with the child as the core, nested systems of influence impact development and affect every facet of a child's life. When writing curriculum, it is important for teachers to understand these influences in order to best support each child's development.

The center of focus in the ecological systems theory is the child. The next level, the *microsystem*, includes the groups a child interacts with on a regular basis, such as family, school, sports teams, and religious organizations. How these groups interact with the child and how the child responds has an effect on the child's growth and development. Bronfenbrenner proposed that the more supportive the relationships within these groups, the stronger the advantage to the child. This is the level where the early childhood classroom has the most influence.

The third circle, the *mesosystem*, illustrates how the many parts of a child's microsystem work together to support the child. For example, when a child's family takes an active role in their education, such as volunteering at the school or attending sports games, they support the child's overall growth. Also, strong friendships promote social-emotional wellness (**Figure 4.2**). By contrast, conflicts between adult caregivers regarding the best ways to raise the child can negatively impact the child's development and thereby alter teaching.

The fourth circle, the *exosystem*, includes other people, places, and events with which the child may not have direct connections, but which nonetheless impact the child's development. For example, if a parent is laid off from their job and cannot afford to pay for a

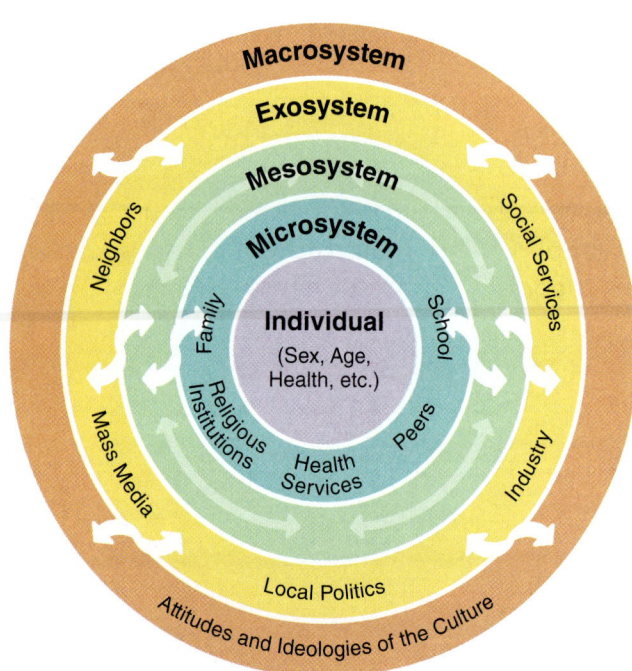

Goodheart-Willcox Publisher

Figure 4.1 Urie Bronfenbrenner's ecological systems theory is represented by these circles. Why is each circle important in developing the whole child?

quality preschool program, the child may be negatively impacted. Alternatively, if a parent receives a bonus and is able to provide school supplies not available before, this can have a positive impact on the child.

The *macrosystem* includes people and events that are not connected to the child but have the potential to have a great influence on the child's development. This includes events like pandemics, wars, the economy, and cultural values. The impact of these factors can be positive or negative.

Bronfenbrenner referred to the outermost ring as the *chronosystem*, which comprises all life situations of the ecological system model. Using the different systems as a guide, teachers can devise a plan to help the child meet developmental needs.

kali9/E+ via Getty Images

Figure 4.2 These two children share a strong friendship. Why are friendships important to a child's development?

Recalling your childhood, what events have shaped your own life? Describe your own ecological system using **Figure 4.1** as a model. Who was significant in your life? What events may have occurred in your extended family, in your community? What historical events (macrosystem) may have affected your microsystem?

STOP AND THINK

 Checkpoint

- ☐ Explain the impact of Bronfenbrenner's theory on child development and learning.
- ☐ Identify the system on which the early childhood classroom has the most influence.
- ☐ Provide an example of an event or experience that would fit into Bronfenbrenner's macrosystem and explain how that may affect a child's development and learning.
- ☐ What impact does Bronfenbrenner's theory have on child development and learning?

4.2 Creating a Community

Not only is building community a part of the developmentally appropriate practice principles, it is also part of NAEYC's Professional Standards and Competencies for Early Childhood Educators. This standard is devoted to the importance of creating strong family-teacher partnerships and community connections, further supporting the importance of creating a community. Teachers create and foster a community of learners when they employ developmentally appropriate practices.

NAEYC GUIDELINES

NAEYC Standard 2 focuses on three key elements (Professional Practices, NAEYC, 2020). The teacher must:

1. know and value the diversity of the children and their families.

Continued

2. use this knowledge to create respectful, responsive, and reciprocal relationships with the family so that they are considered partners in their child's learning and development.

3. use community resources to build connections between the early learning setting and the community organizations to support the child's family and the child's development.

Several supports can be provided to create a caring community. Refer to the NAEYC Guidance feature. The first part of Standard 2 provides the expectation that early childhood teachers use their knowledge of family influences and build on each family's assets and strengths. This element reinforces that the teacher understands all family commonalities, and that each family is unique.

The second part of Standard 2 reflects the importance of relationship building between the teacher and the families. Teachers should elicit the families' expertise about their children for insight into curriculum, program development, and assessment.

Building respectful, reciprocal partnerships in the community is the final part of Standard 2. Partnerships should be created not only with other early learning programs and schools, but also with community organizations and agencies. Intentional activities include field trips to local areas of interest (libraries, museums) and inviting community members to be guest speakers to help children become familiar with those individuals who make a difference in the community. These actions support child and family confidence (NAEYC, *Professional Practices*, 2020).

Integrating Standard 2 into practice helps teachers create curriculum that includes strong classroom communities in which each child, each family, and each person feels respected and included in decisions that impact teaching and learning.

Social-Emotional Foundations for Early Learning

When developing curriculum, teachers must understand the benefits of creating caring communities to support the social-emotional development of a child. The Center on the Social Emotional Foundations for Early Learning's (CSEFEL) *teaching pyramid model* identifies four levels that build upon each other (**Figure 4.3**). The base of the pyramid represents the foundational policies and procedures that are based on solid evidence from the field.

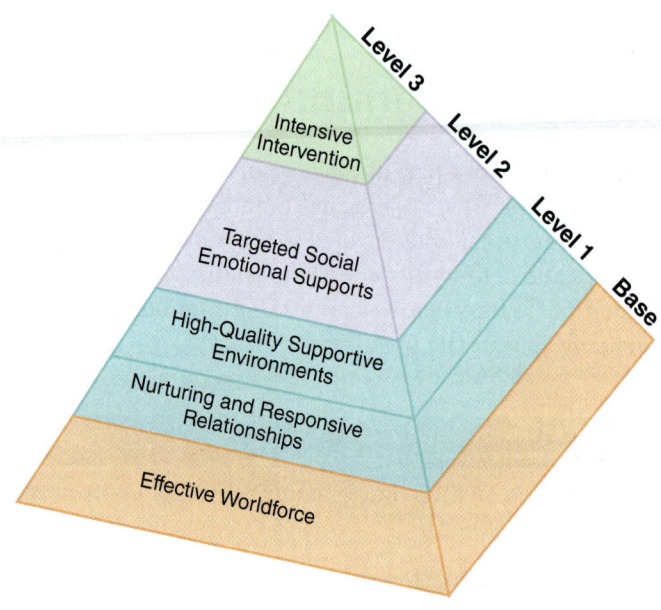

Figure 4.3 The Center on the Social Emotional Foundations for Early Learning's teaching pyramid model. How does each level build upon the one below it?

Goodheart-Willcox Publisher

Level 1, Nurturing and Responsive Relationships, identifies the importance of connecting to all children in the classroom. Research shows that the stronger the child's relationship is with the teacher, the harder the child will work to meet expectations (Fox et al. 2003).

Level 2, High-Quality Supportive Environments, focuses on creating an environment that supports positive outcomes. This includes the curriculum, transitions, routines, and teaching practices as part of the environment.

The Targeted Social Emotional Supports of Level 3 point to teaching practices that promote the formation of positive social relationships. This must be modeled by caring adults. Skills such as conflict resolution and negotiation are embedded into the curriculum and are lifelong competencies. Supporting strong relationships is a common element in all curriculum development.

Level 4, Intensive Intervention, provides interventions for children who need additional support. Research shows that when the three previous levels are fulfilled, additional supports are needed by only 4 percent of children (CSEFEL). This correlation alone is a motivation for creating a caring community where everyone is respected.

Antecedents and Consequences

A young child who breaks rules and pushes boundaries should never be labeled a "bad kid" or held at fault for their actions (Bredekamp 2014). In a nurturing, responsive learning environment, teachers approach the issue as a collaborative effort to ensure that the classroom expectations are appropriate and clearly communicated. They also examine the environment for potential antecedents and consequences to address the challenging behavior.

One common antecedent is telling a young child who is engaged in an activity to stop, without prior warning. This often results in a tantrum (Howell & Reinhard 2015). Providing a transition (see Chapter 8) eliminates that antecedent. "In five minutes, we are going to clean up and get ready for lunch" is an example that supports an appropriate transition. A natural consequence might be that lunch will be delayed until the area is cleaned up. Focus on being proactive versus reactive, and reach out to colleagues, the child's family, or community experts if there is a continued issue with engaging a child in daily classroom learning experiences.

 **Checkpoint**

- ☐ Identify several ideas to involve the outside community in your own classroom community.
- ☐ Share an example of an antecedent and consequence. How might this knowledge change your reaction to classroom behaviors?

4.3 Engaging with Children

When children see themselves represented in the classroom, their understanding of being part of a group, their sense of belonging, and their belief that they are important are strengthened. Building a classroom community involves many opportunities for the children to get to know each other and work together. The teacher is the conduit to building a community, engaging the children in conversation, and creating learning opportunities that build shared experiences. Classroom practices that provide strong communities of learning have the following characteristics in common:

- Shared discussions of what "community" means
- Knowing each child's characteristics
- Creating opportunities for children to work together and collaborate
- Shared classroom responsibilities
- Shared decision making
- Development of class rules

THE TEACHER'S LENS

Teacher Myong is aware of how important it is to build relationships with the child and family and between the children. The roster the director provided prior to school starting lists 15 different families, each from a different set of experiences, cultures, and traditions.

Prior to the first day of school, Teacher Myong mailed each family a letter. She introduced herself and included her email address, inviting families to write her and describe their children in "one million words or less."

"No one knows your child better than you," the letter read, "and I want to learn everything there is to know about your child. No detail is too small!" Teacher Myong also invited the families to share anything they would like about their family traditions. She knows that the minimal time investment in reading the families' emails will pay huge dividends on the first day of class as the children settle into a learning environment that is designed to meet their individual needs.

Reflecting on the culture and background of each child forms strong learning experiences. Integrating a variety of experiences with varied teaching strategies supports all learners. The teacher considers the range of children's differences in development, languages, skills, abilities, prior experiences, needs, and interests (NAEYC, *DAP*, 2020). Intentional teaching strategies ensure that all children and their families feel safe and wanted in a caring community of learners. Examples include greeting each child and family when they arrive and sharing positive feedback to the families at the end of the day.

When children are part of a nurturing learning community, they feel safe as they make, keep, and test relationships. The focus is on children's positive, socially acceptable behavior (*Texas Child Care*, Quarterly, 2016). An example of a caring community is seen in the classroom display from the first week of school shown in **Figure 4.4**. The learning experiences are built around creating a community of learners and is proudly placed on the wall for all families and visitors to enjoy.

Communication

Early childhood teachers work to foster positive relationships among the children. Supporting small group learning experiences provides an opportunity for all children to develop conversational and critical thinking skills while building on one another's ideas and sharing their own. ***Critical thinking*** questions often do not have a yes or no answer and encourage the child's response to be more thought-provoking. These questions also build language and thinking skills that would not otherwise be tapped. Providing daily opportunities for extended and engaged conversations between the teacher and the child also creates a sense of community.

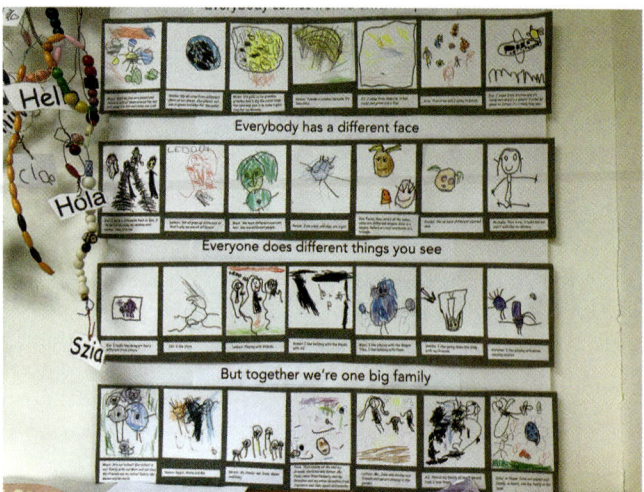

Ginny Harmelink

Figure 4.4 Created as a first week of school documentation, the International School in Even Yehuda, Israel, displays graphic images and statements to reflect a caring community. *Why do you think they included both statements and images? Explain your answer.*

NAEYC GUIDELINES

Families should be offered multiple ways of participating, including weighing in on any program decisions about their children's care and education. If families cannot communicate with educators during drop-offs and pickups, alternative means provide frequent, ongoing communication. (NAEYC, *DAP*, 2020)

Cooperative learning teaches children to work together, which is a core element of building a community and is also an instructional strategy. Examples of cooperative learning are creating a mini-book with the child's art or acting out roles during dramatic play. Encouraging cooperating pairs to discuss different perspectives and practice asking questions teaches the value of considering alternative points of view, a lifelong skill.

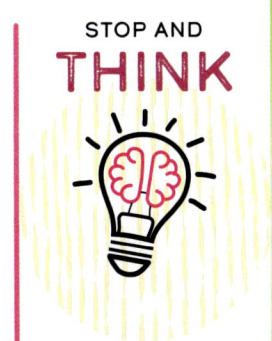

Examples of open-ended questions to drive inquiry:
- How does it work?
- Why do you think...?
- What else might work?
- What do you think would happen if...?
- Tell me about it....
- How might you do it differently?

How would you intentionally embed open-ended thinking questions into your teaching?

When teachers use open-ended questions, they are presented with opportunities to learn what a child is thinking and feeling. Open-ended questions do not have a *yes* or *no* answer and are worded to encourage deeper reflection when answering. A question such as, "What color is that crayon?" prompts a one-word, right-or-wrong answer and may stifle children's engagement. "Tell me about the crayons you are using" encourages children to use their language to describe the crayons or what they are doing.

- ☐ Design an example of classroom rules. How will you involve the children in the creation? How can you ensure that the rules reflect positive actions?
- ☐ Explain the impact Bronfenbrenner's theory has on child development and learning.
- ☐ What does a caring classroom community mean to you?

4.4 Engaging with Families

NAEYC considers family and community engagement as a necessary component of high-quality early childhood programs for children (**Figure 4.5**) (NAEYC, *DAP*, 2020). To provide the best experiences for children, engaging with the whole family is intentional from the beginning. This builds strong learning communities.

NAEYC GUIDELINES

Teachers strive to make sure that each child's home language and culture are reflected in the daily interactions, activities, and materials in the early learning setting (NAEYC, *DAP*, 2020).

Supervisors should support teachers' efforts to engage families in the educational plans for their children, including curriculum, implementation, and assessment. Early childhood teachers have the responsibility to get to know each child well and understand them as individuals with unique qualities and abilities. Involving families as a source of information about the child (both before beginning a program and during the program) is a quality guideline in an early childhood program. The teacher must ensure that the curriculum is comprehensive and that each child has individualized goals.

Researchers at the University of Oxford found that children whose parents participated in the early childhood program "made significantly greater progress in their learning than children whose parents did not participate." These strides were found in children ages three to five and included progress in vocabulary, language comprehension, understanding of books, and print and number concepts. In addition, the children exhibited higher self-esteem in comparison to children of nonparticipating parents (Evangelou & Sylva 2003).

Teachers include the family to ensure that the child's home culture(s) and language(s) are embedded in the learning community. Intentional strategies enhance each child's communication, comprehension, self-expression, and learning (NAEYC, *DAP*, 2020). Consider learning how a family eats or the music they listen to or their bedtime rituals to provide a deeper understanding of their home culture. Tips on how to draw and attract family participation include:

Rawpixel/istock via Getty Images

Figure 4.5 This parent is visiting her child's classroom. Is it beneficial to the child for a parent to visit the classroom? Explain your answer.

- Provide a short biography about your interests. Parents are often too hurried at drop-off and pickup time to get to know their child's teacher.
- Parents/caregivers can feel more at ease, reducing stranger anxiety, when teachers share some of their interests and special talents.
- Create a private social-media page to upload pictures for parents during the week.
- Inquire about talents or skills parents/family may be interested in sharing.
- Ask if there are family members who may be interested in volunteering in the classroom (remember that grandparents are often an untapped source of time and energy).
- Provide classroom support outside of class time; for example, compiling resources to support learning.
- Ask the family how they might like to be part of their child's day.
- Encourage the family to provide snapshots of important people in their child's life, and frame these on a family shelf. Some children will find comfort looking at those familiar faces, especially when they need time to adjust.
- Create a monthly classroom newsletter or blog with pictures and fun classroom activities to share.

Parent involvement and regular communication is considered a hallmark of a high-quality early childhood classroom. At least two of the Division for Early Childhood (DEC) Recommended Practices are relevant to this point:

- F1. Practitioners build trusting and respectful partnerships with the family through interactions that are sensitive and responsive to cultural, linguistic, and socioeconomic diversity.
- F2. Practitioners provide the family with up-to-date, comprehensive, and unbiased information in a way that the family can understand and use to make informed choices and decisions (DEC 2014).

Family Participation

Communication with the family should be frequent and two-way with an open-door policy that welcomes all family members into the classroom. An open-door policy ensures access to the child by the family or guardian at any time during regular classroom hours and is one way to create trust, providing accessibility at any time (**Figure 4.6**).

Open-door policies are a compelling practice. Providing guidelines for parents regarding the open-door policy will ensure positive experiences for all:

- Establish blocks of 30–60 minutes for visiting the classroom to minimize distractions and prevent visitors during rest or naptime.
- Reinforce that the class follows rules that the children helped create. A child will often act differently when family is in the room. Parents should reinforce the classroom rules.
- Provide parents with times when their involvement will be especially helpful. For example, during active learning times, an extra pair of hands is helpful. You may also create room-parent roles for volunteers with more time to commit. They can put together weekly newsletters, update the class blog or social media page, or create community events to involve all the families.

Parent and family engagement with their child's learning environment and regular communication are hallmarks of a high-quality early childhood classroom.

Sandbox Early Learning Center, Tucson, AZ

Figure 4.6 An open-door policy allows grandparents to stop in and read. How is this practice beneficial to children and to their families?

Forms of Communication

Early childhood teachers know that communication is the key to quickly overcoming misunderstandings, and to helping ensure that all families are provided opportunities to participate in learning activities. While face-to-face and verbal connections are valuable, today the use of written and electronic information sharing is common.

Some teachers, especially new ones, may struggle with communicating with all families in a meaningful way (Gauvreau & Sandall 2017). Begin by asking each to complete a family questionnaire to help them share their interests. Consider these examples:

- Please share prior knowledge and experience about [blank].
- Do you have any props that the class might borrow (nothing valuable or breakable) as we explore [blank]?
- Please share if you have any ideas for field trips that connect to the learning, or if you would be interested in attending.
- Would you or another family member, such as a grandparent or relative, be interested in being a guest reader or sharing a special skill?
- Is there a specific topic of interest you would like to see us learn about this year?
- What are any specific questions you have about what your child will be learning?

Apps for Mobile Devices

Written communication comes in many forms and varieties. Many classrooms engage the families using technology such as phone apps to provide everything from the current topic of interest being studied to assessments and photos of learning in action. Informational

REAL-WORLD CLASSROOM

For the following events, teachers invited families and the community to participate with the children in their classrooms. Posters were made as invitations and short event descriptions were published in the class newsletter that goes home to every family.

Grandparents' Day

Grandparents' Day (**Figure 4.7**) provides an opportunity for grandparents to engage with their grandchildren in their school setting. Grandparents are given the opportunity to read and share stories with small groups of children. Lunch and simple-to-prepare craft projects are available for grandparents and children to enjoy together. Staff facilitates play and assists with craft projects so the grandparents can simply enjoy spending time with their little ones. So special!

Veterans Day Celebration

The Veterans Day Celebration Luncheon (**Figure 4.8**) honors veterans, past and present, who have given their service to our country. Families bring their honored loved ones to be acknowledged and celebrated.

The children present each veteran with a special thank you card as a small token of appreciation. Lunch and cake are provided, and afterwards the children proudly sing songs for everyone. Heartfelt and endearing.

Imagine an event you could plan that invites families to engage with their children in the classroom environment. What is your event called? What theme will you use? How will you engage children and parents in authentic conversations and connection? How will you highlight the children's learning?

Sandbox Early Learning Center, Tucson, AZ

Figure 4.7 Grandparents' Day announcement.

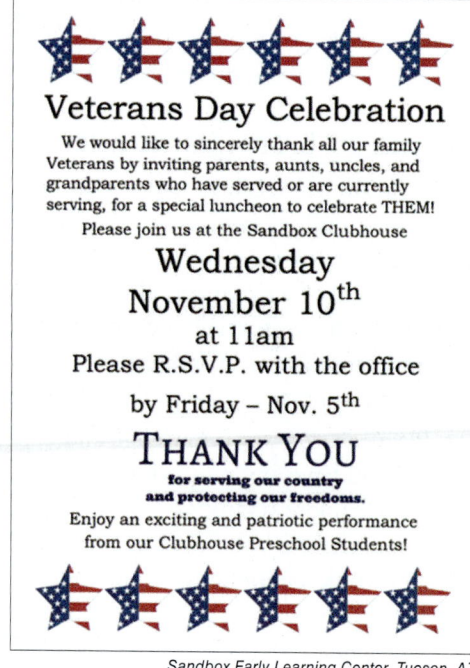

Sandbox Early Learning Center, Tucson, AZ

Figure 4.8 Veterans Day announcement.

paper copies may be posted on the family bulletin board (**Figure 4.9**) and then posted on a password-protected website or social media page.

"Unfortunately, early childhood education teachers, including those that serve children with special needs, have fewer technology tools available to support teacher-parent communication" (Ho et al. 2013). Some of the reasons for this are limited access or money to purchase these tools. Involved advocacy practices by the teachers and school administrators to enrich the classroom can help connect to local agencies for assistance.

Many teachers experience uncertainty about how to communicate effectively with families, especially with those whose cultural or linguistic backgrounds are different than their own (Sewell 2012). Teacher and parent communication apps make sharing information especially valuable in the busy lives of parents and teachers. The use of **digital applications (apps)** has opened up many opportunities to engage with families and increase family involvement. This can be especially useful for families whose children have disabilities or are considered at risk for delayed development (Beecher & Buzhardt 2016). Although there are apps that can communicate in different languages, be mindful that this alone may not create the clear communication a family needs. Tapping outside resources is encouraged.

wavebreakmedia/Shutterstock.com

Figure 4.9 Family bulletin boards should be displayed in common, high-traffic areas of the school or early learning center. How do family bulletin boards promote strong school–family relationships?

Numerous widely used apps can provide inside views of the child's learning day. Common features show the child's progress in learning the curriculum, as well as opportunities to engage in the classroom. Doing a quick search on the internet brings up dozens of apps, all with special features for various mobile devices. Today, keeping families engaged is easier than ever using technology, making this an area to be highlighted. Everyone likes to be informed, regardless of their busy lives.

Other Forms of Communication

Newsletters provide an opportunity to share classroom learning news in a different format. Involving the children in the classroom newsletter provides another learning opportunity that will create a classroom community as well as connect with the writing area. Throughout the year, children can learn about interviewing peers, using editorial skills, and using the computer as a tool for producing content. A "Kid's Corner" column that is child-created will be a feature all families look forward to.

Calendars are another popular communication tool used to inform and engage families. Calendars are commonly found on the child's home refrigerator. To help organize the month (and make it easier for the busy parent), each day of the week focuses on a theme that connects with the curriculum (**Figure 4.10**). Notice how October 25 lists one of the children's parent's birthdays as well, another connection of family to the class. The monthly calendar of events involves the family and the child. Note that different days of the week follow a similar focus, which helps families stay connected and plan for learning opportunities:

- Monday: Share and tell
- Tuesday: Field visits
- Wednesday: Wear a certain item
- Thursday: Home-play (family involvement)
- Friday: Special events

Ginny Harmelink

Figure 4.10 This preschool calendar is designed for a refrigerator! How might this calendar promote family engagement?

 **Checkpoint**

☐ Identify ways to embed different home languages in a classroom. Share examples.

☐ Following your own search for digital apps, share two and explain how they may engage the family.

☐ How does the teacher involve working families who are unable to volunteer in the classroom? Share three examples.

4.5 Engaging with Colleagues and Community

Early childhood teachers intentionally involve their colleagues and the broader community when appropriate, especially when creating curriculum. **Collaborations** are connections with people, business, organizations, and institutions that provide additional resources. They are a valuable part of creating a classroom community, and they provide a network of support for the children as they consider the concept of sharing. Collaboration is a dynamic element that occurs at all stages of learning and teaching. Collaboration can happen among children in the classroom or with outside entities, including colleagues and the broader community.

Colleagues

Collaborating with colleagues provides mutual support for professional development, as well as enhancing the curriculum (**Figure 4.11**). Peer colleagues are valuable subject matter experts who can offer innovative ideas from a different perspective. Carve out time each week to consult with another teacher, co-teacher, or assistant to brainstorm ideas related to improving your classroom and instruction.

Teachers are part of a team, and discussing current areas of interest supports the classroom curriculum in many ways. Another teacher may have books or materials that can be shared to enhance your classroom. Examples of collaborating with colleagues include:

- Invite other teachers to participate in planned experiences; for example, observing a puppet show the children have been working on or going on a field trip together.
- Work collaboratively in staff meetings to share ideas around curriculum development.
- Invite guest colleagues into the classroom to share specific learning experiences and expertise with children.
- Observe another teacher's instruction and offer strength-based ideas to implement or consider.
- Hold staff development sessions that provide opportunities to develop connections between classrooms.
- Attend early childhood conferences to stay up-to-date on new findings in the field.

Sandbox Early Learning Center, Tucson, AZ.

Figure 4.11 These colleagues are collaborating by attending a staff development workshop together. *Why is staff collaboration so important?*

Community

Teachers should continually be learning about the community in which they work. The community serves as an important resource for enhancing the curriculum and linking families with a range of services based on identified priorities and concerns. Early childhood teachers look for ways they can contribute to the ongoing development of the community as well. Use the community in three ways:

- Share resources for upcoming classroom events.
- Provide resources for the classroom.
- Become a resource to the community.

Community resources for the classroom can provide a wealth of exciting additions to support learning. Local businesses are a first go-to when planning around different topics of interest. They are often able to supply theme- or curriculum-related items, depending on the topic. Local businesses are also places of interest around which field trips can be planned.

- Studying pizza? Contact the local pizza parlor for a tour.
- Studying faraway places? Contact the local travel agency for brochures.
- Studying transportation? Invite the bus driver to read a book about buses after children sit on a real bus. (Be sure to have the driver autograph the book when finished.)
- Studying animals? Take a tour of a local animal shelter (**Figure 4.12**).
- Studying bones? Request a local doctor visit to show how casts are applied.
- Studying plants and flowers? Visit a local greenhouse or botany laboratory (**Figure 4.13**).

From local businesses to the school bus driver, creating a list of contacts will provide the resources needed to reinforce learning. The use of community resources supports efforts in the future learning of the child in untold ways.

Being active in the community can also create connections to support your work in many ways as you create a reputation for making a difference. Some ideas to explore include hosting a neighborhood recycling event, donating pet food to the local humane society, visiting a local orthopedic office, or visiting the biology lab at the local college.

Ginny Harmelink

Figure 4.12 These children are visiting a local veterinarian's office.

SID Productions/Getty Images

Figure 4.13 These children are visiting a local plant nursery.

STOP AND THINK

Look around your neighborhood. How can your classroom of learners connect to the outside community as part of your curriculum? Make a list of business and places where community and curriculum can connect. How creative can you be?

Offering active engagement in the community as part of learning makes everyone visible and reinforces a sense of belonging to the community. Community-based participation can provide extraordinary learning experiences for children and everyone involved. The extra effort required to plan and implement the field experiences or guest appearances will enrich and engage the children, the families, and the community.

REAL-WORLD CLASSROOM

CityKids educational center in Tel Aviv, Israel, offers a community library including all genres of books, from infant to adult, for all community members that live or work in the neighborhood (**Figure 4.14**). The center offers school enrichment, holiday camps, English-language courses, parenting workshops, and professional development for early childhood educators. "Mommy and Me" classes are held weekly to support parents. Shared spaces within the program are utilized for yoga classes. CityKids strives to show community members that they are welcome in the learning space and highlight their many efforts using social media.

CityKids

Figure 4.14 This is the community library within CityKids in Tel Aviv, Israel.

Outreach

Many businesses include community outreach to visit and educate children about their services, including government agencies such as police and firefighters (even Smoky the Bear) and nonprofit agencies. Keep in mind that many outside entities will need support and education on developmentally appropriate presentations and how to capture a child's attention. Providing guidance for those who are not experienced working with groups of young children is advised. Remember to follow-up and send child-created thank-you notes to guests and businesses who supported your requests. Consider having personalized thank-you notes that are illustrated by the children (**Figure 4.15**).

czarny_bez/iStock/ Getty Images

Figure 4.15 A thank-you note.

Chapter 4 Review and Assessment

Chapter Summary

4.1 Explain how the ecological systems theory supports community and family engagement.
- Creating a community of learners includes many different facets. Bronfenbrenner's ecological systems theory can provide a basis with the child as the core.
- The microsystem includes the family, the school, and people and events with which a child interacts regularly.
- The mesosystem describes how the different parts of a child's microsystem work together to support the child, such as when a family member is actively engaged in the child's events.
- The fourth system is the exosystem, which includes people, places, or events that may not have a direct connection to the child, but may impact them in other ways, such as a parent winning a large sum of money that influences decisions made.
- The macrosystem includes people and events that do not directly impact the child but could influence the child's life, both positively and negatively.
- The chronosystem refers to all the systems of this model.

4.2 Summarize practices that create communities in the classroom.
- NAEYC Standard 2 for early childhood practitioners focuses on fostering community connections. Within this standard are the elements that provide for an inclusive classroom and build a caring community.
- Standard 2 criteria support a foundation toward understanding why creating strong relationships is a key element in the early childhood classroom.
- The CSEFEL teaching pyramid introduced high-quality practices that support a teacher while building an eager community of learners. This begins with nurturing relationships in supportive environments to targeted social-emotional supports.

4.3 Describe methods to engage children to become part of the classroom community.
- Involving children in their own learning begins with asking "How do you teach children to manage their own learning?"
- Engaging with children to build a community requires making sure they are visible in the classroom and acknowledged as participants.
- Using small groups encourages communication skills and is a common practice in the early childhood classroom.
- Cooperative learning fosters strong relationships and is encouraged.

4.4 Discuss the variety of communication practices to support family engagement.
- Family engagement is one of the most important pieces when working in the early childhood field. Connecting with each family and involving them in all aspects of curriculum development ensures that they are partners in all areas that involve their child.
- Guidelines to ensure open communication include multiple forums for correspondence, including digital apps.

Copyright Goodheart-Willcox Co., Inc.

4.5 Describe strategies to engage colleagues and the broader community.
- Collaborations with the larger community provide opportunities for teaching and learning and are a valuable part of the classroom community.
- Intentional practices when working with colleagues reinforce ways to integrate both into the daily curriculum and influence learning.
- Guest speakers and field trips provide real world learning applications that support the curriculum and provide enhanced opportunities to learn.
- Integrating into the community enriches learning while involving the true spirit of the neighborhood: the child.

For Further Reflection

1. Drop-off and pickup times are often rushed, and there is little time to talk about current learning experiences. What is a solution?
2. A new family does not speak English well, making communication difficult. How can you support this family so they can understand the curriculum?
3. Look around your own community. Where are some places where a group of children could learn what the word *altruism* means? In what ways could you integrate helping others into your curriculum?
4. Speaking to a group of young children is different from speaking to older children. What are key talking points you would share with a potential guest speaker? How would you prepare the children?
5. Identify guidelines to share with a community resource spokesperson around keeping a group of young children engaged during a presentation.
6. What are other specific practices and structures in the classroom that will support a caring community and enrich the curriculum taught?

Recall and Application

1. Which circle of the ecological systems theory includes pandemics and wars?
   A. microsystem
   B. mesosystem
   C. exosystem
   D. macrosystem
2. Which circle of the ecological systems theory includes parents either losing their jobs or receiving a promotion?
   A. microsystem
   B. mesosystem
   C. exosystem
   D. macrosystem
3. **True or False.** The ecological systems theory is based on the social development of the child.
4. **True or False.** The CSEFEL pyramid provides a tiered look at expected cognitive development.
5. Identify an open-ended question.
   A. What day is it today?
   B. Can I help you with your zipper?
   C. Is this blue or black?
   D. Can you tell me about your picture?

6. **True or False.** Cooperative learning encourages children to work individually.
7. An open-door policy is a policy that ____.
   A. provides access to information that may be in a child's file
   B. encourages families to visit as interested
   C. advocates for video viewing of a child during instruction
   D. requires the door to the building to be propped open during the day
8. **True or False.** Including each child's home culture(s) and language(s) is part of the shared environment of the learning community.

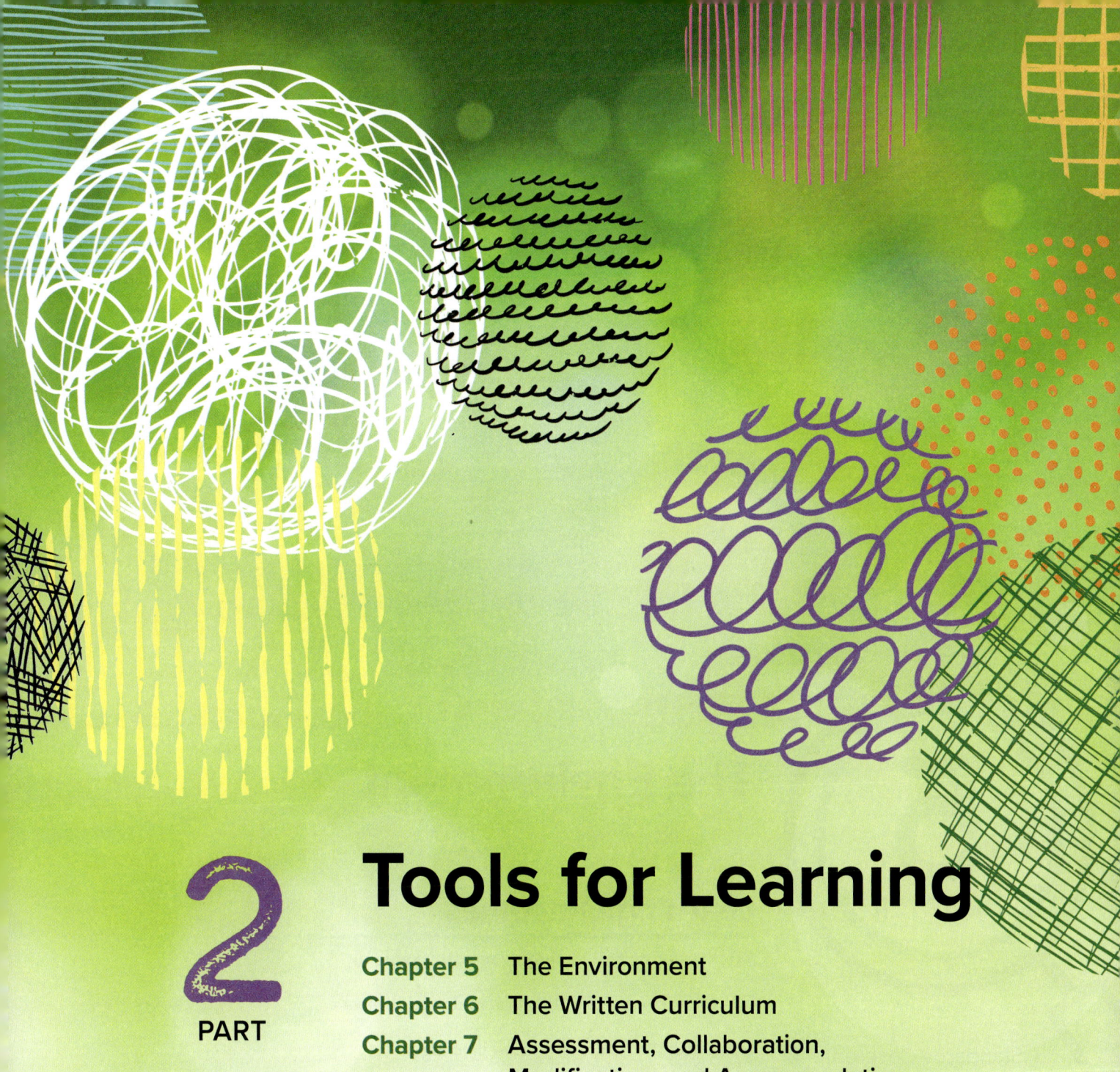

Tools for Learning

PART 2

Chapter 5 The Environment
Chapter 6 The Written Curriculum
Chapter 7 Assessment, Collaboration, Modification, and Accommodation
Chapter 8 The Implementation Phase

CHAPTER 5

The Environment

Learning Outcomes

After studying this chapter, you will be able to:

5.1 Identify early childhood room design elements.

5.2 Define the use and value of labeling.

5.3 Explain the role of culture in the early learning environment.

5.4 Distinguish components to consider when planning the environment.

5.5 Compare learning areas in the early childhood classroom.

Standards Covered in This Chapter

NAEYC

1c, 1d, 2b, 2c, 4b, 4c, 5b, 5c, 6a, 6e

DAP

Principle 2, Guideline 7;
Principle 4, Guideline 1

Image credit: rilueda/iStock via Getty Images Plus

Miss Alma

SNAPSHOT

FatCamera/E+ via Getty Images

"If you're happy and you know it, clap your hands!" is a common tune in Miss Alma's room. The children enrolled are excited, and their engagement is evident to anyone observing. Miss Alma spent hundreds of hours observing other classrooms during her early childhood studies to arrive at the perfect classroom setup. Considering the children's interests, the physical space, and the curriculum needs, the classroom represents her philosophy of education.

The physical space is predetermined, and using it wisely begins with a class layout. This was an exciting part of her planning: where to place which learning area, and how to ensure supervision of everyone. Miss Alma knew that the many learning areas should be able to integrate many different academic subject areas with play, and she was also aware that some areas go better together than others, depending on the learning experiences planned.

Miss Alma recognizes that children learn social-emotional skills in the context of their relationships with others through observing, interacting, imitating, and responding. The classroom environment and the different learning areas support the development of skills that build a strong social-emotional foundation, and placement of the learning areas could provide many opportunities to support the children as they develop. Miss Alma also is aware that the dramatic play area is a core learning area in the classroom and wanted to be sure it provided an ever-changing look to support the children's different cultures and interests. School is set to begin in 10 minutes, and this teacher and the children enrolled are ready to learn!

Give It Some Thought

1. What are ways that Miss Alma can involve the children in the design of her classroom? Share examples.
2. Miss Alma has created a flower shop in the dramatic play area that can host eight children. How might Miss Alma structure the morning learning experiences if all children want to participate in the dramatic play area and still support self-direction of making choices to support agency?

Key Terms

adaptations	forest schools	learning area placement
authentic learning	group dynamics	loose parts
availability	individual grouping	modifications
engineering	intentional teaching	pairing
environmental print	invented spelling	prosody
facilitator	invitation table	supervision

Introduction

"Look what I made, Opa!" shouts four-year-old Ledoux to her grandpa, pointing to a sketch displayed outside the classroom door. "It's a picture of us. It says, 'I love you.'" The display includes highlights of the children's work and makes both the children and their family proud. Displaying children's work brings the classroom to life.

Tables and wall displays are an important part of early learning environments. Many early childhood professionals consider the environment to be "the third teacher," meaning the environment is as influential as the educator who created it. Environment planning in the early years starts with a *discernment* (ability to judge) for design.

Children learn best in well-arranged classrooms that support secure relationships with caring and responsive adults. They also thrive in classrooms that provide routines or schedules that are consistent. Additionally, research suggests that a high-quality classroom environment can help close the achievement gap. The environment serves as a rich context within which children can gather, analyze, and begin to understand the many facets of life.

5.1 Designing Early Learning Environments

Early learning environments consist of the physical space, the social interactions, and the *temporal* (time-based) elements (**Figure 5.1**). Each component depends on the others. The different elements, with an emphasis on the physical environment, include connections to and integration of each child's culture. This chapter describes the physical environment. The social and temporal elements of the environment are explored in Chapters 6 through 8.

Classroom design affects how children learn. Everything a child looks at should hold visual appeal—but how much? From the ceiling to the floor and across the walls, the design choices are arranged to provide interest and reflect the children who spend their time in that space. A balanced display supports learning without over- or under-stimulating the young learner.

It is important to consider all the sensory elements that come into play, including lighting, color, sound, smell, and texture. Many studies show that there is a relationship between the quality of the designed physical environment (for example, size, well-defined learning areas, a variety of design features, and the quality of outdoor play spaces) and the child's cognitive, social, and emotional development. The way a room is set up—including elements such as a sense of welcoming and movement from one area to another—can enhance or impede learning (Department of Education and Training 2022). Infants need a lot of floor space to practice rolling. Toddlers require space to move, climb, and explore. Preschool rooms require the addition of learning areas. The early grades (K–3) are challenged with classroom sizes that might have to accommodate thirty or more children.

Planning spaces that ensure access to materials within reach of children is not as easy as it may sound. Researchers looked at classrooms and how the environment affected children's ability to maintain concentration and learn. Children in highly ornamented classrooms

Figure 5.1
Components of the Early Childhood Environment.
Why is each important?

Designing an Early Learning Environment	
Components of the Early Childhood Environment	**Definition**
Physical environment	The overall design and layout of an area, including its learning areas, materials, and furnishings
Social environment	Grouping of children, including the interactions that occur between peers, teachers, and family members
Temporal environment	The daily learning experiences, schedules, timing, length of routines, and child-to-teacher ratios

Goodheart-Willcox Publisher

(**Figure 5.2a**) were likely to be less focused or on-task and showed smaller learning gains than children in classrooms where décor was kept to a minimum (**Figure 5.2b**) (Association for Psychological Science 2014).

The environment supports play and displays of children's work to reflect their importance in the classroom. Examples of children's work should be chosen as a design feature over teacher-created motifs that are sold in mass supplies. One example is using children's self-portraits to support each child as an individual (**Figure 5.3**).

Different educational philosophies have different views on learning environments. Notice how the educational philosophies and curricula from Chapter 3, "Curricula and Approaches," embrace different views of the learning environment in **Figure 5.4**.

Sensory Elements

In early learning environments, spaces that are inviting begin with sensory-related elements. Many classrooms have overhead fluorescent lighting that casts cool white light. Studies suggest that this type of lighting has harmful effects on behavior and learning. The rapid fluctuation of light from fluorescent lamps is known to affect the way our eyes move across a page and can interfere with the performance of visual tasks (Wilkins 2019).

Children who are affected by the flicker see an improvement in the clarity of text when a sheet of colored plastic is placed on the page. Children who use colored overlays find they can read more quickly and often report a reduction in eye strain and headaches. One possible reason is that a colored filter can reduce the variation in color that occurs with the old-fashioned fluorescent lighting (Wilkins 2019). Additional warm lighting provides an appealing feel to the space. Table lamps provide soft lighting that can define a space much like a divider and create a feeling of separation between areas, much like a rug can do. Tape electric cords securely to the floor so there is no danger of tripping. Using natural light brings the outdoors in.

Think about the power of color. Color connects to emotions, learning, and memory. In designing spaces, warm colors (red, orange, or yellow) are connected to energy and optimism while cool colors (green, blue, or purple) are associated with calming environments. A gallery wall to display the children's work can be painted and repainted multiple times and is easily changed, providing visual interest through the year.

The sound of learning is evident in an engaged classroom, and nothing sets the stage as much as music. It might be children's musicians such as Raffi or Joe Scruggs playing in the block area or Mozart lightly playing in the background during quiet times. Intentional music selection can provide a subtle definition of space. Music sets a tone that is difficult

sandsun/Shutterstock.com

Figure 5.2a, 5.2b The learning environment has a strong effect on learning. *Which environment do you think is more conducive to learning? Why?*

Sandbox Early Childhood Learning Center, Tucson, AZ

Figure 5-3 Self-portraits displayed on wall focus on emotions. *How does this display engage children, family, and guests as they enter the classroom?*

to achieve using other tools. A well-stocked collection of tunes should be part of a teacher's toolbox.

Smell is another element to be considered when planning the environment. Smell is our most powerful sense and continues to be fine-tuned for the first eight years of life. Compared to sight, which develops over the first months, an infant's sense of smell is well developed from birth. Just as the smell of baking bread can make a house feel warm and cozy, pleasant odors in an early learning environment can inspire positive feelings about education.

Texture produces interest and invites exploration, whether it is on a table, on the wall, or on the floor. Design should include contrasting and complimentary textures in the classroom and learning areas. For example, burlap, different fabrics, textured paper, and mesh will interest the children.

Filling vertical spaces can captivate attention while differentiating learning areas, provided it does not distract the children (**Figure 5.5**). It is important to check with the local fire marshal, as some states regulate and limit how vertical space is decorated. The type of flooring is also part of the vertical space. Rugs or carpets should be placed on top of non-slip mats to reduce slip-and-fall hazards. Rugs add visual appeal and soften the sound in a space. They are flexible to move around while also providing a comfy spot to play or rest.

Figure 5.4 Comparing Educational Approaches' Views of the Environment. *Which view aligns best with your teaching philosophy?*

Comparing Educational Approaches' Views of the Environment	
Approach	**View of the Environment**
Reggio Emilia Philosophy	The classroom environment is considered the third teacher, in addition to the team of two teachers. Children's work is displayed on all the walls, and their work is one of the main contributions to shaping the space of the school (The Hundred Languages of Children).
Waldorf Curriculum	Soft, plain wall colors are quiet enough to allow the children a sense of inner freedom. Brighter colors are found in play capes or cloths. Comfort and space are key factors in creating an experience designed around the child to inspire curiosity and embrace free thinking (In a Nutshell).
HighScope Curriculum	Environment is arranged with diverse, open-ended materials, reflecting home, culture, and language, that are organized and labeled to promote independence and encourage children to carry out their intentions (HighScope.org).
Tools of the Mind Curriculum	The dramatic play area is the core of the classroom, which supports mature, imaginative play. Encouraging mental tools to build self-regulation skills is a hallmark in this environment (ToolsoftheMind.com).
Project Approach Philosophy	With different kinds of learning activities in progress at any one time, intentional placement of quiet spaces and use of wall space and horizonal elements can help organize the room (ProjectApproach.org).
Montessori Curriculum	The *prepared environment* can be designed to facilitate maximum independent learning and exploration by the child with a focus on practical skills. All furnishings are child-size and match the developmental needs and interests of each child (Montessori.org).

Goodheart-Willcox Publisher

How and where materials are stored will be determined by the space available and where windows and doors are located. Many early childhood classrooms have closets to store boxes that connect to specific learning areas. Creating an inventory using labeled containers will make it easier to find those items and will save time during setup of the learning area.

Displays

A unique way to stimulate curiosity is to arrange different items that are connected to the topic of interest in some form of presentation. Displays in the early childhood environment include items placed on the walls, tables, or counters to reflect the children's learning. Displays can be child-directed, adult-directed, or both. Table spaces set up to display specific interests are called *invitation tables*. Often placed near the entry to the class, these are spaces that provide multiple elements to elicit interest and are built around what the children are focusing on that day or week. Just as the name implies, these collections provide an invitation for both children and adults to explore materials related to the current learning or to give a preview of what is to come. Invitation tables can spark conversation and can even become a *catalytic event*, or a trigger that sparks a child's interest in learning (see more about catalytic events in Chapter 6, "The Written Curriculum").

Some invitation tables become their own learning areas for a small group of children to explore a certain characteristic they find interesting. For example, a display table on the topic of automobiles might include car magazines, trays with car parts to disassemble, images placed on a wall to show car-related activities, and of course, a children's book to learn more about this topic of interest.

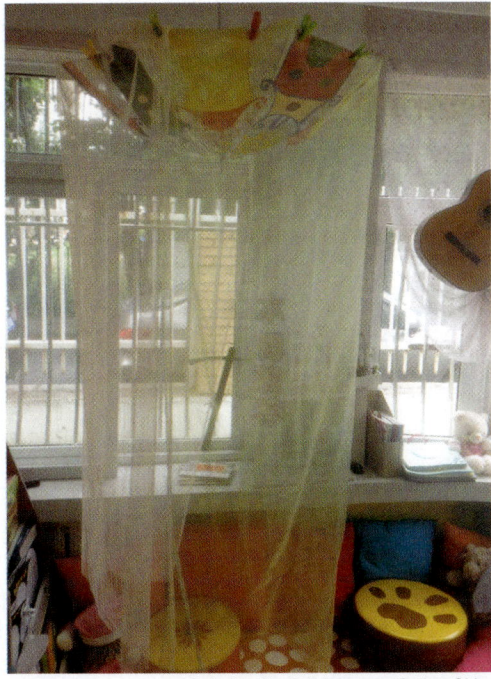

Submitted by Deb Lawrence/Dalian, China

Figure 5.5 The vertical space in a classroom includes space above the heads of the children. These sheer curtains define the space between the floor and ceiling. How would you embrace space when designing an environment?

STOP AND THINK

- How does the classroom design promote learning outcomes?
- Are the aesthetics appealing to any person that visits?
- Are the different learning areas inviting?
- What does your classroom space say about you? What does it say about the children?

 Checkpoint

☐ Identify examples of the physical elements in a classroom.
☐ Describe two examples of the social environment.
☐ Why are the temporal components an important consideration when planning?
☐ Name and describe three sensory elements in the classroom.
☐ What is an invitation table?

5.2 Labeling

Labeling is the act of pairing a written term or graphic with an item in an early learning environment. One common form of labeling is using each child's name throughout the classroom. Children's names and their photos should be prevalent in common areas that include a cubby for each child to store items and a place to hang a jacket. Laminate names at the writing learning area to support children who are interested in practicing writing their own or other's names. Including children's names throughout the classroom affirms this as their space and is one element that supports the creation of a community of learners (**Figure 5.6**).

THE TEACHER'S LENS

Teacher Jennings was pleased with the responses from families about the invitation table as they walked in the door. The display reflected many of the items the class was learning about.

The table contents created interest and were a great conversation starter. Two families offered items to display! Teacher Jennings pondered asking how the families celebrate holidays and wondered how that might create a meaningful conversation.

Labels with Images

Labels that include an image help inform children, families, and visitors what they might expect to happen in each classroom area. Pictures of items aid in word recognition and help children put things away in the correct place. If the toys or manipulatives are in a basket, the attached label helps them make the connection, recognizing the image.

Figure 5.6 Appropriate Versus Inappropriate Uses of Labels in Early Learning Environments. *Why are appropriate labeling practices important?*

Labeling	
Appropriate Uses of Labels in the Early Learning Environment	**Inappropriate Uses of Labels in the Early Learning Environment**
• Creating and placing labels in the classroom *with* the children—starting with a blank slate each year. • Using images that correspond to learning materials that are stored in bins or on shelves. • Using all the languages represented in the classroom. • Signifying different elements such as *white wall* or *blue chair*. • Including images that correspond to learning materials that are stored in bins or on shelves. • Creating signs that designate a learning area, with maximum numbers when needed to limit overcrowding. • Using children's names to support learning one's own name. Use them on cubbies, coat hangers, tables.	• Including too much information…make it simple. Example: Instead of labeling "Assorted Dolls" simply say "Dolls." • Using labels only to decorate and cover the walls. • Creating teacher-made labels with little help from the children. • Using the same labels repeatedly year after year. • Writing labels only in English when other languages are spoken at home.

Goodheart-Willcox Publisher

Environmental Print

Labeling is a common type of environmental print within the classroom. **Environmental print** is defined as the print of everyday life and includes all the letters and words the child sees, including the 'M' for McDonald's, the 'W' for Walmart, and the "S-T-O-P" letters on the street sign. Some teachers feature the alphabet comprising common words in the child's neighborhood. Early Years Foundation Stage teacher Lisa Atkinson says, "We love this alphabet featuring brand logos to represent each letter. Children love recognizing logos and it's a fantastic way to start a discussion around sounds and to spark their interest in reading and mark making."

Virginia Harmelink

Figure 5.7 The early childhood classroom should reflect the home languages of the children enrolled. How would you involve the families in the creation of different labels that are meaningful?

The process of creating and placing labels around the classroom should start over every year because involving the children will give meaning to what the labels symbolize. A label on the door can display all the languages that are reflected in the classroom enrollment (**Figure 5.7**). Supporting the development of a rich and shared vocabulary involves creating language-rich environments. Using labels is one of many ways to support the children's home language in the environment. Picture labels are helpful as the teacher works to address communication differences in the classroom. A well-designed learning area is engaging and full of life. The environment should reflect the home culture and languages of the children, while strategically embedding opportunities to enhance a child's expressions, understanding, and learning.

 **Checkpoint**

- ☐ What are some examples of environmental print in your neighborhood? How might these be connected to your curriculum?
- ☐ Why does supporting environmental print make sense in the early years?
- ☐ How can labels support the child's home language?
- ☐ Name an inappropriate use of labeling in the classroom.

5.3 Culture

A person's culture shapes and is inseparable from development (Reid et al. 2017). A first step to support multicultural learning in an early learning environment is for teachers to examine their own cultural beliefs. How were they expected to interact with others? How did they address important adults in their life? Were they encouraged to fit in to different situations or to stand out? For instance, some children are expected to address adults with "Yes, sir" or "Yes, ma'am," while others are encouraged to refer to adults as "Mister" or "Miss" using last names. Still others are expected to address adults by their titles, such as "Teacher." If a child is asked to follow the teacher's cultural beliefs—for example, calling the teacher by their first name—it may feel disrespectful to them. For this reason, it is important for teachers to have open discussions with children and to reach a class agreement. For younger children, it is appropriate to have this discussion with the families.

Intentional Teaching

The focus on culture should be reflected in each of the different learning areas. Through *intentional teaching*, which means always thinking about teaching efforts and how they support or enable children's development and learning, the teacher blends opportunities for each child to exercise choices within the context of a planned learning environment and supports the family's culture.

Social Dynamics

In well-planned learning areas, children learn powerful lessons about social dynamics. They observe the interactions that educators have with children and sometimes the interactions teachers have with one another. Well before age five, most young children have some ideas about their own social identities and the social identities of others. These ideas may include biases regarding gender and race (Skinner & Meltzoff 2019).

Consider the practices in the classroom environment that support individual cultures. These may include labeling objects in both English and other languages spoken by students, displaying images that reflect diverse backgrounds, singing songs from different cultures, and reading books in a child's home language. Early childhood teachers need to understand the importance of creating a learning environment that helps children develop social identities that are not biased toward one group over another. This chapter explores additional ideas to embed cultural diversity as it focuses on each of the specific learning areas.

Checkpoint

☐ How would *you* define *your* culture?

☐ Identify two different cultural experiences that might be included in the block area.

☐ Understanding your own biases is critical in the early childhood classroom. What are some biases you are aware of?

5.4 Setting the Stage

There are five main factors to consider when setting up an early childhood classroom:
- learning area placement
- supervision
- group size
- adaptations
- availability

THE TEACHER'S LENS

Teacher Flores noted that the children were not visiting the block area. This learning area was popular the previous year, and additional space as well as manipulatives were added this year. As the teacher evaluated the block area, the recent change in how the classroom was lit cast a shadow on the area, and the many manipulatives were not organized.

Freshening up learning areas is often accomplished by rotating and changing the materials, or by switching the location with another learning area. Just like moving furniture around in your home, changing the look and location sparks renewed interest.

Learning Area Placement

Learning area placement refers to where the different learning areas are located (**Figure 5.8**). Placement can have a direct effect on children's behaviors. For example, if children have been running too much in the classroom, their teacher may want to consider arranging the classroom in a way that leaves less space for running. Noisy learning areas, such as the block area and the music area, should be placed in proximity to one another and as far away as possible from quiet learning areas, such as the library area and the math area.

Sometimes finding a good balance takes a little redecorating. A well-defined physical arrangement promotes a positive learning environment that will teach children to respect physical boundaries, identify which specific types of activities are appropriate in particular areas of the classroom, and learn which behaviors are acceptable and expected.

Changing the Learning Areas

While children like consistency, they also sometimes enjoy change. Allowing the children to be part of redesigning a room is a great community-building experience. Some reasons to consider changing the layout include:

- The learning spaces are not large enough to meet the needs of the children who choose to play and work there.
- Some learning areas are extending into the next space. For example, if the library is located near the block area, the children may begin to use the library space for additional building.
- Children have lost interest in what was once a favorite learning destination. Changing the location can renew interest.
- You notice that children are cross-playing or combining materials (such as dramatic play and blocks), so putting those centers next to each other will make the integration easier for the children.

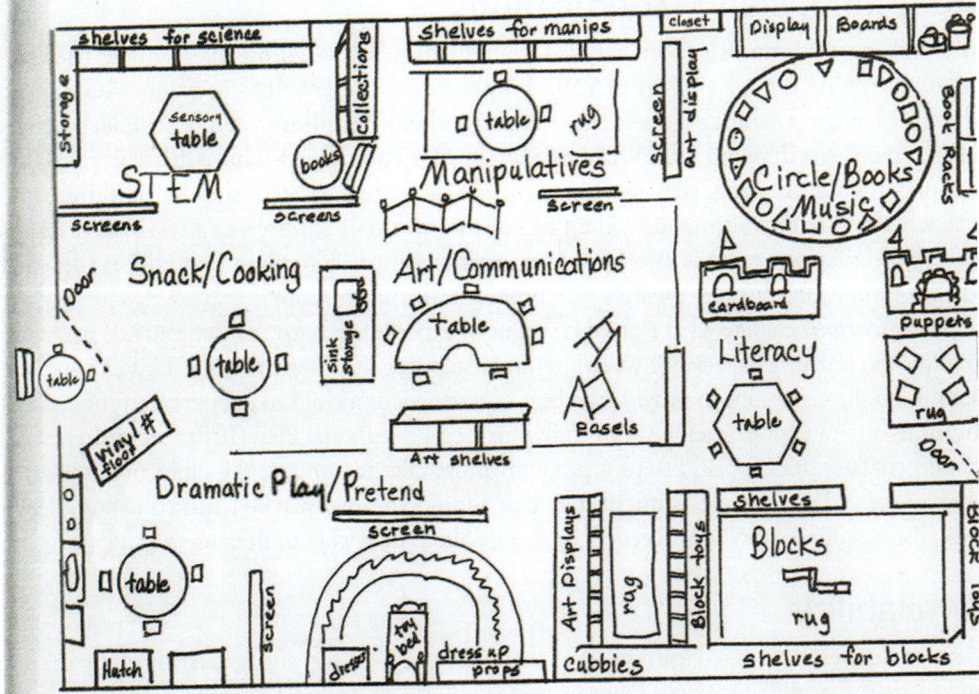

Goodheart-Willcox Publisher

Figure 5.8 This is an example of a layout for an early learning environment. Do you think this layout follows best practices?

STOP AND THINK | What would happen if you moved the art area next to the blocks? How about moving the dramatic play area near the music area?

Supervision

Supervision refers to monitoring the children and their activities. Planning for supervision includes determining how much autonomy children should have in each learning area, and using low shelves that allow the teacher to scan the entire room as needed. Some learning areas require minimal supervision, while others require full supervision. The amount of supervision is an important factor when developing learning experiences in the learning areas. Plan no more than one learning experience that will require direct teacher oversight at one time. While best practice supports enlarging learning areas if there is interest, some large-group activities are not appropriate if children need to wait quietly, if the teacher needs to provide individual responses, or if children need to take turns (for example, in cooking experiences).

One way to increase supervision is to involve family volunteers. An extra pair of hands can go a long way, especially when a teacher does not have a partner to co-teach. Teachers should plan ahead and give volunteers specific jobs that will help keep the learning environment running smoothly.

Group Size

Group dynamics refers to groupings of individuals. These include large groups, small groups, pairing, and even individual experiences. *Pairing* is a dynamic in which children with differing abilities can support each other and is an effective way to encourage peer learning. *Individual grouping* provides children a time to be alone. Group size as a main instructional strategy is explored in depth in Chapter 8, "Implementation Strategies."

Adaptations and Modifications

Adaptations and modifications require thoughtful plans based on the needs of the children occupying the space (**Figure 5.9**). *Adaptations* are alterations in an environment to maximize engagement and meet the needs of individual children. For example, teachers affix papers to a drawing table with tape or clips for children who have difficulty holding the paper while coloring; they rearrange the learning areas to accommodate children who use wheelchairs or walking aids; they add a stool so small children can wash their hands at the sink. An art easel is another common adaptation. Knowing and addressing each child's limitations ensures positive outcomes for all the children.

Modifications change what a child is taught or expected to learn. Sometimes it is necessary to alter the learning experience to ensure understanding at different levels. This can include setting up the classroom to provide the best experience for a child to support learning. Modifications often include developing an Individualized Educational Plan (IEP) for children. This document identifies specific steps a program must take to support the child in all areas of development. For example, it might state that additional time may be required to complete a task, list specific sensory tools needed, or specify alternative ways to measure success.

Availability

Availability refers to which learning areas are open on a given day and is determined by the lesson plans, the areas that may need direct supervision, and group size. Using these indicators helps ensure optimum learning experiences. Although it is ideal to have all learning areas open at all times, it is not always possible because some areas may require more supervision than the teacher as time to provide. Placement, supervision, and group size are conscious decisions a teacher should make when writing the curriculum (more on this in Chapter 6, "The Written Curriculum," and Chapter 8, "Implementation Phase").

Checkpoint

- Why does learning area placement matter in the early childhood classroom?
- Provide an example of group size and why it may impact a certain learning area.
- Share an example of an adaptation that might be created in the classroom.
- Share an example of a modification that might be made to the classroom.

olesiabilkei/Istock via Getty Images Plus

Figure 5-9 There is ample space in this learning environment to accommodate this child's wheelchair. What other accommodations could be made for this child?

5.5 Learning Areas

There are nine common learning areas in early learning environments. Remember that the learning areas can be organized to integrate multiple subjects to meet different learning outcomes (and standards). The learning areas focus on the following four characteristics:

- definition and purpose of the play area
- teacher role for the play area
- culture and the ways it can be explored within the play area
- furnishings that support learning for the play area

This chapter explores in depth the nine common learning areas. Note that all of these can easily be modified to meet the needs of different age groups. The basic learning areas are:

- dramatic play
- blocks
- sensory-texture
- outdoors
- music/movement
- creative arts
- writing
- library
- STEM
- bonus area

The music-movement, creative arts, writing, library, and STEM areas are also considered academic-content areas and are featured in Chapter 9, "Academic Disciplines." While some teachers might add a specific manipulative area or quiet-time area to the learning areas listed here, others commonly merge manipulatives with the blocks area and quiet time with the library area.

Dramatic Play Area

The dramatic play area is the most supportive of children's social-emotional development, which is the foundation of all learning. Integrating academic subjects into the dramatic play area is easy because children recreate real-life scenarios in this area. **Figure 5.10** reflects a traditional dramatic play area space set up as a restaurant table. The space can be anything that supports learning.

In dramatic play, children are able to acquire the foundations of phonemic and phonological awareness, vocabulary, grammar, and reading by integrating multiple learning activities such as

Figure 5.10 This dramatic play area looks like a table at a restaurant. *What skills can children learn by playing "restaurant"?*

Ginny Harmelink

reading pretend menus in a pretend restaurant, writing prescriptions in a pretend doctor office, and creating a shopping list in a pretend grocery store, to name a few.

The dramatic play area is a space where children can pretend. Pretending enables children to take risks and identify with someone or something other than themselves. Early childhood researcher Vivian Gussin Paley stated, "Pretend often confuses the adult, but it is the child's real and serious world, the stage upon which any identity is possible and secret thoughts can be safely revealed" (Paley 2009). When children are pretending, they are making strides in each of the developmental domains: physical, cognitive, and social-emotional.

In the dramatic play area, children learn to:

- explore human relationships.
- experiment with humor, such as wearing silly clothes.
- expand their ability to plan, predict, and organize.
- develop empathy through roleplay and understand how others feel, think, and act.
- use social skills to communicate, negotiate, cooperate, compromise, take turns.
- develop symbolic thinking.
- extend vocabulary as dramatic play is social in nature.

Teacher Role in the Dramatic Play Area

The teacher's role in this area is often that of *facilitator.* This means the teacher provokes additional ideas to support children's play. A facilitator guides the children and provides props or other items to support their learning. Children naturally have active imaginations. Teachers who create learning areas that support the active mind provide a jumpstart to learning new concepts. The following three strategies can spark children's interest in the dramatic play area (Colker 2015).

Strategy 1: Combine two play areas. Combining another learning area with the dramatic play area is a great way to keep children interested while covering more than one learning domain at once. For example, incorporate math by adding a menu with prices in a play restaurant area. Pretend to call the restaurant and ask the children how much it will cost to buy two $1 muffins. Incorporate writing by helping the children create a recipe. Ask them which items should be included, and spell them out on a sheet of paper.

Strategy 2: Provide picture and informational books. Children's picture and informational books should always be part of the dramatic play area. Change the books once a month based on the subjects students are currently interested in. Based on interests, changing this area each month is appropriate: restaurants, pet shops, camping sites, doctor offices, grocery stores, farmer's markets, beaches—the ideas are endless. Asking families to loan or donate books from home will enrich the area further and support student connections to the topics.

Strategy 3: Incorporate story plans into play. Creating story plans and assigning specific roles to children provokes thinking and provides a starting place when children first arrive at the dramatic play area. Story plans should start with a problem to solve, and the teacher should identify roles to remove any possible conflicts. Consider a dramatic play area created around the topic of shoes. The area is set up as a shoe store with lots of child-created signage, shoes, and associated shoe store items donated by families or loaned by the community.

- **Problem**: Customer comes in and is searching for a special pair of shoes for dancing. The store does not have any specific dancing shoes, so the salesperson must convince the customer to buy what the store has. The customer must be convinced.
- **Roles**: Salesperson, Customers

The teacher remembers to support the changing roles and different scenarios as they emerge. These are child-led opportunities to try out different ideas.

Culture in the Dramatic Play Area

Signage in the children's home languages, clothing and costumes from different lands, and assorted props that represent many different cultures will provide a setting that is respectful and inclusive of all. Dolls that reflect different skin colors, genders, and other items that reflect different abilities, for example, eyeglasses with lenses removed, walking aids for people with physical disabilities, or child-sized crutches are easily merged into dramatic play. These measures promote *authentic learning*, or learning in which children reenact activities and events from their own family life.

Placement of Furnishings in the Dramatic Play Area

The dramatic play area needs a larger space than many of the learning areas due to the activity and number of children that visit and stay involved for long periods of time. The furnishings change depending on the topic of interest and can include many unique items, depending on the overall theme. For example, teachers may add props such as menus or signage to a restaurant theme or live flowers to a flower shop theme. Creating the sense of having actual walls also supports efforts of sustained play and can often be accomplished using low shelves.

Block Area

The value of a well-stocked block area is supported by multiple studies that demonstrate a positive correlation between preschool block play and math achievement in later school grades. While there was no correlation between block performance and standardized

---

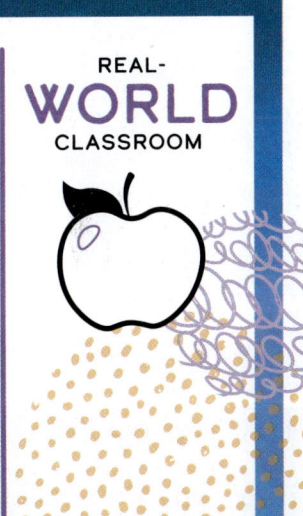

REAL-WORLD CLASSROOM

Children's need for dramatic play is universal. Below are some examples of dramatic play areas in classrooms from around the world.

Styling Salon

This dramatic play area is complete with shampoo sink, child-created signage, smocks, sprayers, unbreakable mirror or even tinfoil on the wall with a bulletin board frame, and towels. An appointment book is also essential. The dramatic play area has been turned into a hair salon (**Figure 5.11**). Providing authentic tools support connections to real-life scenarios. Children bring their own experiences when they play hair styling, as most will have visited a salon. Including children's picture books and hair styling magazines will extend literacy into this area Families may be able to offer an old-fashioned bonnet hair dryer to add realism to the salon.

Maple Images/Shutterstock

Figure 5.11 A hair salon theme in the dramatic play area encourages connections to real-life experiences. What are some props you could add to make the learning more authentic?

Continued

REAL-WORLD CLASSROOM

Not only are the children learning social skills, but they are also practicing with money, time, and creativity, all connected to the early learning standards and outcomes. This dramatic play idea is popular with all children.

Bakery and Store-Front Setup in China

The pastries in the bakery (**Figure 5.12**) were made and painted by the teachers to be as real as possible and to reflect the Chinese culture. The integration of math with literacy is reflected in the store-front with labels placed on shelves (**Figure 5.13**).

Submitted by Deb Lawrence/Dalian, China

Figure 5.12 A bakery is ready for customers in this dramatic play area. Identify ways to connect a bakery theme can connect to other learning areas in the room.

Submitted by Deb Lawrence/Dalian, China

Figure 5.13 A store front is neatly arranged with prices displayed. What props would you add to this dramatic play area that are authentic?

Two More Examples

In the home center play area in Wyoming (**Figure 5.14**) and a campground area in Oregon (**Figure 5.15**), serious play is occurring. Taking on real roles allows children to practice skills using familiar scenarios.

Shelby Miskimins/Foundations Early Care & Education, Wyoming

Figure 5.14 The dramatic play area is set up as the "home corner." Identify items that create a feeling of home to support the developing child.

R. Taylor/Chemeketa College Early Childhood Laboratory School, Salem, OR

Figure 5.15 A camping play area introduces children to the facets of connecting to the great outdoors. How might families be involved in this learning area?

math tests or grades at the elementary school levels, by the beginning of middle school (seventh grade) and in the high school grades, a positive correlation between preschool block performance and math achievement was demonstrated (Wolfgang et al. 2009). It is no surprise that the block area is a staple in every classroom.

Educator and researcher Harriet Johnson (1867–1933) detected that children progress through a series of developmental stages when playing with blocks (**Figure 5.16**). The first three stages are carrying blocks, then stacking blocks, followed by creating bridges that resemble actual structures. The fourth stage involves the ability to use blocks to enclose a space, which requires a level of cognitive skill. This is followed by building complex structures that combine all the earlier stages and includes symmetry and pattern.

Block Stages

Stage	Characteristics
Stage 1: Exploration Age: 0–1	Exploring and using blocks to create sensory connections occur as they are carried, pulled, and simply felt/tasted. This stage lays a foundation for future block play despite the blocks not being used to represent anything yet.
Stage 2: Repetitive Age: 2–3	Manipulating the blocks as they are stacked, creating rows and towers define the repetitive stage. Engaging with blocks and patterning is a common practice.
Stage 3: Active Experimentation Age: 3+	Stage 3 reflects blocks set apart to support a third, creating a tunnel or bridge. Learning to balance a block takes repeated attempts and improves as their coordination develops. Adding props to the block area are often a strong support!
Stage 4: Enclosures Age: 3+	Children will often move to creating enclosures around their bridges during stage 4. Closing up spaces require larger areas as the play expands. Closing the space requires spatial abilities, and the start of actively including zoo animals in cages or cars in garages.
Stage 5: Symmetry and Patterns Age: 4+	Designing the builds requires matching and sorting of colors and shapes to create a sense of balance and symmetry. Patterns are evident and defined only by one's imagination.
Stage 6: Naming of Structures Age: 4+	Children use block structures they build to understand the growing world around them. During this stage, the child builds detailed representation and dramatic play elements are inherent.
Stage 7: Later Representational, Complex and Symbolic Age: 4+	Increased detail reflects structures that can reach great heights and involve multiple manipulative toys in a play plan. Creating buildings that have specific purposes such as the Eiffel Tower, Golden Gate Bridge, the local post office or their own homes are possible. Symbolic play is evident.

Figure 5.16 The typical stages of block play for children. *How does understanding these stages help teachers assess children?*

Goodheart-Willcox Publisher

Figure 5.17 A well-stocked block area provides learning across content areas. Why are blocks considered a staple in the early childhood classroom?

Caroline Pratt developed wood blocks in multiple shapes and sizes that are the basis for the blocks used in many settings today. Purchasing a set of wood unit blocks is one of the best investments a teacher or school can make (**Figure 5.17**). There are many varieties of blocks that can be added; for example, foam, magnetic, cardboard, and plastic blocks. Each adds a different building element, inviting new ideas for trying out different plans. Sending out a family inquiry requesting sanded wood blocks with certain dimensions should gain family cooperation. Investing in blocks can integrate all curricular areas and will last a lifetime.

When children play in the block area, they learn:

- how to reason and test hypotheses.
- about measurement and building.
- drawing new ideas for the world.
- creativity when experimenting with different building structures.
- geometry (shapes), length, estimation, and balance.
- spatial awareness.
- fine and gross motor development.
- self-expression.
- how to use their imagination.
- how to represent ideas using physical items.
- problem-solving skills.

Teacher Role in the Block Area

Based on the potential for learning many concepts when building with blocks, the teacher should model block play for children who may start preschool without building experience. The block area should be intentionally appealing. Challenging the children to create complex structures by using open-ended questions, and including literacy building experiences—for example, naming their creations—is another way to add to their learning. Children may tend to neglect the block area, so keep it interesting for them by connecting it to many different learning experiences. When possible, support the children to keep their structures up for longer than a day.

Culture in the Block Area

Connecting to different cultures is possible in many ways. Placing photos of landmark buildings (such as the London Bridge, Eiffel Tower, Empire State Building, Great Pyramid of Cholula, Great Wall of China) will challenge children to recreate and then design their own buildings with a unique name and location. When several children work together, they can create an entire city (**Figure 5.18**). Reflecting cultural diversity might include adding toy figures that represent people of different ages and ethnicities. Another idea is laminating pictures of children "head-to-toe" onto a wood block to enable them to place themselves in their play and really connect to their block experience.

Figure 5.18 These children are working together to build a city with blocks. How do blocks encourage cooperative play?

Placement of Furnishings in the Block Area

In the classroom, the block area is located near the noisier learning areas due to the conversations and activity that occurs. The block area needs unimpeded space for children to move around without interfering with other builders, and a flat surface to build on. A carpeted area reduces noise. Sturdy shelves are important to store and label the different shapes. Storing the blocks in a visual way demonstrates mathematical relationships between them, related to length, volume, and shape.

When building with blocks, children may use other materials, called *loose parts*. **Loose parts** can be a wide range of items including pinecones, seashells, old toys or parts of toys, spools of thread, or chunks of wood (**Figure 5.19**). Loose parts are found in many learning areas. They support a child's love of play, experimenting, discovering, and inventing. "In any environment, both the degree of inventiveness and creativity, and the possibility of discovery, are directly proportional to the number and kind of variables in it" (Nicholson 1971).

Lauren Ryan/Childspace, New Zealand

Figure 5.19 A selection of loose parts ready for play at Childspace, Wellington, New Zealand. What skills can children develop by playing with these items?

Loose parts fit especially well in the block area although loose parts can stand alone or be included in many other learning areas. When considering the value of loose parts, remember that children's inventiveness is enhanced by the range of variability and number of loose parts in the environment. The learning is open-ended as children explore endless possibilities.

Sensory-Texture Area

Nothing can hold the imagination and engagement of a young child more than empty boxes, a sink full of water, or a mound of dirt. The sensory-texture area combines the senses as children explore and connect to the materials while engaging with each other. (**Figure 5.20**) This area provides time to explore a variety of mediums and is a popular destination for children.

When children play in the sensory-texture area, they learn:

- fine motor skills.
- to organize, match, and classify objects.
- a sense of balance while sorting out items.
- conversation skills with friends.

Teacher Role in the Sensory-Texture Area

The teacher input includes open-ended questions that encourage and support deeper thinking in regard to the children's findings. Daily set up for this area is minimal. Children are easily engaged in their learning while they discover and manipulate the medium and assorted items provided (**Figure 5.21**).

Culture in the Sensory-Texture Area

Adding a variety of items and media in the sensory table provides diverse experiences. A Wyoming program displays a nature-based small world, created from an emerging interest in rock collecting and insects found in the area. The polished rocks are a sensory experience

Submitted by Mis Manos Montessori/Tucson, AZ

Figure 5.20 These children are playing with fake snow in a sensory table. How do sensory tables aid in a child's development?

Sensory-Texture Area

Containers	Medium to Add	Items to Add	Experiences
• plastic tub • bowls • empty box with trash bag lining • sensory table • roasting pans • clean cat litter pans • dishpans	• water or water with food coloring • water with bars of soap • water with bubbles • bird seed • cracked corn • whole corn • cornmeal • dirt/potting soil • mud • cornstarch • sawdust • colored (or white) rice • Easter grass • dried leaves • straw/hay • shaving cream • snow	• spoons of assorted sizes • cups of assorted sizes • funnels • measuring cups • straws and bubble wands (to blow bubbles) • strainers, colanders, and sieves • turkey basters • flour sifter • pie pans (with or without holes punched in bottom) • seashells • tongs • plastic dishes and drainboard • plastic boats • plastic animals (dinosaurs, fish, and so on) • artificial flowers • magnets/magnetic letters • hand mixer	• use paintbrushes with cornmeal and large bones to practice being a paleontologist • dig for items such as coins (gold coins for St. Patrick's Day, pennies for Lincoln's Birthday, and so on) • insert paper clips onto plastic or laminated fish, tie string to sticks, put a magnet on the end of the string, and have the children "go fishing" • use straw with pumpkins and gourds in the fall and compare weight • use earthworms and dirt; bury the worms and let the children dig, releasing them into the outdoor play yard when the day is over

Goodheart-Willcox Publisher

Figure 5.21 Sensory-Texture Table (Wet and Dry) Ideas. What other ideas can you think of?

when children discover the rock's smooth surfaces. Adding small faux insects, feathers, and toy woodland animals provoke conversations about colors, patterns, and counting, adding a new level of learning to discussing local nature.

Placement of Furnishings in the Sensory-Texture Area

This popular learning area is located where multiple children can access the play simultaneously. While specific texture tables (such as sand and water tables) are a great investment. They can be replicated easily depending on space and budget. Chairs pulled up to a sink can provide ready sources for water-related play. Low tubs are affordable and can provide similar experiences, and even a box lined with a plastic trash liner can contain elements to explore. The freedom of experimenting with the contents of the sensory table supports new learning and is truly an open-ended learning experience. (**Figure 5.22**) A slip-proof mat is suggested in this area because wet play can produce puddles. The sensory area should be placed near cleanup facilities if a messy experience is planned. This area creates a lot of conversation between children and is best positioned closer to the noisier areas in the class.

Sensory experiences in the infant room can take advantage of natural light. A window can expand visual interest by using metal disks

Submitted by Mis Manos Montessori/Tucson, AZ

Figure 5.22 These children are making bird feeders out of pine cones. Do you think it is important for children to touch items from nature, rather than always playing with plastic toys? Why or why not?

REAL-WORLD CLASSROOM

In a Montessori classroom, toddlers learn about the environment in the sensory area. Try filling a sensory table with fake snow composed of baking soda and white hair conditioner. The combined ingredients make a consistency like snow without the temperature issues. Add animals that may be found in regions where there is constant snow. The children learn about weather, animals, habitats, chemistry, and so much more. Vocabulary is often introduced with objects rather than pictures. The ability to share with others and to voice opinions and desires is exercised in all areas of the prepared Montessori environment.

decorated with glass beads. The sun shining through the window is reflected by the disks, creating a disco ball display around the room. Rainbow sensory bottles and rainbow scarves can add a beautiful touch to this sensory space. The feel of the sheer scarves on little bare feet creates another layer to this sensory experience. A basket is filled with textured rugs to place around the room when the infants need a new view.

Outdoor Area

There is no place more powerful than being outdoors in nature for discovering endless learning opportunities. Outdoor play is considered spontaneous play that builds self-esteem, supports a child's natural curiosity, and creates a love of discovery. Large, open spaces support a child's ability to develop physical skills and coordination. ***Forest schools*** are an example of the outdoor learning environment in which children spend most of their day outside. Traditional outdoor education differs from forest schools in that learning is led by the child's curiosity and interests in unstructured ways, rather than being focused on scientific inquiry. While forest schools are still unusual, they are gaining popularity across the world, and these opportunities to experience nature can be part of any program or school (**Figure 5.23**).

When children play in the outdoor area, they learn to:

- run, jump, skip, and hop as they develop gross motor skills.
- play with friends in a wide-open area and practice boundaries.
- have empathy for the natural world.
- appreciate weather and the seasons.
- have confidence and take smart risks.

Teacher Role in the Outdoor Area

Teachers who engage with children in outdoor play counteract the increasing tendency of children to perceive the outdoors as an unsafe and frightful place. Teachers report that behavioral issues among children decrease dramatically; family involvement greatly increases, and teacher satisfaction is at an all-time high in programs that support environments that emphasize outdoor play (Rosenow & Jaffe 2014). The teacher should plan at least sixty minutes per day for active play. Using that time outdoors, weather permitting, is supported for all.

The National Association for Sport and Physical Education (NASPE 2000) states that the development of physical activity is sequential. For example, two-year-olds cannot hop on one foot until they have mastered all the physical skills required (balance, able to jump). The sequencing principle includes all gross motor actions, such as kicking, running, skipping, and jumping. This is one reason the role of the teacher is to provide for and model different physical skills while offering children time to practice during planned and unplanned activities. Milestones of development

Kate Yeomans/Merrohawke Nature School, MA

Figure 5.23 Nature is an important element of learning. *What outdoor experiences might be part of learning in your area?*

include skills that are typically mastered at different ages and are a valuable resource for teachers when planning outdoor experiences.

Culture in the Outdoor Area

Planning different learning experiences outdoors can take on global awareness as children make connections to their own backyards. Plan outdoor events to embrace different games from different lands. For example, you may plan a festival outdoors to display specific cultural connections, tapping into the children's family stories and cultures, including food and games.

Placement of Furnishings in Outdoor Areas

The nature-outdoor area can range from a fully equipped playground to a neighborhood park, from a backyard to an entire forest. The outdoors includes all of nature. Many of the same materials provided indoors can also be used to promote engagement outdoors, with multiple ground covers or surfaces to provide different types of play. Outdoor equipment should be child-size, with a quantity of various items so all children can be active (**Figure 5.24**). Outdoor play can include indoor gear, including dramatic

Laura Hintze/Little Cherub's Preschool, Spring Arbor, MI

Figure 5.24 Shovels are lined up, ready for the next snowfall. How does this reflect the culture of this program?

REAL-WORLD CLASSROOM

Here are five examples of outdoor play from around the world.

Mexico

Vibrant colors (art) and multiple shapes (math) are integrated in the outdoor space, encouraging different activities shown in an outdoor play space in Guadalajara, Mexico (**Figure 5.25**). The different ground covers used include sand, pea gravel, rubber mats, and artificial turf or actual grass. Playsets are strategically placed to provide safe play while supporting independence.

Alaska

A boat was installed in the playground more than 30 years ago; a student-teacher added the fishing equipment and props. Fishing is common among many families in Alaska. Even in the landlocked interior, families are out on boats in the summer and ice fishing on the lakes in the winter. Drowning is a serious problem for young children in Alaska: at one time, the state had the highest rate in the nation, per capita. The use of the life jackets was an important part of this outdoor lesson. According to Pammy Fowler, longtime teacher for the Early Childhood Lab School in Fairbanks, "[The] children have been all over the world in that boat (**Figure 5.26**).

Continued

Robin Stirling

Figure 5.25 An inviting, challenging, and colorful outdoor play space. How many different learning experiences can you imagine occurring in this area?

Patty Merrit

Figure 5.26 Learning about boats connects to the geographic and cultural connections in Alaska where fishing is a prevalent occupation. How could your playground feature support imaginations and local culture?

They've visited grandparents, they've taken trips into fantasy worlds, fighting dragons and swimming with mermaids. Some of them just like to sit and observe, almost all of them love to be the Captain, and will happily throw anyone overboard that stands in their way."

REAL-WORLD CLASSROOM

Ginny Harmelink

Figure 5.27 These children are learning about the pioneers who once lived in their area. What other social studies lessons can they learn via play?

Deb Lawrence

Figure 5.28 This active outdoor playground in China reflects multiple areas to support learning. Identify a favorite playground memory.

Lauren Ryan

Figure 5.29 Outdoor equipment promotes gross motor development through play. What are some other skills children can develop through outdoor play?

Wyoming

Located down a long country road, the chuckwagon was the first thing one saw when entering the early childhood program land, west of town. The wagon is a favorite play destination for children, offering rich learning and play experiences (**Figure 5.27**).

Visiting the indoor writing area, children created their own license depicting whatever game they hoped to capture for dinner to eat on tin plates. The children learned respect for and safety amidst wildlife, and about the many different licenses required (hunting, fishing, marriage, drivers) while creating rich play scenarios and integrating literacy with nature.

China

Soft landing materials and different outdoor surfaces support the children engaged in active play and assorted learning experiences in China (**Figure 5.28**). The many pieces of play equipment further gross motor development, including running, swinging, climbing, and jumping, all with adult supervision.

New Zealand

Creating an inviting outside space is as important as designing the indoor classroom. Note this inviting, challenging, and colorful outdoor play area at Childspace, Wellington, New Zealand (**Figure 5.29**). Risky play (refer to Chapter 2, "Play") is evident in this outdoor space. A sailcloth provides shade and there are multiple areas to navigate. Colored panels provide an aesthetic element.

play props, sand and water tables, pencils and paper, a basket of books in the shade, and blocks or natural materials for building.

Sidewalks, turf, pebbles, sand, and soft and hard surfaces need to be thought out to maximize learning opportunities while providing for safe play. Each state provides guidelines around outdoor safety elements and should be consulted when designing learning spaces. The outdoor learning area is an extension of the classroom and needs the same attention as other learning areas.

Music-Movement Area

Music is the art of arranging sounds in time to produce a composition through the elements of melody, harmony, rhythm, and timbre. It is one of the universal cultural aspects of all human societies (Dictionary.com). Movement is the physical actions of our bodies and a natural fit with music. Music-movement as a curriculum is explored in Chapter 9, "Academic Disciplines," where music and art are integrated; however, it also has its own learning area in the classroom (**Figure 5.30**).

When children play in the music-movement area, they learn to:

- move to a rhythm.
- create a beat and keep time.
- connect to emotions.
- discriminate sounds.
- build confidence skills.

Teacher Role in the Music-Movement Area

Children love to listen, move, and sing along to music. Research shows that children need planned movement experiences (Pica 1997). The early childhood teacher knows that music exposure for young children includes play-based engagement within a developmentally appropriate curriculum that is attentive to gender, ability, and culture. The National Association for Music Education (NAFME) supports music education and encourages embedding music into the curriculum and environment.

The teacher should plan activities that introduce a range of physical movements to promote healthy growth and development. Teachers create opportunities for children to embody abstract concepts by physically experiencing them. Children gravitate to music, as the teacher who can strum a guitar will attest.

Music connects to every discipline and strengthens learning. An area that includes a variety of instruments with labels of what they are will further educate children. Studies point toward the positive effects of music on the human body and brain. Music activates both the left and right brain at the same time, which can amplify learning while also improving memory (NAFME 2019).

Culture in the Music-Movement Area

Music is a universal language, with each note connected to culture in some way. The music-movement area should reflect many genre posters that suggest different styles (zydeco, jazz, hip-hop, pop, country, classical, rock, and Native American, to name a few) as well as instruments used around the world. Introducing children to different sounds can be expanded by using a library of musical tunes

Creation Preschool, Vail, AZ

Figure 5.30 Perhaps to the relief of the people in the building, this music area is located outdoors. *Why do you think this teacher has chosen pots and pans, rather than toy musical instruments, for this area?*

that vary from traditional kiddie tunes. Background music is a great way to create mood and can be listened to through class computer speakers.

Consider some of these recordings:
- *Raffi in Concert*—Raffi (Assorted)
- *Choo Choo Boogaloo*—Buckwheat Zydeco (Cajun)
- *Cado Niño/Every Child*—Tish Hinjosa (Spanish)
- *Native American Songs*—Sue Straw (Native American)
- *The Mozart Effect* (Classical)
- *A Child's Celebration of Song* (Assorted)

Placement of Furnishings in the Music-Movement Area

Locate this area near the other noisier areas, such as the block area. Low shelves holding different instruments, along with a non-breakable mirror in which to watch oneself, will encourage children to visit this area. The teacher should keep the music area interesting by periodically changing posters and instruments. Providing a small carpet will help define this space. Due to the large size of this area, it is also a great space for circle time and large group activities. When integrating learning, creating an area for music outside will extend the influence of the music.

Creative Arts Area

The creative arts area is where creativity flourishes, and it is central to a child's development. Art is both intrinsically and extrinsically rewarding and has a strong influence around all domains of development. The creative arts area is often a favorite space to play and learn.

When children play in the creative arts area, they learn:
- to foster creativity.
- to play with ideas and explore.
- divergent thinking and the realization that problems can have many solutions.
- to revel in the process of creating without concern about an end product.
- how to acquire new skills.
- to feel joy and pride in their work to feel good about themselves.

Teacher Role in the Creative Arts Area

Inspiring children to experiment with the visual arts while providing a range of materials in the creative arts area is important (**Figure 5.31**). This area is usually available every day to provide many opportunities to explore. The teacher's role in the creative arts area is to create a space where children feel open to express their feelings and try out different media. Encouraging children to describe their creations, focusing on their use of line, color, or design, supports their experience of art as a process rather than as a product.

Early childhood educator Lisa Atkinson commented on a classroom experience: "We introduced the children to some ammonite fossils yesterday and they definitely created an air of 'awe and wonder.' We provided some black fine pens, charcoal, and different pencils (soft and hard). We talked about noticing—looking carefully at shapes and patterns, looking carefully at light and shade."

Submitted by Lisa Atkinson/Martongate Primary School, Bridlington, England

Figure 5.31 These arts and crafts supplies, which are safe for children age three and up, are a treasure trove for young, creative minds. Think of a learning experience that could begin with these supplies.

Culture in the Creative Arts Area

The creative arts area supports connecting to different cultures in the most natural of ways. Art is as individual as each child and reflects perspectives from every walk of life. The creative arts area includes a variety of tools and media to empower the child's imagination and creativity and can be set up for one or many children. Resources from art history help make cultural connections as the teacher shares different artistic techniques and artworks.

Placement of Furnishings in the Creative Arts Area

The creative arts area should be a beautiful space, placed near a sink, and open daily to promote creativity. Furnishings in this area include low shelves to store needed utensils, paint, paper, and clay. Art easels, stools, and tables with mats can be placed on the floor for easy cleanup. Display the children's art at the child's eye level, where all children can enjoy them. For the infant-toddler age, art can be placed near the floor behind plexiglass to protect it. The entire classroom can be a space where every child is valued within the community of learners.

Writing Area

The writing area integrates all early literacy forms: language, speaking, listening, reading, and writing. The skills practiced at the writing area support later kindergarten readiness. Children practice their fine motor skills and pencil grip as well as communication skills in a well-stocked writing area. Notes written to friends or family, pretending to order a pizza, and practicing writing one's name are all common occurrences.

When children play in the writing area, they learn:

- to strengthen hand-eye coordination.
- that symbols (letters) hold meaning.
- how to hold a pencil for muscle development.
- that writing is a strong communication element.

Teacher Role in the Writing Area

Teachers should rotate materials and foster children's connections to the writing area to encourage participation (**Figure 5.32**). Creating engaging scenarios provides opportunities for choices while meeting a range of interests. Including multiple writing tools supports invented spelling during the preschool years. **Invented spellings** are self-directed and spontaneous attempts to represent words in print. Over time, a word such as *eagle* will be presented first as random letters, then as *E* or *EG*, then as *EGL*, then as *EGUL*, and eventually *eagle* (Gentry 2017). Do not correct the children's practice, as it may discourage them. Conventional spelling will be part of the kindergarten experience.

Culture in the Writing Area

Providing examples of different forms of alphabet letters provides opportunities to make connections to a child's own language. An *A* can be written in many ways, and when it is combined with other letters, children learn the concept of creating words. A bulletin board above the writing area can depict different writing professionals from different backgrounds, different ages, as well as different workspaces.

Placement of Furnishings in the Writing Area

The writing area should be located in a quieter part of the room, away from distractions that other learning areas may create. This area is often set up for one child at a time to provide a private feeling that encourages purposeful writing experiences.

Ginny Harmelink

Figure 5.32 Building a writing center doesn't need to be expensive! This writing center is stocked with donated office supplies for the children to explore. What can you add to this writing area to reflect diverse occupations?

Props include general office supplies to create real-life experiences. Consider ways to incorporate writing into many different areas—for example, in the dramatic play area. Props may include:

- telephones, telephone books
- paper cut in different sizes (recycle when possible)
- different textures of paper
- stencils
- tape
- mailbox
- different writing utensils, such as pencils, markers, pens, crayons

The writing area empowers children to try out writing skills and practice many real-life roles they are familiar with, such as answering the phone, pretending to look up a phone number, or pretend-writing a book. Including a dedicated writing area yields lifelong benefits as children practice early literacy skills.

Library Area

The library area includes many genres of books and magazines for children to look at and be read from. The different genres include poetry (Mother Goose rhymes, lyrics, limericks), fairy tales, fantasies, fables, tall tales, nonfiction (science and nature, arts and leisure, history). Books from the library area should also be part of every other learning area, to integrate literacy.

When children play in the library area, they learn:

- different perspectives.
- to make connections between the spoken word and written word.
- to strengthen language skills and vocabulary.
- about different people, places, and ideas.
- to foster attachments to the people who read to them.

Teacher Role in Library Area

The teacher needs to be a prosodic reader in the library area. **Prosody** is reading with expression, and it takes practice. Reading to a group of young children while keeping everyone engaged is more difficult than it sounds. Using different voice intonations and embedding different children's names will help. Showing the pictures while reading will also help. The teacher who creates such an atmosphere is providing a balance of experiences and a model for children.

Culture in the Library Area

All parts of the world and its people should be reflected in the library. Books, magazines, and catalogs should represent different races, cultures, ages, types of families, men and women engaged in many different occupations, and people with different disabilities through picture and informational books. Chapter 10, "Infant-Toddler Integrated Curriculum," is devoted to literacy and language.

Placement of Furnishings in the Library Area

The library area is often located near quieter learning areas, such as the music-movement area. Books are displayed in an attractive manner that makes them accessible to children. This area should include beanbags or comfy seating, low shelves, and carpeted floors. The library area might also provide the space where large groups gather if space is limited. The library area is a place where a child can go to look at picture books and be alone when desired.

Science/Technology/Engineering/Math (STEM) Area

Science, technology, engineering, and math are collectively known by the acronym *STEM*, which has a standalone learning area. Some early childhood classrooms might also offer these focuses as separate math, science, technology, or engineering learning areas. The integration of these four subjects into one area provides children a chance to explore topics that are truly integrated. STEM experiences provide opportunities to develop and practice a range of core skills and attributes, including hypothesizing, investigating, analyzing, reasoning, and problem-solving.

When children play in the STEM area, they learn:

- how to solve problems.
- to experiment with different ideas.
- how things work, such as turning a light switch on and off.
- about different concepts such as volume, weight, and space.

Teacher Role in the STEM Area

Children's curiosity and need to make the world a more predictable place certainly drives them to explore and draw conclusions and theories from their experiences. Children are born scientists but need to practice science—to engage in rich scientific inquiry by observing, measuring, experimenting, and repetition.

The primary role of the teacher is to intentionally embed different experiences that will challenge children in the STEM area (**Figure 5.33**). Current research from National Science Teachers Association (NSTA) indicates that young children have the capacity to construct conceptual learning and the ability to use reasoning and inquiry. Unfortunately, the opportunities and experiences to foster science skills and build this conceptual understanding are often lacking in the early childhood class.

NSTA recommends that teachers and other providers who support STEM learning concepts in young children be given professional development experiences to engage them in learning science principles in an interactive, hands-on approach. Teachers need age-appropriate and science-specific strategies to help children understand STEM practices.

Submitted by Lisa Atkinson/Martongate Primary School, Bridlington, England

Figure 5.33 This basket of items, where children can learn about sunflowers, was placed in a STEM area of a preschool. How might these items help students learn concepts such as volume, weight, and space?

Support for technology in the early childhood classroom is relatively new. The teacher's role is to use technology responsibly and intentionally because interactive media and digital resources can be valuable tools for supporting children's development and learning (NAEYC, *DAP*, 2020).

Emerging evidence correlates negative impacts between too much screen time and childhood obesity. Further, excessive screen time has been shown to negatively effects toddlers' performance in skills related to fine motor development, communication, and social skills (American Association of Pediatrics). The early childhood teacher has a responsibility to inform families of current research in this area. Studies reveal no evidence that development is enhanced for children under age two when they independently view screen media or use digital devices, and it is the teacher's role to reinforce these cautions.

The teacher of older children should use technology to support children learning to be producers rather than consumers. A *producer* uses technology to create items, while a *consumer* uses technology to play games and occupy time, with no actual learning expected. Technology and interactive media are tools to expand a child's access to new content, but these tools should never replace direct experiences.

Engineering is the process of finding out how things are built and why. It is about finding ways to construct things better and solving problems through the development of new technologies. In early childhood, engineering is all about play. Engineering for young children develops early concepts they can build on as they grow. The early childhood teacher's role is to be aware of current research in the area of engineering and embed practices that are developmentally appropriate (**Figure 5.34**). Unfortunately, a lack of current research leads to challenges, such as lack of guidance on how to create early engineering experiences that are productive, inviting, inclusive, and engaging (Pattison et al. 2020). Self-initiated research must become part of the teacher's scope and should include the concept of reverse engineering, or taking things apart.

Math focuses on numbers, shapes, measurement, and patterns, and the teacher needs to provide spontaneous as well as planned math experiences that are developmentally appropriate. The teacher plays an important role in influencing and being a role model for children by providing opportunities for children to learn and develop new skills. Children need opportunities to:

- discover and create.
- use number concepts and skills to explore.
- develop confidence in their ability to think things through.
- solve meaningful problems.

Math is an important part of learning for children in the early years because it provides life skills that help children solve problems, measure, and develop their own spatial awareness. It also teaches them how to use and understand shapes. The early childhood teacher should be aware of the National Council of Teachers of Mathematics (NCTM) as a resource to develop curriculum that is challenging and age appropriate. Studies suggest that students who are taught math primarily through memorization and rote learning are more than a year behind those who have been taught by relating math concepts to their existing knowledge and reflecting on their own understanding (Boaler & Zoido 2016). Children thrive when the environment includes language promoting mathematic thinking and curiosity.

Submitted by Child-Parent Centers, Prince Head Start, Tucson AZ

Figure 5.34 This architecture area is designed to give children an idea of what it is like to be an architect. What else could be added to this area?

Culture in the STEM Area

Pathways to connect culture to STEM include comparing authentic examples of plant and animal life around the world and studying climates and temperature to learn how they affect people based on geography. Cultural connections can arise from using technology through live cameras (cams) across the globe, from viewing museums to visiting national parks. STEM supports learning the different elements of engineering and basic arithmetic skills that impact lives across the world. Every developmental domain and academic discipline intersects with STEM in some way and connects to different cultures and opportunities to explore diversity.

Placement of Furnishings in the STEM Area

The STEM area is best located near the quieter learning areas due to the focus and concentration often required. Adding items to the STEM learning area, especially weighing scales, measuring tapes, counting items, manipulatives, items from nature, goggles, gloves, measuring cups and spoons, magnifying glasses, tweezers, rulers, class pet (fish, rabbit, or hamster), magnets, and a computer, can provide real-life applications that will support in-depth investigations around STEM. Real-world applications are a requirement in technology and engineering; science and math are no different. It is important during the early years to provide children with stimulating firsthand experiences in an area that can encompass STEM elements. Making connections to real-world applications reflects integration of multiple topics and engages the next generation of learners.

Bonus Areas

Many areas that fit in this category can be found in early classrooms and programs. These spaces include bathrooms, corners, even stairwells, which may not fit into one of the learning areas or existing spaces identified above (**Figure 5.35**). Ideas might include creating a

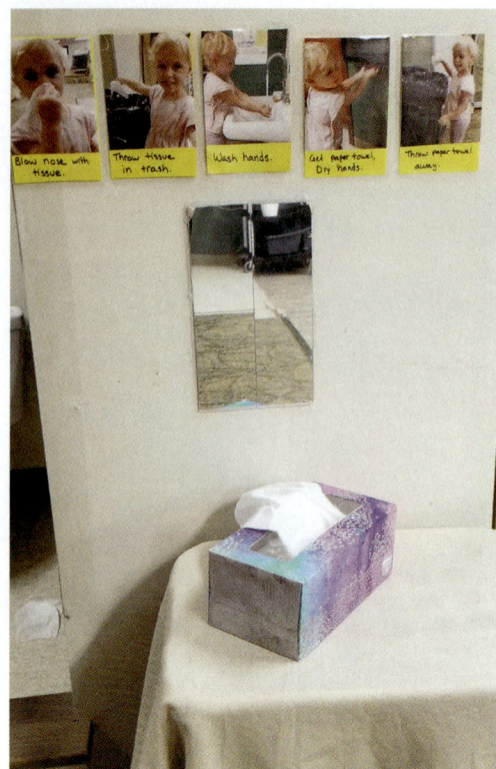

Lisa Morley/Westshore Community College, MI

Figure 5.35 This "Booger Corner" serves not only as a bonus area, but as a reminder to children to practice personal hygiene. What else could you add to this area to encourage germ control?

cave or night sky under a table covered with blankets to make it dark, and affixing stars to the underside, then providing props such as a pillow, books, and a flashlight. Other ideas include using empty corners or spaces at the entry of the classroom or an otherwise unused space under the stairway that will enhance learning or provide a place for a child to be alone.

When children play in these other "bonus" areas, they learn:

- unexpected things.
- to try out different practices.
- about hygiene and flushing the toilet.
- life skills.

Teacher Role in Bonus Areas

Innovative and open minds support multiple learning possibilities. There are endless opportunities for learning in the bonus area that touch upon all domains of development. Look around the classroom, imagine where new learning can occur, and build it.

Culture in Bonus Areas

The diversity found in bonus areas is limitless. Making connections to the community or the families and staff that frequent the early childhood program and classroom should be intentional and unique (**Figure 5.36**). The bonus area provides open-ended ideas and the perfect space to highlight a family or upcoming community event as well. Thinking creatively is a staple in the early childhood classroom.

Lisa Morley/Westshore Community College, MI

Figure 5.36 This native sturgeon is being fostered and cared for by the children who attend this school. What scientific concepts can children learn by observing an animal on a daily basis?

✓ Checkpoint

- ☐ Identify your LEAST favorite learning areas in the classroom. Why are these your least favorite? Provide two opportunities in your least favorite learning area to engage children.
- ☐ How might the dramatic play area and the sensory area be utilized when studying a "food" topic of interest?
- ☐ Compare learning in the STEM area to the learning in the dramatic play area. What are the similarities? What are the differences?
- ☐ Provide three examples of embedding culture into the art area.
- ☐ What are "loose parts"?

Chapter 5 Review and Assessment

Chapter Summary

5.1 Identify early childhood room design elements.
- Many people consider the environment to be "the third teacher" because of the role it plays in supporting learning. The process of examining the different curriculums and approaches that focus on the environment supports the teacher in making connections.
- Supporting positive relationships between adults and children is critical to support learning.
- Having policies that can be depended on by families and children is an important temporal component. It is important to be aware of the elements that differ in various curriculums and approaches.

5.2 Define the use and value of labeling.
- Labeling provides the children with an opportunity to make connections to print, as well as participating in the classroom community.
- Creating labels to reflect the home languages of the children enrolled ensure that everyone is respected and helps build a positive community in the classroom.
- Labeling makes connections between a word and one of its elements—the letter.

5.3 Explain the role of culture in the early learning environment.
- Understanding one's own culture is important to be able to accept and support the cultures of other people as an intentional and inclusive practice.
- Intentional teaching ensures that the learning opportunities integrate all cultures and blend experiences through the learning areas.
- When engaging with the children and the family, understanding each culture is critical to building a curriculum that reflects everyone.

5.4 Distinguish components to consider when planning the environment.
- One important component of room design is learning area placement. Some areas are best located together because they are noisy, while others are best located near cleanup sources.
- The supervision factor of being able to easily scan the room is important when a teacher is working alone with many children. Planning low shelves is one way to accomplish this.
- The size of the group of children affects decisions made about which learning areas are open on a specific day and how many children a learning area can host.
- Adaptations and availability are important parts of planning the environment, ensuring that all areas are accessible to all children.
- Intentional planning of the foundation ensures an environment that provides the best possible space for learning.

5.5 Compare learning areas in the early childhood classroom.
- There are nine common learning areas, each with specific factors to be considered while setting up the classroom.
- The dramatic play area is considered the core of the classroom, where social and literacy skills are evident through pretending. The role of the teacher as facilitator encourages children to seek out new ideas and learning. Including props that represent different cultures provides authentic learning experiences built around the curriculum. This area requires a lot of space in the classroom.

- The block area exposes children to multiple real-world applications. The teacher's role is to encourage thinking and provide ideas to keep this learning area engaging. Connections to cultural aspects are easily incorporated. Creating low shelves to store the blocks and a carpeted area are two ideas to consider.
- The sensory-texture area is easily a favorite area in the classroom and the teacher's role is to encourage curiosity and thinking because discoveries are frequent. Integrating different cultural elements into the area produces lively discussions as well as exploration. This is an active area and can include water play. Placing this area near a source of easy cleanup is suggested.
- An outdoor area provides spontaneous play opportunities with forest schools built around only learning in nature. The benefits of outdoor play are evident, and different cultural events are easily located outdoors. The teacher takes on the role of observer in most instances, engaging when requested.
- The creative arts area is also both an academic subject and an exclusive learning area. The teacher should provide daily opportunities for children to experience different artistic media. Connections to culture are everywhere in this area. Locating this area near a cleanup source is recommended.
- The writing area provides opportunities to build literacy skills. Including this area as part of the curriculum can be easily accomplished as the teacher fosters connections to writing. Invented spelling is encouraged as children practice multiple literacy skills. Exposure to different cultures and letter symbols is a best practice. Locate this area in a quieter part of the classroom.
- The STEM area includes several academic subjects (science, technology, engineering, and math), with a focus on each or all of these. This area invites curiosity and provides many different learning opportunities based on the subjects. Culture is an inherent element in many discoveries, and placing this area in a quieter area is recommended.
- The bonus areas consist of spaces that are often unused for curriculum needs, such as stairways, corners, and bathrooms. Considering where your classroom might have an additional area to use is recommended.

For Further Reflection

1. Research your own state's licensing rules to review the minimum space requirements for the infant-toddler and preschool age groups. What did you find?
2. Placement of learning areas in the early childhood program depends on available space. Consider ways to rotate materials and share between learning areas. Is there a local nonprofit that offers a toy lending library you can access?
3. Why is it important to create labels with the children versus having the classroom labeled when the class begins each year?
4. Music has the power to instill enjoyment and wonder in a child's life. What happens when the rules are sung? How does music make you feel?
5. What is one book example that you could include in the dramatic play area if you were studying the solar system? What are your sources for quality books that are developmentally appropriate for children of different ages?
6. Is there one view of the outdoor environment you might embrace, or several? How does the outdoor space support the curriculum?

Recall and Application

1. Which answer indicates how an invitation table supports learning?
   A. reflects safe learning areas
   B. provides learning extensions
   C. creates physical activities
   D. discourages outside participation

2. Which example represents environmental print?
   A. billboards
   B. sign on restroom door
   C. names above coat hooks
   D. All of the above

3. Which of these statements does *not* support learning when the teacher is placing labels at the beginning of every school year?
   A. Labeling with children helps them make connections.
   B. Labeling identifies different items in the room.
   C. Labeling aids in word recognition.
   D. Labeling decorates the walls.

4. What is a first step to support multicultural learning in the classroom?
   A. enroll in a language course to ensure that home languages can be spoken
   B. meet with families to identify their expectations
   C. reflect on your own beliefs and experiences
   D. identify heroes from different cultures to learn about

5. **True or False.** Culture is defined as a practice of supporting patterns of beliefs, practices, and traditions associated with a particular group of people that evolves over time, reflecting the lived experiences of people in particular times and places.

6. Identify five factors to be considered when creating learning areas.
   A. supervision, room for all children at one time, timer to rotate learning areas, props available, accessibility
   B. supervision, group size, interest of majority, placement, availability
   C. supervision, group size, availability, adaptability, placement
   D. supervision, availability, placement, inclusion of children's help, parent participation

7. **True or False.** Learning areas and learning subjects are the same.

8. How does the teacher impact play/learning areas?
   A. Creating learning areas that are based off teacher's knowledge.
   B. Defining learning areas that use labels and pictures.
   C. Promoting input from families regarding learning areas.
   D. All of the above.

CHAPTER 6

The Written Curriculum

Learning Outcomes

After studying this chapter, you will be able to:

6.1 Define measurable outcomes that align to learning standards.

6.2 Describe how backward design and graphic organizers are used when planning.

6.3 Describe the daily learning plan and catalytic event.

6.4 Define the components of the topic of interest and focus topic.

Standards Covered in This Chapter

NAEYC

5a, 5b, 5c

DAP

Principles 2, 5, 7, 8
Guidelines 3, 5

Image credit: SDI Productions/Getty Images

Bryce

SNAPSHOT

MBI/Shutterstock.com

During his college program, Bryce was introduced to his state's early learning standards. He had experience writing learning outcomes that were measurable, and he was confident in his skills. Bryce always wanted to work with children and thought he understood what they needed.

Bryce was offered a position to teach the three-year-old classroom at a local accredited program. An exciting year was in the works! Bryce was excited to work on daily learning plans to guide his teaching. "I bought an entire curriculum kit from an internet source," Bryce said. "It was full of items that I thought the children would enjoy. But no one was interested. Not a single child wanted to play with any of the items. Maybe I should have asked them first."

Bryce just assumed that providing learning materials was important and making connections to the children's interests was an afterthought. He found out quickly this was not so. He met with his peer teachers and came up with a plan to ask families to complete a short questionnaire of what their children's interests included. Then, he created an order of new supplies for the classroom. Bryce learned the value of including children when defining the focus of learning.

Give It Some Thought

1. How could Bryce inform the families of the learning standards the children are working on as they play?
2. Meeting with peer teachers is a strong best practice. Would it be worthwhile to create staff training around writing measurable learning outcomes that are guided by the standards? If so, what would the agenda look like? Would you invite families to attend?

Key Terms

backward design	daily learning plan	learning sequence
Bloom's taxonomy	early learning standard	storyboards
catalytic event	family-initiated catalytic event	teacher-initiated catalytic event
child-initiated catalytic event	focus topic	topic of interest
concept diagram	graphic organizer	Universal Design for Learning (UDL)
concept web	KWHL chart	
constructivism	learning outcomes	Venn diagram

Copyright Goodheart-Willcox Co., Inc.

Introduction

Think about the goals people set for themselves. Examples include fitness goals, New Year's resolutions, and saving up money for a special purchase. People set these goals because they desire a specific outcome. The more specific they are when defining and planning how to reach their goals, the more successful they are in achieving them.

Similarly, when teaching young children, educators have intentional goals in mind. Some of those goals come from vast knowledge of how children develop and what will support their growth. Other goals come from the programs or the states in which educators teach. This chapter explores how to establish, write, and implement measurable goals and outcomes; how to plan strategies to use as resources; and how to introduce the daily learning plan, which is a tool designed to support teaching and learning.

6.1 Standards and Learning Outcomes

When parents walk into a preschool classroom, they may notice children playing store, a child reading a picture book, and another child building a bridge with blocks in the corner. What they do not see is the extensive planning and intention that goes into the activities of the day. In order to make every day meaningful for the children in the classroom, purposeful goals are set and then activities are built or planned that will help children meet those goals (**Figure 6.1**). NAEYC guidelines set the expectations. It is also important that teachers become thoroughly familiar with their own state's early learning standards, as well as other mandates that may affect their work (NAEYC, *DAP*, 2020).

Thus, the first step in creating quality learning goals is to know the standards for the year or grade level being taught. Think of the standards as building blocks to focus on so children learn what they need to prepare for the next age or grade. An ***early learning standard*** is an agreed-upon list of skills that children need to develop a foundation for higher levels of learning. These are defined by the early childhood experts in each state. Early learning standards, both in the past and today, are known by a variety of names, such as developmental standards and early learning guidelines. Each state has its own set of early learning standards that include infant–toddler, preschool, and kindergarten–third grade categories.

The standards are maintained by the State Department of Education and can be accessed via the Center on Enhancing Early Learning Outcomes (CEELO) website. While each set of state standards may have some unique elements, all early standards include a focus on the importance of social and emotional development. These are based on recommendations from the jointly authored NAEYC and National Association of Early Childhood Specialist in States Departments of Education (NAECS/SDE) 2002 position paper "Creating the Conditions for Success." Notice how the different concepts are presented in the example illustrating similarities between preschool programs in Arizona and Indiana (**Figure 6.2**).

The teacher will refer to the standards many times when considering the multiple ways to provide learning experiences. The standards connect to all domains of development and all subject areas to support learning experiences. These are not assessment tools, nor are they designed to be a checklist. They are not the end point, but the beginning.

Chemeketa Community College Child Development Laboratory School, Salem, OR

Figure 6.1 This learning experience begins with a map. How does reading a map connect to learning?

Creating Learning Outcomes

Child development and learning goals in an educational setting are referred to as *learning outcomes*. **Learning outcomes** are statements that describe what the child will be able to do after participating in a learning experience. They are the end result of student experiences and should be measurable, meaning the teacher can use an assessment tool to determine the child's level of proficiency or learning.

Figure 6.2 Side-by-side comparison of the mathematic standards in two states. *What do your state's mathematics standards include?*

Early Childhood Standards in Arizona Versus Indiana

Arizona	Indiana
Strand 1: Counting and Cardinality • Counts out loud • Knows number names and symbols • Compares numbers and quantities • Counts to tell number of objects	**Mathematics Foundation 1: Numeracy** Early learners develop foundational skills in learning and understanding counting, cardinality, written numerals, quantity, and comparison
Strand 2: Operations and Algebraic Thinking • Explores addition and subtraction • Patterning	**Mathematics Foundation 2: Computation and Algebraic Thinking** Early learners develop foundational skills in learning and understanding mathematical structure and patterning.
Strand 3: Measurement and Data • Sorts and classifies • Data analysis • Measures	**Mathematics Foundation 3: Data Analysis** Early learners develop foundational skills in learning to understand concepts of classification, data collection, organization, and description.
Strand 4: Geometry • Shapes • Spatial Reasoning	**Mathematics Foundation 4: Geometry** Early learners develop foundational skills in learning and understanding spatial relationships and shape analysis.

Goodheart-Willcox Publisher

STOP AND THINK

"Child will be able to demonstrate differences between a trumpet and a guitar." Consider this preschool learning outcome, identifying standards from two different subject areas that could be used to support the outcome. Focus on mathematics and one other subject area. What would you select?

Determining learning outcomes should be based on the teacher's knowledge of early learning standards, as well as family input, which includes the child's background knowledge and experiences. The learning outcomes (and experiences) used to reflect understanding for a 12-month-old will be much different than those for a five-year old, which further illustrates why knowledge of child development is so critical. In Bloom's taxonomy, represented by the pyramid in **Figure 6.3**, locate the foundational level, *remember*, and note how each step up becomes increasingly more complex as you move toward *create*.

Follow these steps to write measurable learning outcomes:

1. Identify the state standard(s) that will be the focus of the learning outcome.
2. Select the most appropriate action verb from the list in Bloom's taxonomy (you can find a more extensive list of verbs for each cognitive level in an online search).
3. Begin a statement that describes the knowledge or abilities to be demonstrated. The learning outcome describes the intended outcome for learning and often begins with: "Child will be able to…."
4. Insert a verb that describes the measurable action the child will use to demonstrate learning.
5. Complete the statement with the knowledge or skill that should be learned.

Again, thinking of your personal life, if you do not have a specific, measurable goal in mind, how do you know when and if you have reached your target? Using verbs that are

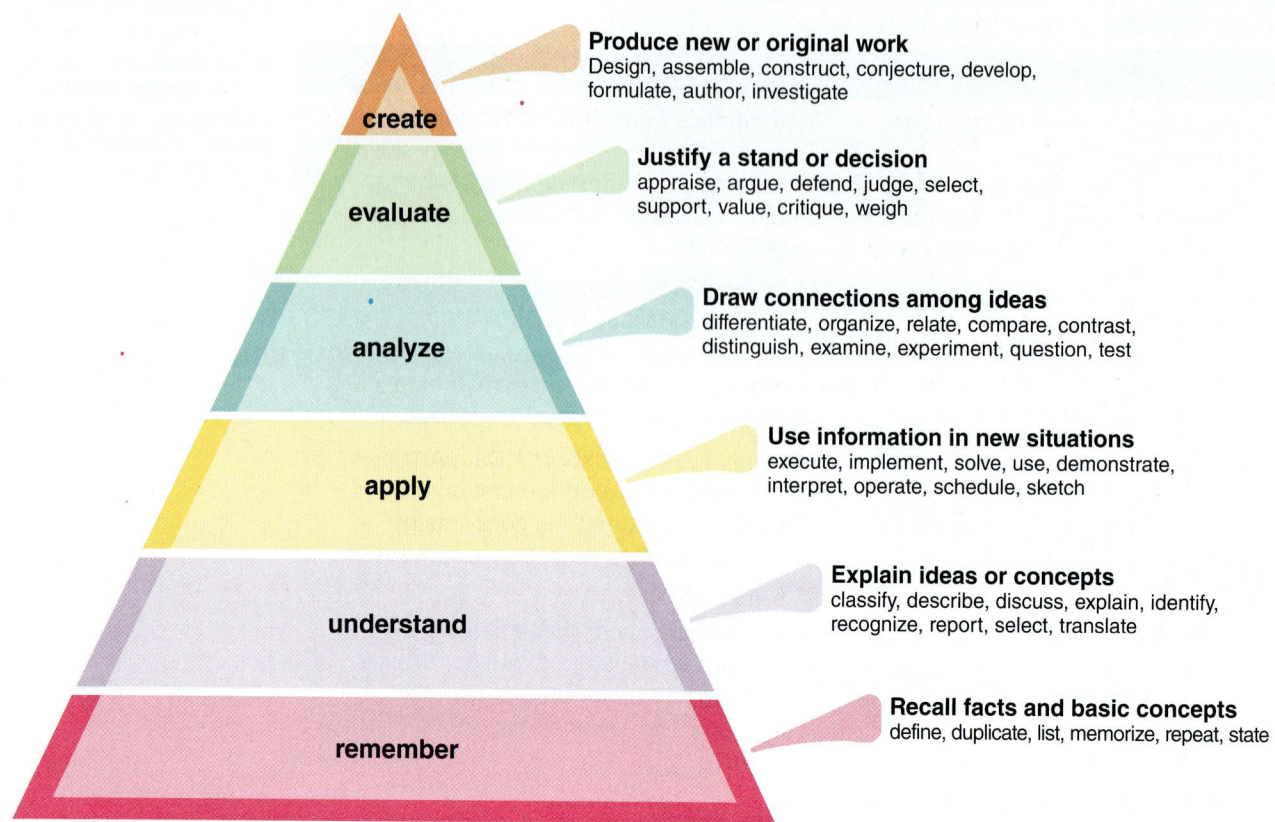

Figure 6.3 There are six levels of complexity in Bloom's taxonomy. How can each level be used to enhance teaching and learning?

intentional, specific, and reflect the level of understanding are the key. Bloom's taxonomy is a resource tool that many teachers find essential when creating learning outcomes.

Bloom's Taxonomy

Bloom's taxonomy is a system to define and distinguish different levels of thinking, learning, and understanding. It was developed to provide common language for educators to discuss and exchange ideas about learning and assessment methods. Bloom's taxonomy is a great tool to keep learning outcomes consistent and measurable. Note that there are six different levels of cognitive connections to consider. These range from rote memory to actually applying what was learned and creating something.

Bloom's taxonomy includes a list of measurable action verbs that are particularly valuable when writing learning outcomes. The verbs distinguish the level of expected learning for the child by accurately reflecting cognitive abilities. Extensive lists of appropriate verbs for each level can be found through an online search. When writing learning outcomes, it is valuable to refer frequently to lists of typical words at each of the Bloom's taxonomy levels. This is helpful to both new and veteran teachers.

Bloom's taxonomy verb charts provide many verbs to support the teacher in using authentic assessment tools to assess the children's proficiency. Different verbs align better to different assessment tools. As an example, verbs such as *define* or *list* require different assessments than *design* or *argue*. Additionally, different verbs may be used with different ages and capabilities.

Avoid verbs that are not easily measured or observed, such as *understand*, *know*, *learn*, *believe*, and *comprehend*. It is also important to use only one of Bloom's verbs when measuring understanding and writing each learning outcome. When determining the verb to use, choose one that has a clear connection to the content being taught. For example, use

"Child will be able to *classify* fruits and vegetables" or "Child will be able to *distinguish* between fruits and vegetables" rather than "Child will be able to *understand* differences between fruits and vegetables."

The verb you choose will be helpful in identifying the authentic assessment tool and in designing the learning experience. After the standard and the learning outcome are defined, the best assessment tool is determined for measuring learning. **Figure 6.4** reflects how standards and outcomes align with the different authentic assessments used to document performance and with the accompanying learning experience.

Eventually, the teacher will expand the early learning standards and learning outcomes in the learning plan to include an entire daily or weekly learning plan, with many different planning strategies used throughout the learning process. Child development and learning are both advanced when children are encouraged to aim just above their current capacity and when they are offered multiple opportunities to practice their new skills (NAEYC, *DAP*, 2020). Assessment (explored in Chapter 7, "Assessment, Collaboration, Modification, and Accommodation") becomes the evidence of the child's efforts.

Making connections between the early learning standards and learning outcomes provides the framework for connecting to authentic assessment (Chapter 7). These connections will yield data that will inform the teacher about the child's learning and future needs, as well as provide insights into planning for the day or weeks to follow.

Checkpoint

- What is a standard? How many early learning standards are supported in your state?
- Define *learning outcome*. Share an example.
- Bloom's taxonomy is a tool that is commonly used to write measurable learning outcomes. How many levels of questions are there?

6.2 Planning Strategies

There are many ways teachers can plan their day to meet the learning outcomes, but regardless of the method, the effective teacher always keeps in mind the desired learning outcome. Learning plans contain many different elements. While there are many differences in planning strategies, there are many more similarities, depending on the structure of the classroom and the teacher's preferences.

Standards/Learning Outcome Alignments

Early Learning Standard	Learning Outcomes	Appropriate Assessment	Learning Experience
Approaches to Learning: Initiative and Curiosity Concept 2: Curiosity Shows interest in learning new things and trying new experiences	Child will be able to *identify* preferences among fruits	Individual chart (using smiley faces)	Food-tasting–science area
Math: Measurement and Data Concept 1: Sorts and Classifies Sorts and groups objects by a variety of characteristics/attributes	Child will be able to *classify* fruits and vegetables.	Checklist	Play store plastic veggies and fruits–dramatic play area

Figure 6.4
Components of backward design, beginning with the standard, followed by writing a learning outcome using a measurable verb. How can the process of starting with the standard create effective goals for the child?

Goodheart-Willcox Publisher

Backward Design

Backward design is the process of constructing a lesson by first deciding what the desired outcomes are, then planning assessment strategies, and finally selecting learning experiences. Extensive research reinforces the success of backward design as a planning tool. When considering the multiple ways to design learning, many teachers follow the components of backward design that outline the process for writing learning outcomes (Bowen 2017). Backward design can be an effective framework for ensuring that various early learning standards are covered. With a focus on what children will learn rather than what the teacher will teach, backward design begins with the steps shown in **Figure 6.5**.

As an example, consider two early childhood teachers, Miss Olga and Mr. Ben, who are both planning learning experiences around the idea of sharing. They are responding to an event that occurred on the playground that resulted in a conflict over a jump rope. Miss Olga plans many activities that she thinks will expose the children to the concept of sharing. Her curriculum planning is focused on the learning experiences. Because of this, assessment becomes an afterthought; it is not directly tied to the early learning standards or the activities in which the children will participate. Therefore, there is no way for Miss Olga to measure whether students truly grasped the idea of sharing during these experiences. This is common when curriculum planning begins with a focus on experiences.

In contrast, Mr. Ben plans using the backward design model. He first identifies what he wants the children to learn by referring to his state's early learning standards. Then he identifies what the learning outcome will be, followed by the most appropriate assessment, and lastly, he plans the learning experiences. While Miss Olga and Mr. Ben may have similar learning outcomes, Mr. Ben has been deliberate in selecting experiences that will enhance the learning outcomes, as well as provoke deeper thought processes during discussions with the children. Mr. Ben will have strong examples of student learning that are measurable using assessments that are intentional.

Planning Tools and Graphic Organizers

Graphic organizers comprise an additional planning tool that can be used at the beginning, middle, and end of the planning process. ***Graphic organizers*** present information in text and graphic formats, including charts, diagrams, webs, and story boards. An effective teacher might use these to help determine how best to engage children in the experiences related to the learning outcomes or to illustrate a point using an illustration or image. Graphic organizers are valuable tools that engage the children based on their interests and prior experiences and provide the teacher with information to inform teaching.

Graphic organizers are central to ***Universal Design for Learning (UDL),*** which creates flexible and diverse ways to engage learners by incorporating the foundational principles of UDL: engagement, representation, action, and expression (Brilliante 2018). Much of the research on graphic organizers has focused on the powerful learning impact they have for children with learning disabilities and special needs (Dexter et al. 2011).

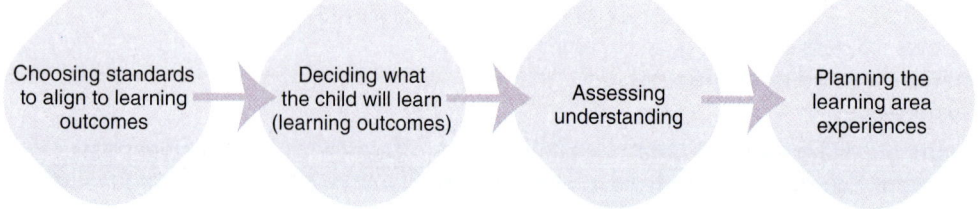

Goodheart-Willcox Publisher

Figure 6.5 The backward design process. What are the key steps involved in the backward design process, and how can they be applied to create a successful learning experience for a child?

KWHL—Know, Want, How, Learn

A widely used graphic organizer called a **KWHL chart** allows children to share their knowledge of what they already **k**now, what they **w**ant to know, **h**ow they can find out, and what they **l**earned during the learning experiences. The KWHL records the children's existing knowledge and provides the teacher with a direction to guide the learning based on what new knowledge the children want to explore (**Figure 6.6**).

The KWHL example focuses on the shared and common experiences of children who are living in the American Southwest. What the child tells the teacher may be incorrect, but the teacher should include all statements children make, even when they are wrong. Through the children's own process of inquiry and exploration, they will come to see their misconceptions, and this will become a valuable part of the learning process. Keep the following points in mind when using a KWHL chart:

- *What I Know* column includes anything the child associates with the topic. Elements that the children may have experiences with will be varied because the children come from diverse backgrounds. Be prepared for connections that are quite different from what you expect and may be incorrect.

KWHL Chart: Coyotes

K What I Know	W What I Want to Know	H How I Will Learn	L What I Learned
Coyotes live in the desert	What do coyotes eat?	Research web	Respect for the land
Javelinas	Why do javelinas stink?	Visit Desert Museum	There are many different cacti, i.e. saguaros, barrel, organ pipe, ocotillo.
Lizards-snakes	Can a Gila monster hurt you?	Contact entomologists	Some lizards are protected, which means you must not hurt them.
Big spiders bite you!	Are tarantulas dangerous?	Books	Tarantulas are friendly and so is the Desert Museum guest speaker—the study of spiders is called *entomology*.
Monsoons-Haboobs!	Is a monsoon just a thunderstorm? What does the word *Haboob* mean?	Children's museum Watching the Weather Channel	
Lots of Snakes			Dogs can be trained to steer away from rattlesnakes.
Cactus	How many kinds of cactus live here?		
Mariachi	What instruments does mariachi include?		Mariachis include music instruments such as trumpets and guitars and people sing Spanish lyrics.

Goodheart-Willcox Publisher

Figure 6.6 KWHL chart. *What is the purpose of a KWHL chart, and how can it enhance learning?*

- *What I Want to Know* column is completed using discussions with the children; the teacher should record actual statements and can include the emphasis on these concepts during the learning experiences.
- *How I Will Learn* column is dynamic and develops as colleagues and family share information about resources available in the community and elsewhere. Teachers should ask children for ideas to help complete this list.
- *What I Learned* section is not completed until after the learning has been exhausted; this column is then used to reflect on the different perspectives of the children.

Concept Webs

Concept webs (also called *webs*, *concept maps*, or *bubble maps*) are visual diagrams that connect abstract ideas. They are used to brainstorm links between central concepts as a teaching tool to generate ideas and explore connections (**Figure 6.7**). At the center is the main idea, with supporting ideas branching out from it. In this example, the teacher is using concepts to make connections around water as a learning focus. Note how the content subject topics are shown closer to the center bubble, and concepts to create learning experiences related to the subject topics extend from the individual topics.

Concept webs are valuable tools for making connections between topics with children. The next example of a web was created with the children following the reading of a book called *Heckedy Peg* by Don and Audrey Woods. The book title is placed in the center, with elements related to the story situated around it (**Figure 6.8**). Webs can be valuable prompts for discussions. When you create concept webs about books for younger children, using pictures from the book allows them to make inferences.

Concept Diagrams

Another popular graphic organizer is the ***concept diagram***. This teacher-created tool provides the teacher with many different pathways connected to learning and ideas to explore in the days and weeks to come, while providing a snapshot of where the learning has come from and where it might be going.

When exploring the concept diagram, note how the children's different KWHL entries around living in the Southwest (refer to **Figure 6.6**) are captured and built upon further (**Figure 6.8**). There can be multiple opportunities to add to the concept diagram, including asking the family for input; it is a dynamic and evolving graphic organizer.

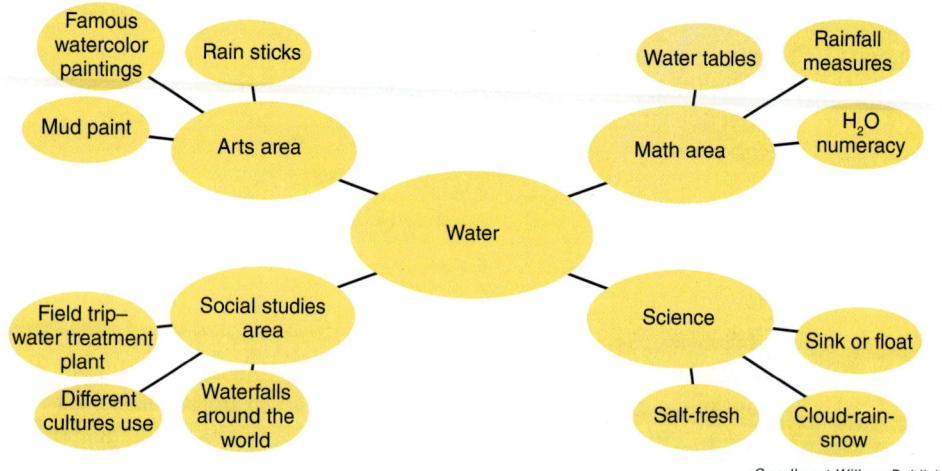

Goodheart-Willcox Publisher

Figure 6.7 Concept webs start with a main concept and branch out to show relationships among related concepts. *How can a teacher use this with children when brainstorming a new topic of interest?*

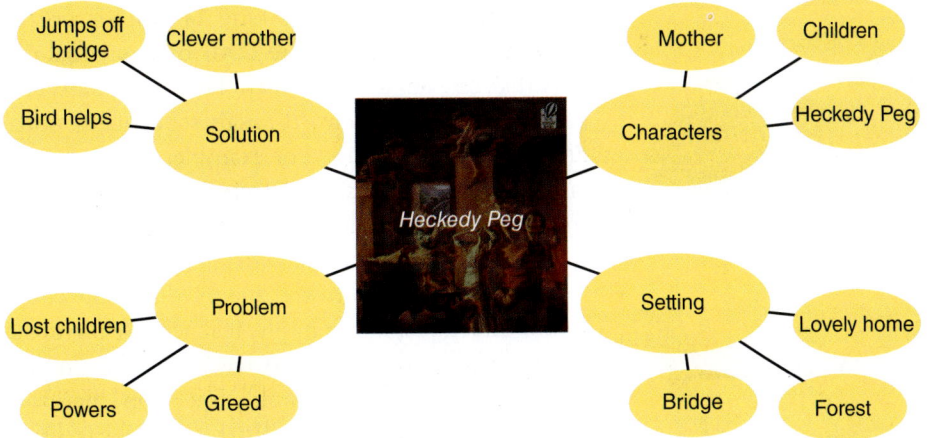

Figure 6.8 Select a book around which to design a concept web. What concepts would you include?

Figure 6.9 Concept diagram. Make connections to your own part of the world—what would it include?

Venn Diagrams

Venn diagrams provide a simple way to show relationships between a set of items using circles that overlap. items shown in the portion of the circles that overlap share common attributes. For example, the class is studying fruits. The children are asked to share their favorites, those who like both are shown in the middle (**Figure 6.10**). Venn diagrams are one way to show relationships, and using photos or illustrations instead of (or in addition to) text provides quick connections for young learners who do not read yet.

Goodheart-Willcox Publisher

Figure 6.10 This Venn diagram explores the differences and similarities of oranges and bananas. Create a Venn diagram on the topic of your choice with pictures that reflect relationships.

Storyboards are another kind of graphic organizer presented as a set of picture cards or sequential drawings that can tell a visual story. The use of storyboards supports the curriculum through sequencing, sorting, and matching activities. For example, teachers support language and social skills by creating a copy of pages from a recent read-aloud and encouraging children to retell the story while sequencing.

Storyboards also provide images that help children follow directions. For example, teachers use picture cues during whole group time to teach children to "look" (eyes), "listen" (ears), "think" (question mark), and "speak" (lips). To remind a distracted child to listen, a teacher can simply point to the picture of the ears without saying a word or disrupting the class.

Backward design and graphic organizers reflect intentionality in planning learning experiences. NAEYC's program accreditation highlights the expectation of **daily learning plans** (also called *lesson plans*), citing sixteen different criteria under its program Standard 2: Curriculum. Alignment among the disciplines and learning areas with early learning standards, learning outcomes, and assessment becomes clear through the sample daily learning and the evolving written curriculum. (See this textbook's Digital Companion Resource Log for a blank daily learning plan template.)

 **Checkpoint**

☐ Describe the backward design process.
☐ List three examples that are central to Universal Design for Learning (UDL).
☐ Create an example of a KWHL using your area of the country as the topic of interest.
☐ Create a concept web chart to show connections that might be made using a favorite book.
☐ Describe the value of using Venn diagrams with young children.
☐ How are concept diagrams useful when planning curriculum?
☐ How do storyboards support learning? Provide two examples.

6.3 The Daily Learning Plan and Catalytic Event

Written daily learning plans meet the expectation that each school and early childhood program offers its curriculum in written form while also creating a curriculum that is built on the children's own shared experiences. Additionally, most states require early childhood programs to have a planned learning environment for the children enrolled. All of these constitute best practices. The daily learning plan is undeniably one of the most important documents the teacher or teaching team creates.

Elements of a Daily Learning Plan

Some early childhood programs and classrooms use published or purchased curricula, which is developmentally appropriate as long as teachers can adapt learning experiences based on the children's interests. "It is most important that teachers be supported to have the flexibility to adapt units and activities to meet the interests and experiences of each group of specific children. Rigid, narrowly defined, skills-focused, and highly teacher-scripted curricula that do not provide flexibility for adapting to individual skills and interests are not developmentally appropriate" (NAEYC, *DAP,* 2020).

Children's previous skills and interests are defined and used to create developmentally appropriate curriculum. A curriculum that includes rigid, narrowly defined, skills-focused, and highly teacher-scripted elements does not take into account individual skills and interests, nor does it provide flexibility for adapting to individual children (NAEYC, *Professional Standards and Competencies,* 2020). It is important for teachers to design curricular experiences that are coherent and aligned to the tenets of developmentally appropriate practice (DAP) and to build on what the children learned previously. A daily learning plan includes all of these elements.

Launching the learning from the children's prior knowledge is a tenet of good teaching and a foundation of constructivism in the early childhood classroom. Knowledge is constructed based on personal experiences (Cooper 1993). **Constructivism** is based on the view that learning is an active, personal, and experiential process of structuring knowledge, which the catalytic event (a concept or event that sparks the learning idea) typifies.

A challenge that may arise is how to create curiosity for a topic when only part of the class is interested. Having alternate ways to approach different learning experiences is a strategy that many teachers employ. One solution might be to add items to the block area or suggest a new way to paint at the easel. Discussing different interests with a child may create additions the teacher never thought of. Be open to this, and be flexible to support the individual child's ideas. Sometimes a child may want to be alone, to look at books, or to read if the child is older. Support these times; alone time is valuable.

THE TEACHER'S LENS

The children are focused on the topic of interest "zoo," and some are actively exploring monkeys on a live camera at the San Diego Zoo after a class trip to the zoo the week before. Halfway through the morning, it begins to snow for the first time that year and many children have stopped their work and play to watch the white particles fall from the sky. Understanding the value of teachable moments, Teacher McGuigan suggests that everyone pull their coats on and head outside to see who can catch the most snowflakes on their tongue. Outside, Teacher McGuigan explains that snowflakes are just tiny pieces of ice and that no two snowflakes are exactly alike. Back inside, the learning will shift to observing how quickly snow can melt and the children will be challenged to paint white snow images on black paper.

Catalytic Events

The daily learning plan starts with a catalytic event and ends with reflection of what worked or needed additional attention. **Catalytic event**, also known as *teachable moment*, is defined in early childhood education as an experience or material that sparks children's interest and motivates them to want to learn more. It is often associated with the Project Approach (refer to Chapter 3, "Curricula and Approaches") but is also evident in many other curricula and approaches.

Throughout a child's day there are many events that could become a catalyst for learning. They are sometimes spontaneous, often fleeting moments such as observing a bug crawl under a chair or noticing a reflection in a puddle. These events or experiences provide opportunities for learning something new. While children may learn lessons from these moments on their own, the teacher who capitalizes on them will intentionally enrich learning.

A catalytic event can influence meaningful learning and form a strong foundation of shared experiences. These can be teacher-initiated, child-initiated, or family-initiated. Catalytic event examples include:

- a new building being constructed near the school
- a garbage truck picking up trash outside
- crossing paths with a critter on a walk
- snow falling for the first time in the season
- a puddle showing a cloud's reflection
- a community fishing derby

There are times when the early childhood teacher believes it is important to teach around a certain topic and might introduce an idea, in which case the catalytic event becomes a *teacher-initiated catalytic event*. Ideas include inviting a visiting author to read a book about a certain topic or placing a prop box that is full of related items in the dramatic play area to garner interest in a new topic of interest, such as fishing.

Child-initiated catalytic events occur across all ages. Children see the world through a different lens. Encouraging children to investigate their ideas may uncover topics and concepts not otherwise considered. This level of engagement is the pinnacle of emergent curriculum. Recall that emergent curriculum (refer to Chapter 3, "Curricula and Approaches") is learning that is created from the child's interests.

Examples of *family-initiated catalytic events* include the birth of a new baby or a recent family trip. Alternatively, any experience the family might want to share with the children in the group can possibly become a catalyst. Family-initiated catalytic events are very common when working with infant and toddlers who do not yet have the language skills to share interests or experiences to build on. Embrace and encourage family participation whenever possible; the teacher plays a central role in collaborating with families on their children's learning and development, regardless of the age.

Recognizing opportunities for learning begins with understanding that children learn about the world and their place in it through their interactions with materials and other people (**Figure 6.11**). Be sure to provide a variety of opportunities for children to play together, explore materials, and engage in meaningful conversations with adults. It is in these moments that teachable moments will emerge (Asasher 2021).

✓ Checkpoint

- ☐ Consider the meaning of constructivism in the early childhood classroom. How does your own philosophy include the value of constructivist concepts?
- ☐ Identify an example of a teachable moment.
- ☐ Compare a teacher-initiated, child-initiated, and family-initiated catalytic event.

6.4 Topic of Interest and the Focus Topic

A **topic of interest** is the main idea that results from the catalytic event and from which many smaller learning opportunities, or *focus topics*, arise. **Focus topics** are the possible concepts that create engaging learning experiences. The length of time (hours or days) spent on a focus topic should be determined by the engagement of

wavebreakmedia/Shutterstock

Figure 6.11 These two children are looking at a rock through a magnifying glass. Do you think this could be a catalytic event? Why or why not?

to be used and come in many forms. Early childhood teachers analyze assessment results from a variety of assessment documentation and then use that data appropriately to inform best-practice teaching strategies and to set learning and developmental goals for young children (NAEYC Professional Competencies and Standards 2019c).

Authentic assessment can be either formative or summative. It includes teacher-made assessments that are based on the standards and aligned to learning outcomes. Authentic assessment takes into consideration factors such as a child's facility in each language they speak and uses assessors and settings that are familiar and comfortable for the child. Authentic assessments are considered a strong representation of learning and provide valuable documentation, also called *artifacts*, that reflect the child's skill level and efforts at a point in time. Artifacts are actual evidence of learning. They are a concrete result of an assessment observation that reflects evidence of the child meeting the learning outcome measured. Visualize artifacts as something you can hold and share with a family at a conference to reflect the child's learning. When a child is observed being successful at a task, it is documented somewhere; the teacher does not rely on memory.

Artifacts

There are many different types of authentic assessment artifacts to be compared based on how they embody the unique characteristics of the individual child when measuring understanding. Work samples are child-created examples of learning experiences that include original drawings, paintings, and graphs. Work samples that include the teacher's written transcription and date on the back are a commonly used authentic assessment artifact. These provide a valid measurement of learning outcomes and standards. Making a copy of the actual sample, while allowing the child to take the original home, is a best practice.

Work samples are not worksheets. Worksheets are teacher-created pages that are often copied year to year for children to practice a set of skills. Worksheets do not allow for a great deal of creativity or divergent thinking, and in most instances, they do not support children in expressing their learning in their own way. While they are a great prop for playing school and make good templates to practice cutting skills, their use should be minimized.

A child's drawing of a girl, the sun, and a ladybug (**Figure 7.2**) can be used to demonstrate understanding of two different learning standards: art and literacy. On the back of the drawing, the teacher should write an inscription to show clear alignment to the standards and the learning outcome. While this was created in the art learning area, the learning is not confined to art. Drawing stages are part of literacy in many standards and, depending on the learning experience, can be relatable to social studies or science.

Work samples can show the progression of writing one's name collected by the teacher at the beginning, middle, and end of the year (**Figure 7.3**). Using work samples to illustrate the child's progression from the scribble stage of drawing to the basic shapes stage is a strong documentation of early literacy. Writing one's name is a common focus in the early years as children develop a sense of autonomy.

Ginny Harmelink

Figure 7.2 Child-created work samples can be connected to multiple learning outcomes. Create a learning outcome that this work sample might measure.

Checklists

Checklists provide a quick and easy way to collect data and make a record of a large group of children. In the case of an individual child, a checklist might include a developmental focus. Checklists are especially useful when the teacher is looking for common abilities.

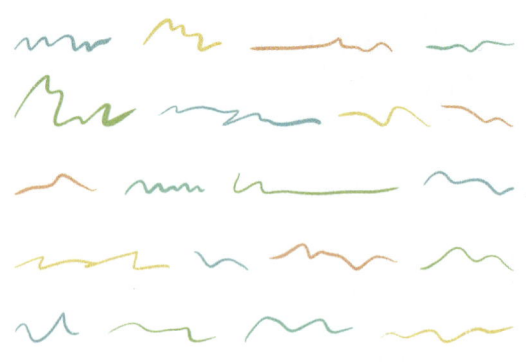

Marina Leer/iStock via Getty Images Plus   *ideabug/iStock via Getty Images Plus*

Figure 7.3 Work samples that reflect beginning scribbles are valuable examples of early literacy. Consider the different writing materials that should be available to document writing.

Checklists are widely used and can be easily adapted to many forms of learning and domains of development (**Figure 7.4**).

The strengths of checklists include providing teachers with the opportunity to document large amounts of information quickly. The challenges of checklists are their lack of qualitative data and the difficulty in correcting erroneous checkmarks afterward. Errors and edits are a challenge because they require recall of who did what, with no reference to return to later to see actual progress for an individual child. Additionally, another person, or even the original assessor looking at a checklist later, might make assumptions that are not correct because minimal data is recorded.

Annotated Photographs

Annotated photographs collect dynamic views of real-time learning. They are quick, easy, and require little advance preparation. Adding written notes to explain context and provide detail takes additional time but is achievable and adds to the data. Photographs are meaningful artifacts to assess and document children's learning. The challenge is that notes reflecting the learning need to be kept with the photograph. The use of digital cameras makes capturing the moments and aligning to a file name much easier, but with less flexibility for notes.

Checklist: Scissor Skills

Name	Snips	Cutting Straight Lines	One Complete Cut	Cuts on Curved Line	Cuts Out Figures	Holds Paper Properly	Holds Scissors Correctly	Holds Both Correctly	Improves with Assistance
Henry	X	X	X	X		X	X	X	
Cooper	X		X				X		
Evie	X	X	X	X	X	X	X	X	Mastered
Landon	X	X	X	X		X			X
Scarlett	X		X				X		X

Goodheart-Willcox Publisher

Figure 7.4 Checklist measuring the learning outcome: "Child will be able to cut with scissors." Standard: Physical Development, Health and Safety; Strand 1 Fine Motor: Uses hands, fingers, and wrists to manipulate tools (AZ Early Learning Standards). What is a learning experience you could create to assess this skill?

Video

Video recording provides opportunities to revisit the learning and note things not observed in real time in the busy classroom. Videos are also enjoyed by families and are often used to reflect learning. The main challenge of using videos to capture learning is the time it takes to review long periods of footage to capture specific learning outcomes. Annotating the learning in the video is important for quick retrieval if reflection is needed. Storing videos digitally is a quick solution to archiving what can be an overwhelming library of evidence; however, privacy and security must be ensured. Videos are becoming a favorite authentic assessment for teachers because they allow others to view the learning and share in the observation/assessment process.

> Videos capture an objective record of a child's behavior, skills, and development. How does the early childhood teacher ensure confidentially when saving and sharing videos?

STOP AND THINK

As teachers plan to use videos in the early childhood educational environment, the following steps are important (Edelman 2014):
- Identify the ways in which digital video will be used.
- Decide what equipment will be needed and purchase it.
- Learn how to shoot quality video.
- Develop consent forms.
- Obtain written and informed consent.

Anecdotal Notes

Anecdotal notes are written, individual reflections about children that are quickly noted during class activities. Anecdotal notes provide short records to consider later and are readily personalized. Strengths include how quick and easy it is to record all types of learning, while making direct observations to record all events in the classroom. The challenges include the time it takes away from interactions with the child, and the notes can be easily misinterpreted if writing is not clear and objective.

Documentation Panels

Documentation panels (similar to posters) are widely used to document entire class learning and are an assessment artifact that can be used in many ways. Documentation panels include original works of art from the children around the provocation combined with actual dialogue and photographs. The photographs focus on classroom practices that occurred and are used to educate classroom visitors about actual learning experiences. Documentation panels begin with a *provocation,* which is an Emilio Reggio term akin to asking open-ended questions to encourage deeper thinking or inquiry.

This assessment artifact includes many different learning experiences and is a visual that children can revisit long after they have moved onto a new topic of interest (**Figure 7.5**). The challenges include the time it takes to create, design, and capture the many learning artifacts and dialogues, although teachers often find the work deeply satisfying, as they reflect on the learning process.

Project work   Teaching environment   Project documentation

Visual Generation/iStock via Getty Images Plus

Figure 7.5 Documentation panels provide many examples of learning. How can this form of authentic assessment be used to inform families and guests entering the classroom?

Dynamic Assessment

Dynamic assessment is based on Lev Vygotsky's concept of the Zone of Proximal Development (ZPD). The focus of dynamic assessment is on awareness of what the child is able to do independently and using that knowledge to probe what skills the child is on the verge of grasping, with and without teacher support. This is much different from most assessments, which focus on measuring what the child completed correctly.

The teacher's cues, questions, and hints are recorded, along with the child's responses. Examining the assistance needed to support the child's understanding often reveals the child's skill level and the impetus for future teaching. Dynamic assessment starts with where the child is having difficulty and is then used to provide responsive teaching (McAfee 2016). The foundations of *responsive teaching* are inquiry and knowledge of individual children to inform their practice. One strength of dynamic assessment is the focus on responsive teaching; a challenge is the need to know each child's individual abilities.

Participation or Frequency Charts

Participation charts, also called *frequency charts*, are artifacts that provide details around children's preferences and participation patterns. These can include documenting which children visited the dramatic play area over time, participation in different groupings during the day, or tallying and tracking behaviors (**Figure 7.6**).

The strengths of using this type of assessment include the children's ability to record their own participation and the ease with which the teacher can create them. One challenge of using them as a learning artifact is that the information could be misleading. An example of providing potentially misleading information could come from a chart that captures the number of verbal interactions during large group time without acknowledging the dynamics of talkative peers taking over the conversation.

Rating Scales

Rating scales are an assessment artifact used to evaluate a child's performance based on the specific characteristics under consideration and then ranking the child along a predetermined continuum of high to low frequency (McAfee et al. 2016). Rating scales are often used to indicate degree or frequency of behaviors or skills. The strengths in using rating scales include provision of a quick way to capture data, judgments, and evaluations. The challenges include the difficulty of constructing your own rating scale artifact and potentially inserting assessment bias.

Rubrics

Similar to rating scales, *rubrics* use a specific set of criteria to evaluate performance. Rubrics include a fixed measurement scale with detailed description of levels of understanding

Participation Chart							
Activity	Jaelyn	Enrique	Lily	Sienna	Amal	Lucia	Aidan
Reading to self	XX	X		X		XX	
Dramatic play		X	XX		XX		X
Blocks		XX	X		X	XX	
Writing center	XX		X	XXX	X		XX
Music/movement		X	X	X	X	X	X
STEM	X	XX	X	XX		X	X
Art	X		X	XX		X	

Goodheart-Willcox Publisher

Figure 7.6 Participation chart. How does the chart inform the teacher about the different children's participation preferences?

for each level of performance. They may be used to assess individuals or groups and, as with rating scales, can be compared over time. Rubrics are defined by two characteristics: criteria for the child's work and descriptions of performance level. Different levels of performance or different criteria being assessed are frequently used with some variations. For example:

- A = exceeds expectations
- B = meets expectations
- C = developing
- D = does not meet expectations

Rubrics are more common in the K–3 primary grades when specific criteria must be met. The challenges and strengths of rubrics are similar to those of rating scales. The one distinction between rating scales and rubrics is that rating scales lack descriptions of performance quality.

Interviews

From the child's perspective, interviews are conversations that occur naturally. The teacher conducts interviews in the context of play, group activities, or teacher-directed times (**Figure 7.7**). This form of interview should not be confused with an adult interview with scripted questions. Open-ended questions that are part of active conversations elicit responses from the child that can reveal thinking and learning processes and allow the teacher to gain new insights into how the child thinks. "Tell me about the field trip to the honey store" or "What are some other ways you might try to make this work?" will encourage more lengthy responses than a question that requires only a *yes* or *no* answer.

Interviews often involve notes jotted down to inform the teacher about the child's understanding of something

FatCamera/E+ via Getty Images

Figure 7.7 Interviews with children occur naturally throughout the day. During which parts of the day do you think interviews are the most appropriate?

and are much different than anecdotal notes that occur randomly during the day. The interview notes are intentional, as the teacher is seeking specific information. The strength of interviews is the teacher's ability to use the responses to evaluate the child's level of understanding that may not be seen otherwise. The teacher is able to support engaging and differentiated curriculum based on the child's responses, with no preparation required. The challenge is capturing actual dialogue to revisit later and put it in context for assessment purposes.

Common Charts

Graphing charts are common in the early childhood classroom, encouraging everyone to participate (**Figure 7.8**). Common charts are another way to create a community of learners while querying on a topic to support planning of learning experiences that connect to various children. Charts can include children's names or be used to do a count or even to support a focus of study. The strengths and challenges of various types of authentic assessment artifacts are compared in (**Figure 7.9**).

Checkpoint

☐ Describe authentic assessment, including dynamic assessment.
☐ Specify a learning outcome that would align to using work samples to document learning.
☐ When might a rubric be used in an early childhood classroom? Provide examples.
☐ Specify a learning outcome that would align to using interviews to document learning.

STOP AND THINK Formal assessment can be valuable to the early childhood teacher when the teacher has concerns about a child's development delays. Identify a scenario in which the teacher might consider having the child assessed using a standardized assessment.

7.3 Formal Assessment

Formal assessments are used to measure what a child has learned. Formal assessments include standardized tests, screening tools, and other forms of diagnostic evaluations. Formal assessments require specific training to use and are based on large populations to create a baseline. A *baseline* is a reference point for comparing performance data before and after an assessment to get an average.

Formal assessments are generally not considered appropriate assessments for measuring understanding in the infant-toddler or preschool years. These early years include daily changes in all developmental domains, which makes it difficult to arrive at an accurate decision

Figure 7.8 Common assessment chart.

Common Chart			
Food	Would Eat for Lunch	Would Eat for Breakfast	Has Family Ever Eaten?
Spinach	Y-2 N-13	0	Yes-10
Eggplant	N-14 Y-1	0	Yes-9
Tomatoes	Y-12 N-3	5	Yes-15

Goodheart-Willcox Publisher

Authentic Assessment Chart

Authentic Assessment	Strengths	Challenges
Work Sample	Shows actual abilities of the child—useful for many learning experiences	Making copies of originals
Checklists	Documents large amounts of information quickly; easy to use	Inability to correct previous checkmarks; data recorded is minimum, with no context
Photograph	Multiple uses; easy to capture events	Including data that supports learning
Videos	Family favorites for viewing in personal social media spaces; ideal for observing actions not noted initially	Time to review and annotate learning; retrieving and connecting to learning observed
Anecdotal Assessment	Quick and easy to record all types of learning, direct observations	Takes time away from interactions with the child; easily misinterpreted if writing is not clear and objective
Documentation Panel	Strong artifact to reflect classroom learning to inform current focus	Time to create, design, capture many learning artifacts and dialogues
Dynamic Assessment	Focus is on what child has mastered to scaffold independent learning experiences	Need for awareness of all children's abilities in the classroom
Participation or Frequency Chart	Ease of creating; child's ability to be part of recording	Minimal connections to learning; misinterpretation of data
Rating Scale	Quick and easy way to record inferences and opinions of others	Rater bias; difficult to construct; relies on numerical or proficiency levels to determine mastery
Rubric	Quick and easy way to record mastery of criteria being measured	Time-consuming to construct; fair amount of subjectivity possible
Interview	No preparation needed	Capturing and recording actual conversation
Common Chart	Quick and easy, children can record own names as well	Duplicating other's responses

Goodheart-Willcox Publisher

Figure 7.9 Authentic assessment chart. *Which assessment would you select around the learning outcome 'Child will be able to compare a worm and a snake'?*

concerning abilities using formal assessments. Formal assessment is more common in the kindergarten through third grade with standard tests to measure understanding might be available.

One type of formal assessment is called ***standardized assessment***, which requires that the procedures for assessment be the same for every child (McAfee et al. 2016). Each child is asked the same question and asked to do the same thing in the same way. The term *standardized* is often used interchangeably with the term *formal* due to the specific training assessors need. Standardized assessments usually have a scoring system that compares results to a specific population of children of the same age; in addition, they often have specific time constraints. Formal assessments are used to make important decisions in the life of a child and are not appropriate in the early years without a strong rationale due to the daily developmental changes and impact of the environment that occur.

Standardized screening and diagnostic assessments are types of standardized assessment completed by an assessor trained to use the assessment. These types of assessment are used to identify a child who may have a disability or an individual learning or developmental need. Screening is commonly used to identify issues that need more thorough examination by individuals who are qualified to do so and should not be used to diagnose or label children. Some examples of standardized screenings include:

- Denver Developmental Screening Test (DDST)
- McCarthy Screening Test (MST)
- Developmental Indicators for the Assessment of Learning (DIAL-4)
- Early Screening Inventory (ESI)
- Dynamic Indicator of Basic Early Literacy Skills (DIBELS)

However, a teacher who has all the children draw a self-portrait the first week of school and then repeats at the end of the year is not performing a standardized assessment. While all children are asked to do the same thing, the differences in their work will be valued. This is an authentic assessment.

Criterion-referenced assessments measure how well a child has mastered a specific learning goal (or outcome). The child's performance is judged by how closely the performance matches specific criteria, not by how the child compares to others. This type of assessment is often considered *high-stakes* because it is used to make important decisions., A group of individuals with specific backgrounds, different from that of the child, may determine the score of proficiency in an area. If an assessment that uses common terms from a rural area is used to assess children that live in an urban community, the result may not reflect their understanding and their lack of understanding the rural terms would be counted against their comprehension. An example of an unfair assessment question might be to ask an urban child to identify characteristics of the different kinds of chickens.

Examples of high-stakes assessments are the requirements to pass a certain exam to enter college or to receive a high school diploma. Children can span many different levels of mastery from day to day, depending on factors such as their current mood and experiences around them, so it is important to use more than one assessment. Examples of early childhood criterion-referenced assessments are:

- Hawaii Early Learning Profile (HELP)
- Early Childhood Prekindergarten Assessment

Assessments that compare individual performance with the average performance of a group, such as all four-year-olds, are called ***norm-referenced assessments***. Because you can see how well one child scores when compared to the group, norm-referenced assessments usually cover a broad range of content. Some examples of norm-referenced assessments include:

- IQ tests
- Ages and Stages Questionnaire (ASQ-3)
- Bayley Scales of Infant Development

Evidence and research caution that many tests and test procedures are unfair to children who are poor, from a localized racial minority or marginalized background, considered creative or divergent thinkers, or English-language learners (Dixon-Roman et al. 2013). This includes high-stakes, criterion, and norm-referenced assessments.

"When standardized assessments are used for screening or evaluative purposes, the measures should meet standards of reliability and validity based on the characteristics of the child being assessed. When these standards are not met, these limitations must be carefully considered before using the results. Using assessments in ways that do not support enhancing the child's education is not developmentally appropriate practice" (NAEYC, *DAP*, 2020). **Figure 7.10** provides an overview of the different types of assessments.

Assessment Types and Purposes

Assessment Type	Description	Purposes	Examples	Comparison
Informal—Authentic	Teacher-created Often collected to showcase learning	To inform instruction To support children's learning	Work samples Checklists Photographs Videos Anecdotal assessment Documentation panels Dynamic assessment Participation charts Rating scales Rubrics Interviews Common charts	To self
Formal—Criterion-Referenced	Compares child to a preset standard or criterion Specific training required to administer Usually quantitative	To focus on a specific set of learning outcomes To measure knowledge to inform classroom instruction	Teaching Strategies Gold High Scope COR Head Start Ounce Scale Social Emotional Assessment Measure (SEAM)	To a standard or criterion
Formal—Norm-Referenced	Compares child with peers of same age Uses only quantitative data Specific training required to administer	To screen for developmental delays To provide data for program evaluation To determine needs for the classroom	IQ Tests SATs Classroom Assessment Scoring System (CLASS) ASQ-3	To others

Goodheart-Willcox Publisher

Figure 7.10 Assessment types and purposes. Identify two major differences between formal and informal assessments.

Checkpoint

- When are formal assessments appropriate in the early years?
- Identify an example of a baseline.
- Define *standardized assessments*, *screening*, and *diagnostic assessments*.
- Why are criterion-referenced assessments considered high-stakes?
- Explain the value of norm-referenced assessments.

7.4 Portfolios

After assessment artifacts are collected, the next question is how they will be compiled to make sense of what they are measuring. This section explores the different types of portfolios used to collect assessments for each child. Remember that all types of assessments have a purpose, and knowing what you want to achieve is critical when making any assessment decision, including how you showcase the results.

A ***portfolio*** is an organized, purposeful compilation of assessments that documents a child's development and learning over time and can include both authentic as well as formal assessments. A portfolio can be a folder, file, box, or electronic collection stored on a computer; all of these provide evidence of a child's learning. Portfolios are part of many program practices and are popular with teachers, children, and parents at all levels of education due to their effectiveness in showing the child's experiences, efforts, progress, unique capabilities, and accomplishments. "Conceptually, a portfolio is an evolving concept rather than a term with an agreed-on, precise definition" (McAfee et al. 2016).

Portfolios themselves are not an assessment. Rather, they are a way of compiling information from many assessment artifacts. They provide a basis for evaluation and a guide for further learning and development. Programs that involve the child and the family in the compilation of the portfolio will have compelling, positive results. Shared goals for future learning strengthen the family relationship, which is known to enrich the classroom. Portfolios that are indexed to align the early learning standards to assessment artifacts showing abilities can provide valuable information to update the family at conference time. Because they reflect the development of the child, portfolios are often shared with the next teacher when a child moves up a grade or into an older classroom.

There are four major types of portfolios: showcase, evaluation, documentation, and process portfolios. The ***showcase portfolio*** contains a child's best or favorite work and should be created with input from the child and family. These portfolios are primarily created to show evidence of learning and the different learning experiences in the child's day.

The ***evaluation portfolio*** contains mostly specified and scored material. Evaluation portfolios (also called *assessment portfolios*) contain assessment artifacts that align the learning outcomes to standards and reflect understanding of what was experienced. Graded papers and other evidence that was evaluated and contributed to a score or grade are included. These portfolios are considered more formal, are more common in the primary grades, and can be a combination of teacher and child insertions.

The ***documentation portfolio*** holds evidence of a child's work and progress. Included items are selected to build a comprehensive description of each child. These portfolios often include assessment artifacts that align to the different developmental domains, as well as learning standards. Some teachers start the new year with a child completing a self-portrait and return to this throughout the year to reflect abstract and fine motor control (**Figure 7.12**).

A ***process portfolio*** is a purposeful collection of a child's work that documents growth from novice to proficiency. It contains ongoing work (or work in progress) for a larger project, usually chronicled and commented on by the child (Valencia et al. 2014). Successful process portfolios include assessment artifacts that actively engage children in their creation, especially in determining their goals, selecting work to be included, and reflecting on how each piece demonstrates progress toward their goals and a popular type of portfolio. Today, there are many software packages designed to capture and display children's authentic and formal assessments and create a seamless level of sharing with families, which helps to create stronger relationships between the home and the early childhood program, benefiting the child. The different types of portfolios are compared in **Figure 7.13**. While considering the type of assessment and types of artifacts that will document learning, think about how collaborating with colleagues, the families and the community can provide additional information to support planning.

Creation Preschool, Vail, AZ

Figure 7.11 Work samples to share on family night. What is one element the teacher might share regarding use of work samples as part of a portfolio?

✓ Checkpoint

☐ Identify the types of assessment that would be contained in a showcase portfolio.

☐ Compare the similarities and differences between an evaluation portfolio and a documentation portfolio.

☐ What types of assessment would be contained in a process portfolio?

7.5 Differentiation, Modification, and Accommodation

Foundations Early Care and Education, WY

Figure 7.12 Photographs and work samples combine to increase the value of an assessment. What would one strength of this dual assessment be?

The next section in the daily learning plan sequence addresses ways to involve all children and the distinction between modification and accommodation. Each child must be provided with supports as needed in the best-practice early learning classroom.

Children need learning opportunities that are appropriate to their development and readiness to learn. A child who is developing above what is considered a typical range is considered gifted, and a child who is developing below a typical range is considered a child with a differing ability. It is essential that teachers have complete understanding of typical and atypical development to meet each child at the child's readiness to learn and provide the appropriate support for the child's development. All children learn at their own pace and level, and early childhood teachers must be aware of the importance in offering different levels of instruction for all children. Theorist Lilian Katz notes, "When a teacher tries to teach something to the entire class at the same time, chances are, one-third of the kids already know it, one-third of the kids will get it, and the remaining third won't. So, two-thirds of the children are wasting their time" (Katz, n.d.).

The term *differentiation* reflects a planned curriculum that takes into consideration the individual needs or interests of each child. It is important to expect changes to the daily learning plan by altering instruction and learning environment as a consistent practice. Differentiation supports all children, regardless of capabilities, by tailoring learning approaches to teaching, learning experiences, and assessment. Teachers utilize evidence-based practices through a range of strategies and use assessment results to adjust instruction.

Portfolio Types		
Types	Strengths	Unique Features
Showcase	Active child involvement to show off favorite works	Created to reflect strengths and involves family input
Evaluation	Specific scored material	Often used in primary grades
Documentation	Comprehensive collection of work	Aligns to different domains or to shows the child meeting specific standards
Process	Active child involvement	Dynamic, ongoing collection of work

Goodheart-Willcox Publisher

Figure 7.13 Comparison of portfolios. Which portfolio do you find most valuable? Why?

Multiple Intelligence Theory

Understanding different learning approaches provides additional information to support diverse ways of thinking and learning. The early childhood educator supports and encourage learners through rich, meaningful, and varied opportunities for engagement (Gardner 1997). Dr. Howard Gardner, a researcher at Harvard University, has spent his life investigating the different ways in which people learn and how teachers can support different learning styles. Dr. Gardner struggled with the idea that children were expected to learn in one way with little recognition that there are other ways to learn the same thing.

Gardner's *Multiple Intelligence (MI) Theory* suggests that no one set of teaching strategies works best for all children at all times (Armstrong 2009). Gardner found that any particular strategy is likely to be successful with several children, but not all. Gardner's framework identified nine "intelligences" to show the many ways a person can reflect intelligence and learning in different ways. Teachers are best advised to use varied teaching strategies as a response to the individual variations among child intelligences. When teaching young children, it benefits teachers to understand their own intelligences and preferences for learning as well. One reason for this is that teachers often tend to teach the way they learn. Review **Figure 7.14** for examples of each intelligence.

Most people can develop each intelligence to an adequate level of competency, and virtually everyone has the capacity to develop all intelligences to a reasonably high level of performance if given the appropriate encouragement, enrichment, and instruction (Armstrong 2009). Gardner says, "Intelligences usually work together in complex ways and

Figure 7.14 Multiple intelligences support differentiated learning. *To which intelligence are you most connected?*

Activities to Support Multiple Intelligence Theory

Type of Intelligence	Key Skills	Activities
Verbal-Linguistic	Using words and language	• Repeating rhymes • Oral storytelling • Creating scenarios in dramatic play • Listening games • Listening to stories throughout the day
Logical-Mathematical	Using logic and numbers	• Problem-solving story problems at learning areas • Measuring lengths and learning units of measurement • Sequencing activities • Thinking out loud
Visual-Spatial	Using space and images	• Creating collections • Studying photographs for differences • Playing with words and metaphors • Creating 3D projects • Painting using different tools, such as a paintbrush • Illustrating books
Body-Kinesthetic	Using body and physical movement	• Playing freeze tag • Playing red-light-green-light • Marching to music • Dancing to different genres • Pantomiming • Exercising and leading the class in jumping jacks • Following an obstacle course

Continued
Goodheart-Willcox Publisher

Type of Intelligence	Key Skills	Activities
Musical	Using music, sound, and rhythm	• Humming • Learning notes on the musical scale (do-re-mi) • Rapping • Playing instruments • Singing • Discussing how music affects emotions • Attending a musical performance • Learning piggy-back tunes (well-known tunes and adding new words)
Interpersonal	Understanding others' feelings	• Practicing assertive reactions to conflict • Planning classroom parties • Cooperative learning activities • Circle time activities • Role-playing different scenarios • Creating collaborative group books • Playing tag and other games outside
Intrapersonal	Understanding your own feelings	• Learning personal responses • Setting individual goals • Working on individual projects • Working independently • Sharing responsibilities in the classroom • Writing and illustrating your own book
Naturalistic	Identify, classify, and manipulate elements of the environment, objects, animals, or plants	• Reading outside • Watching clouds • Identifying trees • Identifying insects • Visiting parks, zoos, and botanical gardens • Going on nature walks to observe • Using binoculars, magnifying glasses, and microscopes • Dissecting
Existential	Reflective and deep thinking, design abstract theories	• Yoga • Imagining alternate ideas • Creating fantasy tales • Questioning deep topics such as, "What it is like to grow old?" • Design a room of your dreams

Goodheart-Willcox Publisher

points out that no intelligence exists by itself in life (except perhaps in very rare instances in savants and persons with brain-injuries)" (Gardner 1997). In other words, a person who does not excel at sports may excel in another kinesthetic activity, such as knitting. A child who is having a hard time learning to read may actually be highly linguistic with an impressive vocabulary.

VARK Learning Approach

Another popular learning theory, known as **VARK**, defines learning styles that include visual, auditory, read/write, and kinesthetic learning. Learning styles are the way children store and remember new information. The acronym *VARK* defines the four modalities of learning (Cherry 2019).

- Visual—Learn through seeing
  - Show pictures to reflect focus topic
  - Provide images that connect to topic
- Auditory—Learn through hearing
  - Provide learning through music and song
  - Provide times to work with others
- Read-Write—Learn through reading or writing
  - Encourage to practice writing what was learned
  - Provide written instructions
- Kinesthetic—Learn through direct, interactive learning
  - Create experiences that are concrete
  - Provide opportunities to move around while learning

The overlap between the multiple intelligence theory and the VARK learning approach is apparent. Teachers need to know about both approaches but should assess the child's learning style as soon as possible to help develop their different intelligence factors (Prashing 2005). Understanding these factors will ensure the development of a classroom that is engaged and responsive to all children, regardless of abilities.

Modification and Accommodation

Learning approaches provide a valuable tool; however, when a child is unable to complete tasks at the same level as other children, then a modification or accommodation may be required. In simple terms, modification changes what is being taught. Modification supports a child with a disability in a developmental domain to demonstrate success through appropriately adjusted skills and measurement. There is a possibility that the learning outcome will need to be altered if the level of learning is beyond the child's current abilities. **Accommodations** are adaptations that provide access to the curriculum, but do not alter the learning outcome. Accommodations may apply to children with all abilities (Tomlinson, 2022; Jung, 2018). Some children may require both modifications and accommodations, only one of them, or neither.

Example of modification:

- Revising the learning outcome to a simpler language for the child; for instance, rewording the learning outcome from "Child will be able to compare a rectangle to a triangle shape" to "Child will identify a rectangle shape and a triangle shape" The more difficult task is at the analyze level of Bloom's Taxonomy, while the modified learning outcome is at the remember level.

Examples of accommodation:

- Allowing extra time to finish.
- Posting pictures that show a sequence of events to follow.
- Providing a stool to gain access to the sink area (**Figure 7.15**).

Example of combined modification and accommodation:

- Learning outcome is modified and picture cards (considered assistive technology) are used to scaffold learning during transitions.

Nina Unruh/Shutterstock.com

Figure 7.15 Placing stepping stools near the sink is an accommodation. Identify two additional accommodations that may be present in a classroom.

Assistive Technology

Resources to support children who require modifications or accommodations are collectively known as **assistive technology (AT)**. These tools can help children with disabilities develop skills that may be challenging for them. Some AT tools are high-tech, such as devices that can "speak" the thoughts of someone who has verbal communication challenges. Other AT tools are low-tech, such as a foam grip on a pencil to make writing easier for a child with fine motor challenges (Pacer.org n.d.).

Remembering that accommodations change how a child learns content, and modifications change what a child is being taught or expected to learn, AT can improve daily routines and learning experiences in numerous ways:

- bowls or plates with suction cups to increase stability
- headphones that block noise to reduce overstimulation
- weighted blankets to provide calming affects and increase focus
- apps that "speak" when selected on a computer screen
- high-contrast paper and pens for children with visual impairments

Individual Education Plans

Some children with disabilities might need additional accommodations or modifications to learn the concepts and skills being taught. Specific AT can be included in a child's individual education plan (IEP) or 504 plan. An **Individualized Education Plan (IEP)** is a written plan used to delineate an individual child's current level of development and learning goals, as well as to specify any accommodations, modifications, and related services that the child might need to maximize learning (Tomlinson 2022). A **504 plan** is developed to ensure that a child with an identified disability, who does not meet the specific criteria for special education, can receive accommodations appropriate to the disability. Both plans are created by a team that may include special education or general teachers, the child's parent, and others who may be familiar with the needs of the child. Both plans are covered under the **Individuals with Disabilities Education Act (IDEA)**, a law that ensures that individual education plans are in place for children who need them. This law makes available free, appropriate public education to eligible children with disabilities throughout the nation and ensures the availability of special education and related services to those children. By law, states are required to educate children with disabilities.

The Division for Early Childhood (DEC) of the Council for Exceptional Children recommends the following practices to help improve learning outcomes for young children (birth through age five) who have or who are at risk for developmental delays or disabilities:

- Practitioners provide services and supports in natural and inclusive environments during daily routines and activities to promote the child's access to and participation in learning experiences.
- Practitioners consider Universal Design for Learning (see Chapter 6, "The Written Curriculum") principles to create accessible environments.
- Practitioners work with the family and other adults to modify and adapt the physical, social, and temporal environments to promote each child's access to and participation in learning experiences.
- Practitioners work with families and other adults to identify each child's needs for assistive technology to promote access to and participation in learning experiences.
- Practitioners create environments that provide opportunities for movement and regular physical activity to maintain or improve fitness, wellness, across domains.

Well-planned environments, curriculum, and assessment approaches will produce rich and meaningful experiences for all children. These intentional practices will be especially useful in the next chapter as you explore strategies and complete the implementation and reflection phase of the daily learning plan.

Checkpoint

- ☐ Share an example of atypical development.
- ☐ What does differentiated curriculum look like? Share an example.
- ☐ Why is Multiple Intelligence theory (MI) helpful to know when providing differentiated curriculum?
- ☐ Explain the differences between modifications and accommodations.
- ☐ Provide three examples of assistive technology.

Chapter 7 Review and Assessment

Chapter Summary

7.1 Summarize how the NAEYC Code of Ethics supports anti-bias assessment.

- Developmentally appropriate assessment measures the individual, not the entire classroom.
- Assessment bias includes explicit and implicit bias; it is important to be aware of your own biases when creating assessments to measure understanding.
- The NAEYC Code of Ethics (COE) plays an important part in ensuring a process that is fair to all children and families, while maintaining confidentiality.
- The COE supports decisions made based on equity and best practice.
- The impact that assessment bias has on decisions made in the classroom is evident and should be a core element when using various assessments.

7.2 Classify the types of authentic assessment artifacts.

- Authentic assessments are the most appropriate type of assessment to use in the classroom. They have many strengths as well as challenges to consider, but they provide rich data to inform teaching and learning.
- Teacher-created assessments are authentic assessments.
- Work samples provide evidence of 100% child ability. Although they are not the best assessment artifacts to measure some outcomes, they are a valid measurement for many. Writing one's name is a common focus in the early years, and using a work sample, or even a photo or a photocopy of the child's own signature is strong proof of ability. Work samples are child-created and are not worksheets to be completed. Work samples are the exception to an authentic assessment being teacher created.
- Checklists are especially useful when a teacher is observing a large group of children and their abilities. Checklists are widely used and easily adapted to many forms of learning and domains of development. While they can capture a large amount of information, they lack the details that a teacher may want to focus on later.
- Adding written notes to explain context and provide detail to photographs takes additional time, but is achievable. Photographs are meaningful artifacts to assess and document children's learning.
- Videos are always appreciated by the family and can document elements in a busy classroom that might otherwise be missed. Strategies to enhance using video as an assessment artifact provide guidance to ensure that their use is meaningful. Taking quick videos is easily achieved with today's technology.
- Anecdotal notes can be written quickly and provide individual reflections when a teacher is observing children. A strength is that they are easily retrievable later; challenges include the time it takes away from interactions with the child and the possibility that they may be misinterpreted if the writing is not clear and objective.
- Documentation panels include many different learning experiences. These panels are comprehensive, combining photography with annotations of learning in a display that engages not only the child, but other visitors to the classroom. Strengths include the ability to group many learning opportunities; a challenge is the time required to document and create each panel.
- Frequency charts provide details around children's preferences and participation patterns. These can include documenting which children visited a play area over time, participation in different groupings during the day, or behaviors tracked.
- Rating scales are often used to indicate degree or frequency of behaviors or skills. They provide a quick way to gather data and evaluations, but the possibility of inadvertently inserting one's own bias provides challenges when creating.

- Rubrics evaluate performance with expected levels of attainment. They are common in the early grades and are rarely seen in the 0–5-year-old classroom.
- Interviews can be quite valuable and are often combined with anecdotal notes afterward to document a conversation. These are dynamic exchanges that occur in the context of a conversation and are not a planned event in most cases.
- Charts that contain data that provides whole-class participation reflect interest and are most valuable for determining future learning opportunities.

7.3 Classify the types of formal assessment and how they are used.
- Standardized and diagnostic assessments are used to make important decisions that can affect a child throughout life. Their use requires a strong rationale because the decisions can be "high-stakes."
- Criterion-referenced assessments measure how well a child has mastered a specific outcome, not how they compare to other children.
- Norm-referenced assessments generally include a broad range of content and are comparisons made among children; for example, the assessment might compare all four-year-olds.
- Caution is needed when using standardized or formal assessment regarding children who may come from poor or a marginalized population, including children who are divergent thinkers or not familiar with the language of the assessment.

7.4 Classify the types of portfolios and how they are used.
- Four different types of portfolios demonstrate a variety of skills to support the child; they also provide examples (artifacts) to inform the parent and the teacher.
- Showcase portfolios are created to show a child's best work, with families contributing. This type of portfolio is primarily used to reflect the many different learning experiences; it does not show connections to early learning standards.
- The evaluation portfolio includes work that aligns with early learning standards and includes scores or grades received. These are common in the primary grades and can include insertions by the child as well as the teacher.
- Documentation portfolios are common in the 0–5 year range and connect to the early learning standards and developmental domains. This type of portfolio includes assessment artifacts selected by the teacher to reflect meeting early learning standards.
- A process portfolio is child- and teacher-driven and includes insertions from both. These portfolios document mastery of learning and actively engage the child in items selected as well as goals identified.
- Many assessment portfolios are electronic today, enabling the teacher to upload documents to share with families digitally while informing teaching and learning.

7.5 Explain how differentiation, modifications, and accommodations support learners in the daily learning plan.
- Collaboration involves working with someone to produce or create something; it is an expected element in the daily learning plan.
- Collaboration with families is at the heart of a classroom that is built on respectful communication. Including families in their child's day provides opportunities to develop stronger classroom community and is a best practice.
- Community collaboration serves as a valuable resource not only for the curriculum, but also for the entire classroom culture.

7.6 Explain how differentiation, modification, and accommodation support learners in the daily learning plan.
- Differentiation of curriculum highlights the importance of planning curriculum based on the individual needs and interests of the child.

- Gardner's Multiple Intelligence (MI) Theory provides valuable connections to the many ways children learn to support individual learning.
- VARK is an alternate learning approach that focuses on learning styles.
- Clear distinctions can be made between modification and accommodation to inform teaching.
- A variety of assistive technology tools can be used in the classroom to benefit a child with either accommodations or modifications.
- Individual Education and 504 plans covered under the Individuals with Disabilities Education Act (IDEA) provide specific criteria for items that are required to be offered by law to support young learners.

For Further Reflection

1. List some of your biases. Describe how they might affect what you see when you observe children and how they might affect your interpretations of your observations.
2. Secure one or more work samples from a preschool. What does the work sample tell you about the child? What interpretations can you draw from these samples? What are possible outcomes to which you can align?
3. Teacher Gbenga has been asked to share portfolio contents for a staff development training. What should the teacher's reaction to this request be?
4. A parent is interested in placing a non-mobile child with cerebral palsy in your classroom. What process is necessary to stay within the law?
5. Following the Multiple Intelligence theory, what is one strategy in your classroom that will support all children's learning?

Recall and Application

1. **True or False.** To provide all children with responsible assessment practices, teachers must agree on ethical practices when assessing.
2. **True or False.** The Code of Ethics principals reflect the aspirations of practitioners, while the Ideals guide the conduct and assist practitioners in resolving ethical dilemmas.
3. **True or False.** Authentic assessments require specific training to implement.
4. Formal assessments include ____.
   A. anecdotal notes
   B. participation charts
   C. IQ tests
   D. rubrics
5. A baseline refers to the ____.
   A. distance between beginning to learn and understanding
   B. line that measures growth from an assessment
   C. reference point for measuring data from an assessment
   D. first assessment performed in a school year
6. What is the difference between an evaluation portfolio and a showcase portfolio?
   A. Showcase portfolios include work screening results.
   B. Evaluation portfolios include scored work.
   C. Showcase portfolios include connecting to standards.
   D. Evaluation portfolios include examples of art created.
7. **True or False.** Collaborations involve working with someone to produce or create something.
8. **True or False.** Assistive technology includes only electronic devices designed to support different learners.

8 CHAPTER

The Implementation Phase

Learning Outcomes

After studying this chapter, you will be able to:

8.1 Explain how the characteristics of the learner factor into planning learning experiences.

8.2 Describe the importance of schedules.

8.3 Identify the different instructional strategies, including transitions, scaffolding, and learning formats/group sizes.

8.4 Explain the CIRCLE acronym and the importance of circle time in the daily learning plan.

8.5 Discuss key elements of the learning areas and experiences during the implementation phase in the daily learning plan.

8.6 Outline the components and strategies of a completed daily learning plan.

Standards Covered in This Chapter

NAEYC
4a, 4 b, 4c, 5a, 5b, 5c

DAP
Principles 2, 5, 7, 8
Guidelines 3, 5

Image credit: kali9/E+ via Getty Images

MBI/Shutterstock.com

SNAPSHOT | **Miss Marisol**

Miss Marisol is a sought-after teacher. Her skills include being bilingual, which provides many connections for the children, the families, and her colleagues. In addition to her early childhood program of study coursework, she also volunteers and is involved with the local chapter of the National Association for the Education of Young Children.

When Miss Marisol graduated, she was offered a position as a lead teacher in a program that included a high proportion of children whose home language was not English. Because she had a background in common with many of the families, she was able to create strong relationships and a curriculum that reflected the children's needs and past experiences.

Being bilingual has numerous benefits, including enhancing communication skills, fostering cultural understanding and tolerance, and improving overall academic success. Miss Marisol is able to facilitate better communication with families who may not speak English as their first language, creating a more inclusive and welcoming learning environment.

Give It Some Thought

1. How do bilingual teachers cater to the learning needs of preschool children who do not come from bilingual or multilingual households?
2. Can you provide some examples of how a bilingual teacher can promote cultural awareness and sensitivity among young children?

Key Terms

agency	learning plan reflection	resources
disposition	nonverbal cues	scaffolding
engagement strategies	one-on-one	story problems
funds of knowledge	props	transitions
implementation phase	reflection	verbal cues
instructional strategies		

Copyright Goodheart-Willcox Co., Inc.

Introduction

As 9:00 approaches, the children eagerly await the start of circle time. They want to find out about the learning areas that will begin their day. They are not aware of the planning that has occurred, or the strategies considered to support their learning. Their parents, however, *are* aware. The teacher has informed each family of ways to engage and support their child's learning. The daily learning plan and schedule is posted on the parent bulletin board with a list of classroom needs, volunteer opportunities, and exciting events that are planned for the upcoming month.

This chapter brings the daily learning plan form to completion with emphasis on the implementation and reflection phases, covering the characteristics of the learner, instructional strategies, and schedules. The chapter also describes implementation components and the final reflection on what worked well in the day of an early childhood classroom.

8.1 Characteristics of the Learner

Using what we know about children to build a daily learning plan is essential to ensuring success. Making learning experiences interesting, engaging, and meaningful encourages children to participate and helps the teacher to create a daily learning plan that supports all learners. Recall that NAEYC defines *developmentally appropriate practice* as a framework that promotes the child's development and learning with a strength- and play-based approach to engaging and enjoyable learning. Daily decisions should take into consideration core content of knowledge in the following areas:

- child development
- developmentally appropriate practices
- social and cultural contexts of the children and their families

Building learning experiences based on social and cultural contexts of each child's funds of knowledge is crucial to excite interest and engage curious explorations. **Funds of knowledge** are the child's skills and knowledge that have developed through family dynamics, interests, culture, history, and community. Classroom activities based on funds of knowledge and dispositions create a rich learning experience for children (Bodrova & Leong 2018). Making connections to a child's own fund of knowledge can create rich connections to children from all backgrounds and experiences.

STOP AND THINK | What are your funds of knowledge?

Examples of funds of knowledge may include learning how leather is tooled or how to make pasta from scratch. It may include knowing how to repair a timepiece or understanding the significance of lighting a menorah during Hannukah. Perhaps one of the children has a new sibling and is learning how to hold a baby's head; perhaps another child has a new pet and is learning how to care for it. Children with strong home-to-school connections thrive at school. A framework that is culturally relevant builds new learning experiences. Inclusion of funds of knowledge encourages the teacher to be a researcher and broadens the scope of learning for all children while also making connections to the families.

Disposition

Disposition refers to the child's innate traits and emerging knowledge, skills, and voluntary, as well as the child's habits of thinking and learning. It is an attitude about learning that becomes a life skill. Further, Lilian Katz defines *disposition* as "a pattern of behavior exhibited frequently ... in the absence of coercion ... constituting a habit of mind under some conscious and voluntary control ... intentional and oriented to broad goals" (Katz 1993).

During the ***implementation phase*** supported learning experiences that invite inquiry are derived from the teacher's understanding of the different dispositions of children. For example, a child who is provided appropriate opportunities to make decisions gains independence, problem-solving skills, and critical thinking skills. As another example, supporting collaboration with peers in pairs and small groups encourages children to value the opinions of others.

Effective teachers in early childhood settings notice, recognize, and respond to the children's dispositions. Characteristics that are positive for learning include courage, curiosity, trust, playfulness, perseverance, confidence, and responsibility (**Figure 8.1**). The child's disposition is reflected in the way the child approaches learning. Among the child's strengths may be expressing interest; getting involved; persisting through difficulties, challenges, and uncertainty; and expressing a point of view.

A child's disposition can also be negative, resulting in disengagement that may be related to the child's interests, abilities, or level of confidence. Since dispositions are not fixed, the teacher has an opportunity to adjust learning opportunities and reinforce positive dispositions. Effective early childhood teachers model positive dispositions to encourage desirable dispositions in children. Educators know their actions and attitudes send implicit messages. When they model and value curiosity and creativity, the children's dispositions are likely to flourish in the classroom.

The teacher considers the many elements that affect learning, including the dispositions of the children. When a teacher relies on drill and decontextualized activities to achieve mandated learning outcomes instead of fostering skill development through meaningful integrated learning, the children's dispositions are likely to be less positive (Hatch 2002).

Sample Dispositions and Traits

Disposition	Trait
Curiosity results in	Exploration
Exploration results in	Discovery
Discovery results in	Pleasure
Pleasure results in	Repetition
Repetition results in	Mastery
Proficiency results in	New skills
New skills result in	Confidence
Confidence contributes to	Self-esteem
Self-esteem increases	Sense of security
Sense of security results in	Curiosity

Figure 8.1 Positive dispositions for learning. Identify a trait you most value—do you find that the disposition aligns?

Agency

In early childhood education, a child's *agency* is the ability to make choices about the activities they will engage in and how they will engage in those activities. Child-based choices must be widely available for all children, not offered as a reward after completing other tasks or limited to those who are considered to be high achievers. The daily learning plan includes learning experiences that support and cultivate agency by providing multiple choices to select from in the learning areas.

Early childhood teachers promote children's agency by providing experiences that are achievable, and that motivate and challenge the children. The daily experiences should be guided by the children, including which learning areas they choose to visit during the active learning time.

A child should not be required to rotate learning areas, despite the teacher's desire for all children to share the experience. When children are actively engaged in their learning, they can make deeper connections (Self 2018). Teachers need to "plan the daily schedule with generous amounts of time for play and long enough play periods for children to become engaged in the kind of rich, sustained play is at the heart of optimal learning" (Levin 2016). NAEYC promotes organizing the use of daily and weekly schedules that provide extended durations for sustained investigation, exploration, interaction, and play.

The overall structures and routines in early learning environments remain mostly predictable, but the environmental elements are dynamic and changing. Creating a framework around which to plan supports the teacher's ability to maintain some sort of organization, while incorporating the need to be flexible. The daily and weekly schedule provides this support.

 **Checkpoint**

☐ Make connections to your own funds of knowledge. What five factors will you include?

☐ What are the primary reasons why rotating learning areas/centers is *not* supported?

8.2 Schedules

The daily schedule identifies a general framework of time around which the family, teachers, and older children can plan (**Figure 8.2**). Schedules are a way to communicate routines, although not at the same depth as the daily learning plan. Most days follow a generic schedule, similar to what is posted on a family bulletin board. However, the need to be flexible is important.

Daily schedules are characteristic of those found in the early years. A schedule is important for the child, the family, and the teacher to:

- help families schedule appointments around class events, ensuring that their children are able to fully participate.
- support the teacher when planning.
- create a routine for the children.

The infant-toddler schedule (**Figure 8.3**) is open-ended and more a guide for practices; there may be six different lunch times based on hunger, sleep cycles, and play-learning throughout the day. Flexibility is woven throughout this schedule as the infant-toddler teacher provides an environment that is safe and geared to meet each individual child's needs. The preschool schedule (**Figure 8.4**) reflects a sample full-day enrollment, although many programs offer half-day enrollment as well, most commonly occurring during the morning hours.

Chemeketa Community College Child Development Center, Salem, OR

Figure 8.2 In this early learning environment, children are encouraged to find and attempt to write their names as part of their morning routine. Do you think this is beneficial to children who cannot form letters yet? Why or why not?

The K–3 primary grades schedule (**Figure 8.5**) is more rigid; the school defines many events, with set times for specials (music, computer lab, art, PE), recess, and lunch. Providing learning experiences that are primarily covered on the same day each week allows the teacher and family to plan ahead.

If a planned learning experience takes longer than planned, a special event occurs that enthralls the children, or a certain learning area is not interesting to a child, the learning plan is set aside to follow the direction of the child's interest. The responsive teacher connects the child and the learning experiences in meaningful, respectful, and effective ways, based on the teacher's understanding of and positive connections with each child.

Infant-Toddler Schedule

Time	Activity
7:30 a.m.–9:00 a.m.	Individualized welcomes, breakfast option, child choices and teacher responsive playtime varies
9:00 a.m.–9:30 a.m.	Greeting songs, snack, playtime for those interested
9:30 a.m.–11:30 a.m.	Indoor and outdoor playtime–child choices with teacher responsive playtime; songs and stories with small groups or individuals as interested
11:30 a.m.–12:30 p.m.	Lunch–varies
12:30 p.m.–2:30 p.m.	Naptime–varies
2:30 p.m.–3:00 p.m.	Quiet playtime, children waking, snack time varies
3:00 p.m.–end of day	Follow common good-bye rituals for each individual child (i.e. common bye-bye, tune, snapshot of day written and placed in cubby)

Goodheart-Willcox Publisher

Figure 8.3 Infant-toddler daily schedule. How does this schedule support the individual?

Preschool Schedule

7:30 a.m.–9:00 a.m.	Open Choice	Early arrival with open choices of learning experiences inside and outside available as children arrive, routines–some programs offer children breakfast
	Transition	
9:00 a.m.–9:20 a.m.	Large Group	Circle time
	Transition	
9:25 a.m.–11:30 a.m.	Small Group	Active learning, open snack; choices inside and outside
	Transition	
11:40 a.m.–11:55 a.m.	Large Group	Closing circle time
	Transition	
12:00 p.m.–12:45 p.m.		Lunch
	Transition	
12:50 p.m.–2:30 p.m.		Storytime followed by quiet time or quiet activities (allowing children to have a picture book helps some children settle down. Many programs allow children who do not fall asleep within 40 minutes to play quietly in a different location). Some states limit rest time–check those regulations!
	Transition	
2:30 p.m.–4:00 p.m.	Open Choice	Afternoon active learning, snacks and stories

Goodheart-Willcox Publisher

Figure 8.4 Preschool daily schedule. Identify the different components of the preschooler's day. Which is most structured?

K–3 Primary Grade Schedule		
8:30 a.m.–9:00 a.m.	Large Group	Morning Message Routine
	Transition	
9:00 a.m.–10:00 a.m.	Small Group	Monday: Music Tuesday: PE Wednesday: Spelling—Vocabulary Thursday: Social Studies Friday: Open Focus
	Transition	
10:00 a.m.–10:30 a.m.	Large Group	Recess
	Transition	
10:30 a.m.–11:30 a.m.	Small Group	Reading Circles
	Transition	
11:30 a.m.–12:30 p.m.	Lunch	Lunch
	Transition	
12:30 p.m.–1:30 p.m.	Small Group	Math
	Transition	
1:30 p.m.–2:00 p.m.	Large Group	Recess
	Transition	
2:00 p.m.–3:00 p.m.	Large Group	Monday: Art Tuesday: Science Wednesday: Technology Thursday: Engineering Friday: Drama
	Transition	

Goodheart-Willcox Publisher

Figure 8.5 K–3 primary grades schedule. Identify three elements that are different from the preschool schedule.

 **Checkpoint**

☐ Create comparisons among the three different schedules described in this section and the ages they support.

☐ Why is the infant-toddler schedule open-ended? Identify three reasons.

8.3 Instructional Strategies

The daily schedule provides multiple experiences in various areas that require multiple instructional strategies to guide the children's learning. ***Instructional strategies*** are intentional practices that support learning. Essential planning processes with which the early childhood teacher should be familiar include transitions, scaffolding, and learning formats.

Transitions

Knowing effective ways to change directions in a spontaneous manner is difficult when working with children of any age. Providing a warning of what is about to happen in the early learning environment is called a *transition*. **Transitions** are intentional, well-thought-out activities that signal an upcoming change that involves stopping what you are doing and starting something else. Planning and using transitions are considered a best practice.

Transitions support children when they move from one environment or learning experience to another. The term *transition* is also used for the changes and shifts that are part of daily life. Sudden changes that occur without warning can create feelings of anger, sadness, worry, or confusion in young children. Advance notice of an upcoming change allows the children to prepare and be ready. For children with ADHD, anxiety, autism, or sensory processing challenges, transitioning is particularly crucial and can make the difference between a good day and a bad day (Martinelli 2020).

Classroom transitions are recognized as central to young children's experiences; but the number of transitions should be minimized whenever possible due to the need to shift actions. Constant change is not good for anyone, especially a child. Teachers are often surprised at the amount of time spent in transition in the classroom.

There are many predictable transitions in the average child's day:

- getting out of bed
- getting dressed
- eating breakfast
- leaving home to start school
- entering school
- joining opening circle time
- moving to active learning areas
- having a morning snack
- joining closing circle time
- eating lunch or leaving school (half-day)
- having quiet or nap time
- participating in afternoon active learning time
- having an afternoon snack
- leaving school for home
- returning home
- having supper
- going to bed

One way to minimize the number of transitions is to provide open snacks during the active learning time, thus removing two transitions (**Figure 8.6**). Having a specific area with finger foods that are available when children are hungry also supports agency and provides an opportunity to teach children to be aware of thirst and hunger while listening to their own bodies. Teaching children that washing hands is part of the eating process should become a natural occurrence, and handwashing should become synonymous with eating.

Consider the following transition practices to provide advance notice to children. Each of these practices supports the early childhood classroom when making transitions.

- Use **verbal cues** to announce upcoming changes.
  - Sing the same tune.

Zurijeta/Shutterstock.com

Figure 8.6 Open snack time. What are the benefits of supporting open snack time?

- *Caution:* Choose your words carefully when giving verbal cues. Instead of saying, "5 more minutes," state "It's time to clean up the table, 5 more minutes"; avoid ending your alert with "OK?" which signifies that children have a choice. (This takes practice.)
- Use **nonverbal cues** to announce upcoming changes.
  - Strum an instrument.
  - Hold up a picture card that signifies an upcoming change. This is especially helpful for children with learning disabilities.
  - Set a timer.
  - Clap your hands in a rhythm.
  - Turn lights off.
- Minimize wait time.
  - Reduce the amount of time children have to wait.
  - During transitions, challenge children who are expected to wait with a critical thinking question. For instance, ask children to "Imagine being a balloon and looking down. What do you see?"
- Plan ahead.
  - Have materials ready at the next event. If the children are transitioning from circle time to the active learning areas, have the areas ready to go. This applies to all subsequent events.

Scaffolding

Scaffolding is an instructional technique in which the teacher, peers, or materials provide support children as they practice a skill within the child's zone of proximal development (ZPD). Scaffolding requires a teacher to identify when a child needs additional support and—once the child has mastered that skill—is ready for more challenging experiences. Understanding different ways to scaffold learning provides flexibility for different levels of support.

Deep knowledge of the individual child is based on what the teacher has learned from close observation and from what the family has shared about the child's interests, skills, and abilities, plus practices of importance to the family. These sets of knowledge are critical to matching curriculum and teaching experiences to each child's emerging competencies in ways that are challenging but not frustrating (NAEYC, *DAP*, 2020).

Identifying the right amount and type of scaffolding entails general knowledge of child development and familiarity with the paths and sequences that children follow in developing specific skills, concepts, and abilities. An appropriate scaffold makes it easier for a child to complete a task and influences construction of mind. Scaffolding helps children develop the mental categories and processes necessary for attempting tasks (Bodrova & Leong 2018).

Consider ways in which educators use scaffolding with a child learning to use scissors. Methods may include verbal cues, modeling, providing hand-over-hand support, providing alternate scissors, and other assistance. The examples range from least amount of assistance (verbal cues) to the maximum amount of assistance (physical support and alternate tools). Some of the scaffolding techniques involve materials, while others are provided by the teacher and might also involve peers.

Figure 8.7 Practicing cutting with scissors. What are two safe ways to encourage cutting skills in the early years?

damircudic/E+ via Getty Images

- Verbal cues and modeling: Share how a paper can be separated in many ways: by tearing it into strips, or cutting with scissors, for example. Teacher Nguyen might say, "The scissors have finger holes to place your fingers, like this" and model what to do (**Figure 8.7**). Provide support only as needed and allow wait time for the children to try the technique on their own.

- Hand-over-hand support: Teacher Qadir may provide physical support by gently placing hands over hands to practice the cutting motion. After a few times, remove hands and allow time for the children to try the technique on their own.
- Alternate tools: Provide special scissors with three finger holes to practice the cutting motions of scissors.

Teachers often provide scaffolds for a child without even being aware of it. Beginning with least amount of support is always a best practice. This allows the children to show what they are capable of without assistance.

Learning Formats/Group Size

The term *learning formats* refers to the size of a group; group size is a key part of the planning process. The teacher's role is to ensure that each child has the opportunity to pursue individual interests and benefit from the learning opportunities. Teachers consider which learning format is best to help children achieve learning outcomes based on their individual characteristics, ages, dispositions, and abilities.

One-on-one times in the early childhood classroom are opportunities for a child to have the full attention of a teacher. These can be unplanned events, such as reading a book together in the literacy area, or planned events, such as assessing a specific skill.

Pairing is defined as "a group of two." There is compelling research that supports the value of pairing in the early years. Especially useful for children who are bilingual or multilingual, paired learning experiences cultivate relationships with peers, particularly those of different social and ethnic groups. Pairing children can further support peer learning in which children with different abilities can scaffold each other (Alanís et al. 2015). When pairing is used during large group activities, children can have each other's full attention. Sharing information in pairs during the large group format supports assertiveness and confidence skills when children are speaking in front of a larger group.

Small groups (usually 3 or 4 children) are most common during indoor and outdoor active learning times. As with pairing, child-selected or teacher-chosen small groups can be beneficial for children who are bilingual or multilingual to strengthen relationships with peers.

Large group occasions include outdoor time or recess, as well as lunch and circle time. Each of these venues offer different opportunities to engage with the entire peer group. Outdoor time and recess provide experiences with the natural world in addition to learning and enjoying games that include gross motor skills. Lunch is an opportunity to gain experience with social skills. Circle time is described in the next section.

Checkpoint

- Identify two reasons why it is important to provide children with transitions.
- Suggest a learning experience that might include different groupings of children.

8.4 Circle Time

Circle time is the gathering of the whole class in a large group. It is the foundation of the learning day and provides an opportunity for all children to hear the same message, listen to the same stories, sing songs, discuss the soon-to-be-open learning areas, and connect to meaningful activities. Circle time builds strong, caring communities. The implementation section of the daily learning plan begins with opening circle time (with the full group), followed by the active learning time (in small groups) that comprises the learning areas and experiences, and ends with the closing circle (with the full group).

Opening Circle

Gathering the children together to discuss the daily focus topic is a common component of the early childhood classroom and signals the start of the day. Sometimes called *morning meetings* or *large group time*, these events build the children's sense of being part of a larger group. Opening circle time should always precede the planned active learning experiences and provide an opportunity to discuss items common to all the children (**Figure 8.8**).

Large group instruction periods are limited to align with the shorter attention spans of young children (NAEYC, *DAP*, 2020). Opening circles should be no more than 15 to 20 minutes due to the developing attention spans of the children. The rule of thumb is approximately five minutes for each year up to age five. Remember the importance of being flexible if there are circumstances that warrant it.

Children younger than three have short attention spans and should not be expected or required to attend circle time unless they are interested in a song or play activity. Small groupings are sometimes found in the infant-toddler room, but do not necessarily follow a set sequence. Older K–3-grade classrooms often have a routine that focuses on abstract concepts, such as weather or daily word wall (vocabulary) activities; however, it is not usually referred to as "circle time," but as "morning message time" or something similar.

Robin Stirling/Creer School, Rio de Janeiro

Figure 8.8 Circle time at an early learning center in Rio de Janeiro, Brazil. What are the benefits and disadvantages of changing the circle time shape?

Meaning of the CIRCLE Acronym

Circle time is a chance to be creative and have fun; it should be a stress-free time for the teacher(s) and the children to come together as a classroom community. The opening preschool CIRCLE acronym is useful when planning to ensure a seamless start to the implementation phase. The CIRCLE acronym stands for:

Come

Invite

Routine

Concept

Learn

Exit

Following the CIRCLE sequence is a valuable way to create structure and make connections to the learning experiences that follow the opening circle time. Over time, the teacher will see which circle time activities are the best fit for the children.

The first half of the acronym, C-I-R, is repeated each day with some common elements, while the last half, C-L-E, focuses on the day's learning experiences and material. The length of each component is driven by the children's interest and the ideas that the teacher suggests.

Come

Get the children's attention using the same transition signal every time. The signal should take about one minute. Transitions provide gentle reminders throughout the day that it is time to move from one area of the room to another. They help children change directions. As an example, for the **C**ome segment, children can be taught that after a transitional nonverbal cue such as turning the lights off, they should wash their hands, find and sit on their name, and count their fingers and toes while waiting for friends to join the circle.

Invite

Once everyone has come to the circle, plan a lively movement exercise for about two minutes to work the wiggles out. The **I**nvite segment is the time to invite and welcome everyone into circle time as soon as all are seated and ready. Begin with a traditional "Come to Circle" song that includes everyone's name.

"Good morning, good morning!
I am so happy you are here—
I say good morning to
(Name each person's name)"

Children approach group events in different ways, much as adults do. Plan the circle time to be short, fun, and a time to learn of the experiences waiting; this should encourage most children's interest in participating. However, if you have children of differing abilities, providing a quiet table to look at books or make a puzzle is advised. A teacher should never require a child to participate; instead, consider ways to engage the child in a different way. What if a child does not want to participate in the circle time?

Routine

Following a predictable series of events with the opening circle time, the **R**outine segment creates a structure to provide a sense of belonging for the children, as well as an awareness of what comes next. The routine section should only last about 3 to 5 minutes. Consider meaningful routines that support activities. For example, during calendar time, invite children to draw a picture of something they saw on the way to school that day and place it on the calendar. This is preferable to focusing on abstract symbols such as numerals or counting days of the month. There are many ways to teach numeracy that are more significant but do not involve counting to thirty-one, taking up valuable circle time. Chapter 9, "Academic Disciplines," explores many hands-on methods to add to your toolbox.

Preschool children live in the present. The more authentic and true-to-life the learning is, the more valuable and appropriate it will be.

Connecting children to classroom tasks by assigning classroom jobs creates a sense of community. The goal is to have a meaningful job for each child. Examples of classroom jobs include:

- Be a friend when someone is sad (empathy).
- Feed the class pet.
- Set the table.
- Help set out the rest mats.
- Water class plants.
- Help solve disputes (conflict resolution).

What are additional responsibilities that you may include when creating a class jobs jar?

Concept

In the **C**oncept segment, share with the children what concept(s) they will learning from the focus topic (3 to 7 minutes). Some teachers start with an engaging book or finger play around the focus topic. Plan to introduce the focus topic concept by including:

- a creative approach
- use of all five senses
- open-ended questions
- element of surprise
- good eye contact
- lots of enthusiasm

Learn

During the **L**earn segment of circle time, the various planned learning area experiences are described to the children so they may choose where to begin their active learning time (10 to 15 minutes). They should be free to choose where they begin and should not be required to stay in one area for the duration of active learning time.

Some curriculum models, such as HighScope and Tools of the Mind (ToM), actively include the children in planning their upcoming play in the learning areas as part of their curriculum. ToM teaches the children to draw their plan of what they will be doing, integrating art and literacy. HighScope has children verbalize what their plan of action is when beginning play, then actively review the plan during the closing circle as part of the plan-do-review process described in Chapter 3, "Curricula and Approaches." How to excuse the children to participate in the active learning time is the teacher's decision and can change frequently.

Exit

The **E**xit segment is the beginning of the transition to active learning time. The exit includes children selecting where they want to start (and remain for the entire learning segment if they choose) after the teacher has shared the choices of learning areas. It is a good idea to identify and plan for space limits in case everyone wants to start at the same area, such as the sensory table. Each child should be encouraged to announce where they plan to go when excused. The teacher can confirm that the child knows which is the correct area (this should take 2 to 5 minutes).

Be creative when children are excused to their destination by using different methods. Examples include:

- If you are wearing red today...
- If you are sitting next to Lee...
- Everyone who had toast for breakfast...
- If your name starts with *R*...
- If you chose the sensory table...

Engagement Strategies

Capturing and retaining the interest of a large group of children requires strategies to keep everyone actively involved. Recalling the instructional strategies of transitions, scaffolding, and learning formats are helpful when the teacher is exploring intentional engagement strategies to use during circle time.

Engagement strategies are methods to keep children interested in the happenings around them. With planning, the teacher will find that engagement strategies become second nature.

While each child taking a turn to share is a common occurrence in many circles, even the most well-behaved child can lose patience waiting for a turn. The *turn and share* strategy allows children to answer the question a teacher has posed to the group by turning to the child sitting next to them and sharing their answer. Even the children sitting at the back will be engaged and disruptions will be kept to a minimum when using this strategy.

Another practice to keep the children's interest is including the children's names as active characters when reading books, telling oral stories, or singing tunes. This strategy works especially well if changing the character's name does not challenge the integrity of the story and the teacher is intentional to include everyone.

Props are physical items used strategically throughout circle time to engage children during storytelling. Some teachers use props to assign *talking rights*. Props such as curiosity suitcases and empty boxes become visual aids to help the children make connections that cement thinking about the topic being explored.

Another strategy is to consider the many ways to prepare the circle time space. "Switching it up" in this context means to physically change things around. As an example, instead of circle time, call it "triangle time" or "square time" one day and have the children sit in a formation of those shapes. Regardless of the shape or what it is called, the following ideas may help with engagement:

- Lay carpet squares on the floor in a circle (or other shape, or even a zigzag) to define individual spaces.
- Allow children to define their own seating arrangements.
- Use a tablecloth or blanket to sit around.
- Describe what a personal bubble is and have all children sit an extended arm's length away from each other.
- Plan circle time outside, weather permitting.

Story problems are scenarios that give children a starting direction and problem to solve when arriving at the dramatic play area. This can also be used in other learning areas, such as blocks, to make connections and give the children a starting point in their play. The story problem chart builds a set of teacher-constructed critical thinking and problem-solving skills scenarios that challenge the children when they arrive at the learning area. Provoking critical thinking is a strategy to initiate deeper play and learning.

Just as story problems are used in math to consider different ways to solve number problems, they can be used in a critical thinking context during play. The example in **Figure 8.9** shows story problems built around a pretend airport or airplane and connected to a topic of interest around travel.

Creating multiple and varying engaging activities helps ensure that circle time is a favorite group activity to which all of the children look forward. Other supports include changing the routine while maintaining a balance of familiar and new activities and keeping it flexible. The teacher would not spend time reading a picture book that does not engage every child from beginning to end. Enjoyment and engagement make the minutes memorable and worth everyone's time. Circle time is the foundation of active learning time and should be a favorite of everyone, including the teacher.

The learning areas are always prepared and set up by the teacher before the children leave the opening circle time. Some teachers are able to set up the next day's learning areas the day before, while others must wait until the morning due to the structure of the program. Some preschool rooms are shared spaces that require cleaning or will have other occupants after the preschool time is done. Whatever the circumstances, when the opening circle reaches the exit stage, the learning areas must be ready.

Story Problems: Travel

Learning Area	Roles and Props	Scenarios of What Happens	Props	Story Problems—Provocation	Literacy, Science, and Math Extensions
Dramatic-Pretend Play Area	6+ Participants 1) Pilot: Fly plane 2) Co-Pilot: Fly plane 3) Flight attendant: Greet and take care of passengers 4) Ticket agent: Sell tickets 5) Security agent: Check suitcases 6) Travel agent 7) Passengers 8) Control tower	For example: Pilot greets the passengers, sits at the front of the plane, talks on the intercom, shares destination	Chairs to make plane rows; block for intercom; maps; hat; nametags, tickets, travel brochures (ask families to share); maps; airport signage; compass, binoculars; aisle rope; headphones; ticket scanners, suitcases, baggage tags	1) Travel agent has a *special* to go to XXX for XXX money, customer needs more money 2) Security agent will not allow passenger to pass with water bottle 3) Passenger wants to fly to a different place; or sit in a different seat 4) Customer does not have enough money 5) Crying baby is bothering one passenger 6) Pilot cannot land due to weather issues	1) Schedule of arrivals and departures 2) Name of airport signage 3) Creation of tickets/nametags 4) Menus of food items to order 5) Maps with destinations and travel distances

Goodheart-Willcox Publisher

Figure 8.9 Story problems; the topic of interest is travel. The teacher will read the travel-themed book *Where Are We Going* during circle time. Possible dramatic play extensions include a ticket counter, airport signage in different languages, and passports.

Special Events

Special events are a fun part of the early childhood experience. Before you decide which events to celebrate in the classroom, make sure you understand the cultural background of the children and their families. Not all cultures, for example, celebrate birthdays.

Some examples of special events include:
- birthdays
- visitors to the classroom
- field trips

Checkpoint

☐ Provide an example of each C-I-R-C-L-E segment around a common topic of interest.

☐ Create a story problem for the dramatic play area around a common topic of interest.

8.5 Elements of the Implementation Phase

During the active learning time portion of the daily learning plan, multiple learning areas are open for children to experience the environment in small groups. This is typically the core of the morning, and ideally lasts between two to two and a half hours. Providing longer lengths of times in the active learning areas is supported by many researchers. Learning environments are created to reflect children's interests (**Figure 8.10**). Planned areas provide time for children to engage in individual self-directed play as well as play in small groups (NAEYC, *DAP*, 2020). Sustained *synchronous interaction* in which the child is interacting with others in some continuous process supports initiative (Rabinowitch & Knafo-Noam 2015).

Younger children are more likely to learn through interactive processes than through passive, receptive, and reactive practices. A curriculum for young children should include abundant interactive experiences with peers and with materials in the environment (Katz 2007).

Tardos (2013) emphasizes that uninterrupted play not only helps to let young children move and play independently, but also assists in creating a relationship in which the child is not "considered as a helpless being, but is thought of instead as another person, a partner." Learning experiences should be designed to sustain interest and allow for initial and then deeper investigations. Children learn through concrete experiences, needing many opportunities to practice skills as they are acquired. The planned experiences should be responsive to each child to create strong connections to the learning outcomes outlined in the daily learning plan.

During the active learning block of time, children may participate in various self-selected learning experiences with the teacher scaffolding the learning of each as needed (**Figure 8.11**). Observing the dynamics of the children and tracking individuals' connections to the learning outcomes creates a very quick two hours of teaching and learning. The teacher will be actively assessing certain areas, providing guidance in other areas, and teaching problem-solving skills in yet other areas.

A five-minute transition signals the end of active learning time. Children know to prepare to return to the closing circle. The transition gives the children time to clean up and help put the area back into some order. There are times when signals at 10 minutes then 5 minutes are supportive for some children to prepare.

The closing circle provides closure for the children and provides an opportunity for the children to reflect on their learning. During the closing circle, children are encouraged to share their experiences with one another as well as the large group. The turn and share tactic is a great way to limit wait time during large group time. Engaging everyone at the same time also provides the teacher time to discuss the most important part of their morning collectively.

The children's song from opening circle time is sometimes sung again, or a new or familiar finger play practiced. Other activities during the closing circle time include sharing a teaser of what is expected the next day and ends with the children singing their traditional closing circle song.

"Good-bye. Good-bye. Until tomorrow once again.
Have fun, learn much, and remember to think kind thoughts
Good-bye. Good-bye. Until tomorrow once again."

kate_sept2004/E+ via Getty Images

Figure 8.10 Active learning environment. *How many different learning areas are evident in this image?*

SDI Productions/E+ via Getty Images

Figure 8.11 Dynamic learning. *Provide three examples that represent active and engaged learning.*

Materials and Resources

Having supplies on hand helps ensure that all the learning experiences will go as smoothly as possible. ***Resources*** include the supplies needed in the learning areas as well as any books and magazines that might be of interest to the children. Think of this as a shopping list for learning experiences. Consider the different genres of books around the focus daily topic, making sure that both picture and informational books are part of the list. Placing different books as part of each learning area will increase interest and support early literacy.

Learning Plan Reflection

Learning plan reflection describes the final section of the daily learning plan, in which the teacher evaluates what worked well and what might need improvements or adjustments. The learning plan reflection can take many forms, such as jotting down notes to attach to the template itself or writing an extensive narrative to guide future teaching. Learning plan reflections serve as a record for future instruction. As the children say their goodbyes or transition to getting ready for lunch, the teacher reflects on the morning learning and may jot down notes to revisit later.

The daily learning plan reflection is an important part of the day, providing notes on what needs more emphasis and on those elements that went especially well. Teachers should make time for this reflection at the end of the day. While time is always a concern, noting what needs to be considered the next day, reviewing individual children's interests, and communicating with one another is extremely important. Many things may have occurred that might not fit into the focus topic, and a responsive teacher will want to take advantage of any teachable moment that might be present, while having a framework in place.

Checkpoint

☐ Identify key components of the implementation phase.
☐ Explain the value of a daily group reflection.

THE TEACHER'S LENS

Carving out time at the end of the day to file different assessment artifacts in the individual children's portfolios allows for additional reflection on practices to implement in the coming days and weeks. Teachers should provide portfolios at parent-teacher conferences as valuable evidence of each child's progress. Looking at portfolios provides a sense of satisfaction for teachers and families

8.6 Components and Strategies of a Completed Daily Learning Plan

Consider a class that has spent three weeks on the topic of interest "fish." The class was part of a community fishing derby (catalyst) a few weeks before and all the children showed interest in the topic of fish. Shortly after the catalytic event (fishing derby), a query was sent home that resulted in many families sharing various experiences and items of interest.

The teacher created intentional learning experiences that target the different abilities and interests of the children. The learning outcomes are aligned with the state early learning standards the teacher will use to support learning. The children arrive, excited for a new day. Different learning areas are open where they can play and learn while families sign in and drop off their children.

Fish: Weeks 1 and 2

Using a graphic organizer, the teacher created a fish-related KWHL (What I **K**now, What I **W**ant to Know, **H**ow I Will Learn, What I **L**earned) chart with the children during the morning circle (**Figure 8.12**). When creating a KWHL chart, children who state misconceptions should not be corrected; they will learn through the process of inquiry what is correct.

Following the creation of the KWHL chart, the teacher created a concept diagram, which was shared with families, encouraging input. The teacher used the concept diagram to build learning experiences and to connect to the different learning areas. A concept diagram (**Figure 8.13**) another the of many planning strategies that can be used to display or document learning. It can be dynamic, meaning a teacher can add on to it based on additional interests and input.

During the first two weeks, the dramatic play area was turned into an airplane that was flying across the globe for fishing expeditions. The children were busy creating props, and families donated (safe) fishing gear to make it come alive. Destination images were printed from the internet and the children used the computer to customize their own travel brochures and itineraries (new vocabulary) with a little help from the teacher.

The children were fascinated with visiting different locations and researching the fish that live there. The teacher set up a computer displaying a live webcam of the Great Barrier Reef in the art area, which the children enjoyed watching as they created their own fish (**Figure 8.14**). Also at the art center, children were introduced to famous paintings of fish and fishermen such as Winslow Homer's "The Fisherman's Return." In the library area they explored favorite fish books such as *Rainbow Fish*, *Big Al*, *Swimmy*, and *The Pout-Pout Fish*. Informational books full of photographs were borrowed from the library and placed in different learning areas. Children were encouraged to design their own fish and then tell a story about it. With help from the teacher, mini books were created. Multiple learning outcomes were used to connect to the early learning standards around social studies and valuable authentic assessments were collected and placed in the children's portfolios.

The children have learned many facts, including that fish are *vertebrates* (new vocabulary word), that they are different from other animals because they have gills and fins, and

KWHL Chart: Fish

What I Know	What I Want to Know	How I Will Learn	What I Learned
• We eat fish • Goldfish are fish • Some cats are fish • People fish • Fish like worms • Some fish live in the ocean • I do not like fish • Fish can talk • Fish can breathe	• What fish are pets? • What do fish eat? • How many different fish are there? • How do fish breathe under the water? • What are some foods made from fish? • How do fish breathe?	• Asking families if they have fish • Visiting the fish hatchery • Guest speaker from Game & Fish • Researching fish that live in the ocean and rivers • Investigating fish gills	• Fish have gills • Fish breath with gills • Minnows are pets • Goldfish are pets • Fish lay eggs

Figure 8.12 KWHL chart. Note the learning that has occurred about fish. What are two additional ideas to which you might make connections?

Goodheart-Willcox Publisher

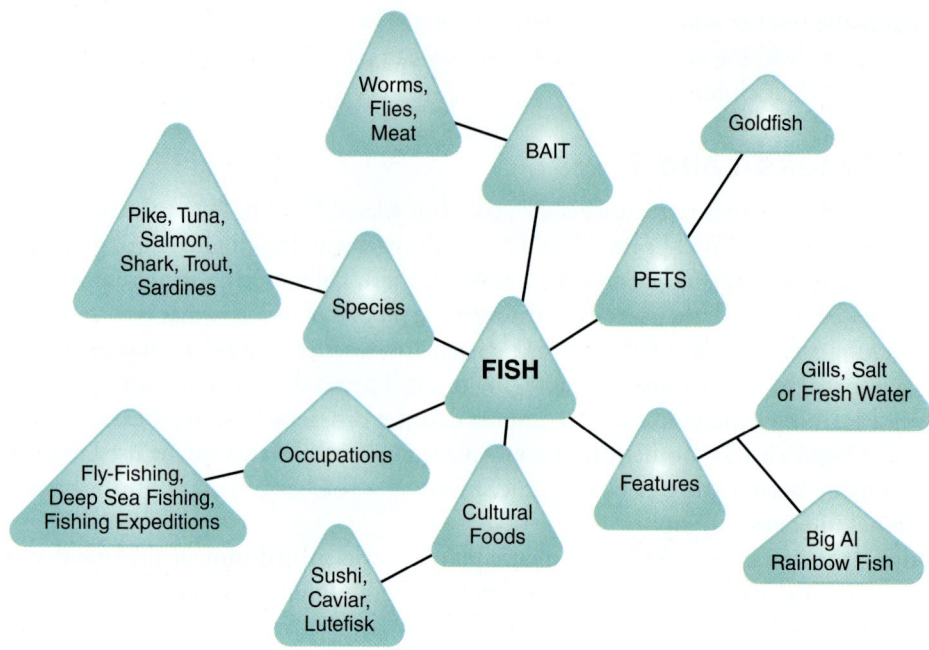

Figure 8.13 Concept diagram. What are additional connections you could make to focus on fish?

Figure 8.14 A child has drawn this image of a fish. How does this activity support learning under the topic of interest?

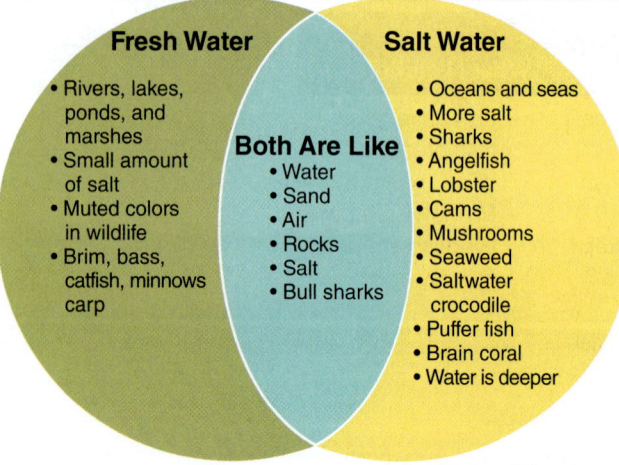

Figure 8.15 This Venn diagram displays some of the similarities and differences of freshwater and saltwater fish. How does a Venn diagram support literacy?

that they are *aquatic* (living only in water). The class explored fish species from across the world, as well as fish in their own area, while the teacher learned along with the children. A deeper dive into the ocean topic compared freshwater to saltwater fish. Learning about deep-sea fishing and fly-fishing provided opportunities for many comparisons not only to fish species and their habitat, but to the different elements of water.

The children were introduced to fish similarities and differences using a Venn diagram, as well as common graphing charts. A Venn diagram example of freshwater fish vs. saltwater fish (**Figure 8.15**) illustrated these facts. Providing many ways to make connections to the different learning experiences offered multiple opportunities for children to make inferences. Cut-out pictures of the different fish were used to manipulate and make connections to the Venn diagram, to make it as authentic as possible.

Common graphing charts using a table format with rows and columns were created to reflect different children's answers to a question. **Figure 8.16** reflects how children responded to questions about their inclination to own a pet fish. The graphing chart has captured different reactions that were recorded during a circle time discussion of freshwater and saltwater fish. Common graphing charts are used in the early childhood classroom to encourage all children to participate and are another way to create a community of learners.

The planning, which started with an early learning outcome located at the sensory table that integrated science and math, evolved as the progression of learning continued.

Graphing Chart: Fish			
Type of Fish	Would Want One for a Pet?	Fresh or Salt Water?	Family Ever Eaten?
Salmon	Yes: 7, No: 8	Both	Yes: 15
Tuna Fish	Yes: 1, No: 14	Salt	Yes: 15
Sardines	Yes: 12, No: 3	Salt	Yes: 15
Shark	No: 15	Salt	Yes: 3, N: 12
Goldfish	Yes: 15	Fresh	No: 15
Trout	Yes: 10, No: 1, Maybe: 4	Fresh	Yes: 13, No: 2
Pike	No: 15	Fresh	Yes: 5, No: 10

Goodheart-Willcox Publisher

Figure 8.16 Common graphing is useful for children to identify differences as well as similarities. How else could common graphing be used to support learning?

The learning outcome, *Children will be able to make comparisons of different fish*, used the early learning standard as the guide to create the outcome, then the assessment, followed by connecting all of these to the learning experience. The teacher may have decided to use a photograph, or video, or any of many other types of assessment to align to this outcome as well (**Figure 8.17**).

In the learning activity, the children's observation of minnows was followed by comparing the minnow's size with that of a whale's image that was displayed on the wall. Anecdotal notes captured the children using words such as *big, bigger, biggest* and *small, smaller, smallest*. New vocabulary words were used by the teacher, including *massive, immense,* and *miniature* (**Figure 8.18**).

Fish: Week 3

At the beginning of week 3, the children found that the airport in the dramatic play area had been replaced with a fish market, with a display that reads "Catch of the Week." A price list, cash registers, telephones, signage, and aprons supported play and learning. The "Fish for Sale" signs were created at the art center and replicated many of the fish the children had been studying. The children did a lot of research about different species of fish. Informational books, as well as popular children's books, were scattered across all learning areas.

Distant lands and how fish are prepared and eaten exposed the children to sushi, lutefisk, and caviar, which provided a deeper connection to social studies. A food-tasting event was created to sample salmon, sardines, and tuna with crackers at the end of one day, with family invited. Taste preferences were predicted prior to the event and then actual reactions were recorded to review later.

Some of the highlights of week three included a field trip to the fish hatchery to observe fish, creating prints with frozen fish that one of the children's grandparents caught, and comparing how many inches long the different specimens were. Ocean music was played in the classroom, with wave sounds crashing to shore, while the children investigated how fish breathe. They

SDI Productions/E+ via Getty Images

Figure 8.17 Authentic experiences support learning. Identify an additional authentic experience that can be created around the topic of fish.

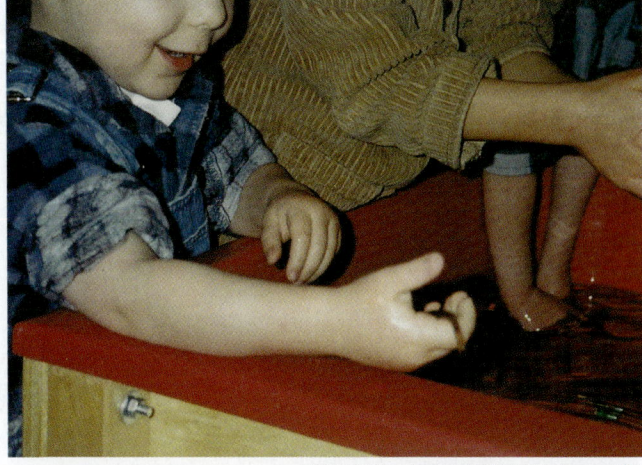

Ginny's Preschool and Child Care, Casper, WY

Figure 8.18 These children are touching minnows at a sensory table. Imagine what you would place in this space to support learning. What might you include?

compared gills to lungs by using a balloon that expands and retracts. The teacher offered many open-ended questions throughout.

THE TEACHER'S LENS

Teacher Huditz did not anticipate that the Fish Topic of Interest would last more than two weeks. Using the initial graphic organizers, Teacher Huditz sketched out week 4. Depending on the children's interests, week 5 is also a possibility. However, it is likely that week 5 will cover a new topic of interest due to many different events that have recently occurred that have captured the children's interest.

The teacher predicted interest in fish would wane after two weeks, but the children's interest continued. The children have studied different fish species, fish habitats, and foods made with fish. During the next five days, unless interest wanes, they will begin with a focus topic on worms and how fish and worms are connected. The teacher planned that each day of week 4 would focus on a different worm element to enrich learning around the different integrated academic areas with specific learning outcomes, the children remain engaged in the focus topic.

The completed daily learning plan (**Figure 8.19**) lists the learning areas aligned in one day, in a real classroom. These are identified for illustrational purposes only; having that many learning areas open on the same day would be rare.

Reflection

The final section of the daily learning plan is *reflection*. The teacher reflection section shows the development that spanned the different standards, as well as domains of

Daily Learning Plan
Catalytic Event (Teachable Moment): Fishing Derby
Topic of Interest: Fish
Daily "Focus Topic": Worms
Intended Age Group (Infants, Toddlers, Preschool, Early Grades)

Early Learning Standard	Learning Outcome	Authentic Assessment	Learning Experience
Emergent Writing-Concept 1: Intentionally uses scribbles/writing and inventive writing to convey meaning, ideas, or to tell a story; examples: signing artwork, captioning, labeling, creating lists, making notes	Child will be able to compare two differences between three earthworms (color, length, width)	Work sample	Free Draw Area: (Learning Outcome 1) Draw worms from observing them on the table tray. Compare/measure earthworms and nightcrawlers, and caption (see Figure 8.12) your drawing (4 spaces) Science, Math, Literacy, Art
Math: Concept 2: Counting and Cardinality: Compares two sets of objects using terms such as greater than, less than, or equal to.	Child will be able to predict weight differences using verbal language	Checklist	Math Area: Weighing worms on postage scale—what in the classroom weighs the same as three worms? Predict and chart different items! (1–2 spaces) Math, Literacy

Continued
Goodheart-Willcox Publisher

Figure 8.19 Daily learning plan. Does this plan support all learning domains? Explain your answer.

Implementation Plan (9–11:30 a.m.)
Opening Circle Time (Large Group Time)
Identify **C-I-R-C-L-E** Steps (20–25 minutes)

C Place children's mats as a large circle. In the middle of the circle a towel is covering a small transparent tub and the book that will be read during the concept segment.

I Sing traditional welcoming song.

R Begin with job jar, news of the day, kindness idea, and announce today is National Worm Day.

C Today we are going to learn about WORMS!
- Share a worm you have in a transparent cup under that was hidden under a towel. Remove the towel and pass it around. (Some children will not be interested in touching this—that is okay). Ask open-ended questions, i.e. "How can we find out about worms?" "Turn and share with your neighbor about your experiences with worms." "Imagine being a worm, what it might be like." Allow the cup and active conversation to go around the circle.
- Model thinking aloud about what you wonder about worms! Read Garden Wigglers by Nancy Loewen

Sing to the tune of "I'm a Little Teapot"

I'm a little wiggle worm, watch me go.
I can wiggle fast, or very, very slow.
I wiggle all around and then I go,
Back into the ground to the home I know!

At this yell "*It's dirt!*" each time we finish singing.

L Introduce the learning area experiences that will be open
- Share learning area experiences with story problems for dramatic play that need solved.
- Identify number of children who can occupy space at a time

E Excuse children to go to their choices after washing their hands. Ask each to repeat where they are going and what they are going to do when they get there. Turn on the background music that symbolizes running water in a creek!

Learning Area Choices (Small Group Time)

Materials and Resources (List)

- Circle Time: *The Garden Wiggler*
- Dramatic Play: telephone, signage, cart with signage of different fish for sale, Worms for Sale sign, pencils, paper, fishy smell oil, Fish market aprons
- Writing: telephone, paper, pencils, Worm Farm signage
- Art: tray with 4–6 earthworms/dirt to observe; paper/sharpies to draw worms, ruler, paper
- Math: scale, paper, pencil
- Manipulative: timer, pipe cleaners cut into 4-inch lengths, metal cans with holes punched in plastic lids
- STEM: copies of picture cards to label
- Science/Cooking: Oreos®, instant pudding, gummy worms, cups, spoons
- Technology: computer with internet connection, paper, pencil
- Sensory: 2 dozen worms, earth (dirt), gloves, goggles

Dramatic Play Area: Fish Market: The fish market has run out of worms to feed the live fish and sell to fisher-people who need some NOW. The workers are busy answering the phone and taking care of customers buying fish. Customers are buying lots of fish. Each needs to be weighed and receipts written. Cost for a small fish is $1 per pound and big fish are $5 per pound. (5–6 spaces) Story Problem *Social Studies, Math, Literacy, Language*

Writing Area: Worm Farm: The telephone is ringing off the hook to fill orders for dozens of earthworms and nightcrawlers. The owner needs to write up the orders and have the workers go out and dig for worms and deliver them to the local fish market' ASAP. (3–4 spaces) Story Problem *Language, Literacy, Science, Math*

Art Area: Draw worms from observing them on the table tray. Compare/measure earthworms and nightcrawlers, and caption your drawing. (4 spaces) *Science, Literacy, Art*

Math Area: Weighing worms on postage scale—what in the classroom weighs the same as a three worms? Predict and chart different items! (1–2 spaces) *Math, Literacy*

Manipulative Area: Transfer worms to new homes. Using 4-inch cut pipe cleaners and tweezers transfer worms to new can. Add a timer and challenge pairs to how many can be transferred in 3 minutes! (1–2 spaces) *Math, Physical*

Continued
Goodheart-Willcox Publisher

Figure 8.19 Daily learning plan. Does this plan support all learning domains? Explain your answer.

Block Area: Create worm homes. Encourage children to name the different mounds using paper and popsicle sticks to advertise. (4–6 spaces) *Art, Engineering*

Science/Cooking: Dirt pudding (teacher assistance) Note: All children can participate if desired at alternating times or have their dirt pudding made for them. (4 spaces) *Science, Math*

STEM Area: Using picture cards, investigate and illustrate anatomy of the worm. (4 spaces) *Science*

Technology: Observe a live webcam on nightcrawlers and research the longest worm in the world by doing an internet search with the teacher. Encourage children to make a pictorial journal page of what they learned. (1–2 spaces) *Technology, Science, Literacy*

Sensory Area: Using gloves, dig and measure worms from tub by placing them on a paper and using a tape measure to record how long they are. Measure 3 worms. (4 spaces) *Math, Science, Literacy*

Outdoor Area: Plant a garden plot with soil and add flower seeds. (6–8 spaces) *Science*

Closing Circle Time (Large Group Time)

Following the 5- to 10-minute clean-up transition signal, children return to the closing circle, excited to share their learning. The opening circle book (or a different one) is (re)read and plans revisited to see if they were met. Using turn and share, children are encouraged to turn to the children next to them and provide learning experience details. A teaser of what to expect the next day is shared: a special guest is scheduled: a worm expert with many specimens.

Reflection

- Worm Day 1 was a hit! Note to self: Try to connect worms to a topic of interest next year!
- The connection from dramatic play to the writing center did not work well…too chaotic—children at the writing area wanted to join in the dramatic play area and havoc ensued.
- Dirt pudding was a hit and was easily manageable. ALL of the children were interested and were able to make their own dirt pudding, and we ate dessert at the closing circle for a strong ending! Reminder to inform families in case they have concerns. Stress the difference between eating fake dirt and real dirt!
- Biggest area to play at was the sensory table, engaged children! I need to offer an alternate, a Rubbermaid® tub, next time to accommodate additional spaces. Probably try to keep this sensory open all week.
- Second-biggest interest was the experiences that Outcome 1 connected to draw/compare/measure worms.
- Assessment tools yielded strong connections to the learning outcomes.

Notes

Work with occupational therapist for additional AT devices for CC; provide additional small group and pairing learning opportunities for entire class. Create a word wall to post new vocabulary as we learn new words.

Goodheart-Willcox Publisher

Figure 8.19 Daily learning plan. Does this plan support all learning domains? Explain your answer.

development, mostly because children were interested in fish. In the example followed in this chapter, the teacher became a researcher with the children and their families. The new and exciting discoveries children made reflect the connections between integration and child development and will provide lasting memories for the children.

The reflection might be done on the back of the template, or by adding notes jotted down when the learning was happening, or as a narrative to support later decisions regarding teaching and learning. Attaching this to the template will provide solid documentation to use as a reflection, and keeping notes will provide valuable feedback for future decisions the teacher makes as part of the reflection process.

 Checkpoint

- ☐ Identify the various learning components found in the learning plan. Specify how each component supports the teacher's instruction and the child's learning.
- ☐ What is a DAP topic of learning from your area? What would you want to include in the learning plan?

Chapter 8 Review and Assessment

Chapter Summary

8.1 Explain how the characteristics of the learner factor into planning learning experiences.

- Learning experiences that connect to a child's funds of knowledge create strong learning opportunities.
- A child's disposition develops into life skills and is part of part of every child's development.
- Agency supports independence and should be part of the daily learning environment.
- When the learning environment fosters a sense of belonging, purpose, and agency, motivation for learning is increased.

8.2 Describe the importance of schedules.

- The infant-toddler daily schedule is designed to be open-ended.
- The preschool age daily schedule is flexible, designed to incorporate teachable moments. Offering a framework to provide young children a needed structure is built into the schedule.
- The K–3 daily primary structure is mostly inflexible.
- A weekly schedule provides spaced events for families to plan around and an opportunity to include children's interests in planning.

8.3 Identify the different instructional strategies, including transitions, scaffolding, and learning formats/group sizes.

- Transitions should be intentional and used throughout the day to support shifts that occur; they should include verbal and nonverbal cues, wait time, and planning ahead.
- Scaffolding is important because it provides the teacher with opportunities to teach children how to complete tasks at their level of need.
- Learning formats provide a flexible framework within which teachers can teach and children can learn. These formats include grouping arrangements of one-on-one, pairing, small and large groups.

8.4 Explain the CIRCLE acronym and the importance of circle time in the daily learning plan.

- Emphasis on the six key CIRCLE elements provides an easy-to-remember sequence for the teacher when planning.
- Well-planned circles provide an opportunity to build a strong community of learners.
- Learning areas are built from circle time—the first meeting of the day.
- Engagement strategies during circle time include turn and share, props, and story problems to build engaging experiences.

8.5 Discuss key elements of the learning areas and experiences during the implementation phase in the daily learning plan.

- The active learning time that follows circle time shares the many different learning areas set up for children's participation.
- The closing circle provides an opportunity for the class to rejoin one another and revisit the learning that occurred.
- Including a section to identify materials and resources needed helps the teacher in planning.
- At the end of the day, it is important to complete a reflection to guide future learning experiences.

8.6 Outline the components and strategies of a completed daily learning plan.
- The responsibilities relating to creating developmentally appropriate curriculum go far beyond simply filling out a daily learning plan template.
- Families, colleagues, and community involvement enhance learning.

For Further Reflection

1. Create two experiences that build on positive dispositions to promote imagination and curiosity.
2. What additional instructional strategies can be used to keep all children engaged when forming a line or waiting is necessary?
3. Establishing an open snack time is one way to eliminate one transition. Contemplate how you might offer open snacks and support independence while teaching children to be aware of thirst and hunger and listening to their own bodies. Would you embrace this? Why or why not?
4. Circle time provides an opportunity to explore new ideas as a group and build community. In what ways can you encourage a passive child to interact in large group discussions? Is this an important consideration?
5. Some children engage in routines with no problems. Other children have a harder time. What are some things you can do to help all children make the most of daily routines?
6. Story problems are designed to provide a starting point when children arrive at specific learning areas. Identify a topic of interest and story problem you might create to incite interest.
7. Imagine a learning area that incites excitement and exceeds the spaces it is designed to hold. How would you support multiple children's interests that is DAP during the active learning time?
8. Evaluation of the daily learning plan is a form of assessment and is completed by the teacher at the end of each day. How might the children's perspective of learning and engagement be included in closing the loop?

Recall and Application

1. The term *funds of knowledge* is best described as the ____.
   A. way the brain collects information and disseminates it
   B. knowledge and expertise children have based on their own life
   C. many ways to collect ideas and sell them
   D. practice of studying other parts of the world during social studies
2. **True or False.** Dispositions are frequent and voluntary habits of thinking.
3. Agency is best defined as a child's ____.
   A. connection to a specific part of the community
   B. ability to make art that defines their inner spirit
   C. ability to make and act upon choices
   D. desire to be part of a social group
4. Scaffolding is ____.
   A. the creation of a framework of walls in the block area
   B. the provision of support to practice a skill
   C. the rotation of learning areas
   D. a block-building phase

5. **True or False.** Circle time is the foundation of the day.

6. Story problems are used to ____.
   A. understand different number equations that need to be solved
   B. deepen learning by identifying a problem that needs to be solved
   C. create group books with different endings
   D. help children relax before naptime

7. **True or False.** Closing circle is a time to revisit the learning that occurred during the active learning phase.

Integrating the Learning

PART 3

Chapter 9 Academic Disciplines
Chapter 10 Infant-Toddler Integrated Curriculum
Chapter 11 Preschool Integrated Curriculum
Chapter 12 Kindergarten through Third Grade Integrated Curriculum

9 CHAPTER

Academic Disciplines

Learning Outcomes

After studying this chapter, you will be able to:

9.1 Define integration of academic disciplines.

9.2 Identify the practices teachers use to support a child's understanding of literacy and language.

9.3 Interpret the academic disciplines in the acronym STEM.

9.4 Summarize the importance of teaching social studies to young children.

9.5 List the different elements within creative arts.

9.6 Explain how teaching physical education and health helps in the formation of curriculum.

Standards Covered in This Chapter

NAEYC
5a, 5b, 5c

DAP
Principle 7; Guidelines 4, 5

Image credit: SDI Productions/E+ via Getty Images

Firdous

Dedy Andrianto/E+ via Getty Images

SNAPSHOT

Firdous is the director of a large early childhood center and interviews many families looking for high-quality programs as part of her work. Today she is meeting with the Townsend family whose twins have just turned four years old. The twins' education is very important to them. The Townsends are aware of the play-versus-academics debate, and they want to discuss the matter with the director to ensure a good fit. The parents begin by sharing their hopes and dreams for their children, and then ask about the program's play and learning philosophy.

Firdous shares the program's foundation of supporting play and explains that because a program uses playful ways to increase children's learning does not mean the curriculum is not also academically challenging or fun. On the contrary, the approach reflects that the program is appropriate for the young learner. The director goes on to share examples of developmentally appropriate practices (DAP) across many discipline areas. Firdous reminds herself that it is important to have this conversation with every family that contacts the school.

Give It Some Thought

1. What are important ways to communicate with parents the importance of play in their child's development and learning during their early years?
2. Provide an example of how play can benefit a child's development and learning during preschool.

Key Terms

agility
balance
bilingual
concept
coordination
epistemology
fiction
fine motor skills
force
gross motor skills
invented spelling

math talk
metacognition
morphology
muscular endurance
orthography
nonfiction
phoneme
phonemic awareness
phonograms
phonology
piggyback

playworld
process-focused art
product-focused art
readers' theater
semantics
skill
spatial awareness
syntax
teacher-led
visual arts

Introduction

When families consider placing their children in preschool or other early childhood settings, they have a lot to consider. In the United States, the cost of childcare and early childhood education is a determining factor for many families. On average, US families spend $8,355 per child for year-round child care (Leonhardt 2021). The cost of early care is an investment that will provide a child with a strong foundation for learning. Most important is that society needs to understand the value of this investment and work toward making quality early learning possible for all families. High-quality preschool programs for 3- to 4-year-olds are foundational for developing skills, well-being, and learning, and future success, particularly for those from low-income households (Annie E. Casey Foundation 2021).

The debate between play and academics in early childhood education is an important consideration that can be a determining factor when choosing an early childhood program. Children learn best in play-based experiences, as described in Chapter 2. Advocates of play-based learning argue that play supports a child's social, emotional, and cognitive skills in a natural and engaging way. The debate often centers around finding a balance between the two while ensuring that children have opportunities for both play-based and academic experiences.

Strategies include incorporating academic concepts into play-based experiences by proving hands-on learning opportunities and using a curriculum that includes play-based and academically focused activities to ensure that children have both types of learning experiences. Creating a schedule with unstructured play allows for exploration and supports all domains of development: social, emotional, physical, and cognitive.

9.1 Disciplines

This chapter explores each of the academic discipline areas delineated in Standard 5 of the NAEYC Professional Standards and Competencies. NAEYC defines *competence* in academic discipline within the early childhood curriculum as having knowledge of a discipline's central concepts, methods, tools of inquiry, and structure, including resources. The academic disciplines covered in this chapter are language and literacy; science, technology, engineering, and mathematics (STEM); social studies; creative arts; and physical education/health.

Early childhood educators should have knowledge of the content of the academic disciplines (language and literacy, the arts, mathematics, social studies, science, technology and engineering, and physical education) and of the pedagogical methods for teaching each discipline. It is important for educators to understand pedagogical content knowledge—how young children learn in each discipline—and how to use this knowledge to support young children's learning in each content area (NAEYC, *Professional Standards and Competencies*, 2020).

Additionally, early childhood educators should make a career-long commitment to continuously updating and expanding their own knowledge and skills. The professional standards in content areas provide guidelines for competency and continuing education. Teachers should rely on verifiable resources for their own development, for curriculum development, and for selection of materials for young children in the academic disciplines (NAEYC, *Professional Standards and Competencies*, 2020).

Concepts and Skills

Using their everyday interactions, children build understanding and attribute meaning to people and to their environment, and thus concept development emerges (Illinois ELP 2021). While infants use their senses, physical exploration, and interactions with caregivers to receive information about their physical environment, preschool-age and older children develop concepts in their minds when they link together ideas, experiences, and interactions to build more complex lines of thought. It is important to note that concept development and level of intelligence are not linked. Concept development occurs naturally, and all people develop concepts based on their experiences. Intelligence is the ability to acquire and apply knowledge.

There is a difference between a concept and a skill:

- A *concept* is a mental representation, image, or idea of tangible and concrete objects (a bed, a ball, an ice cream cone), and intangible ideas and feelings that do not have a physical presence.
- A *skill* is the ability to do something intentional (tying a shoe, kicking a ball) (**Figure 9.1**).

Teachers use concept development in the classroom to guide and promote child curiosity and enhance learning by building critical thinking skills.

Integrating Academic Disciplines

Learning experiences (indoors and outdoors) reflect multiple domains: physical, social, emotional, and cognitive. They also include discipline areas, including language, literacy, mathematics, social studies, science, technology, art, music, physical education, and health, integrated across domains and discipline areas.

The teacher plans daily experiences to engage each child's interests in all discipline areas while striving to remain aware of the teacher's own and any systemic gender, ability, racial, ethnic, or religious biases. Early childhood teachers actively reflects on their practice, and how to improve each child's learning opportunities. Young children learn best by direct, engaging, hands-on learning, where they eagerly embrace all types of learning experiences (**Figure 9.2**).

"Having a written curriculum based on children's interests and experiences that is aligned with applicable early learning standards provides a valuable and organized framework through which teachers can ensure that the children's learning experiences are consistent with the program's goals" (NAEYC, *DAP*, 2020). Research in developmentally appropriate practice confirms that even young children understand and can learn more challenging topics. The idea that young children are not ready for academic subject matter is a misunderstanding of developmentally appropriate practice.

Recognizing the value of integrating academic disciplines into the curriculum includes maintaining an intentional approach. For example, when designing a learning experience on making connections to a literacy standard, the teacher may also make connections to a standard from a different discipline. This approach is typically more meaningful than teaching academic disciplines separately and requires going beyond superficial connections. It involves *epistemology*, or the theory of knowledge, and "making rich connections among developmental domains and disciplines, allowing each to retain its core conceptual, procedural, and epistemological structures" (Clements & Sarama 2023).

Ilike/Shutterstock.com

Figure 9.1 Tying shoelaces is an example of a skill. Provide an example of a concept.

Hispanolistic/E+ via Getty Images

Figure 9.2 Learning experiences should engage the learner. Do you think this activity is engaging for the children? Why or why not?

 **Checkpoint**

☐ Explain integration of academic disciplines.

☐ How does a concept differ from a skill?

9.2 Language and Literacy Discipline

Language and literacy learning (oral and written, expressive and receptive) arises out of the earliest gestures and vocalizations and evolve into babbling, single words, scribbling, book manipulation, and dramatic play—are all common during the infant-toddler stages of development (NAEYC 2020). Additionally, exposing infants to **bilingual** (learning two languages) experiences has been shown to increase cognitive abilities, especially problem-solving. According to researcher Patricia Kuhl at the University of Washington, "Science indicates that babies' brains are the best learning machines ever created, and that infants' learning is time sensitive. Their brains will never be better at learning a second language than they are between 0 and 3 years of age" (Bach 2017).

Language and literacy learning are foundational not just for success in school but for lifelong success in communication, self-expression, understanding of the perspectives of others, socialization, self-regulation, and citizenship. Early childhood educators know that listening, speaking, reading, writing, storytelling, and visual representation of information are all methods of developing and applying language and literacy knowledge and skills (**Figure 9.3**).

THE TEACHER'S LENS

Early childhood educators are aware that oral language, print, and storytelling are both similar and different across cultures. They become familiar with literature from multiple cultures and find ways to implement that literature into their curriculum (NAEYC, *Professional Standards and Competencies,* 2021).

Children formulate a concept development of writing, with progressive understanding that the symbols and characters they are seeing have meaning and directionality, and that letters represent sounds. Eventually children understand that when letters are put together in the correct order they compose words, even if the children cannot write a sentence themselves. Opportunities to integrate connections to letter symbols and sounds into a child's day are plentiful if a teacher steps back and considers the possibilities. Letter symbols and sounds can be integrated as the teacher defines the words on a page as they are read aloud without focusing only on a single letter, such as letter of the week. Other methods of integration do not require any additional input from the teacher at all, when children:

- create their own storybooks with illustrations.
- are encouraged to write "kindness" notes to place in each other's cubbies.
- write or draw in a journal/notebook.
- sing songs that use their names using common tunes.
- listen to oral stories and draw what they are imagining.
- are allowed to include grandparents in your literacy program (**Figure 9.4**)

English Language Development

Teachers help children develop skills for reading and writing proficiency when learning English (Block 2015). *Emergent* (early) language and literacy is a required area

Seventyfour/iStock via Getty Images

Figure 9.3 Early literacy experiences include reading books with caregivers. What props can be used when reading a book to children? Share an example.

STOP AND THINK

Imagine being asked to comprehend the following: 你好 or Привет or שלום when your home language is English. Can you tell the teacher what they mean? This is what it is like for a child when first learning about letters. Identify ways to support early literacy as part of your practice.

of study for early childhood education and is explored in greater detail in those courses. The English language can be complex and sometimes confusing, with many different rules about how words are spelled and pronounced. Knowledge of the following concepts provide the teacher with a foundation to support a child's understanding of literacy and the English language.

- *Semantics* refers to what a word means.
- *Syntax* is how the words are arranged in a sentence.
- *Morphology* is the study of where words come from.
- *Phonology* is the speech sound (or sounds) a letter or series of letters makes.
- *Phonemic awareness* is the ability to hear and manipulate sounds in spoken words.
- *Phonograms* are common groups of letters that represent the same sounds, such as –*ight* in bright, light, sight, and so on.

Sometimes sounds are represented in more than one way. The word *of* is often spelled "uv" by a beginning writer. This is because these two **phonemes**, or small sounds in a word that distinguish one word from another, can be spelled as "uv"—it is only through experience that *of* will be spelled correctly. It is recommended that teachers begin teaching phonograms, such as *-ight, –er, -all,* and *–tch*, in kindergarten. Attempting to teach phonograms any earlier than this can interfere with children's process of learning individual letters and their sounds.

Selecting literature to read and integrate into different parts of the curriculum and learning areas requires an understanding of **nonfiction** (informational) and **fiction** (at this age level, usually picture books). Nonfiction books are about real events and people, while fiction includes stories in which animals talk or the story is made up. Both are valuable additions to the classroom. Being familiar with classics as well as new offerings is important to provide rich listening and reading experiences. Use technology to listen to stories aloud by visiting sites such as YouTube®, which provides almost any children's book ever written in audio form, and in most languages. Try searching for your favorite book in a foreign language to find out for yourself.

Ginny Harmelink

Figure 9.4 This man is reading a book to his grandchildren. What is the benefit of inviting grandparents into an early learning environment?

Bilingual Language Development

Teachers should understand how bilingual language develops in young children, including the strong role a child's home language plays as a foundation for academic success. Teachers must also be aware of the damaging effects of a child's home language loss. Myths and truths surrounding bilingual language development are described in **Figure 9.5**. There are many teaching strategies to increase English language comprehension among children who speak different languages, while at the same time respecting their cultures.

Figure 9.5 Facts and errors surrounding bilingual language development. *What is one truth that surprises you?*

Bilingual Language Development: Myths and Facts	
Myth	Truth
Associating each language with a different person is the only way to prevent bilingual children from "confusion and mental fatigue."	There is no evidence that bilingual children are confused by early bilingualism, and the cognitive benefits associated with bilingualism run counter to the notion of "mental fatigue." (De Houwer 2007)
Bilingual preschoolers struggle to understand others' perspectives, thoughts, desires, and intentions.	Bilingual preschoolers have better skills than monolinguals in understanding others' perspectives, thoughts, desires, and intentions (Kovács 2012).
When bilingual children mix words from two languages (*code mixing*) in the same sentence it reflects confusion.	Rather than being a sign of confusion, code mixing can be seen as a path of least resistance: a sign of bilingual children's ingenuity (Pearson 2008).

Goodheart-Willcox Publisher

Invented Spelling

Fundamental knowledge about English orthography enables early childhood educators to effectively respond to young children's reading and writing. **Orthography** is the conventional spelling of a language according to standard usage that includes phonemic and phonological awareness, vocabulary, grammar, and reading (dictionary). However, teachers know that the most valuable early literacy writing skill to encourage in the early years is not knowledge of the alphabet, but ***invented spelling***, which is spellings children create based on their own phonetic understanding (**Figure 9.6**). With time and practice, invented spellings progressively become similar to actual word spellings (Ouellette & Sénéchal 2017).

A child's ability to use invented spelling in early writing is the best indicator of future success as a reader (Ouellette & Sénéchal 2017). Regardless of their existing vocabulary, alphabetic knowledge, or word reading skills, over time children who use invented spelling develop stronger reading. Opportunities to encourage invented spelling include using children's names as a catalyst to learn letters, which promotes early literacy (Kirk & Clark 2005; McNair 2007). The act of handwriting supports the act of thinking.

Ginny Harmelink

Figure 9.6 Invented spelling example: "You are invited to my party" *Why is it important for teachers to support invented spelling in the early years?*

✓ Checkpoint

☐ Identify the practices teachers use when teaching early literacy.

☐ How can teachers ensure that they are providing equal support for language learners in more than one language?

9.3 Science-Technology-Engineering-Mathematics (STEM) Discipline

STEM is the acronym for four closely connected areas of learning: science, technology, engineering, and mathematics. The STEM acronym was first introduced in 2001 by the US National Science Foundation as the disciplines became increasingly integrated. This focus arose out of the perceived underperformance of US students and the need to have a trained workforce to compete in the global economy.

When including the arts as part of teaching STEM concepts, the acronym becomes STEAM. Many believe that adding the arts aids in the process of critical thinking skills and innovation (**Figure 9.7**). Students with a strong foundation in arts perform better academically as a whole (Leeuwen 2018). Many trades require art concepts along with science and technology, such as designing automobiles or houses. Art inclusion is a strong addition to the curriculum.

Early childhood educators have embraced experiences devoted to the STEM disciplines. Integrating these disciplines creates experiences that provide expansive possibilities for challenging the young mind. Teachers use open-ended questions to encourage STEM habits of mind and facilitate learning, and then support children as they investigate for themselves. Withholding adult-supplied answers supports a child's curiosity and requires teacher intention and practice. One of a teacher's most important roles in encouraging children's STEM capacities is to help children persist when they might otherwise give up.

STEM habits of mind include critical thinking and persistence. These habits transfer to real world applications for the learner. Problem solving and other higher-level skills transfer across all domains of development when children have opportunities to practice framing questions, collecting data, and solving scientific problems (McClure et al. 2017).

Jose carlos Cerdeno/iStock via Getty Images

Figure 9.7 Students with a strong foundation in the arts perform better academically as a whole. What is a skill that can be improved through art education?

Science

Although the capacity of young children to grasp and construct conceptual learning is underestimated by many adults, including teachers, current research indicates that young children have the capacity and the ability to use the practices of reasoning and inquiry (NRC 2012). Children have the capacity to learn core scientific ideas and practices such as making predictions and testing those predictions as they connect with and understand natural and human-made phenomena in the early years. Creating learning environments that provide the opportunities to experience different outcomes fosters science skills and builds conceptual understanding. Young children are capable of sustained focus on science explorations (NRC). Effective science investigations can deeply engage young children for extended periods, beyond a single activity or session.

Scientific inquiry develops naturally in young children as they observe, ask questions, and explore their world. Early childhood educators understand the importance of providing opportunities for very young children to engage in sensory exploration of their environments and of supporting their progressive ability to ask questions, engage in scientific practices, collect data, think critically, solve problems, share ideas, and reflect on their findings (NAEYC, *Professional Standards and Competencies*, 2020).

It is important for children to learn skills that support their scientific thinking. Learning how to work through a problem-solving process in a logical fashion is essential to growth in understanding. A child's emerging scientific skills include observing, asking questions, making predictions, testing ideas, documenting data, and communicating thoughts (Larm & Jaros 2021). Providing access to STEM-related projects and scientific thinking to all children is important. In one example, robotics have been shown to generate interest in STEM-related studies among children with disabilities (Lindsay et al. 2020).

Figure 9.8 This child is looking at skin cells using a microscope. *How can looking at things more closely encourage children to ask questions?*

Educator familiarity with materials that help young children conduct experiments, represent theories and ideas, document findings, and build confidence is important for developing positive attitudes toward science. Effective science investigations include up-close looks when possible, using demonstrations or authentic experiences. There are three main questions to ask when learning about science:

- What's there?
- How does it work?
- How did it come to be this way?

For example, looking at skin cells under a microscope can spark children's curiosity and challenge them to look at their skin in a whole new way (**Figure 9.8**).

Technology and Engineering

During the earliest years, infants and toddlers should primarily be interacting with people. However, they also need the freedom to explore, manipulate, and test everything in the environment using all their senses. Most children are drawn to pushbutton switches and controls. Electronic toys should be selected based on their dynamic and interactive nature, combined with the opportunities they provide to engage in conversations with adults.

When infants are distressed, they need the comfort of a caring adult, not the distraction of an electronic toy. There is little research to indicate that infants and toddlers can learn from watching videos. However, when used appropriately, technology can be an active and engaging tool for younger children. While adults are actively engaged and conversing with the child, digital devices may provide comforting access to images of their families and friends. Through technology, they may be introduced to animals, the world around them, and a wide range of images of people. Digital tools offer infants and toddlers an opportunity to encounter things they might not otherwise encounter (for example, photos of children from other countries).

Technology and engineering concepts are explored as young children play with cause and effect, fitting and stacking, dropping, pushing, and pulling physical objects (**Figure 9.9**). Young children's abilities and understanding develop further as they build increasingly complex structures, perhaps experimenting with balance, stability, speed, and inclines in the block corner, dramatic play area, and outdoors. Early childhood educators model the use of science and the language of mathematics to develop children's imaginations, curiosity, and wonder. They know that asking good questions and encouraging young children to express and test their own ideas is often more effective than providing direct information and "right" answers. Knowing that young children have been born into the digital age, educators use technology inside and outside of the classroom and supervise young children in the appropriate use of technology in play and in learning (NAEYC, *Professional Standards and Competencies*, 2020).

Today many children are consuming technology unsupervised or without adult supports from an early age. Studies completed in the U.S. show that 97 percent of children under 4 have used mobile devices, and most started using them before the age of one. By age 4, half of children have their own television and three-quarters have their own mobile device (Kabali et al. 2015).

Figure 9.9 This infant is not dropping the toy to be naughty—he is conducting a science experiment. *How might this action teach this baby about cause and effect?*

As of the most recent published U.S. data from 2014, children aged 2 and under had an increase in screen time, averaging 3 hours, 3 minutes a day, up from 1 hour, 19 minutes in 1997. Three- to 5-year-olds' screen time average 2 hours, 28 minutes a day during that time period in the same study (Chen & Adler 2019). Adults can share technology time as they would when sharing a book, introducing new vocabulary, exploring and conversing about what is being played with to avoid passive screen time.

Technology in the Classroom

For teachers, technology can be integral for their classroom's efficiency. Teachers can incorporate assistive technologies that may be appropriate for children with special needs and/or developmental delays. Using mediators or supported assistive tools can assist teachers in assuring all students are involved. Teachers can record children's stories about their drawings or their play and document their progress.

E-books are available online in any language and teachers can use one-on-one time with individual children to search for photos of people, places, plants, and the world. Teachers can empower children by showing them how to save content to use later in classroom newsletters or to enhance their work.

Video-conferencing to communicate with families and children in other places is common. Though this interaction does not have the same qualities as in-person interactions, it does provide an opportunity to connect with a variety of peoples otherwise not attainable.

The K–3rd grade school years include learning to read, write, and calculate. Children are exposed to many electronic tools including digital and touch screens to further study more in-depth concepts. Digital technologies are part of the developing child's world, and during K–3rd grade, children should learn to be a producer as well as consumer of technology.

Teachers build critical thinking skills as they encourage the children to become proficient in using digital tools as part of their learning experiences. Providing cameras, scanners, recorders, and editing software as tools helps children connect with other children in the community and around the world. Using virtual connections and blogs can help expand the child's sense of social connections and the broader world. Teachers can make electronic recordings of children's stories or to document their progress in the different discipline areas they are learning about. These will become strong evidence of learning, and heirlooms for the family as their child grows.

Preschool Engineering

How is engineering introduced to a group of preschoolers? "Scientific inquiry involves the formulation of a question that can be answered through investigation, while engineering design involves the formulation of a problem that can be solved through design" (NGSS Lead States 2013). The children will become researchers as they define a problem and produce a solution. Being an engineer at the preschool level involves children learning to identify the problem, imagine possible solutions, and design and create final products to model and test (Blank 2018). Engineering with preschool age children is easily captured as they are naturally curious about the world (**Figure 9.10**).

Building and taking apart items encourages children to think out of the box, see how things work, and use parts to create new items. Opportunities to put on the hat of an engineer can also be found in the blocks or art area, where architectural elements are found. Engineering can be embedded across the curriculum.

skyneser/E+ via Getty Images

Figure 9.10 These children are working together to build something. What is a benefit of supporting engineering skills as early as preschool?

Mathematics

The development of pre-numeracy and early numeracy skills, including recognizing shapes and numbers, ordering, sorting, classifying, and sequencing, is the beginning of mathematics. Teachers' math talk correlates to the growth of preschoolers' conventional mathematical knowledge over the school year (Klibanoff et al. 2006). This underscores the importance of using mathematical language, called *math talk*. But what is math talk?

Math talk describes the teacher's use of math-specific language in everyday talking. For example, a teacher might mention that the small hand on the clock is pointed to 9 so it is time to start Circle time. The teacher's use of specific mathematical language can include intentional learning experiences such as counting sets of items, comparing differences of two or more sets (more, less), or conducting calculations, such as "If we have ten children in class and one more arrives, how many do we have now?" Math-specific language can include pointing out page numbers when reading: "Let's turn to page three and see what happens next." The teacher may provide spontaneous mathematical comments about quantity during the day, such as, "Look, there are three birds on the tree limb!" Math talk has the potential to promote mathematical language and concepts in a natural way. Developing math skills at an early age positively impacts a child's cognitive, social/emotional, physical, and literacy development. Concepts such as problem solving, number sense, and spatial relationships help students gain a basic understanding of math to build upon.

Early Math

Children are natural mathematicians; for example, they enjoy sorting items by different sizes and shapes. Math can be a natural part of every academic discipline, integrated into most learning experiences. As children experiment with spatial awareness, measurement, and problem solving, they are exploring math concepts. Early math involves children making sense of the world around them, although when dealing with an abstract subject, the first step is for children to make connections to concrete elements. Open-ended and playful discovery fosters problem solving in real situations (as shown in **Figure 9.6**). Math in early learning is not rote learning of discrete facts, drills, or worksheets with one correct answer. Because the situations are meaningful, children can gain a deeper understanding of number, quantity, size, patterning, and data management (Grossman 2012).

On walks, children compare shapes; they play with quantity at the dramatic play area supermarket; at cleanup time, they may sort materials into correct bins; while creating in the art area, they are exploring patterns and shapes. They play with telling time when imagining what comes next or learning what a beat is in music, and dance patterns to match the tune. Many familiar children's songs, stories, and poems contain mathematical concepts, if the teacher is prepared to focus on them. Some musical examples with math talk include "The Three Little Pigs" and "Hickory, Dickory, Dock." The concept of fractions can be introduced using music (quarter, half, whole) for the older child. Playing guessing games of how many do you think are in the jar can make connections to quantity and numbers.

From the age of 2 or so, children are learning and expressing the language and grammar of counting. They memorize the first ten or so counting words and build on that to learn the rules for counting and naming the higher numbers (Ginsburg et al. 2008). Everyday mathematics is both concrete and abstract; counting is foundational, but math encompasses so much more. Looking around the environment, a skilled teacher will introduce what a number looks like when written (concrete) by pointing to one on the clock and then may sing a counting song (abstract). This helps the child make connections.

Early childhood educators have a grasp of mathematical language and know the importance of modeling it and of fostering positive mathematical dispositions in each child. They know the expected trajectories of mathematical learning, including common misconceptions and errors. They use this knowledge to select scaffolding strategies to advance children's development of mathematical understanding. They know that children learn mathematical thinking through active exploration, conversations, observation, and manipulation of both natural and manufactured materials. They know that play, stories, music, dance, and visual arts can all be used to illustrate and discuss mathematical ideas in ways that are more meaningful to young children than isolated, abstract exercises. (NAEYC, *Professional Standards and Competencies*, 2020).

Math Symbolism

The hardest form of language for children to learn is the written symbols of mathematics, such as 3, +, – or =. Children in preschool learn about counting, that number symbols have names and written numeral symbols. This age understands counting and one-to-one correspondence and can compare different seats of objects (Helmenstein 2019) but a focus on learning math concepts in a rote fashion would not be developmentally appropriate. Make connections to the child and elements in their world to make the abstract math concepts come alive using math talk (**Figure 9.11**).

AlenaPaulus/E+ via Getty Images

Figure 9.11 This child is holding a physical representation of the number "2." Why is using math symbolism an effective learning technique?

Addition and subtraction can be introduced, along with how to write equations (if there is interest) and a common learning expectation in the early grades. Both can be integrated as a natural element when written on a flip chart or other means to show examples. Measuring and data collection includes learning to classify, sort, and group objects, a common learning experience in the early years. Geometry knowledge begins with identifying different shapes and how they are part of the world.

Teachers create environments in the classroom that children recognize as being specific to a discipline area. For example, a well-stocked math area includes objects found in nature as well as purchased materials such as Geoboards® (**Figure 9.12**). Creating a rich math area helps young children acclimate to the concepts of math and fosters belief in themselves as capable mathematicians. Research demonstrates that young children enjoy learning math and can learn far more than was previously assumed—without using flashcards or worksheets. Teachers can encourage the use of math tools and strategies throughout the classroom. Children might use a set of plastic links to measure their buildings in the block area, use play money to pay for a train ticket in the dramatic play area, and use rulers to measure the growth of spring bulbs in the science area. (Carpenter et al. 2016).

When math is incorporated into all areas of the curriculum, children can see themselves as able mathematicians, applying their skills in a number of ways. Early childhood educators bring both their grasp of mathematical language and the terminology to foster positive mathematical dispositions to each child. Early childhood math skills give children confidence and positively impact later school and life. Teacher awareness of the expected progress of mathematical learning supports scaffolding strategies to advance children's development.

NAEYC developed the following high-quality teaching strategies for mathematics education for 3- to 6-year-old children:

- Enhance children's natural interest in mathematics and their disposition to use it to make sense of their physical and social worlds.

Lithiumphoto/Shutterstock

Figure 9.12 This child is using a Geoboard®. How do you think a Geoboard might help teach math concepts?

- Build on children's experience and knowledge, including their family, linguistic, cultural, and community backgrounds; their individual approaches to learning; and their informal knowledge.
- Base mathematics curriculum and teaching practices on knowledge of young children's cognitive, linguistic, physical, and social emotional development.
- Use curriculum and teaching practices that strengthen children's problem-solving and reasoning processes as well as representing, communicating, and connecting mathematical ideas.
- Ensure that the curriculum is coherent and compatible with known relationships and sequences of important mathematical ideas.
- Provide for children's deep and sustained interaction with key mathematical ideas.
- Integrate mathematics with other activities, and other activities with mathematics.
- Provide ample time, materials, and teacher support for children to engage in play, a context in which they explore and manipulate mathematical ideas with keen interest.
- Actively introduce mathematical concepts, methods, and language through a range of appropriate experiences and teaching strategies.
- Support children's learning by thoughtfully and continually assessing all children's mathematical knowledge, skills, and strategies (Early Childhood Mathematics, NAEYC/NCTM Joint Position Statement).

 **Checkpoint**

☐ What are some examples of STEM early learning experiences?

☐ How can engineering education in the early years be inclusive for all children, regardless of background and ability?

9.4 Social Studies Discipline

Social studies focuses on helping children understand their place in the world. As their world expands from their own home environment to the classroom and beyond, children's sense of their place within the world also grows. Group environments enable them to develop, practice, and apply life skills such as cooperation, sharing, and following rules.

Through exposure to a range of cultures, ages, abilities, languages, and family structures, the concept of differences and similarities among people takes shape. The teacher shows each child how differences become a strength when everyone is valued and respected. For example, being sensitive to different family grouping dynamics begins with starting a classroom letter addressed to family rather than parents. Another example is adding each child's home language to labels placed around the room and in curriculum materials (**Figure 9.13**).

Young children have a natural interest in the world, exhibited through their play and daily activities. Early childhood educators can provide experiences related to social studies to cultivate young children's diverse skills and abilities. These experiences cultivate many life skills and capacities, such as forming opinions, identifying and solving problems, negotiating roles, perceiving diversity and inequality, and making connections to the consequences of their behaviors.

There are many opportunities in a day to include understanding the social world by employing developmentally appropriate strategies, materials, and activities using pretend play, games, stories, field trips,

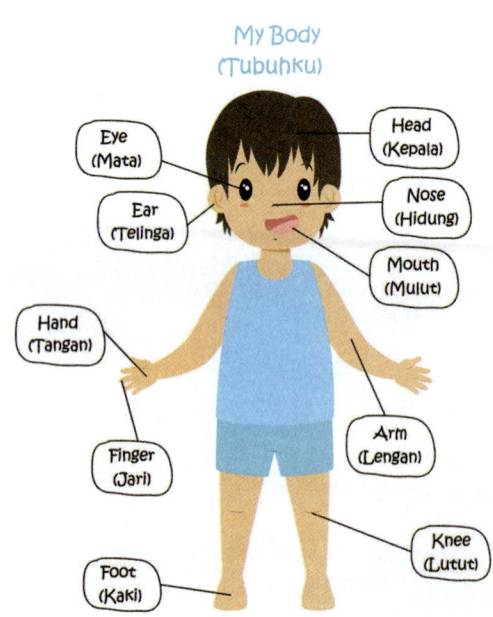

AzuAya25/iStock via Getty Images

Figure 9.13 This body chart is labeled with both English and Indonesian words. *How might this chart be beneficial in a classroom in which some students speak both English and Indonesian?*

and the arts to increase a young child's knowledge. Social studies is a vital part of the early childhood curriculum that integrates well with all other disciplines and is especially easy to embed into the dramatic play area. Children's early experiences shape their mindsets as "citizens of their classroom, their schools, and of the larger community" (Mardell 2011).

Social studies is a science used to understand and think about the past, the present, and the future and about self and identity in society, place, and time. Early childhood educators know that the field of social studies includes history, geography, civics, economics, anthropology, archeology, and psychology.—They also know that all of these areas of inquiry contribute to the ability to make meaning of experiences, think about civic affairs, and make informed decisions as members of a group or of society (NAEYC, *Professional Standards and Competencies*, 2020).

Early Social Studies Development

Beginning with the gradual understanding of self and others, and of individuals and families, the core concepts of what will become social studies take shape from birth. Social studies knowledge will grow to include neighborhoods and communities, time and patterns of time, past/present/future, and an awareness of one's own and others' cultures. Over time, these encounters with the concepts of social studies develop into the intentional study of history, geography, economics, civics, and politics.

Geography as a discipline consists of three major categories: physical, environmental, and human geography. Physical geography is the study of the natural environment, including the landscape and the planet. Human geography is the study of the relationship between humans and their natural environment (National Geographic n.d.), which includes societies, cultures, and economies. Environmental geography is considered the bridge between the two and focuses on how people impact the environment through use, protection, and harm (**Figure 9.14**).

In preschool and early primary classrooms, geography learning is often focused on activities that build skills, such as mapmaking. Other collaborative efforts, such as recycling, volunteering, and interacting with community members, can be part of the child's

Early Social Studies: Concepts of Physical, Environmental, and Human Geography

Physical Geography: Where We Live	Environmental Geography: The Bridge	Human Geography: How We Live and the Concept of Time
• What is Earth? • Where do you live? • Are you near an ocean or desert? Near mountains or prairies? • What are the weather and seasons like? • What animals live in your area? • How do people move from one place to another today? How did they move around 100 years ago? • What is a map, and how can it help us?	• How can we respect and care for our world? • What do people do that is good for the environment? • How do people reuse and recycle? • What do people do that harms the environment?	• How do things and people change over time? • How do we measure time? • How do we talk about time? • How do we talk about the past, present, and future (using terms such as "this morning," "after lunch," and "tomorrow")? • Who are the people in your family? What do they do? • How do you make and keep a friend? • What are the jobs of people in our community?

Figure 9.14 Early social studies concepts. Why is it important for teachers to introduce these concepts in the early childhood years?

Goodheart-Willcox Publisher

early engagement as a member of a caring society. Providing dramatic play props and encouraging pretend play allow the young child to experiment with themes that relate to the family, classroom, community and the larger society. When early childhood educators nurture these values and promote these types of experiences, young children are better prepared for the larger world (Maine Department of Education 2015).

Cultivating understanding of differences and commonalities within a community requires exposure to various cultures, ages, abilities, languages, and family structures. Social studies concepts are central to children's expanding awareness of relationships between people and the environment. Teachers look for ways to explore different geographic aspects of social studies and embed them into the curriculum.

Physical geography in the classroom can be supported by learning about maps and where people live. Making connections to different animals that live in the area and introducing historical events allow children to identify and appreciate where they come from. Investigating how different parts of the world experience different weather patterns is often a new learning experience that can be implemented in the dramatic play or art area (**Figure 9.15**).

Reusing and recycling materials are part of environmental geography and a bridge between physical and human geography. Learning experiences can include taping signs on boxes to create a classroom recycling center near the trash can. Observing Earth Day with planned learning experiences that support the Earth provides insights into how one person can make a difference for all people. Teaching children to respect the Earth is a major tenet of social studies (**Figure 9.16**).

Human geography is often described as providing children with a sense of place, which extends to a sense of belonging. That sense of belonging impacts children's social and emotional development, which is an essential aspect of school readiness (Epstein 2009). Note that space is different from place; *space* is location, whereas *place* describes human attachment to specific locations (Cresswell 2013).

Learning experiences might include learning about the numbers that make up a child's address, where the child feels at home, which is the child's sense of place. Going on neighborhood walks and sketching the different trees or plants also provides children with valuable opportunities to make connections to their own place in the world. The areas they are part of become part of who they are and include who was here before them and who may come after. A sense of time is often explored in the early years and is also part of human geography.

Children develop cognitive skills and begin to understand the world around them through these early geography experiences, such as moving around and through spaces, and direct experiences with the objects in the surroundings. These experiences are the foundation for understanding their sense of place. As result, children see that their sense of place is influenced by the experiences they have had and the thoroughness of their education (Brilliante & Mankiw 2015).

Sergey Novikov/Shutterstock.com

Figure 9.15 These children are learning about weather concepts in the art area. What is another way to teach weather concepts?

Liderina/iStock via Getty Images Plus

Figure 9.16 Globes present an opportunity to reinforce social studies lessons. What concepts can children learn by studying a globe?

Teacher Training in Social Studies

Part of the early childhood educator's training should be social studies-specific professional development, including guidance on how to cultivate bias-free and discrimination-free communities when teaching social studies to young learners. This is another area in which educators underestimate the capacity of young children to form opinions and feel engaged in the cultural and civic life of a community. Without appropriate education, both new and experienced teachers may fail to see social studies as a priority for young children. Further, educators without social studies-specific training will lack confidence in teaching social studies effectively.

Education and continuing professional development experiences need to emphasize developing the teachers' repertoire of practices, materials, and resources for building positive social studies attitudes and dispositions. The result will be educators who value the contributions of young children as citizens who enrich their communities (socialstudies.org).

Checkpoint

☐ What is an example of sense of place?

☐ Provide experiences that reflect physical, environmental, and human geography taught to early learners.

9.5 Creative Arts Discipline

Teachers know that creative and skillful expression and appreciation of the arts begin to develop at birth and continue to grow throughout the early years, evolving from melodic babbling to singing, and from scribbling to drawing. Educators observe the developing child move from bouncing to dancing, and from pretend play to dramatic performances, script writing, and characterization. A recent study presents evidence that a substantial increase in art educational experiences has measurable impacts on students' academic, social, and emotional outcomes (Kisida & Bowen 2019). This applies not only to early education but through adolescence, supporting a lifetime of valuing the arts.

The arts—music, creative movement, dance, drama, and visual arts—are primary media for human communication, inquiry, and insight. Educators understand that each of the arts has its own set of basic elements, such as rhythm, beat, expression, character, energy, color, balance, and harmony. They are familiar with a variety of materials and tools in each of the arts and with the diverse styles and purposes of the arts across cultures. Educators know that engagement with the arts includes both self-expression and appreciation of art created by others. They value engagement in the arts as a way to express, communicate, and reflect upon self and others and upon culture, language, family, community, and history (NAEYC, *Professional Standards and Competencies*, 2020).

There are many opportunities to engage children with diverse art media. In the early childhood classroom, displaying art at the child's eye level provides many opportunities for conversation while the children enjoy artistic talents. For example, simply suggesting that children in the classroom pose like a dancer or pretend to be an artist holding a palette and brush can connect the children's imagination and bodies to an art experience.

As in other areas, it is important for teachers to be trained in a range of materials, techniques, and strategies to encourage children's engagement in and enjoyment of the arts. Teachers and schools have historically recognized the arts as a supporting discipline across the curriculum, especially as young children develop competence in language, literacy, mathematics, social studies, and science (Kisida & Bowen 2019). It is sometimes necessary to identify ways to explain the value of the creative arts to a skeptical family. Providing articles that inform the family of how creative arts can make a beneficial difference may help the family understand their value in other academic disciplines.

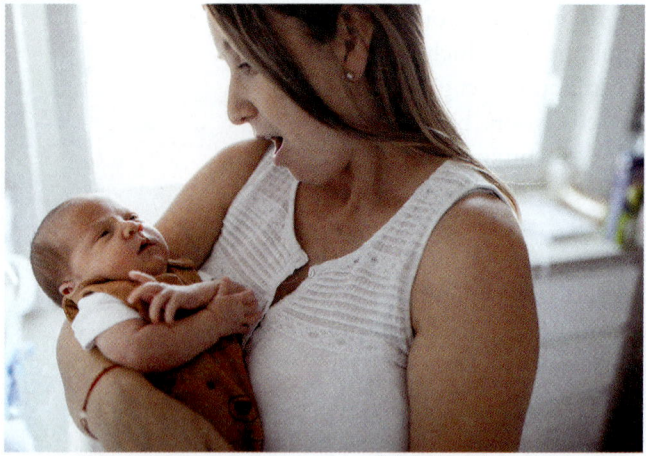

Figure 9.17 This caregiver is soothing this baby by singing a song. In what new ways will this baby utilize music in toddlerhood?

Music/Movement

Music and movement are important in the life of a child. As children grow and develop, music and movement support self-regulation skills, which help them cope with daily life events. A child's awareness of music begins very early—some researchers even say it begins in utero—and studies suggest that infant-toddlers are comforted by quiet singing (**Figure 9.17**) (Corbiel et al. 2013). As toddlers grow, they experiment with their own language and learn to use their bodies in new ways--stomping feet to the beat or clapping to a tune (McElroy 2013). Preschoolers are great composers who love to make up songs, sing, and move to musical beats. They love to hear their voices recorded and played back, and this presents another way to use technology to increase learning. Spontaneously singing silly songs adds another layer of fun to their learning. Joyful, playful, and appealing music and movement activities are central to an early learning program.

Music

Although some teachers avoid integrating music in their classrooms because they presume they need specific skills to use music as a teaching tool, there are multiple ways to implement music in the classroom that do not require any training (Alegria 2017). Integrating music enhances every discipline taught (Sarrazin n.d.). Social studies activities benefit from having music as a lens to teach about cultural traditions and historical events. Consider the topic "shoes" and the connections to melodies like "These Boots Are Made for Walking" or "New Shoes, New Shoes." Many songs include counting, which can help children understand math concepts. In the early grades, changing instruments yet playing the same song can help teach patterns.

Science can benefit from songs like "Dem Bones" to teach about the skeletal system or "Five Green Frogs Sitting on a Log" to teach about amphibians. Music makes a strong contribution when paired with science topics. Literacy improves when children pick up on the patterns and rhymes in the lyrics of songs. Young children have an easier time remembering words when the words are tied to a melody. Music and words go together naturally. The language of music and movement is full of new vocabulary words, such as *tempo*, *rhythm*, and *locomotor*.

Figure 9.18 This child's teachers are playing along to the music the child is making. How does music help children learn?

Strumming and humming along are two simple activities that make connections between music and the brain and are an important part of a music curriculum (Gersema 2016) (**Figure 9.18**). Teaching children how to piggyback a song is a method the teacher can return to again and again. **Piggyback** songs are common tunes with new words added. An example using "Twinkle, Twinkle Little Star" might look like this:

"Baby, Baby, I see you
Smiling, smiling at what I do.
Pick me up, hug me tight
You are just a shining light!"

Including musical notation integrates math and literacy as they are certainly a different language. Provide simple charts to introduce musical concepts when teaching to further enrich the learning experience and introduce clapping to a beat. Clapping games not only teach children coordination and rhythm, but they are also engaging.

Teachers may explore several different genres of music—for example, zydeco, hip-hop, classical, and rock 'n' roll. Instruments from around the world can be placed in the music area to practice making sounds and improvising the music children hear. Musical instruments are often found at yard sales and can be purchased inexpensively. Ask families if they have any old instruments they might donate to the classroom.

Movement

A child's growing physical awareness and excitement about the world are enhanced by movement, dance, and active play. Dance moves combine regional music and movement. Tango, square dancing, flamenco, country swing, tap, and twist are a few of the better-known dances; children may also connect to the macarena and call-out songs such as "YMCA." Using movement and motions along with music helps transfer information to students' long-term memory (Foxwell 2022).

Encourage families to put on different types of music and move to the beat with their baby in their arms and dance together. Tell them to change their actions to match the mood and beat of the music. Young children like going from being on the floor to way up high, as well as swaying, dipping, gliding, and bouncing.

Playing music and dancing when doing simple activities engages the children (**Figure 9.19**). The preschool-age child is often adept at learning new dance moves and is a fully engaged participant. Research indicates a positive relationship between movement and learning, as well as movement and retention (zerotothree.org). The use of movement in the classroom is a cognitive strategy to strengthen learning, improve memory and retrieval, and enhance learner motivation and morale (Jensen 2009).

Studies using brain scans of children suggest that children learn best when they are active. Neurons in the brain respond better to information when combined with movement. These studies show that the brain uses the same connections to move as it does to process reading, writing, and math (Stevens-Smith 2016). Through movement, the child is developing neurological foundations for problem solving, creativity, and the development of language. Creating opportunities for children to move engages all ages in the classroom. Section 9.6 contains more information about the benefits of physical education and health.

Drama

Not surprisingly, all the major theories of human development give special attention to the role of pretend play in the growth and socialization of young children. The most common form of drama in the early childhood classroom is child-led dramatic play that occurs in the dramatic play learning area. The freeform drama that children create together has been a mainstay of the early childhood curriculum for more than a century (Paley 1993). Teachers in the past set the stage for play by providing space, materials, and time; then they observed children's play to learn about their development and mediated the children's disagreements. An alternative role is ***teacher-led*** dramatic play, in which the teacher can be viewed as an improvisational collaborator.

Research on *responsive teaching* (teachers listen to children and enhance and expand on their ideas) found that contrary to long-held assumptions, teachers are less disruptive to play when they participate as coplayers than when they remain in the role of helpful adult. In her study of

Linderina/iStock Getty Images

Figure 9.19 Even very young toddlers can dance. How does movement help keep children engaged?

toddler and preschool classrooms, Carrie Lobman found a similarity between responsive teaching and techniques used by improvisational actors and comedians (Lobman et al. 2015).

In teacher-led creative drama, the work of practitioner-researchers Vivian Paley and Gunilla Lindqvist represent two ends of the spectrum. In Paley's case, the children's own stories are the content for the dramatizations and all the actors are children, whereas Lindqvist's approach draws on children's literature for content and includes the teacher as performer.

Vivian Paley

Vivian Paley found that by observing and acknowledging children's fantasy play stories, helping put the stories into a narrative form, and encouraging children to dramatize them created a classroom environment for drama that stemmed from the children's own life and experiences. Children dictate their stories to a teacher/scribe. The dictated scripts are then performed by a large cast of their classmates (including roles such as family pets to accommodate as many children as possible in the dramatization), theatrically heightening the importance of the children's own words. Through the retelling and dramatization of their imagined or life stories, children's words and perspectives are heard, performed, and appreciated, creating a significant and meaningful experience (Paley 1993).

Gunilla Lindqvist

Gunilla Lindqvist's creative drama pedagogy, called *playworlds*, is based on teacher-led dramatizations of children's literature. Lindqvist (1995) defines the term **playworld** as a dramatic experience initiated by teachers and shared by teachers and students. The playworld is established by a set piece or prop that is relevant to a specific story, or by the presence of a teacher who plays a character from the literature (**Figure 9.20**).

A distinctive feature of most playworlds is their length—the dramatization continues over multiple days or even weeks. This collaborative endeavor results in a meaningful experience that supports aesthetic, intellectual, social, and emotional transformations in adults and children (Marjanovic-Shane et al. 2011).

Readers' Theater

Readers' theater is a style of theater, without props, costumes, or scenery, in which the actors read directly from a script rather than memorizing lines. This form of creative drama is also known as *story theater* or *theater of the mind*. Increasingly, reader's theater has become a learning strategy, with children in a performance space, reading from a prepared text (Moran 2006). Readers' theater is a useful literacy tool in primary grade classrooms, invoking untapped dramatic skills within the context of literacy instruction.

FatCamera/E+ via Getty Images

Figure 9.20 Playworld. Name a story and prop around which you can imagine creating a playworld?

Visual Arts

Visual arts can be product- or process-focused and are a valuable component of the creative arts discipline used for practice, observation, and learning. Visual arts can take on many forms, both two-dimensional and three dimensional, and include electronic art, painting, drawing, sculpting, digital work, and printmaking. Digitally generated art can also be two- or three-dimensional, as well as time-based (video, animation, or audio).

Product-Focused Art

Product-focused art is structured around instructions and has a right or wrong result. The child begins the project knowing what the results should look like. A successful outcome depends on how well the child follows the directions. An example is a teacher-created sample that all the children copy to paint the same thing. Product-focused art typically requires defined skills and techniques for successful completion (educationalplaycare.com). This type of art is beneficial for practice of fine motor skills in activities such as cutting in a straight, curved ,or angled line. Product-focused art can also be a useful approach to teach about specific shapes, colors, and other physical characteristics.

Process-Focused Art

Process-focused art is an open-ended project that provides an opportunity for self-expression through art creation. In process-focused art, the created object is based on the child's discovery and creativeness (**Figure 9.21**).

Process-focused art experiments share the following characteristics:

- The process has no step-by-step instructions.
- Children have no sample to follow.
- There is no right or wrong way or answer.
- The focus is on the experience.
- The goal is exploration of techniques, tools, and materials.
- Each child's outcome is unique and original.
- The experience is relaxing or calming.
- The process and creation are the children's own.
- The experience is entirely the child's choice.

Process-focused art encourages the practice of fine motor skills. Children can practice with scissors, squeeze bottles of paint, or glue. Process-focused art is about playful investigation and discovery. As a result, the child is focused on creativity while gaining confidence to explore and experiment. Process-focused art also provides many opportunities for solving problems (educationalplaycare.com).

Observing Art: A Museum Field Trip

Art is a subject that can be valued equally as an observer. On a field trip, children can explore the experience as observers and delve into what the art is saying to them. The visual world is often thought of as the first language for children. The visual world is the foundation for the Reggio Emilia philosophy (see Chapter 3, "Curricula and Approaches").

Metacognition

In the preschool years, focus on making connections that are as authentic as possible. Engaging children in thinking about why they think what they think is called **metacognition**, and it is another area in which learning occurs. For example, a learning experience can integrate math, art, and social studies when you ask whether a crown is light or heavy. Is the weight due to the size of the object (larger objects are heavy and smaller objects are light) or to the materials (a crown made of feathers is lighter than a crown made of metal).

Young children have a capacity to look carefully and often notice details missed by adults. How can educators guide children to construct meaning from what they see? Children make sense of their world though interactions with their environment and develop knowledge from direct experiences with objects. This connection between experience and

Submitted by Deb Lawrence

Figure 9.21 An outdoor play space at an early learning center in Dalian, China. Identify two indoor activities that can also occur outside.

REAL-WORLD CLASSROOM

The class is going on a field trip to the Ogden Museum of Southern Art in New Orleans. Field trips offer opportunities for a range of learning, from new experiences to increasing literacy skills (Shaffer 2011). In the Ogden Museum project, young children learn about the museum through activities that encourage them to look carefully at paintings or sculptures and imagine the life of the artist or subject, which creates a framework for response and interpretation. Art experiences are easily associated with the physical as well as the cognitive and social-emotional domain.

The preschool teacher offers the children a basket of tools and materials that are used by an artist: a piece of canvas, a palette, a brush, a sculpting tool, clay, and found objects. The children carefully examine these objects and wonder about their use.

Walking through the galleries leads to discussions and discovery related to the objects in the basket. The theme of the trip is "chairs." The journey begins with a reading from a classic children's book, *Peter's Chair*, by Ezra Jack Keats. In the gallery, each child takes a turn sitting on a small wooden chair similar to the one in the nearby painting, "Portrait of Robert Gould," which features a young boy sitting in a chair. The children are encouraged to consider: What is the boy thinking about? How does he feel? As each child takes a turn in the role of the boy in the chair, the children look closely at the painting to get the exact pose and facial expression.

This experience also focuses on the items in the painting. Thinking about chairs continues with the Ogden Museum's exhibition, which explores the design and making of chairs. After the exhibition, the children use popsicle sticks and found materials to create their own chairs. These experiences combine children's literature and objects to support the children's interpretation of paintings.

thinking fosters understanding (Shaffer 2011). Take time to explore a painting or listen to a tune using open-ended questions. Ask:

- What is happening in the painting?
- What is the background of the music playing? How does the tune make you feel?

These types of conversations build on the experience by encouraging the children to make connections. Children readily offer opinions when asked about the relationship between the touchable object and the work of art. When looking at a Degas painting of dancers, for example, children tend to talk about much more than just a dancer.

Bringing attention to the senses supports the creation of new meanings as the child explores a collection of objects gathered by the teacher. When children discover the hard toe of the ballet shoe and look at a Degas dancer on her toes, they form a connection between the firmness of the shoe and the dancer's ability to stand on her toes (*en pointe*). It is this special pair of shoes that enables the dancer to perform, and most children would have no connection to how the dancer is able to do this. Viewing images of other styles of dance or choreography can lead to conversations and curiosity about other types of shoes that might be required.

The child's thought process is important. Advance knowledge of what a crown feels like is unimportant. The thought process and educator-guided open dialogue that explores the child's thinking allow children to create meaning from the situation. The children will learn more about historical eras and the stories around n later school grades when their study of history begins.

 **Checkpoint**

☐ How can an early childhood teacher educate a child's family on the importance of art education?

☐ Identify the difference between process-focused and product-focused art.

9.6 Physical Education: Health Discipline

Physical activity, physical education, health, and safety are essential parts of the curriculum for the well-being of young children. Early childhood educators know that across disciplines, young children learn by doing. Active physical play helps brain development (Kris 2019) and is a primary means for children to learn about themselves, others, and the world. Teachers design physical activities, making sure they support children who need accommodations or modifications to ensure that the activities are inclusive for each child. Physical education and health, while not academic disciplines, are interwoven into all learning experiences and learning areas and are commonly covered by early education teachers.

Physical education, health, and safety have significant effects on children's current and future quality of life. Early childhood educators understand development of fine and gross motor skills; neurological development, including executive function; and the relationship of nutrition and physical activity to cognitive, physical, social, and emotional well-being in young children. They know that the components of physical education include spatial awareness, agility, balance, coordination, endurance, and force. They know about health and safety guidelines and practices for the prevention and management of common illnesses, diseases, and injuries, and they know how to promote wellness in adults and children.

Early childhood educators are able to find and stay current in health, safety, and risk management standards and guidelines for young children from birth through age 8. They are familiar with the processes that help children develop fundamental competence, skillful practices, and physical fitness, including participation in games and sports, aquatics, dance and rhythmic activities, fitness activities, outdoor pursuits, and individual performance activities (NAEYC, *Professional Standards and Competencies*, 2020).

Physical Activity

Early childhood educators understand the learning progression of movement skills beginning with infancy (roll, crawl, creep) through preschool (hop, throw, bend, stretch) to the early grades (engagement in organized and more complex team and individual sports and dance). These skills can be the foundation for enjoying physical activity throughout the lifespan.

All young children strive to be competent in physical skills and to explore the body's capacity for movement. Through movement, children express feelings, manipulate objects, and learn about their world. They take pleasure in their physical achievements while also enjoying movement for its own sake. Physical activity is an important component of life at all stages, and it takes many forms during early childhood (Becker et al. 2014) (**Figure 9.22**).

The brain is activated during physical activity. A rapidly growing body of work suggests that time spent engaged in physical activity is related not only to a healthier body but also to a healthier mind (Hillman et al. 2008).

Antonio_Diaz/iStock via Getty Images

Figure 9.22 These children are enjoying nutritious food.
How can healthy choices be part of your curriculum?

Fine and Gross Motor Skills Movement

Developing and performing *gross motor skills* (large muscle development) is directly related to movement and physical fitness. Children who feel confident moving will keep moving; they will engage in dancing, jumping rope, and swinging at the playground. Children who are less confident may avoid exploring movement. These children are less likely to take part in after-school games or to climb the jungle gym during outdoor time. Deficient exercise habits tend to continue through childhood into adulthood, so a physically inactive child is likely to grow up to be an inactive adult. Given the health hazards related to activity intolerance—obesity, heart disease, diabetes, and other risks—teaching children motor skills is just as important as teaching language skills (Pica 2008).

Opportunities to practice using *fine motor skills* (small muscle development) and gross motor skills need to be an intentional part of planning learning experiences, with accommodations made for children who require them. *Spatial awareness* (ability to explore surroundings), *agility* (speed at performing a task), *balance* and *coordination* (ability to maintain a controlled body position), *muscular endurance* (ability to maintain posture), and *force* (a push or pull that alters, or tends to alter, the state of motion of a body) are all elements of physical education utilized by an informed teacher.

Planning Movement Opportunities

Early childhood teachers plan opportunities for children to move. Movement and play support the child's developing physical fitness, movement skills, and increasing knowledge of movement concepts. Educator-led physical activities and unstructured physical activities are part of the intentional planning to facilitate the maximum participation of all children. Recess and outdoor play are as important as lunch for the developing child.

The informed teacher knows the importance of healthy daily routines and daily practice. Young children need to practice their basic skills and habits related to active and quiet times, meals, rest, and transitions in early childhood settings. Educators are familiar with young children's need for movement, play, rest, safety, along with nutrition. Family and cultural variations in practices are supported and incorporated in the daily planning.

Nutrition

Integrating healthy routines around nutrition includes offering experiences that are inclusive of learning experiences about food, from farm to plate, and supports children's learning through play. It also helps them better understand where their food comes from and the role it plays in their lives and their communities, from planting to harvesting (USDA n.d.). For example, a child who has the opportunity to plant tomatoes in an outdoor classroom might meet a local tomato farmer, go on a field trip to the grocery store to see where tomatoes are sold, and later learn from a chef how tomatoes are prepared. The many authentic experiences will provide a deeper knowledge of and appreciation for food as a precious resource.

The farm-to-early-care-and-education initiative is built around educating young children using the farm-to-table concept. The initiative draws from a variety of strategies to encourage the use of local foods in meals and snacks, creating gardening opportunities for children, and incorporating food-based learning activities that promote health and well-being (USDA n.d.). Teachers can provide developmentally effective ways to help all children think about, express, and reflect on their exercise and nutrition choices. Creating and supporting engaging classroom nutrition and outdoor physical play experiences that are appropriate for each age and child will have lifelong benefits.

 **Checkpoint**

- ☐ Explain the experiences that support fine motor development.
- ☐ Provide examples of gross motor development inside and outside the classroom.

Chapter 9 Review and Assessment

Chapter Summary

9.1 Define integration of academic disciplines.
- The academic disciplines are based on the NAEYC Professional Standards and Competencies.
- Each discipline is highlighted to provide a beginning understanding of the impetus to learn more.

9.2 Identify the practices teachers use to support a child's understanding of literacy and language.
- Language and literacy, including new vocabulary, are emphasized.
- Importance of writing, reading, and communication are stressed.
- The importance of writing is emphasized in a developmentally appropriate manner.
- Invented writing shares the connections children make between symbols and their sounds.

9.3 Interpret the academic disciplines in the acronym STEM.
- Research shows the importance of integrating math, electronics, technology, and science across all learning experiences.
- Emphases on the need for early childhood teachers to embrace and use math and science language is stressed.
- Studies cite the need for active math and science language to be used daily when working with young children.

9.4 Summarize the importance of teaching social studies to young children.
- Social studies from an early childhood lens exposes the many elements of sense of place in the world.
- Embedding strong community awareness provides a foundation for all studies.
- The concept of recycling is an example of a social studies application in the dramatic play area.

9.5 List the different elements within creative arts.
- Creative arts provide enrichment and creativity and include topics from music to movement and from drama to visual arts.
- A strong connection to integrating the arts supports efforts integration easily.
- Child-led, as well as teacher-led, creative drama across the ages is explored.

9.6 Explain how teaching physical education and health helps in the formation of curriculum.
- Physical education and health are important elements when planning curriculum and may include sections on farm-to-table learning and healthy eating habits.

For Further Review

1. Summarize ways to engage families in supporting their children's language and literacy at the different ages of development.
2. Creating times to read aloud to children is important. Design a reading nook and think about what might be included to make it attractive to a child. What elements would you include?
3. Identify a STEM learning experience that will actively engage a family without requiring any supplies.

4. Create a list of ways that technology is present in the classroom. How might the uses for a 3-year-old child differ from the uses for a 7-year-old child?
5. Create a map of your classroom or neighborhood using symbols to indicate areas of interest. Include a key to show what each symbol represents while integrating a mathematical concept.
6. What cultures are represented in your community? What organizations could connect with your early childhood class as guest speakers or field trip destinations (multicultural societies, fine arts groups, service clubs, senior citizens, museums)?
7. Select a well-known painting to show a group of preschoolers. What concrete item can you introduce to help the children make connections between art and science? Art and math? Art and social studies? Art and health?
8. Providing props in the dramatic area to create a mood is one way to support dramatic play. Consider each of the five senses. What could you include around a topic of interest focused on celebrations? How would you integrate literacy into your plan?
9. "Dem Bones" was adopted as a spiritual/gospel song and therefore connects to cultural and historical topics related to Black American histories. Research a favorite tune to connect social studies to enhance your teaching.
10. Identify different outdoor ground mediums and how each contribute to physical education. Which ones would you choose your classroom outdoor area?
11. Connect with food commonly grown in your area to develop learning experiences for the classroom around nutrition.

Recall and Application

1. A child learning to write their name is an example of a ____.
   A. skill
   B. concept
   C. domain
   D. gross-motor activity
2. **True or False.** Epistemology is the theory of humans.
3. Morphology is ____.
   A. what a word means
   B. the study of where words come from
   C. the ability to hear and manipulate phonemes
   D. how words are arranged in a sentence
4. Semantics is ____.
   A. what a word means
   B. the study of where words come from
   C. the ability to hear and manipulate phonemes
   D. how words are arranged in a sentence
5. Syntax is ____.
   A. what a word means
   B. the study of where words come from
   C. the ability to hear and manipulate phonemes
   D. how words are arranged in a sentence
6. Phonemic awareness is ____.
   A. what a word means
   B. the study of where words come from
   C. the ability to hear and manipulate phonemes
   D. how words are arranged in a sentence

7. Invented spelling ____.
   A. represents memorization of sight letters
   B. reflects alphabetic knowledge
   C. supports the act of thinking
   D. decreases phonemic awareness

8. **True or False.** Mixing two languages in a sentence creates confusion.

9. A learning experience that explores how the stars are formed in the sky is an example of a ____ experience.
   A. social studies
   B. drama
   C. language and literacy
   D. STEM

10. Calling out numbers in the classroom and identifying sequencing of numbers in the classroom are both examples of ____.
    A. math talk
    B. early math
    C. preschool engineering
    D. addition

11. **True or False.** Social studies is the study of people and how they relate to the world.

12. Environmental geography includes ____.
    A. jobs present in the community
    B. animals that live in the area
    C. how people measure time
    D. different recycling practices

13. Human geography is the study of ____.
    A. the relationship between humans and their natural environment
    B. maps and where people live
    C. how people measure time
    D. where animals live

14. **True or False.** Readers' theater includes props, costumes, and scenery.

15. **True or False.** The creative arts are focused primarily on painting.

16. An example of process-focused art is a ____.
    A. craft project with instructions
    B. paint-by-number set
    C. fingerpainting activity
    D. coloring book page

17. Tying a bow is an example of a ____ skill.
    A. gross motor
    B. fine motor
    C. math symbolism
    D. preschool engineering

18. Jumping is an example of a ____ skill.
    A. gross motor
    B. fine motor
    C. math symbolism
    D. preschool engineering

19. **True or False.** Healthy nutrition is an important aspect of the overall curriculum.

CHAPTER 10

Infant-Toddler Integrated Curriculum

Learning Outcomes

After studying this chapter, you will be able to:

10.1 Describe infant-toddler curriculum components.

10.2 Create an infant-toddler curriculum using your state standards and guidelines.

10.3 Identify infant-toddler resources that support children in the physical, cognitive, and social-emotional domains.

Standards Covered in This Chapter

NAEYC

1a, 1b, 1c, 1d, 2a, 2b, 3d, 4a, 4b, 4c, 4a, 5b, 5c, 6c

DAP

Guidelines 1, 2;
Principles 1, 2, 3, 4, 5, 6, 7, 8

Image credit: Prostock-Studio/iStock via Getty Images Plus

Machinel-leadz/iStock via Getty Images Plus

SNAPSHOT

Ms. Shenique

The Sandbox Early Learning Center offers care for infants through pre-kindergarten. The infant and toddler rooms are located in a quiet corner of the building, away from the older children. The center understands that the youngest children require different spaces and care than the pre-kindergarten children. The lead teacher at the center, Ms. Shenique, welcomes families as they enter each day, knowing the important role she plays as a resource for the family. A new baby is joining the infant-toddler room today, and her parents are anxious about leaving her at the center. Ms. Shenique reassures the parents that all will be well and promises to text a picture of their baby to them later in the morning. By doing so, Ms. Shenique is building a rapport with the parents and creating a communication plan. She knows that strong relationships are a key factor when providing care. She also understands the importance of schedules and routines as a type of curriculum for infant and toddlers.

At the infant-toddler stage, learning experiences should be influenced by the children's individual needs and interests. For example, an infant who likes looking at his reflection in a safety mirror should be encouraged and supported in prolonging that activity. Ms. Shenique actively seeks to understand infants' needs and desires by recognizing and responding to their nonverbal cues and by using simple language (NAEYC Early Learning Program Accreditation Standards and Assessment, 2019).

An integrated curriculum builds on existing inter-relationships and implies learning that is synthesized across traditional subject areas. The child's learning experiences are connected and overlapping and designed to be mutually reinforcing. This approach supports the child's ability to transfer their learning to other settings.

Give It Some Thought

1. What are ways a teacher can promote language development in young children? Social-emotional development? Cognitive development? Physical development?

Key Terms

benchmark
cognitive domain
dual language learners
emergent literacy
expressive language
indicators

individualized planning
neural connections
parentese
physical domain
rare words
routines

sensory system
serve-and-return
receptive language
social-emotional domain
strategies
temperament

Introduction

Fostering connections between home and the early childhood classroom is a critical element for the newborn or toddler who is not able to control reactions, body functions, or the effects of the world around them. Providing a place to provide nurturing and responsive connections is a best practice for all ages, but none so much as it is for the youngest learners. Creating learning environments that support the individual child is a common element in the infant-toddler classroom.

Knowing what an infant-toddler should be able to do at each stage of development is important for the family as well as the teacher. The focus of the earliest years is primarily focused on domains of development to provide a solid foundation for future learning and development of every child from every background. Providing a curriculum that is responsive and meets the needs of the individual child is best practice.

STOP AND THINK

As you consider the domains of development covered in this chapter, compare them to your own state's infant-toddler standards and recognize the differences as well as the similarities. Being aware of how other states apply curriculum standards will allow you to make connections that will inform your own curriculum planning.

10.1 Infant-Toddler Curriculum

From birth, children are active learners, taking in and organizing information to create meaning through their relationships, interactions with their environment, and overall experiences (NAEYC, *DAP*, 2020) (**Figure 10.1**). Two main goals of the infant-toddler teacher are to:

- provide support for child-led learning and long-term connections.
- build strong relationships with the family and child.

Even though the learning plans for infants and toddlers are not technically a curriculum, the teachers do plan for and create routines and experiences to promote each child's early development and learning. As a result, the terms *learning plan* and *curriculum* are both used in this chapter. Teacher goals focus on cultivating culturally and linguistically responsive relationships with caregivers and family, and they include children's home languages as much as possible (NAEYC, *DAP*, 2020). The interactions and experiences infants and toddlers have in the first years of life provide the groundwork for later academic development across all subject areas.

When an infant-toddler teacher thinks about learning plans, they must incorporate routines and experiences that will promote domains of development:

- social-emotional
- cognitive
- language-literacy-communication
- physical

Rawpixel/iStock via Getty Images Plus

Figure 10.1 Playing and learning. *How does the teacher in a multi-age classroom model sharing with the youngest learners?*

Five Factors for Infant-Toddler Curriculum Development

Teachers of infants and toddlers focus on how to provide an encouraging social, emotional, physical, and intellectual climate, while at the same time supporting a child's learning to help the child build and sustain positive relationships with adults and other children (Lally 2000). The infant-toddler teacher needs to be aware of five key factors when developing learning plans.

Factor 1

All domains of development overlap and influence the others. Changes in one domain often affect and influence other domains. For example, as children begin to master language skills, they can interact socially and influence others. These experiences increase language development while supporting social, emotional, and cognitive abilities. When children begin to be mobile, progressing from crawling to walking, their curiosity expands as they explore their world in new ways, increasing not only their physical abilities but cognitive abilities as well. If milestones are delayed due to disabilities, the effect on the child is evident. This is why assessment and early intervention are so important (**Figure 10.2**).

Factor 2

There are three stages of infant-toddler development, in approximate age ranges. It is important to recognize the three stages of infant-toddlerhood (these age ranges will vary):

- young infant (generally 0–6 months)
- mobile infant (generally 8–18 months)
- toddler (generally 18–36 months)

Factor 3

The curriculum is built on caring and trusting relationships that promote respect among families, children, and the teachers (**Figure 10.3**). When designing the learning environment, infant-toddler teachers rely on their knowledge of what a child finds meaningful and engaging. Each community of learners has its own unique spaces and experiences based on age, culture, and context. Ensuring that practices are developmentally appropriate for each age group, including those with differing abilities, is essential.

Factor 4

The child's home culture and language are integral to the plan. This in an important factor in the development of a child's self-identity. As a result, the curriculum should be inclusive (Lally 2000).

Factor 5

The plan is designed around the routines of infant and toddler development. These routines should help children learn and grow. Typical infant-toddler **routines** include diapering, feeding, and sleeping. Within these routines there are many opportunities for connecting,

Capuski/E+ via Getty Images

Figure 10.2 Providing opportunities to promote muscle development. Identify two activities to promote gross motor development during the first six months of life.

SDI Production/E+ via Getty Images

Figure 10.3 Respect and trust. What are three ways to build trust between the caregiver and the family?

Figure 10.4 Infant daily snapshot. *Are there additional elements a family may want daily information about besides sleeping, eating, and diapering? What might those be?*

interacting, communicating, and accomplishing tasks in cooperation with one another. Most infant-toddler teachers keep a chart of the child's daily activities to share with the family at the end of the day (**Figure 10.4**).

The Biology of Infant-Toddler Learning

The infant-toddler teacher needs to be knowledgeable on all aspects of teaching and learning for this age group. Understanding the value of a targeted curriculum for the earliest stages of childhood is easy when you consider that the basis for all thought, communication, and learning is established during the first three years of life through neural connections in the brain (NSCDC 2018). **Neural connections,** also called *synapses*, are the pathways in the brain that allow cells to connect to each other.

Sensitive and responsive caregivers are attuned to a young child's signals and needs and provide an environment rich in serve-and-return experiences. **Serve-and-return** interactions are responsive exchanges between children and the people who care for them (**Figure 10.5**). These interactions help children develop in all domains of learning and shape the brain's architecture (The Developing Child 2017). Adults' sensitivity and responsiveness to an infant's babble, cry, or gesture supports the development of neural connections that are essential for budding communication and social skills, including self-regulation.

Without responsive relationships a child's development and well-being are at risk (The Developing Child 2017). Even the most attentive, caring adults can find it challenging to keep children safe. There are events outside of the family to consider, such as war, natural disasters, and community violence. Events within the family that may impact a child include domestic violence, physical or sexual abuse, or the death of a family member. The infant is dependent on the adult, which underscores how important consistent and responsive interactions are to the formation of relationships.

For children who have adverse childhood experiences (ACEs), the interplay of biology and environment has particular implications (NAEYC, *DAP,* 2020) (see Chapter 1, "Developmentally Appropriate Practice (DAP)"). Infants who experience a persistent lack of care can experience chronic stress, which can negatively affect brain development. Furthermore, ACEs may delay or impair the development of thinking, learning, and memory, as well as impair the immune system and the ability to cope with stress (NASEM 2015).

Environment as Curriculum

The infant-toddler classroom is designed with soft materials for flooring to support crawling and provide a cushion for the new walker. Furniture and equipment is designed for very young children to promote exploration, sensory stimulation, and social interaction. The environment contributes to responsive caregiving by providing a space that is spacious and welcoming. Creating places where a parent is able to sit down and relax, or even nurse an infant, is a best practice (**Figure 10.6**).

Figure 10.5 Responsive interactions. *What are ways to encourage serve-and-return interactions?*

Consider the infant-toddler classroom and how you can make connections to each child's family. What props or practices might help create and support strong relationships?

STOP AND THINK

Spaces for play, sleeping, and eating provide a variety of experiences for individual children who will often experience different cycles of awake and sleep in the infant room.

Be wary of safety hazards in the environment. All electrical outlets should be covered with plastic stoppers. Heavy items should not be placed on high shelves. Always be cognizant of what toddlers could possibly reach and pull down onto themselves. Toys with strings or small removeable parts are not appropriate in this area.

Because babies and toddlers are still developing their immune systems—and because they love to put objects in their mouths—sanitation is especially important in the infant-toddler area. Toys should be sanitized after every use. The diapering area should not be adjacent to the eating area, and staff should thoroughly wash their hands after each diaper change. Because crawlers are constantly touching the floor, the floor should be kept as clean as possible at all times.

Routines as Curriculum

The daily schedule in the infant-toddler room is predictable, yet flexible and always responsive to the individual needs of the children. This focus topic guides the curriculum development. Many states require childcare programs to have written daily schedules.

Routines offer opportunities to build relationships that promote attachment and trust for the infant-toddler. Consistent and predictable routines may be a common reaction when they arrive every morning or singing the same tune when diapers are changed. Regular caregiving routines are based on when each child has a need, not by the clock or following a precise schedule. The result of these child-led routines in group care settings are responsive activities that give shape to the day.

Individual Learning Plans for Infants and Toddlers

Unlike preschool curricula, which align learning plans to different academic disciplines and content, the learning that occurs in the first two to three years of life is less content-specific and more fundamental to all learning processes, with direct connections to the domains of development. In the United States, states primarily base their guidelines on the domains of development, although some states include academics within the cognitive domain at the emergent level.

Rather than a curriculum that is designed for an age-group or a classroom, infant and young toddler curricula are often documented in individual plans (Zero to Three 2015). *Individualized planning* for infants and young toddlers is based on the daily schedule and routines. Older toddlers are introduced to more group learning experiences when they are ready. The implementation of experiences that support a child's learning plan is conducted through a process of close observation, documentation, and reflection. Individualized planning refers to tailoring a different plan for each child.

Opportunities and interactions to foster social-emotional, cognitive-language-literacy-communication, and

FatCamera/E+ via Getty Images

Figure 10.6 It is important for an infant area to be relaxed and comfortable. Do you think this environment is developmentally appropriate for infants? Why or why not?

physical growth occur during everyday interactions. **Figure 10.7** and **Figure 10.8** are learning plans created for the different ages. Note how the focus on the individual child during the infant stage expands to group learning with toddlers. Then, in the older toddler room, many academic disciplines are incorporated.

 **Checkpoint**

- Provide a rationale for the importance of routines and flexibility in the infant-toddler room. What are two ways to support both for young infants? For mobile infants? For toddlers?
- Identify how serve-and-return interactions support infant development.

10.2 Curriculum Across Domains and State Lines

The different state standards or guidelines for infant-toddler early learning include common categories that can be used as a point of reference for comparisons. Most states utilize benchmarks, indicators, and strategies as guidance to inform and support the development of the individual child.

Educators use a benchmark to track an individual infant or toddler's progress. A *benchmark* explains key skills and behaviors educators and caregivers want a child to be able to achieve within a given standard. *Indicators* are demonstrations that children have achieved the benchmark. *Strategies* reflect ways to support the individual infant or toddler in achieving benchmarks.

Figure 10.7 Infant lesson plan. *What elements do you find most important?*

NAEYC Criteria
One-to one play: 2e.9, 2e.10, 2e.11
Small group time: 3d.5, 3d.6
Physical development: 2c.1, 2e.11, 3d9
Dramatic play: 2j.7
Art expression: 2a.4, 2j.6, 2j.8
Music expression: 2a.4, 2e.9, 2e.10
Book time: 2e.12
Individualized planning: 1c.6, 3e.8, 3e.9, 3e.11, 3e.12, 3e.14, 3g.7

Arizona Infant-Toddler Early Learning Standards
Teaching Strategies and Objectives for Development and Learning

Activity: Give the infants scarves to dance and move with. Play multiculturally inspired music that is upbeat and encourage the children to dance and move their bodies along with the music. Talk about which country the music is from.	**Activity:** Sing "The Color Song" to the infants. If they are engaged, point to the different colors in the room as you sing. Encourage infants to notice and point along with you.
Activity: Read the book *Goodnight Moon* to the infants. After reading the book, take the infants on a walk around the room to say "goodnight" to all of their belongings.	**Activity:** Practice walking in the sand in the sandbox. Depending on the infants' stage of development, either hold their hands or encourage them to take steps on their own. Talk to them about how the sand feels. How is it different from walking in the classroom?
Activity: In this group activity, go around the room singing the name of each infant. Encourage the infants to clap along and help point to who is next.	**Activity:** Bring out the "Family Board." Point to "mamas" and "dadas." Talk about the other family members in the photos.

Submitted by Sandbox Early Learning Center, Tucson, AZ

Toddler Lesson Plan

Week of: Objective 3: Participates Cooperatively Group Situations. Objective 6: Gross-Motor Manipulative Skills.
Theme: Pets Objective 10: Uses Appropriate Conversational/Communication Skills. Objective 16: Demonstrates Knowledge The Alphabet.

CIRCLE TIME	WRITING OPPORTUNITY	CHILD DIRECTED LEARNING	MANIPULATIVES
2D.3/2D.4/3D.6/3G.9	3D.5/3D.6/3G.9	3D.4/3E.13	2A.2/2F.14/2F.15
Spontaneously identifies a story topic. Tells a story with a beginning, middle, and end with assistance. Provides a description of story characters and setting without assistance. Staff counter bias and build understanding of diversity in ages. Discussions about authority.	Alphabet: Can sing most of the alphabet. Can sing all of the alphabet. Copies words under pictures.	Sets simple goals with help—what to make during art. Teaching staff actively teach children social, communication, and emotional regulation skills. Teaching staff help children manage their behavior by guiding and supporting children to learn to take turns.	Teaching staff support children's competent and self-reliant exploration and use of classroom materials.
DI:3 – DI:4 – DIII:1 – DIII:2 DIII:3 – DIII:4	DI:3 – DI:4 – DIII:1 – DIII:2 DIII:3 – DIII:4	DI:2 – DI:2 – DII:4 – DIII:2 – DIV:3	DII:1 – DII:2 – DII:3 – DII:4 – DIV:2
TSG: 18a. – 18c. – 9a. – 9c.	TSG: 7b. – 16a. – 17b.	TSG: 1a. – 2c. – 8a. – 9b.	TSG: 7a. – 11a. – 11d.
Objective 10: Discussions About Pets. Read: "Bark George", "Rainbow Fish", and "Not Norman".	ABC Puzzles, Alphabet Books, Paper, Crayons, Computer Keyboard	Children Are Free to Select an Activity of Their Choice, Chances to Interact with Peers, Completes a Task, Cleans Up and Then Moves On to Another Task.	Geometric Shape Sorters. Colorama Shape and Color Match. Busy Bugs Color, Counting, and Pattern Matching Game.
SMALL GROUP TIME	**DRAMATIC PLAY**	**SOCIAL INTERACTIONS**	**MATH**
3D.5/3D.6/3G.9	2J.7/2J.11/3D.6/3G.9	2E.13/2E.9/2E.10	2A.4/2F.14/2F.15
Teaching staff talk frequently with children and listen to children with attention and respect. Engage regularly in meaningful and extended conversations with each child.	Role playing, rule making, opportunities to foster positive identity and understanding diversity in family structure. Emphasize spatial vocabulary—on top of, over, under, in, out, bottom below, beside, next to.	Takes a turn when asked. Knows when it is his or her turn. Takes turn with another child without being asked. Teaching staff encourage and recognize children's work and accomplishments.	Shapes: Identifies the circle, square, rectangle and triangle. Sorts objects into sets, matching according to color, shape and size. Opportunity for mastery.
DIII:1 – DIII:2	DI:2 – DI:4 – DII:2 – DII:3 – DIV:1 – DIV:4	DIII:1 – DIII:2	DII:1 – DII:4 – DIV:1 – DIV:4
TSG: 2a. – 10a. – 10b.	TSG: 14b. – 21a. – 29 – 30	TSG: 1b. – 3a. – 3b.	TSG: 13 – 21b.
Objective 3: Sounds on the Farm Listening Game. How Much Do You Weigh? Children Will Have the Opportunity to Get on the Scale and Be Weighed (they can also see how much their peers weigh). Objective 10: Dictation: Do You Have a Pet?	Interacting with Peers. Various Stuffed Animal and Doctors Equipment Added So the Children Can Pretend to Be Veterinarians Taking Care of Pets	Objective 6: Children Plays Ball with a Friend (rolls a ball to a friend/plays catch). Children Greets Friends Upon Arrival.	Three in One Shape Pairing. Hi Ho Cherry-O Counting and Color Matching. Teddy Bears in the Ring Counting and Color Matching.
NATURE & SCIENCE	**MUSIC AREA**	**CLASSROOM ART**	**BLOCKS & ACCESSORIES**
2A.4/2G.8/2G.9/2G.10/2G.11/2H.1/3D.8	2A.4/2E.9/2E.10/2J.10	2A.4/2J.6/2J.8/2J.9/3D.3	2A.2/2F.14/2F.15
Recognize the conditions that create changes in the weather-dark clouds mean rain. Temperature warm, hot, cold, freezing.	Music, instruments and dance from other cultures or a language providing a basis for exploring the elements of different cultures.	Children are free to choose the materials that interest them to experience, experiment and examine. Knows mixing primary colors created new secondary colors.	Length (Can you find something longer or shorter than this? Put in order from longest to shortest) Area (Which shape can you cover with most/least # of blocks, Will it take more blocks to cover the table or to cover the book?)
DII:2 – DII:4 – DIII:1 – DIV:1 – DIV:3	DI:4 – DIII:1 – DV:1 – DV:3 – DV:5	DI:4 – DII:2 – DII:3 – DIV:1 – DIC:3 DIV:4 – DV:2	DII:1 – DII:2 – DII:3 – DII:4 – DIV:2
TSG: 24 – 27	TSG: 32 – 34 – 35	TSG: 24 – 33	TSG: 7a. – 11b. – 11c.
Objective 16: Fluorescent Letters on the Light Table	Bells. Drums. Maracas. Shakers	Question of the Week: "How Did You Do That?" Rainbow Fish. Ice Painting.	Multicultural People. Legos. Trains. Wooden Blocks.

Submitted by Sandbox Early Learning Center, Tucson, AZ

Figure 10.8 Toddler lesson plan. What elements do you find most important?

The tables in this section include examples from twenty different states that align learning to specific, unique infant-toddler guidelines and standards. Having a copy of your own state's standards or guidelines is useful for comparison. Be aware that only a small portion of each state's guidelines are highlighted to illustrate their focus. For a full listing of a state's guidelines, visit the state's website.

Figure 10.9 Positive self-worth is evident in a happy, engaged child.

It is important to be aware that states may place different areas of development within different domains. For instance, approaches to learning may be a separate focus or included in the social-emotional domain of development; the focus on self-regulation may be part of the cognitive domain or the social-emotional domain.

Social-Emotional Domain of Development

The *social-emotional domain* is the foundation of all learning. Children's positive sense of self supports undertaking new challenges and provides confidence about their ability to solve the problems or difficulties they encounter (**Figure 10.9**).

Temperament is an important factor of social-emotional development. It impacts all seven social and emotional domain areas. Children's *temperament* is their individual way of responding to the world around them. Temperament plays a big role in how children express their emotions, relate to others, and form attachments. While some children may be outgoing, others may be more comfortable watching from the sidelines or be slow to warm up. With a clear understanding of temperament, the infant-toddler teacher interacts with each child to support their developing emotional and social abilities.

Other characteristics and experiences can impact social and emotional development. Children with differing abilities and those who are bilingual and multilingual often need additional support as they learn to express their emotions and develop positive relationships. Teachers continually strive to support and sustain each child's connection with their family, languages, and cultures (NAEYC, *DAP*, 2020).

The tenets of the social-emotional domain include a focus on the child's family and culture (**Figure 10.10**). In some families, children are encouraged to be more reserved, while other families may consider outgoing characteristics to be a strength. Some families have different expectations for how assertive their children should be, or ways the children show respect to adults.

Understanding the different values and culture of each family is imperative if the teacher is going to support each child's emotional and social development. Remember, the guidelines indicate what an infant-toddler should be aware of in the current stage of development. **Figure 10.11** highlights only a few of many benchmarks in the states that are identified. Teachers use their knowledge about individual children to scaffold learning experiences to support and modify behavior, and to provide the needed individualized attention that is expected from their own state's guidelines.

The social-emotional domain of development comprises seven main areas of focus. These seven areas are represented in every state, although they may be placed in different categories, using differing benchmarks and indicators to guide the infant-toddler teacher. Each state sets up its own guidelines and separates different ages in many ways.

Figure 10.10 Social-emotional concept web. What examples of learning experiences can relate to this concept web?

Domain of Development: Social-Emotional
Featuring: California, Massachusetts, Minnesota, Montana, South Carolina

Social-Emotional Subdomain	Benchmark (What We Want the Child to Be Able to Do)	Indicators (Behaviors We Might See)	Individualized Teaching Strategies
Interactions and relationships with adults	**Benchmark 1** **CA:** At around seven–eight months of age, children purposefully engage in reciprocal interactions and try to influence the behavior of others. Children may be both interested in and cautious of unfamiliar adults. **MA:** SED1. The young toddler has positive relationships with several different adults, including educators and family members. **MN:** S7 Building relationships: Child establishes and sustains relationships. (0–1 year) **MT:** S1B Respond appropriately to familiar adults' greetings. (Toddler) **SC:** ESD-3 Form relationships and interact positively with familiar adults who are consistent and responsive to their needs. (Birth–12 mos.) **Your State:**	**CA:** Engage in pat-a-cake or peekaboo; make eye contact with family; vocalize to get teacher's attention. **MA:** The child may wave, smile, or verbally express acknowledgement when greeted by a familiar adult. **MN:** The actions may vary due to the child's temperament and family cultural practices. **MT:** The child may wave, smile, or verbally express acknowledgement when greeted by a familiar adult. The actions may vary due to the child's temperament and family cultural practices. **SC:** Show signs of separation anxiety when a familiar caregiver leaves. ESD-3d **Your State:**	• Provide multiple opportunities that include singing and fingerplays. • Respond to the child by displaying attention and enthusiasm, imitating actions, and using words such as "Let's wave good-bye to Sammy!" or "Look, Mommy is here!" • Recognize children when they enter the room with a greeting by name (for example, "Hi Mary! I see you have new shoes on!"). Alternatively, respect their anxiety, reassuring them that their loved one will return. Each child's family should be visible using photos throughout the room.
Relationships and interactions with peers	**Benchmark 2** **CA:** At around eight months of age, children show interest in familiar and unfamiliar peers; around 18 months of age, children engage in simple back-and-forth interactions with peers for short periods. **MA:** SED8 The toddler notices and interacts with toddlers their own age. **MN:** S7.1 Shows a preference for a trusted adult. (0-1 Year) **MT:** Standard 1.9: d. Play side by side with another child. (Toddler) **SC:** Goal ESD-4: Children form relationships and interact positively with other children. (Toddler) **Your State:**	**CA:** Children may stare at another child, explore another child's face and body, and respond to siblings and older peers. **MA:** Children may stare at another child, explore another child's face and body, and respond to siblings and older peers. **MN:** Child may cry to be with a person they are familiar with. **MT:** The child may engage in parallel play (playing next to another child using similar materials, but not sharing materials or interacting directly with the peer). **SC:** Notice other infants and children (look at them, turn in other's direction, reach for them, touch them). ESD-4a **Your State:**	• Offer a book to another child, perhaps with encouragement from the infant care teacher. • Provide consistency in the groupings of toddlers. • Don't make unnecessary changes, keep toddlers together as long as possible. The young toddler notices, relates to and engages with children around the same age. • Provide multiples of favorite toys and play materials to allow children to play in the same space when they have not developed skills to take turns or play cooperatively with the same toy. • Be a role model for kindness.

Continued

Figure 10.11 Social development standards of five states. *How does your state support social-emotional development in your infant-toddler standards?*

Social-Emotional Subdomain	Benchmark (What We Want the Child to Be Able to Do)	Indicators (Behaviors We Might See)	Individualized Teaching Strategies
Recognition of self and ability	**Benchmark 3** **CA:** At around eight months of age, children understand that they are able to make things happen; developing an understanding that the child can take action to influence the environment. (18 mos.) **MA:** SED 28. The older toddler demonstrates awareness of behavior and its effects. (12-33 mos.) **MN:** S1.2 Uses voice or body to show likes and dislikes. (0-1 year) **MT:** Standard 1.5: Children demonstrate a belief in their abilities. (Toddler) **SC:** Goal ESD-2: Children express positive feelings about themselves and confidence in what they can do. (Birth–12 mos.) **Your State:**	**CA:** Pat a musical toy to try to make the music come on again. (5–9 mos.) Roll a toy car back and forth on the ground and then push it hard and let go to see what happens. (18 mos.) **MA:** Experiment to see the effects of his actions on other people and on objects. [MN is missing] **MT:** The child may shake or drop a toy to get a desired effect from the toy or caregiver, demonstrating a beginning understanding of causality. **SC:** Show confidence in their ability to make things happen by repeating or changing their actions to reach a goal (move closer to reach an object they want). ESD-2c **Your State:**	• Provide toys that are interactive and require child-power to operate. • Provide activities and opportunities for children to experience cause and effect. • Provide toys and objects that produce different effects when the child acts upon them. Play games, such as retrieving the dropped toy or laughing whenever the child shakes the toy, following the child's lead.
Expression of emotion and empathy	**Benchmark 4** **CA:** The developing ability to express a variety of feelings through facial expressions, movements, gestures, sounds, or words. (8 mos) **MA:** SED13. The young toddler expresses a range of emotions, sometimes with intensity. (12–24 mos) **MN:** S3 Emotions: Child demonstrates understanding of own emotions, others' emotions, and awareness of emotions becoming reactions and behaviors. (0–1 year) **MT:** d. Use gestures, words, or facial expressions to communicate feelings and seek help in order to calm him or herself. (Toddler) **SC:** Goal ESD-6: Children identify, manage, and express their feelings. (Birth-12 mos.) **Your State:**	**CA:** At around eight months of age, children express a variety of primary emotions such as contentment, distress, joy, sadness, interest, surprise, disgust, anger, and fear. **MA:** Experience intense feelings of sadness and jubilation when leaving and reuniting with parents; name some emotions. **MN:** S3.3 Expresses feelings, needs, and wants with nonverbal communication, vocalizations, few words. **MT:** The child may express negative emotions through words, facial expressions, or actions, such as hitting, biting, pulling away, or grabbing, and may turn to and need an adult to help calm and comfort. **SC:** Show when they feel overwhelmed or are in distress or pain (cry, yawn, look away, extend arms or legs, arch their body, fuss). ESD-6b **Your State:**	• Express fear of unfamiliar people by moving near a familiar infant care teacher. (8 mos.) • Stop crying and snuggle after being picked up by a parent. • Play games, read books, have pictures of toddlers showing emotions and use to help toddlers identify feelings as they are occurring. • Label and describe emotions observed during everyday interactions, such as "I feel happy you are here today" or "Sandy looks sad since her mommy said good-bye." Display pictures of people showing all types of emotions.

Figure 10.11

Continued

Social-Emotional Subdomain	Benchmark (What We Want the Child to Be Able to Do)	Indicators (Behaviors We Might See)	Individualized Teaching Strategies
Emotional regulation and impulse control	**Benchmark 5** **CA:** The developing ability to manage emotional responses, with assistance from others and independently. (8 months) **MA:** The toddler progresses in regulating his own feelings and behavior. (Birth–15 mos.) **MN:** S5 Managing emotions and behaviors: Child manages emotions, impulses, and behaviors with assistance from others and independently. (0-1 yr.) **MT:** Standard 1.6: Children manage their internal states, feelings, and behavior, and develop the ability to adapt to diverse situations and environments. (Toddler) **SC:** Goal ESD-5: Children demonstrate the social and behavioral skills needed to successfully participate in groups. (Birth–12 mos.) **Your State:**	**CA:** At around eight months of age, children use simple behaviors to comfort themselves and begin to communicate the need for help to alleviate discomfort or distress. **MA:** SED19. The young toddler begins to develop strategies to manage his/her expression of feelings. **MN:** S5.6 Expands use of sign language, gestures, and a few words or phrases to communicate needs, wants, preferences, and discomforts to adults. **MT:** Fuss or cry when hungry, tired, wet, or overstimulated. **SC:** Control impulses some of the time (look at forbidden object and say, "No, no," allow adult to direct them to a different activity). ESD-5c **Your State:**	• Vocalize to get a parent's attention. (6.5–8 mos.); lift arms to the infant care teacher to communicate a desire to be held. (7–9 mos.) • Provide supportive experiences in which children have valid choices ("You can have water or milk.") • Learn to recognize the type of crying so that you can respond to the child's needs most appropriately. Establish consistent, trusting relationships with each child by responding to the child's appeals promptly.
Social understanding	**Benchmark 6** **CA:** Develop understanding of the responses, communication, emotional expressions, and actions of other people. (8 mos.) **MA:** SED27. The older infant expresses a range of emotions expanding to include more complex emotions. (Birth–15 mos.) **MN:** Child notices and responds to others and their emotions. (0–1 year) **MT:** Learn and practice caregiving strategies that match those familiar to the child at home. (0–18 mos.) **SC:** ESD-2 Children express positive feelings about themselves and confidence in what they can do. (Birth–12 mos.) **Your State:**	**CA:** Control impulses some of the time (look at forbidden object and say, "No, no," allow adult to direct them to a different activity). ESD-5c **MA:** Show a range of emotions including fear, surprise, happiness, and contentment. **MN:** Imitates others' emotions and expressions. (1–2 years) **MT:** Learn and practice caregiving strategies that match those familiar to the child at home. **SC:** Explore the environment with support from a familiar, trusted adult. ESD-2c **Your State:**	• Learn simple behaviors by imitating a parent's facial expressions, gestures, or sounds. • Verbally acknowledge and label emotions ("You were scared when the door slammed.") • Learn and practice caregiving strategies that match those familiar to the child at home.

Figure 10.11

Continued

Social-Emotional Subdomain	Benchmark (What We Want the Child to Be Able to Do)	Indicators (Behaviors We Might See)	Individualized Teaching Strategies
Culture, families, community	**Benchmark 7** **CA:** At around eight months of age, children have learned what to expect from familiar people, understand what to do to get another's attention, engage in back-and-forth interactions with others, and imitate the simple actions or facial expressions of others. **MA:** The infant acts as a social being by engaging with others and the world around them. (Birth–15 mos.) **MN:** S2 Self Awareness: Child demonstrates understanding and appreciation of uniqueness in own family, community, culture, and the world. (0–1 year) **MT:** Distinguish primary caregiver from others. (0–18 mos.) **SC:** ESD-5: Children demonstrate the social and behavioral skills needed to successfully participate in groups. (Older Toddlers 18 mos. +) **Your State:**	**CA:** Smile when the infant care teacher pauses, to get the teacher to continue playing peekaboo or pat-a-cake. **MA:** Vocalize (coo, squeal, babble, or cry) to be held or talked to; look at or watch other children or educators and smile. **MN:** S2 Self Awareness: Child demonstrates understanding and appreciation of uniqueness in own family, community, culture, and the world. **MT:** The child may distinguish differences in caregiving and have preferences for how to be held and comforted. **SC:** Follow social rules, transitions, and routines that have been explained to them, with reminders and practice. ESD-5e **Your State:**	• If possible, use children's home language in daily conversations with them. • Give infants and toddlers many chances to make choices and decisions. Try to avoid telling infants and toddlers "no" by giving them choices that are acceptable. For example, if a toddler tries to grab a toy from another child, offer two other similar toys from which to choose. • Learn and practice caregiving strategies that match those familiar to the child at home. • Hold and talk to babies individually throughout the day, not only during diapering, dressing, and eating times. Cuddle them while reading a book or playing with a toy.

Figure 10.11

STOP AND THINK | Make connections to how various benchmarks influence other developmental domains. For example, review "Expression of emotion and empathy" in Row 4 of Figure 10.11. How might meeting of the listed indicators influence the cognitive domains?

Cognitive Brain Development

With the support of a secure attachment to their teacher, infants and toddlers are able to begin to develop critical self-regulation skills toward gaining control of their body functions and managing their behavior (**Figure 10.12**). With self-regulation and executive function, children are able to pay attention, plan, follow directions, and control their impulses. These skills begin developing in infancy and continue to develop throughout childhood and early adulthood.

To support the development of lifelong skills, children need stable and responsive relationships, healthy routines, and stimulating learning environments. Adults use daily routines and experiences to help children focus their attention, practice self-control, solve

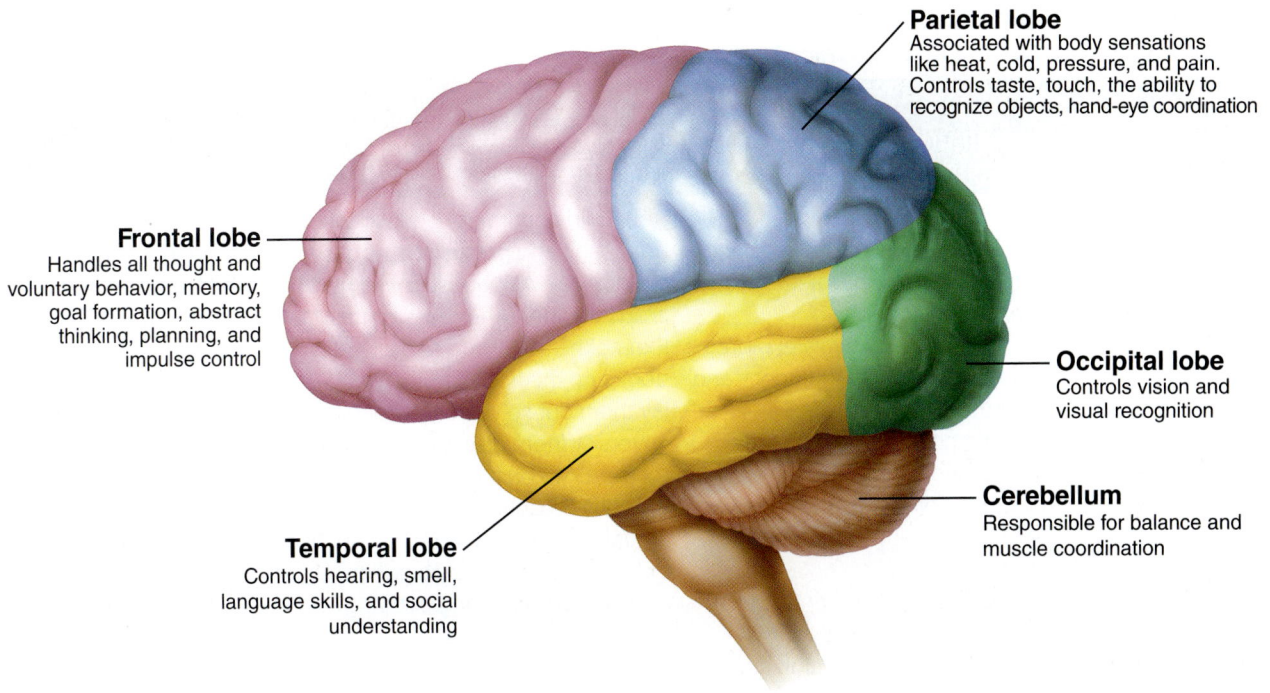

Figure 10.12 Neural development. *How can you utilize knowledge of brain development in your work with children and families?*

problems, and manage emotions (Zero-to-Three 2014). The teacher plays a key role and must be willing to make accommodations that can benefit the children as they learn self-regulation skills, one of many areas that overlaps into the next domain of development: cognitive.

The *cognitive domain*, often called the *thinking domain*, encompasses knowledge and the development of intellectual skills (**Figure 10.13**). This domain includes recall and recognition of facts, patterns, and concepts. Cognitive development supports the infant-toddler in developing self-regulation, executive functions, and emerging connections to academic disciplines. Some states include self-regulation and executive functions under the social-emotional domain.

The infant's **sensory system** is the primary means of gaining information about the world in the early stages of life. The toddler's primary means of gaining information is by trial and error. Through exploration and discovery, the toddler learns what things are and how they work. Making connections to the different components that are part of the cognitive domain provide guidelines to support the infant-toddler teacher in the states that are highlighted in **Figure 10.14**.

Language, Literacy, and Communication Domain

The language, literacy, and communication domain includes expressive and receptive language. **Expressive language** is the language children use to express their wants and needs. Expressive language conveys words combined into phrases, sentences, and paragraphs and includes the use of gestures and facial expressions.

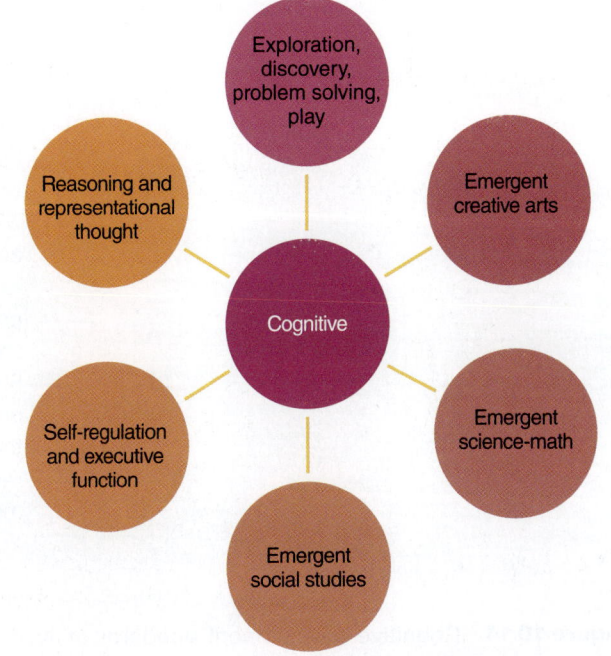

Figure 10.13 Cognitive concept web. *What examples of learning experiences can be connected with this concept web?*

Domain of Development: Cognitive
Featuring: Maine, North Dakota, Ohio, Tennessee, Utah

Cognitive Development Subdomain	Benchmark (What We Want the Child to Be Able to Do)	Indicators (Behaviors We Might See)	Individualized Teaching Strategies
Exploration, Discovery, Memory, Problem Solving	**Benchmark 1** **ME:** Begins to use reasoning and planning to solve problems using a variety of strategies. **ND:** IT-C 1 Child actively explores people and objects to understand self, others, and objects. **OH:** The child will develop an understanding of his or her world through exploration and discovery while developing strategies to solve problems. **TN:** AL.13-24.8 Problem Solving **UT:** Domain III: Cognitive Development- Exploration and Discovery **Your State:**	**ME:** Child continually goes to the bookshelf and puts all the books on the floor. Ask questions to help child consider other possibilities. Example: "You like to see all the books on the floor. Should we lay them out so you can see the covers? Where else could we put them? (6–18 mos.) **ND:** Acts intentionally to achieve a goal or when manipulating an object, such as trying to get an adult to do something or trying different ways to reach a toy under a table. (8–18 mos.) **OH:** In the beginning of this period, I automatically respond in distinguishing between familiar and unfamiliar people. By the end of this period, I can tell the difference between familiar and unfamiliar people, objects and places. For example, I may… …turn toward the sight, smell or sound of my mom. …look back and forth between people or objects, as if comparing them. (Birth–8 mos.) **TN:** Show increasing awareness of his effect on his environment. Pull at caregiver's leg and point to favorite nap item in cubby; say "more" when cup is empty; may indicate when diaper is wet or soiled. (Birth–12 mos.) **UT:** Pays attention to people and objects; Uses senses to explore people, objects and the environment; Attends to colors, shapes, patterns or pictures; Shows interest and curiosity in new people and objects; Makes things happen and watches for results or repeats action. (0–36 mos.) **Your State:**	• Integrate the languages that the child hears at home. • Include books that represent different languages and include interaction in all experiences. • Pair up children to create dynamics that support all languages. • Encourage back-and-forth engagement about pictures and objects. • When possible, connect to the child's personal experiences. • Show enthusiasm when a child makes a discovery. • Talk about what the toddler sees or hears and call attention to new and unusual actions or events. • Provide opportunities for toddler to explore and experience nature while on walks or visits to a park.

Continued
Goodheart-Wilcox Publisher

Figure 10.14 Cognitive development standards of five states. *How does your state support cognitive development in its infant-toddler standards?*

Cognitive Development Subdomain	Benchmark (What We Want the Child to Be Able to Do)	Indicators (Behaviors We Might See)	Individualized Teaching Strategies
Emergent Creative Arts	**Benchmark 2** **ME:** Explores new experiences in a familiar setting. Develops ability to invent, pretend and try new things. **ND:** IT-APL 9. Child shows imagination in play and interactions with others. (Creativity) **OH:** The child will learn the foundations for listening, speaking, reading and writing. **TN:** CA.0-12.5 Dramatic Play and Movement **UT:** Domain III: Cognitive Development: Imitation and Symbolic Play **Your State:**	**ME:** Begins to move to the music of varying rhythms, tempos, and types. Uses a colorful scarf in different to dance. (6–18 mos.) **ND:** Uses pretend and imaginary objects or people in play or interaction with others. Uses materials such as paper, paint, crayons, or blocks to make novel things. (8–18 mos.) **OH:** In the beginning of this period, I use a full-hand grasp to hold a writing tool to make scribbles. **TN:** Begin to discover his/her body. Watches hands; starts to bring things to mouth; kicks and wiggles upon hearing familiar sounds; may attempt to shift onto side towards toy or caregiver. (Birth–12 mos.) **UT:** Observes and imitates sounds, gestures or behaviors Uses objects in new ways or in pretend play. Uses imitation or pretend play to express creativity and imagination. (0–36 mos.) **Your State:**	• Include many genres of music to listen and move to. • Provide crayons, chalk, paint, and writing utensils that are readily available to create. • In the dramatic play area, include different props for the young toddler to experiment with. • Practice closing your eyes and creating a picture in your mind with older toddlers. • Sing. Sing. Sing. Sing. Sing. Sing. Sing.
Emergent Science-Math	**Benchmark 3** **ME:** Discovering mathematical concepts such as: sequencing, size, shape, numbers, amounts of items, spatial relations, patterns. **ND:** IT-C 8.Child develops sense of number and quantity. **OH:** NA **TN:** MA.13-24.2 Comparing Numbers **UT:** NA **Your State:**	**ME:** Uses simple nesting or stacking toys: y nests three or four cups by stacks three or four cups or foam blocks. (6–8 mos.) **ND:** Identifies "more" or "less" with number of items without needing to count them a small. (8–18 mos.) **OH:** NA **TN:** Begin to understand similarities and differences. May mistake another child's pacifier as his own; may notice when another child has the same jacket or shoes. (13–24 mos.) **UT:** NA **Your State:**	• Use mathematical terms when speaking: "bigger, smaller, more, less, many." • Provide items that are similar but different to support making connections to differences. • Include puzzles to practice with shapes. • Provide items that can be taken apart for toddlers. • Provide opportunities to experiment with volume, such as different sizes of containers in the water table.

Continued

Figure 10.14

Cognitive Development Subdomain	Benchmark (What We Want the Child to Be Able to Do)	Indicators (Behaviors We Might See)	Individualized Teaching Strategies
Emergent Social Studies	**Benchmark 4** **ME:** Attention to and exploration of the world around them as it authentically affects them. Learning about their family culture and cultures of others in the classroom or community. **ND:** IT-LC 11. Child recognizes pictures and some symbols, signs, or words. **OH:** The child will learn the foundations for listening, speaking, reading and writing. **TN:** SS.0-12.1 Interactions and Culture **UT:** Language Development and Communication III: Emergent Literacy **Your State:**	**ME:** Engages in immediate and deferred imitation of facial expressions: smiles back at caregiver, smiles when familiar adult re-enters room, responds by patting mirror when sees own image reflected. (Birth–8 mos.) **ND:** Looks at pictures of familiar people, animals, or objects while adult points at and/or names the person, animal, or object. (0–9 mos.) **OH:** In the beginning of this period, I show increased interest in books and pictures. (6–18 mos.) **TN:** Engage with familiar adults. Babble and coo to gain attention of someone nearby; look intently at the face when talked to by a familiar person; smile when someone familiar smiles or make gentle, funny faces; relax when comforted by familiar persons. (Birth–12 months) **UT:** Shows interest in songs, rhymes and stories Shows interest in photos, pictures and drawings. (0–36 mos.) **Your State:**	• Place images of the child's family in picture frames or as part of a bulletin board and describe what you both see. • Provide a consistent and predictable routine; talk about upcoming events or activities and revisit past events. • Use familiar transitions to signal certain learning experiences, such as reading a book to all who are interested in listening. • Place pictures at eye level, including the children's own work. • Label cubbies with child's photograph and name for easy recognition.

Continued

Figure 10.14

STOP AND THINK | Some, but not all, states include emergent academic subdomains in their guidelines for infants and toddlers. How does your state support these concentrations?

Receptive language includes the understanding of both words as well as facial expressions and gestures. Most children learn language on their own, but not all do. Infants and toddlers may have a condition that affects their ability to learn to communicate. For example, those born with partial or full hearing loss or developmental disorders such as autism or severe speech delays may need to rely more on nonverbal communication.

This domain also includes ways to support English language learners (**Figure 10.15**). Understanding and using English is not based on age; instead, it is based on language mastery. Emerging research indicates that children who are learning two languages have stronger executive functioning skills because as they switch between languages they are

Cognitive Development Subdomain	Benchmark (What We Want the Child to Be Able to Do)	Indicators (Behaviors We Might See)	Individualized Teaching Strategies
Self-Regulation and Executive Function	**Benchmark 5** **ME:** Development of the ability to regulate emotions and mood. **ND:** IT-APL 1. Child manages feelings and emotions with support of familiar adults. **OH:** The child will develop an understanding of his or her world through exploration and discovery while developing strategies to solve problems. **TN:** SE.13-24.4 Attempt to manage own behavior with guidance and support. (located under Social-Emotional) **UT:** Language Development and Communication III: Developing Memory **Your State:**	**ME:** Signals (using cues) when full—pushes bottle away, stops nursing, wants to be put down—squirms, pushes away. (Birth–8 mos.) **ND:** Engages with familiar adults for calming and comfort, to focus attention, and to share joy. Looks to others for help in coping with strong feelings and emotions. (0–9 mos.) **OH:** In the beginning of this period, I respond automatically to my environment. By the end of this period, I actively use my body to find out about my world. For example, I may… …cry to get my needs met. (Birth–8 mos.) **TN:** Respond to verbal requests to change behavior and stop unacceptable behavior with a few reminders. (13–24 mos.) **UT:** Shows ability to acquire and process new information; Recognizes familiar people, places and things; Recalls and uses information in new situations; Searches for missing or hidden objects. (0–36 mos.) **Your State:**	• Recognize the type of crying to respond quickly to the child's needs. Establish consistent, trusting relationships with by responding to appeals promptly. • Provide books that show emotions to share. • Nurture the child while paying attention to preferences; gentle touch throughout the daily routine is important to healthy development. • Provide opportunities to identify and meet one's own needs, such as open access to art supplies, open snack table, or individual water bottles.

Continued

Figure 10.14

building their capacity for cognitive flexibility. This research validates supporting a child's home language (Bialystok et al. 2010).

Dual language learners are children who are learning two languages at the same time, including their first (or home-heritage) language (CECER). Caregivers and teachers should create welcoming environments that promote and respect second language acquisition and that preserve the child's home language and cultural identity. Play music or sing songs in the child's first language. If a staff member speaks the child's first language, create opportunities for that staff member and the child to interact.

The number of different applications of language that infants and toddlers experience affects the number of words they will learn and use. This also affects their future success in learning to read and write, and in turn affects their long-range school success. Examples include using **parentese**, which refers to the animated voice parents use to get the baby's attention. Another example is the use of rare words during routine times. **Rare words** are an early literacy strategy that integrates rich and sophisticated or unusual words when conversing with children rather than common terms. For example, "Let's see what happens if you *transfer* the water from the pitcher to the glass." For an infant or toddler, "transfer" is a rare word which they now have the opportunity to interpret as meaning the same thing as "pour." Using rare words is a key predictor of reading success (CAST 2011).

Cognitive Development Subdomain	Benchmark (What We Want the Child to Be Able to Do)	Indicators (Behaviors We Might See)	Individualized Teaching Strategies
Reasoning and Representational Thought	**Benchmark 6** **ME:** Shows interest and engages in active exploration (visual, auditory, tactile) of self, objects, and surrounding. Develops ability to engage others in interaction. **ND:** IT-C 7. Child uses reasoning and plans ahead to solve problems. **OH:** The child will develop an understanding of his or her world through exploration and discovery while developing strategies to solve problems. **TN:** AL.13-24.6 Flexibility and Inventiveness **UT:** Language Development and Communication III: Problem Solving **Your State:**	**ME:** Children are jumping in puddles with their boots on. Example: "What do you think is in those puddles? How big of a splash can you make?" (6–18 mos.) **ND:** Uses own actions or movements to solve simple problems, such as rolling to the side to reach an object or kicking to make something move. (8–18 mos.) **OH:** In the beginning of this period, I begin to learn the properties of objects. (6–8 mos.) **TN:** Use materials in ways other than originally intended. Use toy banana as a telephone; use spoon to bang on table like a drum. (13–24 mos.) **UT:** Experiments with different uses for objects; Shows imagination and creativity in solving problems; Uses a variety of strategies to solve problems; Applies knowledge to new situations. (0–36 mos.) **Your State:**	• Encourage children to touch, bang, shake, and roll objects to help children understand how objects work. • Allow infants time to explore and examine objects and new things. • Offer toddlers a choice of different activities, times, and ways of doing things (builds agency). • Provide a variety of interesting action toys that come apart, move, and can be used in many ways.

Figure 10.14

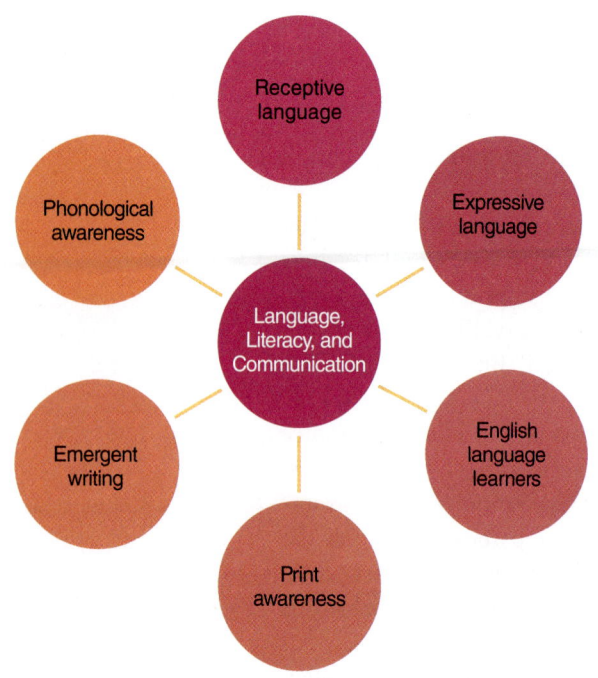

Goodheart-Wilcox Publisher

Figure 10.15 Language, literacy, and communication concept web. What examples of learning experiences can be connected with this concept web?

Infants and toddlers benefit from rich experiences with emergent reading and writing in this domain. *Emergent literacy* is a child's knowledge of reading and writing before the child actually acquires those skills and starts at birth. Phonological awareness, writing, and awareness of print connections start very early (**Figure 10.16**). When an adult reads a book to a child, the child learns that the symbols on the page have meaning. The child also learns that more symbols can be found by turning the pages, and that reading happens from left to right (in the English language).

Physical Domain of Development

Motor skills support children across all domains of development, whether they are exploring their environment or interacting with peers and adults (**Figure 10.17**). The *physical domain* of development includes fine motor skills (small muscles), gross motor skills (large muscles), and sensory skills (development of the senses). Children's physical abilities affect their school readiness and learning (Pan et al. 2019). By demonstrating balance, coordination, and strength, children show that they

Domain of Development: Language-Literacy-Communication
Featuring: Alaska, Arizona, Arkansas, Connecticut, Idaho

Cognitive-Language	Benchmark (What We Want the Child to Be Able to Do)	Indicators (Behaviors We Might See)	Individualized Teaching Strategies
Exploration, Discovery, Memory, Problem Solving	**Benchmark 1** **AK:** LD1.1 Understands and responds to language (in child's home language) **AZ:** Strand 1: Listening and Understanding **AR:** EL1.2 Engages in read-aloud and conversations about books and stories **CT:** Strand A: Early learning experiences will support children to understand language (receptive language). **ID:** Goal 48: Children demonstrate the meaning of language by listening. **Your State:**	**AK:** Responds to noises and voices in the environment (e.g., startles or cries at unexpected sounds; smiles or coos when parentese is used). (0–8 mos.) **AZ:** Turn head to the direction of family voices; Be startled by loud or surprising sounds; Be comforted by voice of family caregivers. Attend to or be comforted by music. (Birth–6 mos.) **AR:** Attends to caregiver's voice when being held and read to. (Birth–8 mos.) **CT:** L.6.1 Respond to facial expressions or voices by changing own facial expression, crying or altering movements. (0–6 mos.) **ID:** Respond to environmental sounds and recognize familiar voices. (Birth–8 mos.) **Your State:**	• Include home languages of infant-toddlers when talking, singing, reading books, doing routine tasks. • Use animated voices and language called parentese. Parentese draws a baby's attention and is very natural to most people as they exaggerate sounds using simple grammar. • Talk with the baby and allow the baby time to respond to you, perhaps by turning to look at you, smiling, or cooing. • Watch for cues that the baby is attending or listening and repeat sounds, gestures or simple language.
Expressive Language	**Benchmark 2** **AK:** LD2.1 Uses increasingly complex vocabulary, grammar, and sentence structure (in child's home language) **AZ:** Strand 1: Listening and Understanding **AR:** LD2.1 Uses increasingly complex vocabulary, grammar, and sentence structure (in child's home language) **CT:** Strand B: Early learning experiences will support children to use language (expressive language). **ID:** Goal 49: Children communicate effectively. **Your State:**	**AK:** Experiments with making sounds (e.g., babbling), often repeating consonant sounds (e.g., da da and ba ba). (0–8 mos.) **AZ:** Observe caregiver's face when being spoken to and shapes mouth in a similar manner; Distinguish other languages from native language, with greater interest paid to nouns. (0–6 mos.) **AR:** Begins to say a number of simple words (e.g., "nana," "go," "hi," and "leche" [milk in Spanish for dual language learners]) (9–18 mos.) **CT:** L.6.4 Use a variety of facial expressions and sounds (e.g., cooing, babbling and varied cries) to communicate. **ID:** Begin communication with facial expressions and vocal play to interact with others. (Birth–9 mos.) **Your State:**	• Provide opportunities to communicate, such as telephones and recorders. • Establish consistent, caring, and trusting relationship by using a steady, soft voice as you interact to meet individual needs. • Introduce and model new sounds, gestures or words for the baby to imitate. • Play naming games with the baby, such as naming animals and making the sounds of the animals. • Look for new ways the toddler uses language, such as for humor or pretending. • Ask questions and allow time for either a verbal or a nonverbal response.

Continued

Figure 10.16 Language, literacy, and communication standards of five states. How does your state support language-literacy-communication development in its infant-toddler standards?

Cognitive-Language	Benchmark (What We Want the Child to Be Able to Do)	Indicators (Behaviors We Might See)	Individualized Teaching Strategies
English Language Leaners	**Benchmark 3** **AK:** LD4.1 Demonstrates progress in attending to, understanding, and responding to English **AZ:** The language skills needed for young English language learners to become proficient in English are fully embedded in the Arizona Early Learning Standards. **AR:** LD4.2 Demonstrates progress in speaking and expressing self in English **CT:** Comprehension of Information Presented Orally—An entire framework for dual language learners is presented. **ID:** Goal 64: Note: This goal statement only applies to children whose home language is not English. Children must continue to grow and progress in their home language while learning another language. Language in this goal only refers to the "spoken word" or oral language and communication. It does not refer to the "written word" such as reading, writing, or other literacy activities. **Your State:**	**AK:** Progression of English Language Development is defined by stages of development rather than by what should occur within a certain age range. **AZ:** Using the standards to plan enriching experiences will enhance children's proficiency in English and enable them to become successful learners in Kindergarten–12 schools. **AR:** *Early Stage*—Relies on nonverbal communication, such as gestures or behaviors, to seek attention, request objects, or initiate a response from others. *Mid Stage*—Combines nonverbal with some verbal communication to be understood by others. *Late Stage*—Demonstrates increasing reliance on verbal communication in English to be understood by others while still making some mistakes. **CT:** DLL.B.1 Demonstrate an understanding of words related to basic and advanced concepts in L1 that are appropriate for their age. May understand a few words in L2. (Beginning) **ID:** Initiate and respond to differences in sounds including intonation. (Birth–8 mos.) **Your State:**	• Integrate the languages that the child hears at home in written communication. • Continually add new vocabulary words in conversations. • Pair up children to create dynamics that support all languages. • Add languages spoken to shelf labels. • Provide books, music, and other play materials in the child's home language. • Encourage peers to learn words, phrases, and songs in the child's home language. • Establish and post predictable daily schedule and routines. • Monitor the child's language use and communicate with family members to ensure that periods of silence are just a time of adjustment and not a reason to be concerned. • Provide a picture or image for children to see at their eye level that represents common actions, transitions, or classroom items. Encourage all children to use these images as tools to reinforce accurate communication.

Continued

Figure 10.16

STOP AND THINK — Using sophisticated or rare words is an emergent literacy strategy that requires the teacher to replace well-known words with new words in context. Identify a list of common words and the rare or unusual words that can replace them when working with infants and toddlers.

Cognitive-Language	Benchmark (What We Want the Child to Be Able to Do)	Indicators (Behaviors We Might See)	Individualized Teaching Strategies
Print Awareness	**Benchmark 4** **AK:** EL3.2 Shows knowledge of the shapes, names, and sounds of letters. **AZ:** Child develops interest in and involvement with books and other print materials. **AR:** EL3.2 Shows knowledge of the shapes, names, and sounds of letters. **CT:** Strand E: Early learning experiences will support children to gain knowledge of print and its uses. **ID:** Goal 60: Children demonstrate awareness that written materials can be used for a variety of purposes. **Your State:**	**AK:** Typical development of these skills tends to emerge after 18 months. However, foundations of this learning goal are built through: • EL1.1 Shows interest in literacy experiences. • EL2.1 Notices and manipulates the sounds of language. • EL3.1 Responds to features of books and print. **AZ:** Look at books, pat the pictures, or bring books to mouth. (0–6 mos.) **AR:** Attends to and recognizes simple environmental print (e.g., recognizes stop sign or Walmart® or Lego® logos, although may not say letters). (19–36 mos.) **CT:** L.24.14 Hold book upright. (18–24 mos.) **ID:** Shows preference for familiar food labels, clothing, graphics, and characters. Enjoys books with clear pictures or photos about daily routines (eating, toileting). Finds comfort and enjoyment in being read to. (6–18 mos.) **Your State:**	• Read books together daily—as many as you can. • Insert the infant-toddler's name into the book if it does not change the integrity of the story. • Point out items and name what you see in the book. "Look, there is a red balloon." • Repeat favorite songs, stories, rhymes or finger plays on a regular basis when interacting with baby. • Make a photo or picture book for the baby with some favorite people, animals, and things. • Sing songs with motions and do simple finger plays that toddlers can imitate. • Show baby pictures of family members or photos of other babies and young children.
Emergent Writing	**Benchmark 5** **AK:** PH2.2 adjusts grasp and coordinates movements to use tools (listed under Physical Domain) **AZ:** Strand 2: Fine Motor Development **AR:** EL3.3 Demonstrates emergent writing skills. **CT:** Strand G: Early learning experiences will support children to convey meaning through drawing, letters and words **ID:** Children use writing for a variety of purposes **Your State:**	**AK:** Holds large writing and drawing tools (e.g., crayons, sidewalk chalk) to make spontaneous dots and scribbles, progressing from whole hand grip to approximate thumb-and-finger grip (may still move whole arm to make marks) (9–18 mos.) **AZ:** Use a crayon to make marks on paper. (6–18 mos.) **AR:** Explores writing tools and movements, making scribble marks with increasing control. (9–36 mos.) **CT:** L.18.11 Use writing tools to make scribbles. (12–18 mos.) **ID:** Explores and experiences environment using all senses. (0–8 mos.) **Your State:**	• Provide safe and interesting items to hold, mouth, and visually explore. • Model writing and drawing with purpose by talking about what you are writing down. • Experiment with healthy finger foods, playdough, and puzzles with knobs that promote small motor skills. • Encourage scribbles that have a meaning, transcribing what the children says it means. • Encourage writing their name on their work and signing in when they arrive.

Continued

Figure 10.16

Cognitive-Language	Benchmark (What We Want the Child to Be Able to Do)	Indicators (Behaviors We Might See)	Individualized Teaching Strategies
Phonological Awareness	**Benchmark 6** **AK:** EL2.1 Notices and manipulates the sounds of language **AZ:** Child shows interest in songs, rhymes, and stories. **AR:** EL2.1 Notices and manipulates the sounds of language **CT:** Strand F: Early learning experiences will support children to develop phonological awareness. **ID:** Goal 56: Children develop phonological awareness. **Your State:**	**AK:** Shows increasing awareness of and interest in the sounds of spoken language by focusing on the speaker. (0–18 mos.) **AZ:** Identifies rhyming words. (6–18 mos,) **AR:** Shows increasing awareness of and interest in the sounds of spoken language by focusing on the speaker. (0–18 mos.) **CT:** L.36.17 Recognize environmental sounds (e.g., animal or vehicle sounds). (24–36 mos.) **ID:** Makes the sounds of animals and moving objects. Vocalizes familiar words when read to. Recites last word of familiar rhymes, with assistance. (6–18 mos.) **Your State:**	• Talk to the child throughout the day about routines, what you are doing, what the child is doing, and what is going on around the child. • Pay attention to the sounds that each child makes and repeat them back as in a conversation without pointing out errors. • Make up silly rhymes to match children's names when singing. • Clap out the syllables in each child's name during the day.

Figure 10.16

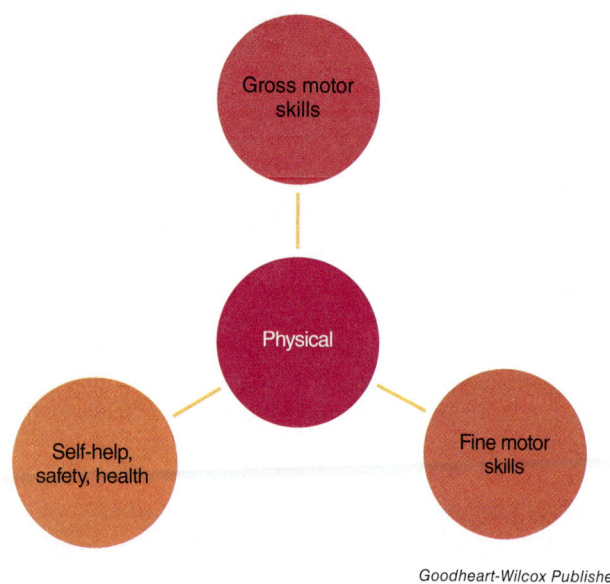

Goodheart-Wilcox Publisher

Figure 10.17 Physical concept web. *What examples of learning experiences can be connected with this concept web?*

have the skills to sit still and pay attention, be stabile on a chair, grasp a pencil, or track their eyes along a line. Children with physical disabilities may demonstrate alternate ways of achieving the goals for gross and fine motor skills. For example, they may use supports such as pedaling an adaptive tricycle, navigating a wheelchair, or feeding themselves with a specialized utensil.

Gross motor skills refer to movement of the larger muscles of the body, including the arms, legs, and core. Infants' physical development progresses through gaining control of their head and neck, then the torso to help them sit, creep, crawl, and stand properly. As toddlers, they mature and develop the strength and coordination to walk, throw, jump, and run.

Fine motor skills involve small muscles such as those in the wrist and hand. Development of fine motor skills include using their eyes, mouth, hands, and feet to learn to control and coordinate small movements and motions such as fastening clothes, drawing, and painting, completing puzzles, or creating small block buildings.

Some individualized teaching strategies in the physical domain include:

- Allow the baby to experience open spaces during playtimes, such as lying on a blanket on the floor in a safe area.
- Show joy when the child tries a new task.
- Provide wedges, pillows, or safe props for the child to crawl and climb.
- Put a toy or object just out of reach and encourage a child to reach for it.
- Provide push and riding toys.
- Roll a ball back and forth to the child.

In guidelines across the states, the physical domain includes skills that represent self-help, safety, and health (**Figure 10.18**). An infant's optimal growth and development is founded on good nutrition and health practices from the beginning. Infants and toddlers depend on their teachers and caregivers to be positive models and make healthy choices for them.

The domains of development provide the infant-toddler teacher with many possibilities for teaching and learning in the first years of life. The opportunities are limitless, and a toolbox filled with resources will ensure that the infant-toddler classroom is engaging and that the infant or toddler feels safe, secure, and loved.

Checkpoint

☐ What does the infant's sensory system include? How is this supported in the classroom?

☐ Share examples of receptive and expressive language.

Domain of Development: Physical Featuring: Alabama, Indiana, New Hampshire, New Mexico, Rhode Island			
Physical Development Subdomains	**Benchmark (What We Want the Child to Be Able to Do)**	**Indicators (Behaviors We Might See)**	**Individualized Teaching Strategies**
Gross Motor	**Benchmark 1** **AL:** PDH1a: Gross Motor Development: Children will demonstrate increasing body awareness, control, strength and coordination of large muscles. **IN:** PHG3.1: Demonstrate development of fine and gross motor coordination **NH:** Strand: Large Muscle Development and Coordination **NM:** Component 11: Large Motor: The infant/toddler moves her body to achieve a goal. **RI:** Component 2: Gross Motor Development Learning Goal 2.a: Children develop large muscle control, strength, and coordination. **Your State:**	**AL:** Demonstrate control and strength of basic body movements such as rolling, reaching and pulling up to standing. (9–12 mos.) Show coordination and control of large muscle movements by throwing or kicking a large ball. (18–24 mos.) **IN:** Develop control of head and back, progressing to arms and legs. (Infant) Begin to develop coordination and balance, requiring less support. (Younger Toddler) **NH:** Develop head and trunk stability and ability to change positions. (birth–9 mos.) **NM:** Moves body, arms, and legs with increasing coordination. (birth–8 months) Demonstrates beginning coordination and balance. (6–18 months) **RI:** Reach and play with toys while sitting > Reach for objects and bring them to their mouth > Pound on a table and other objects. (9 months) **Your State:**	• Allow the baby to experience open spaces during playtimes, such as lying on a blanket on the floor in a safe area. • Show joy when the child tries a new task. • Provide wedges, pillows, or safe props for child to crawl and climb. • Put a toy or object just out of reach and encourage a child to reach for it. • Provide push and riding toys. • Roll a ball back and forth to the child. • Create safe areas for climbing. • Stabilize shelves and furniture to avoid tipping or falling. • Provide toddler-size Lego® blocks and model how to make a tower. • Provide stacking rings or pegboards. • Put out large crayons and paper and encourage children to make marks on the paper.

Continued
Goodheart-Willcox Publisher

Figure 10.18 Physical development standards of five states. *How does your state support physical development in its infant-toddler standards?*

Physical Development Subdomains	Benchmark (What We Want the Child to Be Able to Do)	Indicators (Behaviors We Might See)	Individualized Teaching Strategies
Fine Motor	**Benchmark 2** **AL:** PDH1b: Fine Motor Development: Children will demonstrate increasing strength, control and coordination of their small muscles. **IN:** PHG3.1: Demonstrate development of fine and gross motor coordination **NH:** Strand: Small Muscle Development and Coordination **NM:** Component 12: Fine Motor: The infant/toddler manipulates objects and uses simple tools. **RI:** Component 3: Fine Motor development Learning Goal 3.a: Children develop small muscle control, strength, and coordination. **Your State:**	**AL:** Examine objects and transfer them from one hand to another. (9–12 mos.) Use eye-hand coordination to manipulate objects, feed self, or fill containers. (18–24 mos.) **IN:** Demonstrate hand-eye coordination and participate in a variety of activities to enhance coordination. (Infant) Use hand-eye coordination to manipulate smaller objects with increasing control. (Older Toddler) **NH:** Move from awareness of hands to ability to reach and grasp objects of varying sizes. (birth–9 mos.) Coordinate eyes and hands while exploring or holding objects. (9–18 mos.) **NM:** Uses hands or feet to make contact with objects or people. Begins to coordinate hands and eyes. (birth–8 mos.) Uses hands to explore objects with a variety of actions. (6–18 mos.) Uses hands and fingers in more complex and refined ways. (16–24 mos.) **RI:** > Hold onto a toy when it is handed to them > Reach for, grasp, and shake things > Bring hands and objects to their mouth. (9 mos.) Turn the pages of books and point to pictures while being read to > Hold objects in both hands > Pick up very small objects with their index finger and thumb. (18 mos.) **Your State:**	• Allow the baby to grasp the caregiver's finger while playing. • Prepare a safe environment and remove things that are so small that they could be a choking hazard. • Provide crackers or Cheerios® to pick up with fingers. • Provide opportunities for babies to fill and dump small objects into larger ones. • Offer the baby more than one object at the same time. • Provide pop-up toys or action cubes that require pushing or pressing. • Put out playdough and tools so children can pound, roll, and squeeze it. • Provide opportunities for children to paint with brushes or with hands. • Give children tweezers or clothespin to pick up small objects. • Put out cereal loops or pasta to make necklaces. • Provide opportunities for children to set and clear the table after snack. • Place interesting objects and toys within reach for babies to look or swipe at, hit, or kick.

Continued

Figure 10.18

Physical Development Subdomains	Benchmark (What We Want the Child to Be Able to Do)	Indicators (Behaviors We Might See)	Individualized Teaching Strategies
Self-Help, Safety, Health	**Benchmark 3** **AL:** PDH2a: Healthy Habits: Children will show increasing independence in performing self-care tasks. **IN:** PHG1.2 Demonstrate development of safety practices **NH:** Strand: Self Care **NM:** Beginning to Move and Do: Component 13: Self-Help, Safety, Health, and Physical Well-Being Skills: The infant/toddler begins to care for self and practice personal safety. **RI:** Component 1: Health and Safety Practices Learning Goal 1.b: Children become increasingly able to identify unsafe situations and gradually learn strategies for responding to them. **Your State:**	**AL:** Tolerate hands and face being washed and teeth being brushed. (0–9 mos.) **IN:** Seek reassurance from a trusted caregiver when encountering an unfamiliar person or object. (Infant) Respond to adult guidance and direction regarding safety. (Younger Toddler) Participate, with adult support, to develop safety rules for an activity. (Older Toddler) **NH:** May be able to participate, with adult assistance, in selfcare tasks such as dressing and undressing, and feeding themselves, if culturally appropriate. (18–24 mos.) **NM:** Begins to help with feeding, dressing, and personal hygiene. (birth–8 mos.) Helps with feeding, dressing, and personal hygiene. (6–18 mos.) **RI:** Demonstrates a recognition of the difference between their primary caregiver and a stranger. (9 mos.) **Your State:**	- Name foods while children are eating. - Talk to children while you are wiping their faces and hands with a warm cloth. - Exercise a baby's legs and arms while diaper changing (move them out, then in, up, then down). - Provide a spoon for infant to hold during feeding. - Introduce new foods multiple times. - Establish a mealtime routine. - Sing songs about routines, "It's time to brush our teeth. It's time to brush our teeth…" - Talk about bathroom skills and encourage children's interest in using the toilet. - Describe foods as you eat. - Acknowledge when an infant shows signs of being tired.

Figure 10.18

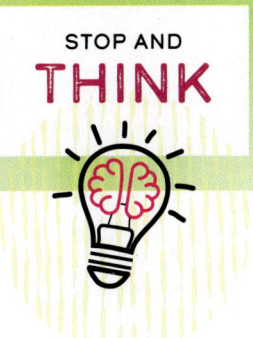

STOP AND THINK

There are many ways to communicate ideas and emotions. Dance and movement provide a method to represent ideas and emotions naturally, as does a game of charades. What are other ideas that are appropriate for the infant-toddler to explore movement?

10.3 Infant-Toddler Resources

The curriculum built in the infant-toddler ages begins with foundational elements of the domains of development: cognitive, social-emotional, physical, and language. It is important for the infant-toddler teacher to have strong knowledge of their state's infant-toddler standards or guidelines.

Using solid and reputable resources provides assurances that expectations are on track to meet each young child where they are and how they can be supported to reach the next milestone of development. During the earliest years, understanding the dynamics of family and the importance of creating strong bonds is crucial. Acquiring valid and reliable resources will support the teacher in their role as parent educator as well as support the child (**Figures 10.19** and **10.20**).

Teacher Toolbox: Curriculum Resources

Resources for Teachers and Caregivers of Infants and Toddlers

Resources for Infant Educarers provides infant-toddler teachers with knowledge around the RIE approach and is aligned with the vision of Magda Gerber. This is a solid source to share with families and professionals working with the very young.

Zero to Three is dedicated to promoting the healthy development of infants and toddlers. They offer a wealth of information, articles, and resources around topics such as brain development, milestones of development, early literacy, and early childhood education.

The Early Childhood Technical Resource Center offers information and resources on development as well as including resources for infants and toddlers with disabilities.

The Child Development Institute includes articles and resources on infant and toddler development, including information on cognitive, social, and emotional development.

BabyCenter is a website with information and resources on pregnancy, childbirth, and parenting, including a section on infant and toddler development.

The National Association for the Education of Young Children (NAEYC) offers resources and information on best practices in early childhood education, including resources for infants and toddlers.

HealthyChildren.org is created by the American Academy of Pediatrics with resources and information on child health and development, including resources for infants and toddlers.

The Center for Early Literacy Learning provides research-based information and resources on early literacy development for infants and toddlers.

National Institute for Early Education Research is a research center that provides information and resources on early childhood education, including resources for infants and toddlers.

Figure 10-19 Credible resources for infant-toddler teachers. How can you utilize these resources to support the children in your care?

Checkpoint

☐ Figure 10.19 includes valuable resources for the infant-toddler teacher. How might you use and share these resources with the family?

☐ The focus of bonding is an inherent element in the infant-toddler years. Identify an example of how this is supported from one of the resources listed.

Rebecca Huguley

Figure 10.20 Infants and toddlers don't come with instructions, and even the most experienced caregivers will sometimes have questions. Having a list of credible sources at the ready will help you find reliable answers to your questions about infant-toddler care. Can you think of any other reliable sources that aren't listed in Figure 10-19?

Chapter 10 Review and Assessment

Chapter Summary

10.1 Describe infant-toddler curriculum components.
- Creating individualized plans is the foundation for learning in the infant-toddler years.
- The domains of development are cognitive, social-emotional, language, and physical. Each of these domains overlap and influence one another.
- The three stages of development from 0–36 months are usually broken into young infant (0–6 months), mobile infant (8–18 months), and toddler (18–36 months).
- Curriculum relies on relationships built on trust.
- The children's home culture and language are integral to all planning.
- Routines are designed around the infant and toddler's development.

10.2 Create an infant-toddler curriculum using your state standards and guidelines.
- The focus of infant-toddler programs vary across different states.
- The early learning standards of various states reflect benchmarks, indicators, and strategies for learning in the social-emotional; cognitive; language, literacy, and communication; and physical domains.
- All standards are built on the premise and understanding that children's development varies widely.
- The infant-toddler teacher plays a key role in identifying concerns that might benefit from interventions.
- Teachers and caregivers should be responsive, intentional, and informed in their everyday work with babies and toddlers.

10.3 Identify infant-toddler resources that support children's physical, cognitive, language, and social-emotional development.
- It is important to identify credible infant-toddler resources.
- Credible and useful resources provide the foundation of a teacher's resource file.
- Making connections to infant-toddler resources provides families with valid information that creates trust and communication.
- The infant-toddler teacher is often the first teacher a family connects with and will become a person that wears many hats: teacher, parent, educator, diaper changer, lullaby-singer, nurturer. It is important for teachers to keep up with the most current information from experts in the field to inform practice.

For Further Reflection

1. Identify examples of questions to pose to toddlers that might expand their knowledge base and encourage their growth and development.
2. Brainstorm ways to incorporate infant and toddler's home languages and cultures through music, drama, and art.
3. How do caregivers arrange the environment and plan the daily schedule to support and encourage toddlers' self-motivated exploration?
4. Why is it important to create a physically safe environment? What elements might be part of an infant room but not part of a toddler room?
5. Identify the factors that influence physical development during the infant-toddler stage of development. Next, explain how you can support and encourage each of the items on your list.

Recall and Application

1. The common four developmental domains include ____.
   A. fine motor, gross motor, literacy, and social-emotional
   B. physical, cognitive, language-literacy-communication and social-emotional
   C. differing abilities, cognitive, social-emotional, and literacy
   D. social, cognitive, emotional, gross motor
2. **True or False.** There are five stages of infant-toddler development.
3. In which domain does learning to walk belong?
   A. physical
   B. cognitive
   C. social-emotional
   D. language
4. **True or False.** The physical domain of development includes scissor-cutting skills.
5. Standards include ____.
   A. benchmarks, indicators, and strategies
   B. cognitive, physical, social-emotional
   C. daycare centers and preschools
   D. gross motor and fine motor skills
6. **True or False.** A child's temperament is the unique way the child responds to the world.
7. Expressive language is ____.
   A. the understanding of words
   B. how gestures have meaning
   C. the understanding of facial gestures
   D. how a child states wants and needs

CHAPTER 11

Preschool Integrated Curriculum

Learning Outcomes

After studying this chapter, you will be able to:

11.1 Define learning plan components.

11.2 Explain the process of building daily learning plan components.

11.3 Demonstrate alignment of daily learning plan components.

11.4 Evaluate academic subject resources.

Standards Covered in This Chapter

NAEYC

1a, 1b, 1c, 1d, 2a, 2b, 3d, 4a, 4b, 4c, 4a, 5b, 5c, 6c

DAP

Guidelines 1, 2;
Principles 1, 2, 3, 4, 5, 6, 7, 8

Image credit: FatCamera/iStock via Getty Images

Real444/E+ via Getty Images

SNAPSHOT

Ms. McKenzie

Three-year-old Chase has spent the morning observing a June beetle he found in the playground sandbox and asks his teacher, Ms. McKenzie, for a container to place the beetle into. Ms. McKenzie frames this as a problem, asking, "How can we ensure that we will not harm the beetle?" Ms. McKenzie helps the boy imagine solutions to placing the beetle in the container and shows him photos of June beetles from around the world. They also look at nonfiction books full of images to introduce the entire class to this beetle's cousins.

For two days, the children investigate June beetles and their life cycle. They create a June beetle habitat in the block area, sketch June beetles in the art area, and create their own June beetle illustrated books. They weigh their June beetle on the scale in the science area and measure the June beetle with a ruler in the math area, The class also views a live webcam from Washington State that shows June beetles in action.

The children's enthusiasm for June beetles has generated interest from their peers and during circle time. On day 3, the class agrees to study insects as a topic of interest. Ms. McKenzie looks forward to guiding the children and plans to learn right along with them. She envisions many ideas to engage her budding group of entomologists (bug experts). Welcome to curriculum integration in the preschool classroom called the *Dragon Room* at Castle Vista Preschool!

Give It Some Thought

1. How does Ms. McKenzie engage the entire class to be interested in a topic of interest around beetles?
2. What will she provide for those children who do not have a shared interest?

Introduction

Curriculum integration builds on existing interrelationships by connecting and overlapping the child's learning experiences. In an integrated curriculum, learning is synthesized across traditional subject areas, along with learning experiences that are designed to be mutually reinforcing. This approach develops the child's ability to transfer learning to other settings (Van-Tassel 2003).

Chapter 11 revisits each of the learning plan components covered in earlier chapters and then explores three integrated topics (museums, weather, great Americans) using three different scenarios. The first scenario includes a completed daily learning plan as a guide, while scenarios two and three provide the template you to complete. When reading each of the scenarios, note the many differences and similarities to your own state standards of practice.

Teachers must also be able to access and assess professional instructional resources, including those available from professional associations representing various disciplines. A comprehensive list of teacher resources that connect to the preschool years invites you to build on that foundation. All educators are expected to understand early learning trajectories and the related developmentally and culturally appropriate teaching and assessment strategies for each area of the early childhood curriculum.

Remember that the role of preschool teachers is to align the learning outcomes to their specific state standards. Assessments assembled in a portfolio collection are categorized by the early learning guidelines and state standards. They are used to reflect the child's proficiencies, which provide compelling indicators for a child's kindergarten readiness.

11.1 Components of a Learning Plan

Developing an integrated curriculum for preschool-aged children is not that different from developing integrated curriculum for elementary school-aged children. Curriculum integration requires a supportive climate of collegiality, a belief in the potential of all children, an expectation of professional growth and involvement, and the resources to make the needed changes operational (Nesin 2019). Preschool educators are aware that when developing curricula they must use their knowledge of each subject area to help children make connections in personally and culturally meaningful ways that reflect their interests (**Figure 11.1**).

Beginning with the catalytic event, the teacher defines the main overarching topic of interest, focusing on one of many options to define the daily focus topic. Next, it is time to create the graphic organizer (commonly a KWHL). The teacher uses children's current knowledge and experiences to select standards that align to measurable learning outcomes and authentic assessments.

Young children learn subjects best by direct, hands-on learning, and because of their innate curiosity, children eagerly embrace all types of engaging learning experiences. The easiest way to incorporate concepts into the early childhood classroom is to integrate them into the planned experiences with questions and prompts. As children move into higher grades, the level of questioning increases, as does the depth of the subject knowledge.

The daily learning plan specifies the state standard used to guide the formation of a measurable learning outcome. You will find many differences and commonalities when exploring state standards, integrating academic subjects, and writing measurable learning outcomes that can be applied to learning experiences. While some states focus more on developmental domains, others focus only on academic subjects, and some focus on

Lordn/iStock via Getty Images

Figure 11.1 This teacher knows that her students love music. *How can she integrate another subject area into a music lesson?*

both. Some states refer to standards as *guidelines*, others as *foundations*, and some states use a combination of different descriptions. Many states also include their standards in languages other than English, such as Spanish or Vietnamese. Each state is unique and reflects the cultures of the families and children that live there.

Because all the elements of a daily learning plan are presented together in this chapter, you should have a copy of your own state's early learning standards and guidelines nearby as a source for comparison. Each topic of interest can be compared to your state's standards to identify similarities and differences. Beginning with the state standards provides a strong start when you are aligning learning outcomes.

An authentic assessment is identified in the daily learning plan. This provides evidence of understanding the learning outcome. The assessment is often placed in a child's portfolio to document the child's understanding for the family or the teacher. Remember that a teacher may use one learning outcome to meet more than one standard and to connect multiple academic subjects, with modifications as needed for each child. The identification of learning areas and the learning experiences occurs last when you are writing backward-design learning plans.

The next sections of the daily learning plan include space to identify ways to involve the family and collaborate with the community, followed by the needs for modifications or accommodations (**Figure 11.2**). The implementation plan outlines the overall learning, beginning with the all-important circle time. The teacher informs the children about the experiences planned and the learning areas that will be used; the children select how and where to start their active learning in the classroom.

The conclusion of the daily learning plan includes a section of needed resources and the educator's reflection of what went well or may need modification in the future. A sample learning plan provides a template to experience how all the elements work together to create a best-practice plan.

Checkpoint

- [ ] Identify a possible topic of interest and a focus topic which a child might find of interest. What would be a potential catalytic event (teachable moment)?
- [ ] Locate your own state standards or guidelines. How does the learning plan support and inform your teaching?

11.2 Putting Together a Learning Plan

The completed preschool learning plan pulls together the elements studied throughout this chapter. The first topic of interest incorporates informed use of internet research to expose children to museums located around the world (**Figure 11.3**).

When guiding a group of preschoolers through a virtual museum experience, teachers introduce them to new vocabulary, media, and artifacts. Each of the museums in the following list has an online collection of artworks for children to explore, always guided by teacher supervision. Take a virtual tour at a museum's website and imagine taking children on a tour, inviting them to select a favorite piece

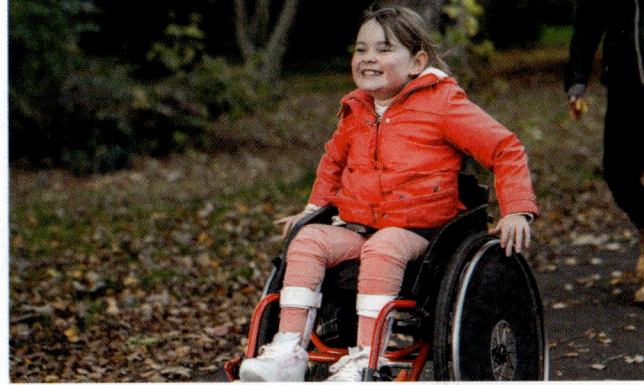

SolStock/E+ via Getty Images

Figure 11.2 When building a daily learning plan, teachers should always document any accommodation or modifications they will need to make for children. What modification might a teacher need to make on a field trip plan for a child who uses a wheelchair?

nicoletaionescu/iStock via Getty Images Plus

Figure 11.3 A virtual field trip can make children feel as though they are roaming the grounds of the world's greatest art museums. In what other ways can the internet be used to broaden children's horizons?

Figure 11.4 These modern-style paintings are located in a museum in Turkey. *How can viewing art from around the world broaden children's horizons?*

of art. Using technology as a tool, children can travel to museums around the world. Curriculum integration with a focus on art in museums begins with a sampling of some of the world's major art museums and the treasures they hold (**Figure 11.4**). The following museums offer virtual tours:

- The Louvre, Paris
- Guggenheim Museum, New York
- Van Gogh Museum, Amsterdam
- Smithsonian Museum, Washington, DC
- The J. Paul Getty Museum, Los Angeles
- The British Museum, London
- Vatican Museum, Vatican City
- The Art Institute of Chicago

Also, visiting an art museum in their home town is a great way to expose children to local culture.

Providing experiences using the internet widens a child's understanding of the world, far beyond the classroom. The daily learning plan embeds technology in the preschool room and allows teachers to explore the global and local sources of art available. Teachers who use technology in their classrooms understand that it is important to supervise children while they are using computers, tablets, or any device that can connect to the internet. When used safely, the internet can not only help children engage meaningfully with technology but can enable children to be active creators (Williams 2017).

When planning a learning experience for "Museums Around the World," one teacher defined multiple standards for visual art, social studies, and math aligned to different outcomes to assess understanding, while intentionally integrating many academic subjects: art, social studies, math, music, physical education, reading, writing, and communication. The teacher took care to individualize the teaching strategies to meet specific needs of individual children, including children with disabilities who require accommodations, as well as children whose learning is advanced, by building upon their interests, knowledge, and skills. State standards are a guide to show what a child should know when entering kindergarten. The teacher used knowledge about individual children to scaffold learning and support and modify learning experiences as needed. The teacher began by creating a KWHL chart (**Figure 11.5**), a complementary concept web (**Figure 11.6**), and a learning plan (**Figure 11.7**).

Figure 11.5 Sample KWHL chart for the "Museums Around the World" topic of interest.

KWHL Chart: Example for "Museums Around the World" Topic of Interest

What I Know	What I Want to Know	How I Will Learn	What I Learned (completed at end of topic learning)
They are big.	What kinds are there?	Field trip, internet search, books, guest speakers	
Museums show off art.	What kinds of art are there?	Paintings, sculptures, drawings, textiles, photographs	
Museums are like cars.	Are they cars?	Lots of new vocabulary words... they sound like limousines, though!	

During the multiweek learning experience built around museums, the teacher planned experiences indoors and outside to support each child's learning. Borrowed books displayed different art styles, and two local artists—a clay sculptor and a painter—presented their skills and techniques to the class. The results of these learning experiences became part of the invitation table to reflect the range of learning opportunities that were explored. The table included some of the artifacts created, including photographs of block area constructions, examples of child-created art, and samples of handmade *My Museum Visit* books. Some of the items were used in the children's portfolios to highlight their individual efforts and reflect which standards they may need to revisit.

For the museum topic of interest, many of the children in the preschool program may have had individualized learning plans that align the local state standards to where they are in their learning and understanding. All children are at different places in understanding concepts, and this is one reason why graphic organizers such as the KWHL chart provide direction for the teacher. For the teacher who differentiates and makes

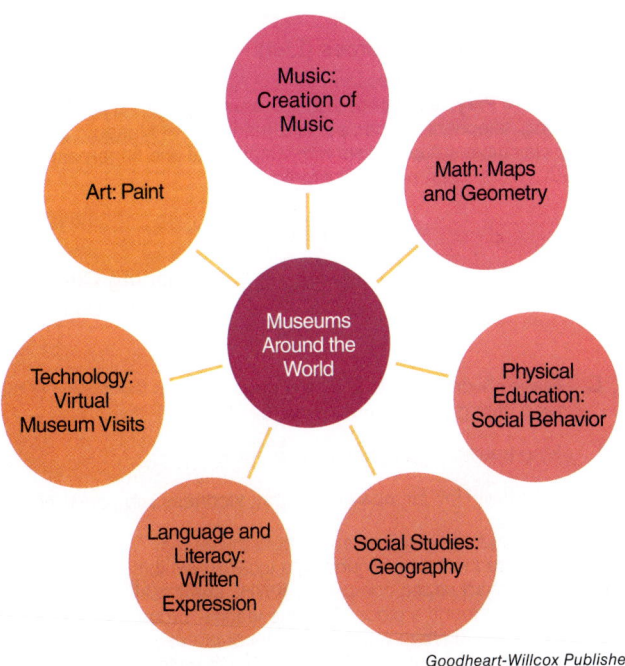

Figure 11.6 Concept web for the "Museums Around the World" topic of interest.

Learning Plan for Topic of Interest: Great Artists
Catalytic Event (Teachable Moment): A local art exhibit is opening in the city
Topic of Interest: Great Artists
Daily Focus Topic: Museums Around the World
Intended Age Group: Preschool

Early Learning Standard	Learning Outcome	Authentic Assessment	Learning Area/Experience
Language and Literacy— Strand 1: Language Concept 3: Vocabulary	Child will be able to identify unique terms connected to museums.	Work Sample	Dramatic Play, Writing, and Art Areas: Role-play docent and curator, and identify different art media: watercolors, chalk painting, fingerpainting, sculpture, as a classroom museum is created (4–8 Spaces). Science, Math, Literacy, Art
Social Studies— Strand 2: Community Concept 1: Environmental awareness	Child will be able to identify different buildings in a community.	Photo	Block Area: Creating museum structure and identifying location of art or local museum in the community (6–8 Spaces). Math, Engineering, Social Studies

Collaborations: (Identify possible role/contribution): Virtual tour guide from a museum?
Community/Colleagues: Donations of variety of frames to frame children's art
Family: Ask families who may be able to donate old paintings, works of art, frames they no longer want
Modifications or accommodations: Alicia requires accessibility through the classroom to maneuver a wheelchair. A table placed in the block area to allow for creating structures will support learning.

Continued

Figure 11.7 Sample daily learning plan for the "Museums Around the World" topic of interest.

Materials and Resources (List)
Circle Time: The Art Lesson
Dramatic Play: telephone, signage, cash register, GRAND OPENING sign, museum worker nametags, art pieces
Writing: telephone, paper, pencils, markers, Art Museum signage
Art: clay table setup, easels with watercolors and fingerpaint, paper/sharpies to create signage, tickets, ruler, paper
Math: rulers, chart paper for predictions

Opening Circle Time (Large Group Time)
Identify C-I-R-C-L-E steps. (20–25 minutes)

C Place children's mats to form a large circle. In the middle of the circle, a towel covers a small, transparent tub and the book that will be read during the concept segment.

I Sing traditional welcoming song.

R Begin with job jar, news of the day, kindness idea, and announce that today is National Museum Day.

C Today we are going to learn about museums!
- Share the flyer announcing a local art exhibit.
- On chart paper, complete a KWHL chart asking, "What do we know about museums?"
- Pass around a piece of art the teacher brought from home and talk about how it was made and who created it.
- "Turn and share with your neighbor about your experiences with museums. Imagine what it is like to be an artist and having your creation in a museum so that many people can admire it." Model thinking aloud about what you wonder about being that artist. Read *The Art Lesson* by Tomie dePaola.

Implementation Plan (9–11:30)
Sing to the tune of "Row, Row, Row Your Boat":

Share, share, share the color,
This is the game we love!
When the little game is through,
The color we will say!

At the end of each verse, point at a child to yell out a favorite color.

L Introduce the learning area experiences that will be open.
- For dramatic play, share learning area experiences with story problems that need to be solved.
- Identify the number of children who can occupy each space at a time.

E Excuse children to go to their chosen areas after washing their hands. Ask each to repeat where they are going and what they are going to do when they get there. Turn on classical background music!

Learning Area Choices (Small Group Time)

Dramatic Play Area: (Learning Outcome 1) Our own Museum: Grand opening of our museum is in the works. The museum is curating new art. The docent is busy answering the phone and taking care of people wanting a ticket to attend. Art pieces need to be priced and marked. The curator helps display each which is important for the artist and the buyer.
(5–6 spaces) Story Problem, Social Studies, Art, Math, Literacy, Language

Writing Area: (Learning Outcome 1)
1) Design and name museum
2) Create invitations to attend an open house at the museum: The docent is answering the telephone, which is ringing off the hook with people wanting to obtain tickets to attend the open house. The museum curator needs to organize the walls for attendees to view, as well as explain to the artists working in the art area what types of art are needed.
(3–4 spaces) Story Problem Language, Literacy, Science, Math

Art Area: (Learning Outcome 1)
1) Clay sculptures
2) Wall displays to frame and hang in our Museum
3) Painting at easels with assorted medium
(4–8 spaces) Science, Literacy, Art

Continued
Goodheart-Willcox Publisher

Figure 11.7

Math Area: Measuring sculpture in playgrounds in inches and feet after being introduced to a tape measure. Chart predictions.
(1–2 spaces) Math, Literacy

Block Area/Social Studies Area: (Learning Outcome 2) Create our own museum and visit those around the community
(4–6 spaces) Art, Engineering, Social Studies

Science/Cooking: Make granola (teacher assistance)
(4 spaces) Science, Math
Note: All children can participate, if desired, at alternating times or have their own granola made for them.

Technology:
1) Observe live webcam of children's museum by doing an internet search with teacher.
2) Children make a pictorial journal page of what they learned.
(1–2 spaces) Technology, Science, Literacy

Outdoor Area: Create stick pictures in the dirt area.
(6–8 spaces) Science

Closing Circle Time (Large Group Time)
Following the five-to-ten-minute cleanup transition signal, children return to the closing circle, excited to share their learning. The opening circle book (or a different one) is (re)read, and plans are revisited to see if they were met. Using turn and share, children are encouraged to turn to their friend and provide learning experience details. A teaser of what to expect the next day is shared: a special guest is scheduled—a real docent or gallery owner.

Goodheart-Willcox Publisher

Figure 11.7

changes as needed, all learning experiences can be modified to make connections within different levels of understanding. In this case, the teacher has used a mix of authentic assessments to provide evidence of understanding. The children engaged in daily learning experiences that included seamless integration of different academic subjects inside and outside the classroom (**Figure 11.8**). Making connections with art through nature could have been included in the study by spotlighting great environmental artists such as Andy Goldsworthy (**Figure 11.9**) or Robert Shilling.

ljubaphoto/E+ via Getty Images

Figure 11.8 This sculptor is sharing her craft with preschool students. How does a visit by a local artist enrich a learning experience about art museums?

 **Checkpoint**

☐ How does a concept web support the teacher's placement of learning experiences?

☐ How is integration of different academic areas supported within a child-led topic of interest? Provide three examples.

11.3 Aligning the Learning Plan Components

With the solid foundation of components that make up a strong learning plan, the following scenarios encourage the creation of unique learning plans built on your own state's standards. A learning plan template can also be found in the Teacher Toolbox.

Chris Oliver/iStockvia Getty Images

Figure 11.9 Andrew Goldsworthy is well known for his stunning nature photography. Creating an artist study using his photographs expands children's connections between nature and art. How would you integrate science and art in your own artist study?

First Step: Choose the Topic of Interest	
Topic Type	Topic
Topic of Interest:	Weather
Focus Topic:	

Goodheart-Willcox Publisher

Figure 11.10 After you have chosen the desired learning outcome for your plan, choose the topic of interest.

Topic of Interest: Weather

Every part of the United States experiences unique weather elements. Begin the learning plan with a catalyst from a regional weather event to create an original daily learning plan (**Figure 11.10**).

When considering learning experiences and outcomes, remember to focus on specific learning standards or guidelines that the children should be able to master by the time they enter kindergarten. Each day the teacher may be working on several different standards, and each child will be observed with different goals in mind. To teach each child at the child's own level of development requires differentiated instruction. Be aware that there are hundreds of possible experiences that can integrate different subjects around each state's early learning standards.

Making connections through children's real experiences is developmentally appropriate practice. A study of weather is relevant wherever one lives. When considering events that might occur outside the neighborhood, look for common themes, such as natural disasters, to support connections.

Over the course of several weeks, children will have multiple learning experiences on the topic of weather and cross many domains of development and academic subjects. The transformation of the dramatic play area into a classroom weather reporting desk may give the learning environment a different look, with a video camera, whiteboard to announce the weather, and props such as a microphone and name tags (**Figure 11.11**). Think outside the box!

In one instance, the focus topic arose naturally due to weather forecasts, and as a result weather dominated current events with the children at the morning circle time. A KWHL chart was created, and the children's conversations revealed what they knew and did not know (**Figure 11.12**). The teacher considered the many possibilities to build on the children's interest when applying this topic to state weather patterns.

Solstock/E+ via Getty Images

Figure 11.11 Transforming the dramatic play area into a weather news center helps the topic of interest come alive for the students. *What other weather-related materials could you add to a dramatic play area?*

In a case like this, the teacher may invite guests from the local news channel or extend learning to include weather from different parts of the world, a great connection with social studies. It is evident that many of the standards and guidelines will continue to be covered as academic subjects and will be integrated during the learning experiences to come (**Figure 11.13**).

KWHL Weather (Blank Template)			
What I Know	What I Want to Know	How I Will Learn	What I Will Learn

Goodheart-Willcox Publisher

Figure 11.12 This is a blank KWHL chart. *What do you think preschool-age children might already know about weather?*

Topic of Interest: Great Americans

The next topic of interest represents the people who live in the United States—local heroes and great Americans. Consider which notable people your state might highlight and which standards could be aligned when completing a daily learning plan with outcomes, assessments, and experiences around which to teach (**Figure 11.14**). Begin with a blank KWHL chart like the one used for the weather topic in the previous section.

Preschool integration strategies using a "Great Americans" topic may be based on the children's interest in an upcoming community event related to a locally significant American, which may provide a possible catalyst for this topic of interest. This topic of interest

Learning Plan for Topic of Interest: Weather (Blank Template)

Catalytic Event (Teachable Moment):
Topic of Interest: Weather
Daily Focus Topic:
Intended Age Group: Preschool

Early Learning Standard	Learning Outcome	Authentic Assessment	Learning Area/Experience
[from your state]	Child will be able to		
	Child will be able to		

Collaborations: (Identify possible role/contribution)
Community/Colleagues:
Family:
Modifications or accommodations:

Implementation Plan (9–11:30)
1. Circle time (large group time) Identify C-I-R-C-L-E steps. (20–25 minutes)
2. Learning area choices (small group time) Example: Dramatic Play, STEM, Art, Literacy, Outdoors, Music, Blocks with planned learning experiences.
3. Identify academic subjects (Music, Art, STEM, Social Studies, Physical Activity, Literacy) to integrate/combine in the learning areas
4. Closing Circle (large group Time) (5-10 minutes)

Reflection:
Notes:

Goodheart-Willcox Publisher

Figure 11.13 Learning plan for the topic of interest: Weather.

embraces unique connections to one's state and in some instances, provides opportunities for exclusive events.

Highlighting important people is one part of social studies that can be integrated across all state lines by connecting to local people who have made different contributions. This topic of interest easily connects to math, literacy, arts, social studies, approaches to learning, science, and physical development and represents true integration of academic subjects supported by the state standards and driven by children's interest. See **Figure 11.15** for examples of some great Americans and their state affiliations.

 **Checkpoint**

☐ Which of the learning area components do you find most useful? Why?
☐ Provide an example of how the final reflection informs your teaching practices.

Goodheart-Willcox Publisher

Figure 11.14 Concept web for the topic "Great Americans."

Great Americans and Their State Affiliations

American/Day	Early Learning Standard	Learning Outcome	Assessment	Learning Experiences (integrate academic subjects)
Amelia Earhart (NC) **National History of Amelia Earhart Day**  *Everett Collection/Shutterstock.com*				
Fred Rogers (PA) **Mr. Rogers' Day**  *Olga Popova/Shutterstock.com*				
Martin Luther King, Jr. (GA) **Martin Luther King, Jr. Day**  *Atomazul/Shutterstock.com*				
Harriet Tubman (MD) **Harriet Tubman Day**  *Photos.com/PHOTOS.com via Getty Images*				
Apollo Ohno (WA) **Mini Olympics**  *Kathy Hutchins/Shutterstock.com*				

Goodheart-Willcox Publisher

Figure 11.15 Creating a chart like this can help you determine how early learning standards, learning outcomes, assessments, and learning experiences can be applied to the topic of Great Americans. Complete the chart with a Great American from the state where you are located.

11.4 Evaluating Teacher Resources

When teachers develop their own curriculum, it is most important that the learning outcomes target identified learning goals and applicable early learning standards, and that they are derived from credible resources. Likewise, if teachers use a published curriculum, it is important that they verify the products as developmentally, culturally, and linguistically responsive for the children served. Using current resources from experts to ensure that curriculum content is accurate and comprehensive is a professional expectation (NAEYC, *DAP*, 2020).

Having reliable resources to guide learning is important in the early years. Creating a resource toolbox is a continual practice for staying current in the field. A resource toolbox can provide engaging learning experiences for the preschool child, as well as be a source of information for families. The internet is full of ideas, and once they are verified as reliable and up-to-date, they can be put to use in the classroom.

Verifying Resources

How can you differentiate between a strong resource and a weak one? When looking for data that will inform practice changes, information should be based on scientific evidence that has been replicated in studies by more than one researcher. Choosing valid resources is an ethical decision that can make a huge impact if you are looking for ideas to support a parent's concern or a new practice you may have learned about at a conference that may or may not apply in your classroom.

Ask yourself these questions when using resources from the internet:

- Is it current?
- Is it relevant?
- Is the author reputable?
- Is it deemed accurate?
- What is its purpose for being posted?

Teacher Toolbox: Curriculum Resources

Maintaining a list of credible resources ensures that the teacher has the most current, valid, and reliable information to support learning and inform teaching. Using common language and concepts provides consistency as well as relevant and current information derived from experts in the field. The teacher toolbox can be expanded and will become a dynamic set of resources that will support decisions made when creating or exploring new curriculum concepts. As a head start toward creating your own toolbox, the following resources have been reviewed and found trustworthy.

Approaches to Learning

National Association for the Education of Young Children (NAEYC): NAEYC promotes research-based, high-quality early learning through publishing guidelines and approaches to practice, and by connecting practice, policy, and research. NAEYC is considered a must-have resource, with credible and research-based journals, articles, and position papers focused on the early years, 0–8.

Early Literacy

International Literacy Association (ILA): The ILA connects research and practice focused on literacy education across the globe. Valuable journals provide current scholarly resources around literacy with position papers ranging from phonological awareness to digital literacy (**Figure 11.16**).

Figure 11.16 International Literacy Association (ILA) is an organization devoted to improving literacy programs for children. Do you think the schools in your area would benefit from this organization? Why or why not?

Figure 11.17 Early Childhood Art Educators (ECAE) is an organization devoted to providing leadership in art education for children ages 0–8. Why do you think art education is important for young children?

Figure 11.18 The Early Childhood Music and Movement Association (ECMMA) promotes meaningful music and movement experiences for children all around the world. Do you think the early learning environments in your community promote meaningful music and movement experiences?

Art

Early Childhood Art Educators (ECAE): The National Art Education Association (NAEA) provides professional activities at state and national levels concerning appropriate art education practices for children from 0–8 years. Relevant information and leadership around art education for young children to early childhood professional organizations, museums and other organizations involved with programs for young children is a focus of NAEA. (**Figure 11.17**).

Early Childhood Music and Movement Association (ECMMA): This organization provides catalysts for meaningful early childhood music and movement practices throughout the world (**Figure 11.18**).

The Dreaming Zebra® Foundation: Encouraging children to embrace their individuality, to express themselves creatively, and to follow their artistic dreams is a common theme of the Dreaming Zebra® Foundation.

P.S. ARTS: The focus of P.S. Arts is on providing opportunities to schools and communities who may not have other resources to support arts education.

Social Studies

National Council for the Social Studies (NCSS): Given the importance of early years, educators create learning environments and experiences that foster young children's skills as active citizens committed to inclusion and equity. NCSS supports young children's progression of social studies learning in early childhood settings and recognizes the developmental continuum of social studies learning.

Science

National Science Teachers Association (NSTA) (**Figure 11.19**): Promotes and provides resources, professional development, and support to improve inclusion of science education. NSTA informs the teacher regarding the many values of including science in the classroom. Ranging from encouraging curiosity to the development of critical thinking skills and creativity, inclusion of science helps prepare children for their future.

Technology

International Society for Technology in Education (ISTE): ISTE provides strategies to support the use of technology as part of the learning experience. ISTE focuses on technology in the classroom to transform learning.

Math

National Council of Teachers of Mathematics (NCTM): NCTM is the leading authority for math-related resources that are current, reliable, and valid. Advocating for a high-quality mathematics curriculum is a focus of NCTM. Publications that include a focus on the preschool years promote accessible math education for all children.

Physical Education and Health

National Association for Sport and Physical Education (NASPE): NASPE promotes knowledge, professional practice and increased support for physical education programs, sports, and other physical activity programs (**Figure 11.20**).

Play

The International Play Association (IPA): IPA provides resources that promote the fundamental right of a child to play. IPA promotes play-based learning with publications and opportunities for increasing the rights of play across the world.

Checkpoint

- ☐ Complete a search and list two credible resources to use when designing a learning plan that includes a focus on social studies.
- ☐ Why is "Approaches to Learning" part of every state standard/guideline written? How do your own state standards/guidelines support this?

FatCamera/E+ via Getty Images

Figure 11.19 The National Science Teachers Association (NSTA) promotes the sciences in the classroom. How would integrating science across the curriculum support critical thinking in other academic areas?

SolStock/E+ via Getty Images

Figure 11.20 The National Association for Sport and Physical Education (NASPE) promotes quality physical education experiences for young children. Do you think children today need more or less physical activity than they are getting? Explain your answer.

Chapter 11 Review and Assessment

Chapter Summary

11.1 Define learning plan components.
- Teachers should consolidate their understanding of the different learning plan components to intentionally integrate curriculum using the backward design approach
- Beginning with the state standards as the guide, learning outcomes are created and measured to reflect proficiency using authentic assessment.

11.2 Explain the process of building daily learning plan components.
- Specific scenarios can connect to more than a dozen different learning outcomes.

11.3 Demonstrate alignment of daily learning plan components.
- The diverse cultures found in every state are an example of possibilities to be considered when building learning that is developmentally appropriate while integrating subjects.

11.4 Evaluate academic subject resources.
- Making connections to credible resources when aligning to academic subjects provides valuable information for teachers when they are planning.
- National organizations and other sources that support teaching for the preschool age teacher are important in a teacher's toolbox.
- It is important for teachers to keep up with the most current information from experts in the field.
- Preschool teachers are a valuable source of knowledge for colleagues and the families they serve.

For Further Reflection

1. Each state has its own written early learning standards. Investigate your own state and become familiar with the standards. On which content areas does your state focus? What does your state call its standards? Is preschool identified as one age group, or are there separate groups (threes, fours, fives)?

2. Individualizing the learning outcomes to challenge some children while providing needed support to others is a common occurrence in the preschool classroom. Identify how one learning outcome in your own state could be modified to meet the needs of many different children.

3. Dual language learners face additional challenges not only when learning to read, but when learning to count. Number words differ between languages. Pay attention and support their learning by helping them compare their home language terms to English number words. Tip: Several internet sites share words in multiple languages. Try it out. In what other ways you can combine two languages to support the dual language learner?

4. Working from a topic of interest and focus topic, select one learning area in the classroom (for example, dramatic play, math area, art area) and create a learning experience that combines two different academic subjects using your state standards as a guide.

Recall and Application

1. The daily learning plan includes which of the following?
   A. lunch menu
   B. catalytic event
   C. transitions
   D. donations needed
2. **True or False.** The daily learning plan uses the KWHL chart to inform practice.
3. Which learning area is *best* suited for a learning experience about how combining the colors red and blue creates a new color?
   A. math area
   B. art area
   C. literacy area
   D. dramatic play area
4. Which learning area is *best* suited for a learning experience about using a ruler to measure objects?
   A. math area
   B. art area
   C. literacy area
   D. dramatic play area
5. Which learning area is *best* suited for a learning experience in which children sketch in their journals what they just saw on a nature walk?
   A. math area
   B. art area
   C. literacy area
   D. dramatic play area
6. Which learning area is *best* suited for a learning experience in which children act out events in the lives of great Americans?
   A. math area
   B. art area
   C. literacy area
   D. dramatic play area
7. **True or False.** Learning plans provide a strong connection to planned learning for a day.
8. **True or False.** An authentic assessment is identified in the daily learning plan.
9. **True or False.** To teach each child at the child's own level of development it is not necessary to differentiate instruction.
10. **True or False.** "Great Americans" is a topic of interest that embraces unique connections to one's state and, in some instances, provides opportunities for exclusive events.
11. Which of the following is *not* a question to ask when verifying an internet source?
    A. Is it current?
    B. Is it relevant?
    C. Is the author reputable?
    D. Does it reinforce what you already believed to be true?

Chapter 12

Kindergarten through Third Grade Integrated Curriculum

Learning Outcomes

After studying this chapter, you will be able to:

12.1 Recognize developmentally appropriate kindergarten–third grade curriculum standards.

12.2 Analyze developmentally appropriate integration strategies across the kindergarten–third grade curriculum.

12.3 Distinguish credible academic subject resources.

Standards Covered in This Chapter

NAEYC

1a, 1b, 1c, 1d, 2a, 2b, 3d, 4a, 4b, 4c, 4a, 5b, 5c, 6c

DAP

Guidelines 1, 2; Principles 1, 2, 3, 4, 5, 6, 7, 8

Image credit: skynesher/Getty Images

Ms. Sanchez

SNAPSHOT

MBI/iStock/Getty Images Plus

Ms. Sanchez's first grade classroom is preparing to conduct science experiments in groups of four to compare the effects of vibration with rubber bands. Her lesson aligns with the mandated physical science standards for what a first grade student should be learning (**Figure 12.1**).

Across the hall, Mrs. Abel's first grade students are also learning around the same standard, but with a very different lesson. The students are making predictions in pairs and using a flashlight beam to observe changes in light waves using a variety of materials. The teachers often integrate academic subjects and standards, when possible, in a way that is engaging and developmentally appropriate for their students.

Give It Some Thought

1. There are many learning experiences that can be created to meet a standard. Which of the experiences described here do you believe is better? Why?

Key Terms

anchoring phenomena
artificial intelligence (AI)
character education
Common Core

crosscutting concepts
lesson plans
performance indicator

social-emotional learning (SEL)
state standards
uniform

Introduction

As established earlier in this textbook, a state standard is the first component of the backward design process. The standard provides guidance and a strong foundation for learning, as reflected in **Figure 12.1**. The planning framework in the early years is commonly called a *lesson plan* to differentiate it from the preschool years and learning plan.

Anchoring phenomena can be described as the glue that holds a lesson plan together. They also provide a strategy to help students make new connections to the information. Anchoring phenomena are introduced at the beginning of the lesson and serve as a reference point for subsequent learning. This helps to "anchor" students' understanding and provides a framework for future learning. An example is a science lesson on vibration. The teacher may start with a video showing how sound is created by vibrations that travel through the air, and how ears turn the vibrations into sound (**Figure 12.2**).

Crosscutting concepts bridge different disciplines and connect them through common themes. One example is cause and effect. Cause and effect can be applied to many disciplines. An example that incorporates cause and effect and vibrations includes:

- Subject: Science
- Topic: Vibrations
- Crosscutting topic: Cause and effect
- Objective: Student will be able to explain and identify the cause and effect of vibrations
- Assessment: Notes
- Learning experience: Group students and give them a worksheet that asks them to identify the cause and effect of vibrations and illustrate their understanding.

The *lesson plans* of both first grade teachers described in the Snapshot align to a specific standard and will provide evidence of meeting expectations as mandated by their state's Department of Education. Teachers in the early grades create their own individual lesson plans while integrating academic subjects (**Figure 12.3**). As students move into higher grades, the level of questioning increases, as does depth of the subject knowledge expected by standards mandated by the state.

Chapter 12 focuses on the different academic standards adopted across fifteen states used to create and integrate curriculum in the kindergarten–third grade classrooms. A section presenting various sources of standards is followed by a section that provides resources and strategies for teachers.

Early childhood education professionals model engagement in the curriculum and support students' curious nature (**Figure 12.4**). They respond to the developmental needs

Figure 12.1 State standards with examples of expectations to meet each.

State Standards for Physical Science

In first grade, students develop an understanding of the effects of forces and waves, and how they can impact or be impacted by objects near and far away. They explore the relationships between sound and vibrating materials, as well as light and materials including the ability of sound and light to travel from place to place.

Standard	#	Description
Plan and carry out investigations	1.P2U1.	Plan and carry out investigations demonstrating the effect of placing objects made with different materials in the path of a beam of light and predict how objects with similar properties will affect the beam of light.
Design and evaluate	1.P2U1.2	Use models to provide evidence that vibrating matter creates sound and sound can make matter vibrate.

Goodheart-Willcox Publisher

of individual students to advance their skills as readers, writers, artists, musicians, mathematicians, scientists, engineers, dancers, athletes, historians, economists, and geographers. All children deserve a caring learning community. When educators develop curricula, they use their solid knowledge in each curriculum area while also helping individual children construct knowledge in personally and culturally meaningful ways (NAEYC, *DAP*, 2020).

12.1 Kindergarten–Third Grade Curriculum Standards

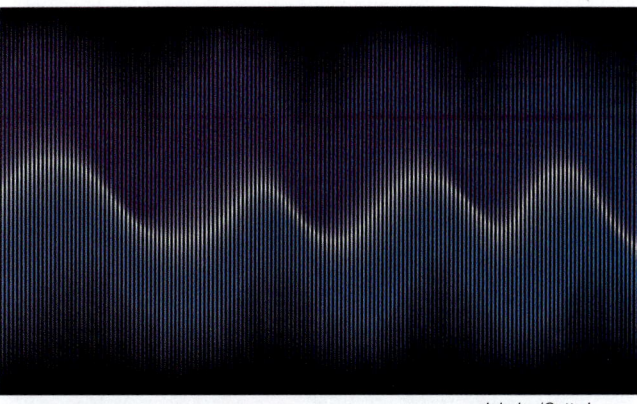

Jobalou/Getty Images

Figure 12.2 This image reflects a visual of sound waves. How can images help students achieve learning standards?

Educational standards are the learning goals for what children need to know and be able to do; *curriculum* is the blueprint for how children will achieve the learning goals. Educational standards are created at the state or national level and are used by all states when writing lesson plans in kindergarten–third grade classrooms. Both state and national standards are developed to set minimum expectations of what students should know and be able to do at each grade level.

State Standards

State standards connect the state's own culture to the curriculum and are developed by education experts and teachers in each state (**Figure 12.5**). These educational standards guide curriculum development and are used by teachers to create lesson plans around the different academic subject areas for all grades. Additionally, some states are beginning to

Lesson Plan Sample: Grade 1
Physical Science I
Supporting module: Balance & Motion

In first grade, students develop an understanding of the effects of forces and waves, and how they can impact or be impacted by objects near and far away. They explore the relationships between sound and vibrating materials, as well as light and materials including the ability of sound and light to travel from place to place.
Core Ideas for Knowing Science:
- P3: Changing the movement of an object requires a net force to be acting on it.
- P4: The total amount of energy in a closed system is always the same but can be transferred from one energy store to another during an event.

Core Ideas for Using Science:
- U1: Scientists explain phenomena using evidence obtained from observations and/or scientific investigations. Evidence may lead to developing models and/or theories to make sense of phenomena. As new evidence is discovered, models and theories can be revised.
- U2: The knowledge produced by science is used in engineering and technologies to solve problems and/or create products.

Science and Engineering Practices	Anchoring Phenomena	Crosscutting Concepts
• Ask questions and define problems • Develop and use models • Plan and carry out investigations • Analyze and interpret data • Obtain, evaluate, and communicate information	• How Are Sleds and Sleighs Different? • Can You Walk a Tightrope? • Why Is Ice Slippery?	• Patterns • Cause and Effect • Structure and Function • Systems and System Models • Stability and Change • Scale, Proportion, and Quantity • Energy and Matter

Goodheart-Willcox Publisher

Figure 12.3 Lesson plan example. Identify an additional anchoring phenomenon and crosscutting concept.

Wavebreakmedia/iStock/Royalty-Free/Getty Images

Figure 12.4 Common Core standards were developed to help students achieve in the areas of literacy and mathematics. *How can teachers use these standards to guide their curriculum?*

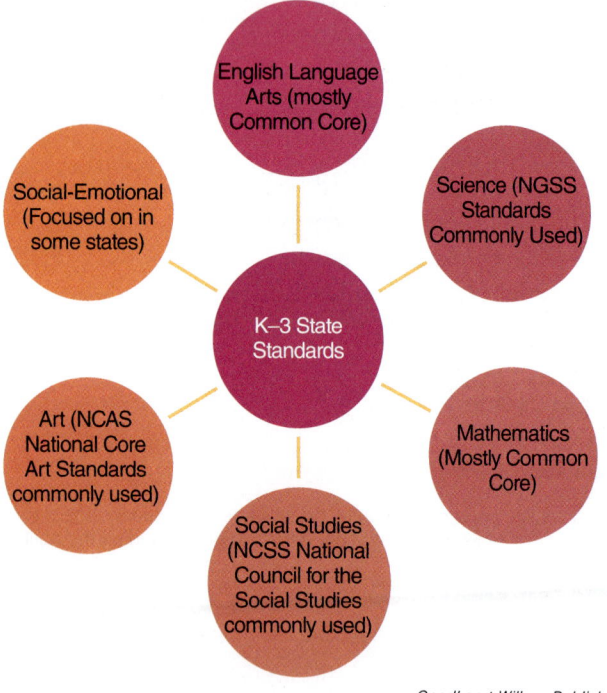

Goodheart-Willcox Publisher

Figure 12.5 K–3 standards concept web. *How do your state's standards connect to your state culture?*

adopt state-created standards for social-emotional development and character education as part of learning.

The federal government does not have authority over the educational systems, based on the US Constitution. States have the sole authority over their educational systems. Each state selects its own standards for defining and connecting learning. States are also authorized to routinely review, and change, or add to the standards to best meet the needs of their students (commoncore.org).

All states have specific standards to guide art, social studies, and science curriculum, although not all align to a set of national standards. Nine states currently use their own state standards or a combination to align to all academic subjects. The remaining states have adopted the Common Core standards to guide curriculum and lesson planning around English language arts/literacy and math.

Common Core refers to a uniform set of education standards that have been adopted in 41 states (as of 2022) and the District of Columbia as a guide to increase skills in math and English language arts/literacy. The Common Core initiative was first introduced in 2010 to ensure that all students would graduate high school with a proficiency in math and English language arts so they could do well in college (**Figure 12.6**). The initiative was sponsored by the National Governors Association and Council of Chief State School Officers and was created after reviewing the state standards that were current at the time.

When used to refer to the Common Core, ***uniform*** means that the learning criteria expectations are the same in every state that has adopted the Common Core standards. Proponents of the Common Core standards believe that having uniform standards that span state lines increases the educational level of the nation. Critics of Common Core claim that focusing on grade-level skills that are highly academic in nature puts pressure on teachers to teach using paper-and-pencil methods instead of learning approaches that are engaging, interactive, and developmentally appropriate.

STOP AND THINK

Making connections to your own state's standards while reviewing other standards is essential and provides alternate perspectives. With the ability of the individual states to modify and change their own educational standards, how does your state currently connect to the English language arts and math Common Core standards?

Performance indicators describe performance expectations of students; this term is commonly used in grade schools. Although in the earlier years, performance indicators are considered *learning outcomes*, both are measurable using valid assessments.

Common Core made big shifts in what students learned in the states that adopted them. It contains detailed standards to specify depth as well as breadth of learning expected across all grades (understood.com). There are 21 to 28 designated standards for each grade from kindergarten to eighth grade. In addition, the standards present an overview of critical areas for each grade in math and English language arts.

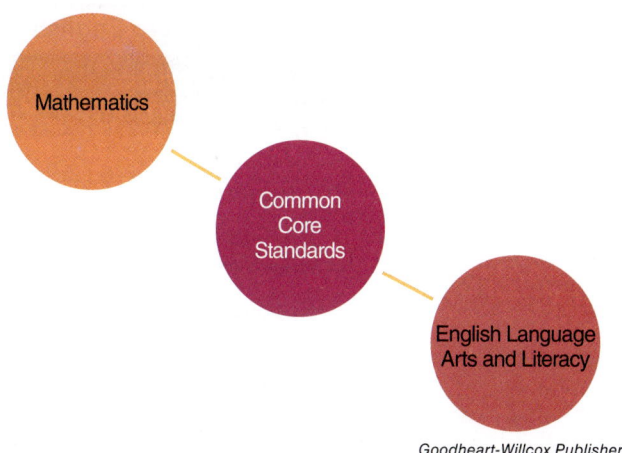

Figure 12.6 Common Core domains. Why do you think Common Core focuses on these two domains?

STOP AND THINK

Before the Common Core, each state had its own academic standards with different learning expectations. A student might have been considered *proficient* (or pretty good) in reading in one state but not even meet *basic* reading standards in another state. What are the benefits to having a uniform set of standards? What might be a concern?

Common Core English Language Arts

Common Core requires students to work more with complex texts. These are books, essays, stories, poems, and other texts that have higher reading levels. They may also have more levels of meaning, require more background knowledge to understand, and use more formal writing.

The Common Core English Language Arts standard (**Figure 12.7**) has also placed greater emphasis on nonfiction texts than have previous standards. For instance, before Common Core, younger students were not introduced to nonfiction texts, because it was believed the student should be learning to read, versus reading to learn. The educational system supported waiting to offer nonfiction books at third grade, but this is no longer the case. Nonfiction books are now offered, along with fiction books, as early as kindergarten. In grade school, the standards require a 50-50 split between fiction and nonfiction. The goal is to build students' knowledge of the world.

Before Common Core, the idea was that before students can gain comprehension of what they are reading, they have to be somewhat proficient readers. This way of thinking continues to influence reading instruction and learning systems in classrooms throughout the world. But should reading for information and comprehension wait until the third grade? Do children make the transition from "learning to read" to "reading to learn" so suddenly? New studies say, "probably not." Research now shows that "learning to read" and "reading to learn" should occur simultaneously and continually throughout a child's elementary and secondary years of education. Reading for information and comprehension should start as soon as a child begins to read—or even as early as parents start reading to their toddler (Loveless 2015).

In writing, citing evidence is now required instead of personal experience. In the past, it was accepted practice for students to write a paper based on their personal experience. Common Core requires that students use evidence in texts to argue and provide examples or explanations. For instance, a student who is writing a paper on immigration must cite news articles, rather than rely on personal feelings.

Common Core English Language Arts				
English Language Arts/Literacy Domain	Kindergarten	First Grade	Second Grade	Third Grade
Reading: Literature	X	X	X	X
Reading: Informational Text	X	X	X	X
Reading: Foundational Skills	X	X	X	X
Writing	X	X	X	X
Speaking and Listening	X	X	X	X
Language	X	X	X	X
Standard 10: Range, Quality, Complexity	X	X	X	X

Goodheart-Willcox Publisher

Figure 12.7 Common Core Literacy Domain. Why do you think speaking and listening are included?

Common Core Math

Previous state standards often required students to cover many different math concepts, without much depth. The Common Core covers fewer math topics but expect students will work more deeply on those topics (**Figure 12.8**). The Common Core standards build on previously learned math concepts. What a student learns in first grade must be applied in second grade, and so on. Students are expected to have a global view of math, not just understand individual topics.

Students should show more understanding of math concepts by third grade. Many previous state math standards focused on simply knowing the right steps to get the right answer to a math problem. For instance, students had to learn a standard way to do long division. Common Core expands the focus to require students to show understanding of the concepts. It is not enough to get the right answer. Students must show how they arrived at the correct answer.

Other National Standards

Common Core standards do not cover science, social studies, art, or social-emotional learning. However, the following widely adopted standards fill the gaps. The Next Generation Science Standards guide science instruction; the National Core Arts Standards guide arts; the National Council for Social Studies guides social studies; and the Social Emotional-Character Education Standards identify guidelines to support the teacher and student in social-emotional learning. Expectations for kindergarten–third grade teaching and learning are much different than those for the first five to six years of life.

Next Generation Science Standards

Most state science curriculum development practices are guided by the Next Generation Science standards. These are considered the gold standard, with performance expectations outlined at each level. The performance expectations build on each other from year to year as students apply and explore the world of science, grouped into four domains: physical science, life science, earth and space science, and engineering.

Common Core Math

Math Domain	Kindergarten	First Grade	Second Grade	Third Grade
Counting and Cardinality	X			
Operations and Algebraic Thinking	X	X	X	X
Number and Operations in Base 10	X	X	X	X
Measurement and Data	X	X	X	X
Geometry	X	X	X	X
Numbers and Operations—Fractions				X
Ratios and Proportional Relationships				
The Number System				
Expressions and Equations				
Statistics and Probability				
Functions				

Goodheart-Willcox Publisher

Figure 12.8 Common Core Math Domain. What do you think geometry looks like at the kindergarten level?

National Core Arts Standards (NCAS)

The arts provide a distinctive path for discovering who we are and embed ways of thinking that are just as disciplined as science or math. The arts are used by and have shaped every culture and individual on Earth, and they are immersed into life on nearly all levels. Examples of how the arts inform people's lives are apparent whenever you hear a loved song, stand in awe of an artist's sculpture, move to music, connect to digital animations, or are inspired by being at a play. Dance, music (including individual elements within technology, composition, harmonizing instruments, ensembles), media arts, theater, and visual arts are the focus of the National Core Arts standards. These standards include four different levels: *create, perform/present/produce, respond,* and *connect* (nationalartsstandards.org). The National Core Arts Standards (NCAS) apply to kindergarten through third grade in each of the states featured later in this chapter, with the exception of South Dakota, which has adopted its own version as shown in **Figure 12.9** and **Figure 12.10**.

National Social Studies Standards

The National Curriculum Standards for Social Studies provides a framework for teachers, schools, districts, states, and other nations, as a tool for curriculum alignment and development. The standards incorporate current research and offer suggestions for improvement from experienced practitioners. They were developed to provide each state with information

Figure 12.9 National Core Art Standards: Artistic Processes

National Core Art Standards (South Dakota) Artistic Processes					
Creating	Performing	Presenting	Producing	Responding	Connection
Conceiving and developing new artistic ideas and work	Realizing artistic ideas and work through interpretation and presentation	Interpreting and sharing	Realizing and presenting artistic ideas and work	Understanding and evaluating how the arts convey meaning	Relating artistic ideas and work with personal meaning and external content

Goodheart-Willcox Publisher

Figure 12.10 National Core Art Standards: Anchor Standards for Children

National Core Arts Standards (South Dakota) Anchor Standards for Children			
Creating	Performing	Producing	Connection
• Generate and conceptualize artistic ideas and work • Organize and develop artistic ideas and work • Refine and complete artistic work	• Select, analyze, and interpret artistic work for presentation • Develop and refine artistic techniques and work for presentation • Convey meaning through the presentation of artistic work	• Perceive and analyze artistic work • Interpret intent and meaning in artistic work • Apply criteria to evaluate artistic work	• Synthesize and relate knowledge and personal experiences to make art • Relate artistic ideas and works with societal, cultural, and historical content to deepen understanding

Goodheart-Willcox Publisher

about what was taught in the previous grade so that states could build on previous teaching (socialstudies.org). The national social studies standards have been adopted by many states.

Creativity is a key element when developing social studies experiences. Integrating the knowledge and skills from the social domain occurs through children's personal experiences at home, at school, and the broader community in which they live (**Figure 12.11**). Social studies, including social skills, socialization, and social responsibility, are essential aspects of children's development and education (Ucus 2018). The national social studies standards are organized into ten themes:

- Culture
- Time, Continuity, and Change
- People, Places, and Environments
- Individual Development and Identity
- Individuals, Groups, and Institutions
- Power, Authority, and Governance
- Production, Distribution and Consumption
- Science, Technology, and Society
- Global Connections
- Civic Ideals and Practices

FatCamera/Getty Images

Figure 12.11 It is imperative for students to play with their peers in order to develop in the social domain. How can teachers foster social play?

For young children, social study themes are explored through play, personal interactions, literacy and project-based learning, collection and analysis of data, and report presentation beginning with the study of self, family, and community. With age, these themes expand to encompass local and national history, economics, political science, and geography in the primary grades to provide meaningful content that helps prepare them to be lifelong learners (Lackaff & Mindes 2013). Some teachers align social studies content to a theme for their instructional grade level (**Figure 12.12**). As instruction progresses through the grades, teachers reinforce previous learning around what was taught earlier while linking content learning to the standards at their grade-level.

Social Studies Themes Arranged by Grade Level	
Grade Focus	Focus Content
K	Sense of Self
1	Family
2	Then and Now (Past and Present)
3	Communities (Local History)

Goodheart-Willcox Publisher

Figure 12.12 This is one way to arrange social studies topics by grade level. Do you think these choices are developmentally appropriate? Why or why not?

Social-Emotional Learning (SEL) and Character Education Standards

Social-emotional learning (SEL) is the process through which children (and adults) understand and manage emotions, set and achieve positive goals, feel and show empathy for others, establish and maintain positive relationships, and make responsible decisions (CASEL.org). *Character education* encompasses many of the same inter- and intrapersonal skill sets as social-emotional learning, and often includes civics and civility components as well.

The five core competencies of social-emotional learning are designed to provide a clear framework from which to teach skills that will benefit students throughout their lives in situations ranging from school and work to families and communities. The competencies were selected to accurately pinpoint the skills required to succeed in multiple areas of life, ranging from achieving academic goals to feeling more confident in social interactions.

The five core categories of SEL competencies are (**Figure 12.13**):

- Social skills
- Social awareness skills
- Social decision-making and problem-solving skills
- Self-awareness skills
- Self-management skills

Character education promotes skills in the following categories:

- Moral sensitivity
- Moral commitment
- Ethical reasoning
- Personal growth

Many existing state policies reflect earlier efforts to build character education, conflict resolution, and similar skills into the fabric of teaching and learning. Although character education and SEL are not fully interchangeable, these policies can support SEL's integration into schools. Altogether, 30 states and the District of Columbia already have statutes and regulations that encourage or require SEL or character education programs in schools. Only 15 of these states, however, mandate the inclusion of such programs in schools (Gabriel 2019).

Nurturing these core competencies in individual students through social and emotional learning is a healthy

Goodheart-Willcox Publisher

Figure 12.13 Social and emotional learning.

and rewarding process that can subsequently have a positive effect on the groups of people to which these students belong (positiveaction.net).

The Collaborative for Academic, Social, and Emotional Learning (CASEL) wheel (**Figure 12.14**) includes the five core social and emotional competencies—broad, interrelated areas that support learning and development. Circling them are four key settings where students live and grow. School-family-community partnerships coordinate SEL practices and establish equitable learning environments across all of these contexts (Casel.org).

A majority of states encourage the inclusion of social and emotional or character development education in the classroom as part of a standard or include them in some part of the instruction. This approach ensures that SEL is embedded into all students' educational experiences rather than just a single lesson or activity.

It is important to remember that standards have a sequential progression, building on what was previously learned. Adoption of new standards occurs at the discretion of the state departments of education. Teachers, school districts, and states decide on the appropriate curriculum and are usually provided with sample texts to help teachers, students, and parents prepare for the year ahead in states that adopt the common core curriculum or develop their own.

STOP AND THINK | Many states are in the process of adopting SEL standards. Does your state support these efforts? Consider how SEL can be integrated into lesson plans.

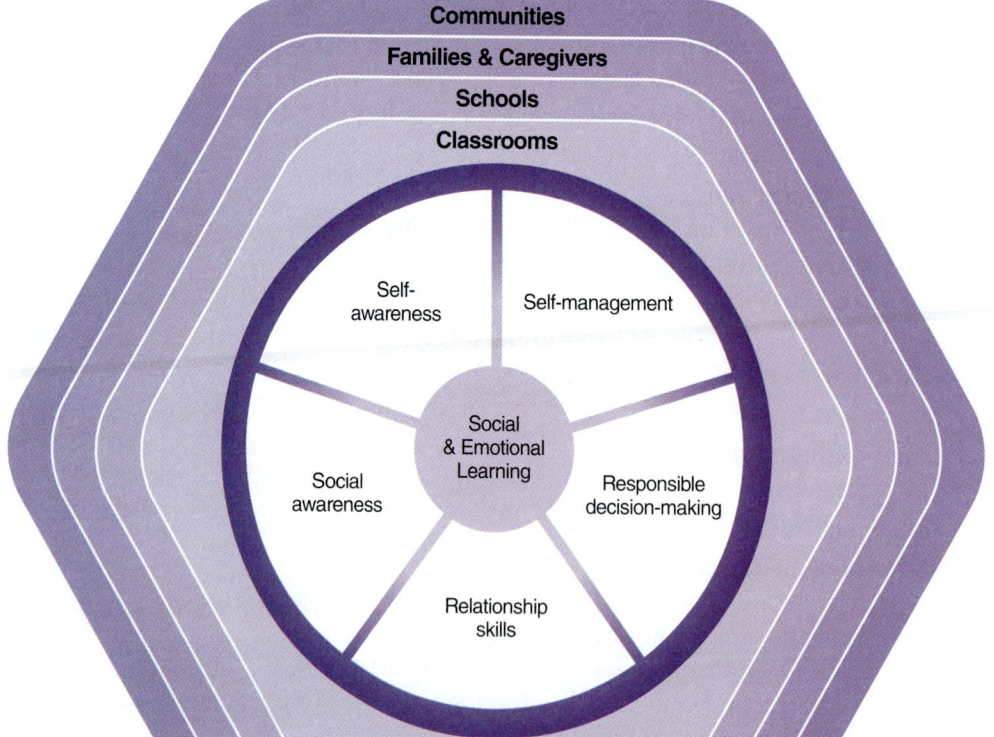

Figure 12.14 CASEL wheel.

Goodheart-Willcox Publisher

Checkpoint

- ☐ Identify your state's practices around social-emotional learning. Are there standards that measure development and understanding? What does that include?
- ☐ Locate your state's kindergarten–third grade standards. How do they support a teacher's lesson plan?
- ☐ How are character education and social-emotional learning different from each other? Provide an example.

12.2 Integration Strategies across Grades and Discipline Subjects

Just as the early ages integrate learning with different standards and academic subjects, the K–3 grades follow a similar planning strategy. To explore each grade level, this chapter showcases different states. Keep in mind that the examples are only a few possibilities presented to inspire curriculum and instruction.

Kindergarten

Starting kindergarten is a rite of passage and is heralded as a time of excitement and many new learning opportunities. Kindergarten can include children four to six years old, although cutoff dates vary by state. The following standards offer a focus for instruction each year and help ensure that students gain adequate exposure to a range of texts and tasks, as well as domains of development. The featured states in this section are Delaware, Kentucky, New York, South Dakota, and Wisconsin.

English Language Arts

Most children are able to use words they have learned from conversations with others or by being read to before kindergarten. Throughout the academic year, the five- to six-year-old child's speech becomes more structured, and reading and writing skills emerge and advance.

During the kindergarten school year, instruction focuses on learning to understand basic sentence structure and punctuation. The Common Core English Language Arts standards include learning that the first word in a sentence is capitalized and that sentences end in periods, question marks, or exclamation points. **Figure 12.15** identifies the states that are used to show examples. At this age, learning how to print letters in both lower and upper case, as well as how to make a word plural, are strong outcomes.

Comprehension and collaboration are among the Common Core themes; the kindergartener is expected to follow agreed-upon rules for discussions (for example, listening to others and taking turns speaking about the topics and texts under discussion). This standard is often difficult for the young five-year-old, who is still developing self-regulation skills. This is one reason some families choose to delay starting their kindergartener until age six.

Remember that *self-regulation skills* are children's ability to control their behaviors and emotions in response to a particular situation. Self-regulation means having the skill to calm yourself down when you get upset, to adjust to a change in environment or expectations, and to manage frustration without outbursts. When children share, listen to others, or wait their turn, they are practicing self-control (Wells 2017).

By the end of kindergarten, most children are reading age-appropriate books by themselves, can name the author and illustrator of a book, and can define the role of each in presenting the ideas or information in a book. Kindergarteners enjoy writing by sounding out words

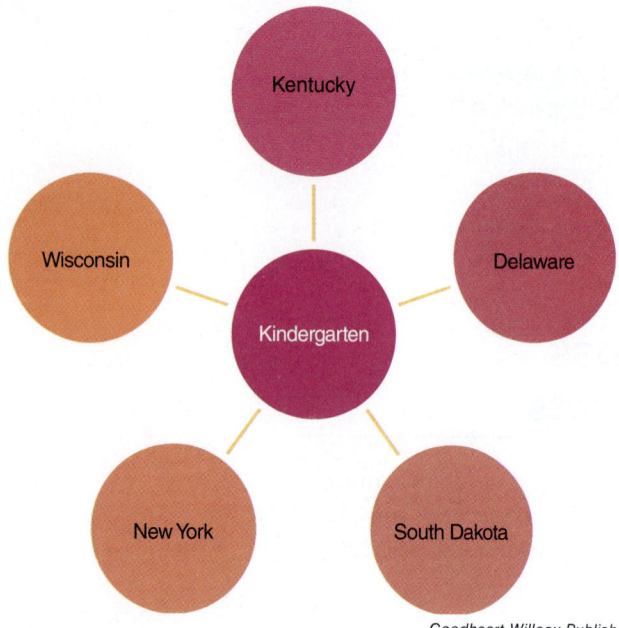

Goodheart-Willcox Publisher

Figure 12.15 Kindergarten states featured.

Drazen Zigic/iStock/Getty Images

Figure 12.16 For some children, kindergarten is their first experience in school. Is it mandatory to send children to kindergarten in your state?

SDI Productions/iStock/Getty Images

Figure 12.17 These students are using a math manipulative called an abacus. Identify two math experiences that are DAP for kindergarten.

and authoring their own short stories. With guidance and support, children of this age can also benefit from being exposed to a variety of digital tools to produce and publish writing, alone and in collaboration with peers across all the disciplines as they become authors and illustrators (**Figure 12.16**).

Math

In kindergarten math, counting and cardinality include children learning to count to 100 by ones and tens, writing the numbers 0–20, comparing numbers using the terms *greater than*, *less than*, and *equal*, and counting them in sequence. Children of this age are also focusing on counting objects and learning to recognize and name shapes such as triangles, rectangles, circles, and squares. Integrating math with other disciplines can be seamless, because math properties can easily be embedded into most learning experiences to create strong connections.

Kindergarteners learn the concepts of addition and subtraction (**Figure 12.17**) using many methods of "putting together" and "adding to" and "taking apart" and "taking from." The Common Core website cautions that the math expectations should be developmentally appropriate. By the end of kindergarten, students learn about math using concrete objects, but it is not developmentally appropriate for kindergarteners to be sitting quietly alone at their desks completing worksheets for 30 minutes.

Science

In the kindergarten performance expectations, students demonstrate grade-appropriate proficiency in asking questions, developing and using models, planning and conducting investigations, analyzing and interpreting data, designing solutions, engaging in argument from evidence, and obtaining, evaluating, and communicating information. Students are also expected to use these practices to demonstrate understanding of the core ideas (**Figure 12.18**).

The performance expectations in kindergarten help students formulate answers to questions such as: "What happens if you push or pull an object harder?" "Where do animals live, and why do they live there?" "What is the weather like today, and how it is different from yesterday?" (Next Generation Science Standards). Students are expected to develop understanding of patterns and variations in local weather and the purpose of weather forecasting to prepare for, and respond to, severe weather. Combining these outcomes into the dramatic play area supports learning forecasting while integrating social studies.

Students should be able to apply an understanding of the effects of different strengths or different directions of pushes and pulls on the motion of an object to analyze a design solution. Utilize the outdoors to demonstrate gravity on the slides and swings. Students are also expected to develop an understanding of what plants and animals (including humans) need to survive and the relationship between their needs and where they live. Making connections to the habitat around the school, integrating art to define and draw and make charts of comparisons from other areas reflect the integration possible. The organizing concepts when integrating math, arts, and social studies include the crosscutting concepts of patterns; cause and effect; systems; and interdependence of science, engineering, and technology on society and the natural world.

FatCamera/Getty Images

Figure 12.18 Science in action. What is one open-ended question you might ask the students shown in this image?

Arts

The National Core Arts Standards support integrating and creating kindergarten lesson plans to measure proficiency around music at the connections level. **Figure 12.19** provides integration and performance indicator examples using the standards from five states.

Social Studies

Kindergarten students apply their knowledge of the geographic themes (location, place, movement, region, human/environment interactions), and skills to demonstrate an

Figure 12.19 Kindergarten art standards.

Kindergarten Art Standards		
State	**Standard**	**Integration–Performance Indicator**
Delaware	Music: Connecting Anchor Standard 1: Generate and conceptualize artistic ideas and work.	Social-Emotional and Literacy MU:Pr4.2.Ka With guidance, explore and demonstrate awareness of music contrasts (such as high/low, loud/soft, same/different) in a variety of music selected for performance.
Kentucky	Music: Connecting Anchor Standard 1: Generate and conceptualize artistic ideas and work.	Social Studies MU:Cr1.1.K a. With guidance, explore and experience music concepts (such as beat and melodic contour).
New York	Music: Connecting Anchor Standard 1: Generate and conceptualize artistic ideas and work.	Literacy and Math PK.ARTS.9. Indicators: a. Explores and experiences music concepts (e.g., beat and melodic contour)
South Dakota	Music: Connecting Anchor Standard 1: Generate and conceptualize artistic ideas and work.	Art, Science (Engineering) K.MU.Cr.1.1a With guidance, introduce, explore, and experience musical concepts using a variety of music; i.e., beat and melodic contour.
Wisconsin	Music: Connecting Anchor Standard 1: Generate and conceptualize artistic ideas and work.	Social Studies (Culture) MU: CR1.1PK With guidance, introduce, explore, and experience musical concepts using a variety of music; i.e., beat and melodic contour.
Your State		

Goodheart-Willcox Publisher

understanding of interrelationships among people, places, and environment. The featured states focus on different strands to teach the kindergarten student (**Figure 12.20**).

Social-Emotional Learning and Character Education

By the end of kindergarten, most children will be able to identify basic emotions, recognize some complex emotions, and associate them with facial expressions, body language, and behaviors (for example, pleasure, ashamed, annoyed, frightened, lonely). The kindergartener also uses richer and more specific vocabulary related to emotions (*happy* can also be *ecstatic, glowing, delighted, blessed*, and so on.). Children of this age are able to express and share feelings in a variety of ways by communicating verbally, writing, acting, or drawing (**Figure 12.21**).

First and Second Grade

For many children, first grade marks the beginning of being one of the "big kids" in the school, and moving from first to second grade reflects students who have grown used to their school environment and are ready to take on deeper learning tasks that are increasingly more abstract. The typical six- to seven-year-old attention span is increasing, as is the ability to learn more difficult concepts in one setting and apply them to other situations. The featured states for first and second grade are Maryland, Missouri, Kansas, Nevada, and Wyoming (**Figure 12.22**).

English Language Arts

By the end of first grade, most students will have demonstrated the ability to write coherent sentences of different types to create a descriptive piece of writing. Students will develop and use a more extensive vocabulary as they learn how to use verbs and adjectives to bring depth to their writing, and they will be able to read simple chapter books.

Figure 12.20 Kindergarten social studies standards.

Kindergarten Social Studies Standards		
State	Standard	Integration–Performance Indicator
Delaware	Citizenship	Language, SEL K.3.a Students will demonstrate the skills necessary for participating in a group, including defining an objective, dividing responsibilities, and working cooperatively.
Kentucky	Citizenship	Literacy, SEL KE.1 Explain how various jobs affect communities.
New York	Civic Ideals and Responsibilities	Literacy, SEL K.SOC.8. [K.4a] Understands children have basic universal rights
South Dakota	Civics Government	Art, SEL K.C.1.1 Identify our country's flag of the United States as a symbol of the nation.
Wisconsin	Civic Engagement	Literacy, SEL SS.Inq5.a.e Explore opportunities for personal or collaborative civic engagement with community, school, state, tribal, national, and/or global implications
Your state		

Goodheart-Willcox Publisher

Figure 12.21 Kindergarten SEL standards.

Kindergarten SEL Standards		
State	Standard	Integration–Performance Indicator
Delaware	Self-Awareness	Art and Social Studies 1A. Demonstrate an awareness of one's own emotions.
Kentucky	Encouraged—not mandated	NA
New York	Self-Management	Social Studies K.SEL.12. Adapts to change K.SEL.12. Indicators: a. Easily separates themselves from their parent or caregiver
South Dakota	Encouraged—not mandated	NA
Wisconsin	Encouraged—not mandated SEL competencies identified.	NA
Your State		

Goodheart-Willcox Publisher

Second grade is a pivotal year in reading. This is the year when students move beyond using decoding skills to figure out unfamiliar words and use context clues instead. Second grade students are able to summarize accurately and have a strong grasp of suffixes and prefixes, using them to decipher the meaning of words they do not know. Other reading skills that develop in second grade include outcome prediction, self-correction, and using a dictionary.

Math

Learning about mathematics occurs in many places in first grade. Students learn how to compute; they also learn about measurements, patterns, shapes, money, and telling time. Six- to seven-year-old students are able to think more abstractly as they make connections between cause and effect.

Second grade students continue to explore the logic of numbers and begin to learn that all the number facts are related in a systematic way as they create real world applications. Expectations include a focus on place value, learning to add and subtract using regrouping, and exploring fractions to learn how they relate to a whole while practicing "skip counting" as a precursor to learning multiplication tables.

Other focus skills include basic money sense, additional units of measure and how those units relate to each other (inches make feet, feet make yards, yards make miles; millimeters make centimeters, centimeters make meters, meters make kilometers), as well as how to use a thermometer in both Celsius and Fahrenheit.

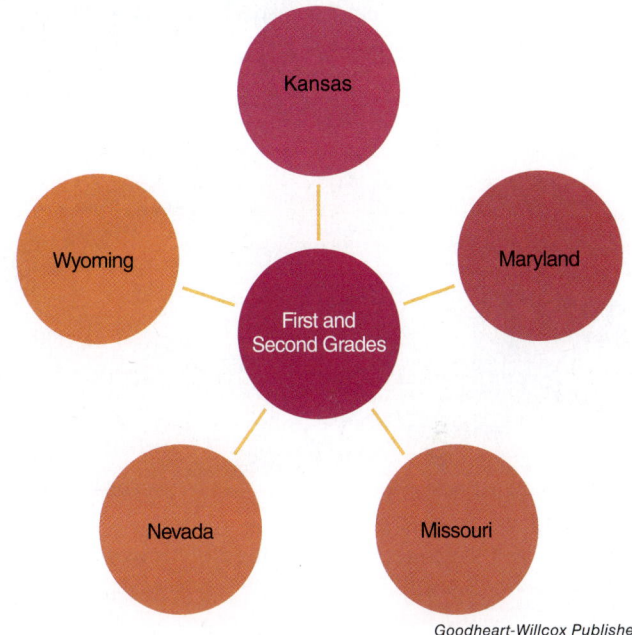

Figure 12.22 Featured states for first and second grades.

> **STOP AND THINK** | What does a classroom that supports science look like? Imagine how to integrate science with all academic subject as you create lesson plans.

Science

The Next Generation Science Standards guide the performance expectations that support teaching science. The performance expectations in first grade help students formulate answers to questions such as: "What happens when materials vibrate?" "What happens when there is no light?" "What are some ways plants and animals meet their needs so that they can survive and grow?" "How are parents and their children similar and different?" In first grade performance expectations, students demonstrate grade-appropriate proficiency in planning and conducting investigations, analyzing and interpreting data, constructing explanations and designing solutions, and obtaining, evaluating, and communicating information.

The performance expectations in second grade help students formulate answers to questions such as: "How does land change, and what are some things that cause it to change?" "What are the different kinds of land and bodies of water?" "What do plants need to grow?" "How many types of living things live in a place?" In second grade performance expectations, students demonstrate grade-appropriate proficiency in developing and using models, planning and conducting investigations, analyzing and interpreting data, constructing explanations and designing solutions, engaging in argument from evidence, and obtaining, evaluating, and communicating information.

The crosscutting concepts of patterns, cause and effect, energy and matter, structure and function, stability and change, and influence of engineering, technology, and science on society and the natural world are called out as organizing concepts for these disciplinary core ideas. **Figure 12.23** and **Figure 12.24** reflect some of these concepts in action.

Ginny Harmelink

Figure 12.23 Science is all around us. What science concepts can students learn by stopping to examine a curious-looking creature?

miroslavmisiura/iStock via Getty Images Plus

Figure 12.24 Pollination in action. What is another discipline that could be integrated when studying pollination? Provide an example.

Arts

Figure 12.25 and **Figure 12.26** connect states with the National Core Arts Standards, providing examples that reflect integrating and creating lesson plans to measure proficiency around visual arts at different levels. **Figure 12.25** focuses on first grade, and **Figure 12.26** focuses on second grade.

Social Studies

First grade standards focus on the common characteristics across cultures and demonstrate the contributions and impacts that human interaction and cultural

First Grade Art Standards

State	Standard	Integration–Performance Indicator
Kansas	Visual Arts	Social Studies Engage collaboratively in exploration and imaginative play with materials. (NCAS)
Maryland	Aesthetic Education	Social Studies, Science Students will demonstrate the ability to perceive, interpret, and respond to ideas, experiences, and the environment through visual art.
Missouri	Visual Arts	Social Studies Engage collaboratively in exploration and imaginative play with materials. (NCAS)
Nevada	Visual Arts	Social Studies Engage collaboratively in exploration and imaginative play with materials. (NCAS)
Wyoming	Visual Arts	Literacy Students create and revise original art to express ideas, experiences and stories.
Your State		

Goodheart-Willcox Publisher

Figure 12.25 First grade art standards.

Second Grade Art Standards

State	Standard	Integration–Performance Indicator
Kansas	Categorize artwork based on a theme or concept for an exhibit. (NCAS)	Social Studies, Mathematics Analyze, select, and curate objects, artifacts, and artworks for preservation, and presentation.
Maryland	Visual Arts: Historical, Cultural, and Social Context	Social Studies Determine ways in which works of art express ideas about self, other people, places, and events.
Missouri	Categorize artwork based on a theme or concept for an exhibit. (NCAS)	Social Studies, Mathematics Analyze, select, and curate objects, artifacts, and artworks for preservation, and presentation.
Nevada	Categorize artwork based on a theme or concept for an exhibit. (NCAS)	Social Studies, Mathematics Analyze, select, and curate objects, artifacts, and artworks for preservation, and presentation.
Wyoming	Creative Expression Through Production: Students create, perform, exhibit or participate in the arts.	Social Studies Create and revise original art to express ideas, experiences and stories.
Your State		

Goodheart-Willcox Publisher

Figure 12.26 Second grade art standards.

diversity make on societies. Some states embed a theme around family in first grade, building off a prior focus on self or oneself (**Figure 12.27**).

In second grade, students apply their knowledge of the geographic themes (location, place, movement, region, and human/environment interactions) and skills to demonstrate an understanding of interrelationships among people, places, and environment. Some states create curriculum around a common theme of *then and now* (past and present) as they continue to support the focus in previous grades on self and family (**Figure 12.28**).

Social-Emotional Learning and Character Education

In first and second grade, standards focus on developing skills to help students identify, define, and live in accordance with core principles that aid in effective problem solving and responsible decision-making. It is important to note that many states are moving in the direction of mandating SEL and character education standards. The states are at varying stages of the legislative process to have them enacted (**Figure 12.29**).

Third Grade

Third grade introduces students to a multitude of concepts combined with national testing to measure understanding as a common outcome. Specific content and skills that children are expected to have acquired by the end of third grade include writing upper- and lower-case letters of the alphabet and being able to comprehend fiction and nonfiction passages.

Third grade is a year of great academic growth. Children who were previously very concrete thinkers are steadily becoming more open to the abstract. Although curriculum may vary from state to state, most states have some commonly taught skills and topics, which are described in

Figure 12.27 First grade social studies standards.

First Grade Social Studies Standards		
State	**Standard**	**Integration–Performance Indicator**
Kansas	Rights and Responsibilities	Literacy, Math 2.1 The student will recognize and evaluate the rights and responsibilities of people living in societies.
Maryland	Political Science	Language, Art Students will understand the historical development and current status of the democratic principles and the development of skills and attitudes necessary to become responsible citizens.
Missouri	School and Community	Language, SEL 1.PC.1.B Identify and explain why cities make laws
Nevada	The Community We Live In & the Work We Do	Literacy SS.1.1. With prompting and support, generate compelling questions to explore the places people live and work.
Wyoming	Citizenship, Government, and Democracy	Literacy SS2.1.3.a Identify how Indigenous Tribes of Wyoming honor people and celebrate through events (e.g., Native American Veterans Day, Native American Heritage Day, Wyoming Native American)
Your State		

Goodheart-Willcox Publisher

Second Grade Social Studies Standards

State	Standard	Integration–Performance Indicator
Kansas	Continuity and Change	Literacy SL 4.1 The student will recognize and evaluate continuity and change over time.
Maryland	Political Science Students will understand the historical development and current status of the democratic principles and the development of skills and attitudes necessary to become responsible citizens.	Language Explain how rules and laws are made and necessary to maintain order and protect citizens.
Missouri	Regions	Literacy 2. PC. 1. B.a. Explain and give examples of how laws and rules are made and changed within the community.
Nevada	The Community We Live In & the Work We Do	Literacy SS.2.1. With prompting and support, generate compelling questions to explore national identity and culture.
Wyoming	Culture and Cultural Diversity	Math, Art SS5.2.3 Identify and describe characteristics and contributions of local and state cultural groups, including Indigenous Tribes of Wyoming, in Wyoming and the region.
Your State		

Goodheart-Willcox Publisher

Figure 12.28 Second grade social studies standards.

First and Second Grade SEL Standards

State	Standard	Integration–Performance Indicator
Kansas	Responsible Decision Making and Problem Solving Identify and apply core principles in everyday behavior.	Social Studies, Literacy Students help create and discuss classroom procedures and consequences (e.g., classroom rules, playground rules, cafeteria manners, etc.)
Maryland	Demonstrates healthy self-confidence. (1st) Initiates and maintains relations. (2nd)	Demonstrates independence in range of routines and tasks Recognize appropriate methods of communication
Missouri	Show Me SEL Initiatives include	NA
Nevada	Encouraged–Initiative linked to CASEL.org	NA
Wyoming	Encouraged–not mandated	NA
Your State		

Goodheart-Willcox Publisher

Figure 12.29 First and second grade SEL standards.

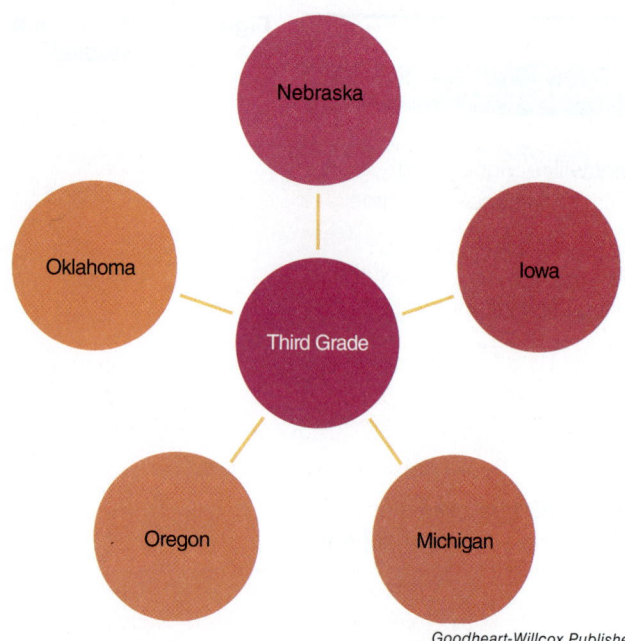

Goodheart-Willcox Publisher

Figure 12.30 Featured states for third grade.

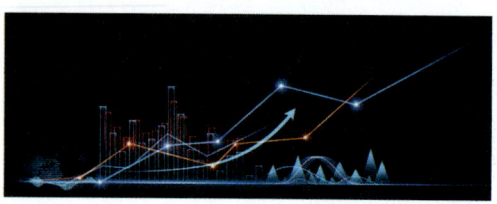

Galeanu Mihai/Getty Images

Figure 12.31 This is an example of a graph. What might a third grade student graph?

Memedozaslan/iStock/Getty Images

Figure 12.32 Science in action. How might this group of students integrate literacy with their learning?

the tables in this section. The featured states for this section are Iowa, Michigan, Nebraska, Oklahoma, and Oregon (**Figure 12.30**).

English Language Arts

Third grade students love the world of "big books," or chapter books. New skills include using graphic organizers; using grammar, text and genre clues to glean information; and summarization. In third grade, writing occurs in all subjects to convey and summarize information. Some states have reinstated some items that had been removed from the Common Core English language arts (Jones 2014). This includes learning to write in cursive, a skill that has been shown to support students with dyslexia. Students begin to use a more sophisticated vocabulary to convey information; their extended vocabulary creates a strong foundation for future grades.

Math

In third grade, focus shifts to more complicated topics: advanced multiplication and division, patterns and number sense, geometry, and probability. By the end of third grade, the skills to complete mental math, work with fractions, estimate, interpret graphs and predict probability and outcomes will be evident (**Figure 12.31**).

Science

In third grade, science is not only conceptual, but hands-on as well. Typically, this is the year that students begin investigating topics that require a lot of observation, measurement, and experimentation (**Figure 12.32**). The focus includes systems, sound, habitats, and natural science. Third grade students learn more about forces of nature, classification, setting up experiments, and organisms and their habitats.

The performance expectations in third grade help students formulate answers to deeper questions, such as: "What is typical weather in different parts of the world and during different times of the year?" "How can the impact of weather-related hazards be reduced?" "How do organisms vary in their traits?" "How are plants, animals, and environments of the past similar to or different from current plants, animals, and environments?" "What happens to organisms when their environment changes?" "How do equal and unequal forces on an object affect the object?" "How can magnets be used?" (NGSS)

In third grade performance expectations, students demonstrate grade-appropriate proficiency in asking questions and defining problems, developing and using models, planning and carrying out investigations, analyzing and interpreting data, constructing explanations and designing solutions, engaging in argument from evidence, and obtaining, evaluating, and communicating information. Third grade is a very important one, because learning becomes high-stakes through statewide testing to measure proficiency.

Arts

Third grade students typically expand their knowledge of visual art—portrait, still-life, seascape, landscape—and learn about depth as they create two- and three-dimensional art. Connections are made among dance, theater, music, and media arts. Many states base their arts standards on the National Core Arts Standards (NCAS), which include standards for visual arts, dance, theater and music as shown in **Figure 12.33**.

> **STOP AND THINK**
>
> Some states support keyboard skills; others support cursive writing and manuscript print. Different parts of the brain are used for each. What does your state support?

Additional skills include how to identify objects of art from different parts of the world or compare works of art that express similar ideas but were created at different times. Students are introduced to art made in many cultures and shown how it can have a functional purpose or convey a certain message. Integration with social studies is very common.

Social Studies

Third grade is the year in which children start to learn more about their country and the world, gaining a basic understanding of economics and about supply and demand. Typically, third grade students spend a lot of time focusing on their own state, its commerce, and its unique qualities, but other geography skills are key. People and places that are significant to American history will further knowledge in the following:

- the world in spatial terms
- exploration of the Americas
- citizenship and government
- chronology

National Core Art Standards		
State	**Visual Art–CREATE**	**Integration–Performance Indicator**
Iowa	Generate and conceptualize artistic ideas and work.	Literacy Elaborate on an imaginative idea.
Michigan	Apply skills and knowledge to create in the arts.	Social Studies Demonstrate how materials, techniques, and processes can be used creatively to communicate ideas.
Nebraska	Students will develop and apply ideas, knowledge, and skills to create, present, respond to, and connect art with the human experience.	Literacy, Social Studies Demonstrate the connections between sensory experience and expressing emotion.
Oklahoma	Practice and refine techniques and skills related to visual arts.	SEL, Social Studies Explore and invent a variety of art-making techniques and approaches.
Oregon	Generate and conceptualize artistic ideas and work.	SEL, Language Generate ideas for narrative or events that could be the basis of art works using personal experiences (e.g., diagram or map places that are part of the student's everyday life).
Your State		

Goodheart-Willcox Publisher

Figure 12.33 National Core Art Standards.

STOP AND THINK

Review the social studies strands listed early in our chapter. Which would you connect to the different lessons from the different state's historical landmarks? What is a landmark in your own state that you might do the same?

The third grade students in the featured states are focusing on the social studies strand "Peoples, Places, and Environments" as they make connections to landmarks in their own regions. Explore ways to integrate literacy to social studies with landmarks from your own state. Connecting to other states reflects the vast diversity across America.

To integrate the social studies standard around people, places, and the environment with literacy, a third grade teacher in Iowa may teach a lesson around Floyd Monument, while a teacher in Nebraska makes connections to Chimney Rock. The curriculum in Michigan may focus on Bond Falls; the Oklahoma instruction may feature Sequoya's home; and the teacher in Oregon might capture the children's interest by reading a book around the Black Mountain Lookout tree (**Figure 12.34**). All teachers are able to make connections to having children write a script in small groups and then create a skit-play around the historical value of the standard, reflecting true integration of literacy and social studies. What would you focus on in your state?

Social-Emotional Learning and Character Education

As previously discussed, states support the integration of SEL at various levels, but not all states mandate them in their standards. The states featured in this chapter for third grade do not include SEL as a standard; instead, they support SEL in various ways to expose students to life-long character-building skills.

Checkpoint

☐ What are three major differences between K–3 standards and preschool standards? Share two examples.

☐ Identify an expectation for the different grades around the English language arts standards. How do they support each other?

Figure 12.34 Third grade SEL standards.

Third Grade SEL Standards		
State	Competency	Integration–Performance Indicator
Iowa	Encouraged—not mandated (Gabriel 2019)	NA
Michigan	Encouraged—not mandated	NA
Nebraska	Encouraged—not mandated	NA
Oklahoma	Encouraged—not mandated	NA
Oregon	Encouraged—not mandated	NA
Your State		

Goodheart-Willcox Publisher

12.3 Credible Academic Subject Resources

As described in Chapter 11, when teachers develop their own curriculum, it is most important that the applicable early learning standards be used to provide guidance. In addition, using current resources from experts to ensure that curriculum content is accurate and comprehensive is a professional expectation (NAEYC, *DAP*, 2020).

It is important that all resources be credible to ensure that the information used is the most current, relevant, and accurate. Like preschool teachers, teachers in the early grades are encouraged to create a resource file of information from which they can build lesson plans. With the information readily available on the internet and now ***artificial intelligence (AI)*** software, after data is verified as reliable and up-to-date, it is ready to be used. See **Figure 12.35** for a list of academic resources that are well-established and valued by early childhood education teachers.

Artificial intelligence is valuable when creating curriculum due to its ability to provide many unique insights for teachers when they create lesson plans. It is also useful to quickly differentiate learning opportunities for individual students. AI can be used to automate tasks such as grading and can suggest alternative assessments based on learning outcomes. The teaching strategies possible using AI as one tool in a resource file are limitless.

Checkpoint

- ☐ The teachers' list of resources includes few resources that are useful to the K–3 teacher. What is one additional resource for each area you would include in your resource files?
- ☐ Sharing resources is common among teachers. How would you share with a family?

Academic Resources for Teachers

Academic Focus	Connecting Resources
English Language Arts Core Standards	The Core Standards site provides the information that represents the next generation of K–3 standards designed to prepare students for success in English language arts. "Teach English Language Arts" provides exercises to develop reading and writing skills at an early age. Silent sustained reading, cursive writing, syntax, thematic writing, and vocabulary are all major focal points of the elementary lessons.
Math	The Core Standards site provides the information that represents the next generation of K–3 standards, designed to prepare students for success in math. "Development and Research in Early Mathematics" (DREME) promotes early math skills with an emphasis on the lower grades.
Science	The National Academies framework provides information for crosscutting, practice, and core ideas supporting science integration across the curriculum. The Next Generation Science Standards, developed by the National Research Council, provides research-based recommendations for implementing the NGSS.
Art	The National Core Arts Standards include anchor standards to guide curriculum decisions in all arts-related content.
Social Studies	National Council for the Social Studies (NCSS) is the source for integrating social studies in the elementary years.

Goodheart-Willcox Publisher

Figure 12.35 K–3 teacher resources.

Chapter 12 Review and Assessment

Chapter Summary

12.1 Recognize developmentally appropriate kindergarten–third grade curriculum standards.

- The early grades encompass kindergarten to third grade, generally children five to eight years of age, although some states enroll older four-year-old children, which may mean a student might begin third grade at age seven.
- Standardized curriculum begins with the standards, which are used as a guide to the knowledge a student should acquire by the end of each grade.
- Connections to the more common standards exploring the differences and similarities are covered.
- The value of seeing other state standards is that doing so provides teachers with a broad look at expectations and provides a glimpse of how other academic disciplines can be integrated across the curriculum.

12.2 Analyze developmentally appropriate integration strategies across the kindergarten–third grade curriculum.

- A variety of resources provide elementary teachers with additional tools to learn more about teaching the early grades.
- The interests of the students is the primary motivator when creating curriculum that inspires the next generation of leaders.

12.3 Distinguish credible academic subject resources.

- Credible and useful resources provide the foundation of a teacher's resource file.
- Artificial intelligence (AI) provides ideas and uses for the next generation of teachers.

For Further Reflection

1. At least 19 states plus the District of Columbia require children to attend kindergarten based on state statutes or regulations, with cutoff dates based on birthdates. Research why many states opt to start kindergarten at age five. What does your state support?
2. Thirty-two states and the District of Columbia define social-emotional learning in statutes or regulations. Explain why this is important.
3. Twenty-seven states and the District of Columbia require or encourage teacher training and professional development in student mental health and trauma-informed practices. How does your state rate in this area?
4. The Common Core standards include instruction in keyboarding, but do not mandate the teaching of cursive handwriting. However, many state standards do include cursive handwriting. What does your state support?

Recall and Application

1. Anchoring strategies may include ____.
   A. concept mapping
   B. graphic organizers
   C. review and reflection
   D. All the above.

2. **True or False.** Crosscutting refers to integrating curriculum across disciplines.

3. Uniformity when discussing the Common Core implies ____.
   A. consistent expectations
   B. clothing worn is of same design
   C. diverse practices
   D. varied curriculum

4. Self-regulation includes students' ability to ____.
   A. control their behavior
   B. spell a word
   C. measure quantity
   D. paint with watercolors

5. What are the major differences between kindergarten and third grade social studies expectations?
   A. Kindergarten focuses on global events; third grade focuses on environmental issues.
   B. Kindergarten focuses on sense of self; third grade focuses on local history.
   C. Kindergarten focuses on local history; third grade focuses on sense of self.
   D. Kindergarten focuses on family; third grade focuses on local history.

6. Using credible resources supports the student's ability to ____.
   A. start school on time
   B. sign up for after-school events
   C. learn from accurate sources
   D. master handwriting

GLOSSARY

504 Plan. A plan that is developed to ensure that a child with an identified disability, who does not meet the specific criteria for special education, can receive accommodations appropriate to the disability. (7)

A

accommodation. Adaptations that provide access to the curriculum, but do not alter the learning outcome. (7)

adaptations. Alterations in an environment to maximize engagement and meet the needs of individual children. (5)

adverse childhood experience (ACE). Potentially traumatic events that occur in childhood. (1)

agency. The ability to choose which experiences one will engage in and decide how those experiences will proceed. (1, 8)

agility. The speed of performing a task. (9)

anchoring phenomena. The glue that holds a lesson plan together and a strategy to help students make new connections to the information. (12)

anecdotal notes. Written, individual reflections about children that are quickly noted during class activities. (7)

annotated photographs. Authentic assessments that provide dynamic views of real-time learning. (7)

anthroposophy. The belief that humans have the intellectual capacity to understand the truths of the universe and the spiritual world. (3)

artifacts. Valuable documentation. (7)

artificial intelligence. refers to the simulation of human intelligence in machines that are programmed to think and learn like humans. (12)

assessment. A systematic process for obtaining information through observations, checklists, portfolios, work samples, and other sources, which are used to make informed judgements about the learners' characteristics, understanding, and/or development. (7)

assessment bias. Attitudes or stereotypes that influences perceptions and behaviors toward others. (7)

assistive technology (AT). Resources to support children who require modifications or accommodations. (7)

atelierista. A studio teacher with a background in education and art. (3)

authentic assessment. Assessment that is age-appropriate, culturally relevant, and written in a language the child understands. (7)

authentic learning. Learning in which children reenact activities and events from their own family life. (5)

availability. Which learning areas are open on a given day and is determined by the lesson plans, the areas that may need direct supervision, and group size. (5)

B

backward design. The process of constructing a lesson by first deciding what the desired outcomes are, then planning assessment strategies, and finally selecting learning experiences. (6)

balance. Ability to maintain a controlled body position. (9)

baseline. A reference point for comparing performance data before and after an assessment to get an average. (7)

benchmark. Key skills and behaviors educators and caregivers want a child to be able to achieve within a given standard. (10)

bilingual. Learning two languages. (9)

Bloom's taxonomy. A system to define and distinguish different levels of thinking, learning, and understanding. (6)

C

catalytic event. An experience or material that sparks children's interest and motivates them to want to learn more. (6)

character education. Encompasses many of the same inter- and intra-personal skill sets as social-emotional learning and promotes moral sensitivity, moral commitment, ethical reasoning, and personal growth. (12)

checklists. Quick and easy authentic assessment to collect data and make a record of a large group of children or individual. (7)

child-initiated catalytic event. A child-led experience that sparks their interest. (6)

chronosystem. The outermost ring of the ecological systems theory which comprises all life situations. (4)

circle time. The gathering of the whole class in a large group. It is the foundation of the learning day. (8)

classism. Any attitude, action, or practice that gives one group of people greater opportunities or resources, or preferential treatment based on economic means. (2)

co-construction of learning. Working cooperatively, the expert and the novice arrive at a shared conclusion or outcome. (3)

cognitive domain. A person's mental skills and acquisition of knowledge. (1, 10)

cognitive flexibility. Includes perspective, critical thinking, and responding to challenges, and involves being able to think about something in a new way. (1)

collaborations. Connections with people, businesses, organizations, and institutions that provide additional resources. (4)

Common Core standards. A uniform set of standards that are a guide to increase skills in math and English language arts/literacy. (12)

commonality. Current research and understandings of processes of child development and learning that apply to all children. (1)

community of learners. A group of people who want to learn. (4)

concept. A mental representation, image, or idea of tangible and concrete objects, and intangible ideas and feelings that do not have a physical presence. (9)

concept diagram. A teacher-created tool that provides the teacher with many pathways connected to learning and ideas to explore, while providing a snapshot of where the learning has come from and where it might be going. (6)

Note: The number in parentheses following each definition indicates the chapter in which the term can be found.

concept web. Visual diagrams that connect abstract ideas. (6)

constructivism. The view that learning is an active, personal, and experiential process of structuring knowledge, which the catalytic event typifies. (6)

context. Everything discernible about the social and cultural contexts for each child, each educator, and the program as a whole. (1)

cooperative learning. Children working together. (4)

cooperative play. Play in which children work together to solve a problem or complete a task. (2)

coordination. Ability to maintain a controlled body position. (9)

creative arts area. Art is both intrinsically and extrinsically rewarding and has a strong influence around all domains of development when experiences are planned in this area. (5)

criterion-referenced assessment. A type of assessment that measures how well a child has mastered a specific learning goal. (7)

critical thinking. Questions that often do not have a yes or no answer and encourage the child's response to be more thought-provoking. (4)

crosscutting concepts. Concepts that bridge different disciplines and connect them through common themes. (12)

culture. Patterns of beliefs, practices, and traditions associated with a particular group of people. (2)

D

daily learning plan. Lesson plans. (6)

developmentally appropriate practice (DAP). Methods that promote each child's optimal development and learning through a strengths-based, play-based approach to joyful, engaged learning. (1)

differentiation. A planned curriculum that takes into consideration the individual needs or interests of each child. (7)

digital applications (apps). Technology that can make it easier for teachers and parents to communicate. (4)

disposition. The child's innate traits and emerging knowledge, skills, and habits of thinking and learning. (8)

documentation panel. An assessment artifact similar to posters that are used to document entire class learning. (7)

documentation portfolio. A portfolio that holds evidence of a child's work and progress. (7)

domains of development. Social-emotional, cognitive, linguistic, and physical development. (1)

dramatic play area. The most supportive of children's social-emotional development, which is the foundation of all learning. (5)

dual language learners. Children who are learning two languages at the same time, including their first language. (10)

dynamic assessment. Teachers consider the zone of proximal development of each child to guide decisions about when and to whom to offer scaffolding. (3)

E

early learning standard. An agreed-upon list of skills that children need to develop a foundation for higher levels of learning. (6)

ecological systems theory. Bronfenbrenner's theory that a child's growth and development is affected by everything in their environment. (4)

emergent curriculum. A process in which teachers plan the activities and projects based on the children in the classroom, considering the children's skills, needs, and interests. (3)

emergent literacy. A child's knowledge of reading and writing before the child actually acquires those skills and starts at birth. (10)

engagement strategies. Methods to keep children interested in the happenings around them. (8)

engineering. The process of finding out how things are built and why. (5)

environmental print. The print of everyday life and includes all the letters and words the child sees. (5)

epistemology. The theory of knowledge and "making rich connections among developmental domains and disciplines, allowing each to retain its core conceptual, procedural, and epistemological structures." (9)

evaluation portfolio. A portfolio that contains mostly specified and scored material. (7)

executive function. The mental processes that regulate thought and action in support of goal-directed behavior. (1, 2)

exosystem. The fourth level of the ecological systems theory which includes other people, places, and events with which the child may not have direct connections, but which nonetheless impact the child's development. (4)

explicit bias. Conscious attitudes, beliefs, and stereotypes that influence perceptions, actions, and decisions. (7)

expressive language. The language children use to express their wants and needs. (10)

F

facilitator. A teacher who provokes additional ideas to support children's play. (5)

family-initiated catalytic event. A moment in which a family event sparks interest in a child. (6)

fiction. Picture books. (9)

fine motor skills. Small muscle development. (9)

focus topic. The possible concepts that create engaging learning experiences. (6)

force. A push or pull that alters, or tends to alter, the state of motion of a body. (9)

forest schools. A type of outdoor learning environment in which children spend most of their day outside. (5)

formal assessment. Used to measure what a child has learned. (7)

funds of knowledge. A child's skills and knowledge that have developed through family dynamics, interests, culture, history, and community. (8)

G

graphic organizer. A tool that presents information in test and graphic formats, including charts, diagrams, webs, and storyboards. (6)

gross motor skills. Large muscle development that is directly related to movement and physical fitness. (9)

group dynamics. Groupings of individuals. (5)

guided play. A form of play in which teachers provide materials and resources to support play choices. (2)

H

HighScope curriculum. HighScope curriculum is an open-framework approach that encourages teachers to follow children's interests. (3)

I

implementation phase. A phase in which supported learning experiences that invite inquiry are derived from the teacher's understanding of the different dispositions of children. (8)

implicit bias. Happens automatically and without the person's awareness that there is an underlying belief or prejudice occurring. (7)

indicators. Demonstrations that children have achieved the benchmark. (10)

individual grouping. Provides children with time to be alone. (5)

individuality. The characteristics and experiences unique to each child, within the context of their family and community, which have implications for how best to support their development and learning. (1)

Individualized Education Plan (IEP). A written plan used to delineate an individual child's current level of development and learning goals, as well as to specify any accommodations, modifications, and related services that the child might need to maximize learning. (7)

individualized planning. Tailoring a different plan for each child. (10)

Individuals with Disabilities Education Act (IDEA). A law that ensures that individual education plans are in place for children who need them. (7)

inhibitory control. Includes focus and self-control and self-directed and engaged learning. (1)

instructional strategies. Intentional practices that support learning. (8)

integration. The process of combining multiple learning experiences that include multiple subjects. (1)

intentional teaching. Teaching that involves always thinking about teaching efforts and how they support or enable children's development and learning. (5)

interviews. An authentic assessment with open-ended questions that are part of active conversations the elicit responses from the child. (7)

invented spelling. Self-directed and spontaneous attempts to represent words in print. (5) Spellings children create based on their own phonetic understanding. (9)

investigative play. A form of play that provides time to tinker, explore, and experiment. (2)

invitation table. Table spaces set up to display specific interests. (5)

K

key developmental indicators (KDI). Behaviors that reflect the child's developing mental, emotional, physical, and social abilities. (3)

KWHL chart. A graphic organizer that allows children to share their knowledge of what they already know, what they want to know, how they can find out, and what they learned during the learning experiences. (6)

L

labeling. Images that help inform children, families, and visitors what they might expect to to happen in each classroom area. (5)

learning formats. Refers to the size of a group; group size is a key part of the planning process. (8)

learning objectives. Align to a standard and provide evidence of meeting the expectations in grades K–3. (12)

learning area placement. Where the different learning areas are located. (5)

learning outcomes. Statements that describe what the child will be able to do after participating in a learning experience. (6)

learning plan reflection. The final section of the daily learning plan, in which the teacher evaluates what worked well and what might need improvements or adjustments. (8)

learning sequence. The time allotted to learn and study each topic before moving to another idea. (6)

lesson plans. A teacher's plan for teaching a lesson. (12)

linguistic domain. Focuses on languages, including bilingual and multilingual development. (1)

looping. Children remain with the same teacher and the same classmates for many years. (3)

loose parts. Materials that children pick up to use in their play including pinecones, seashells, spools of thread, or chunks of wood. (5)

M

macrosystem. The level of the ecological systems theory that includes people and events that are not connected to the child but have the potential to have a great influence on the child's development. (4)

manipulatives. Small handheld items. (3)

math talk. The teacher's use of math-specific language in everyday talking. (9)

mediators. External, tangible tools to support children's learning, such as cards with pictures. (3)

mesosystem. The third level of the ecological systems theory which illustrates how the many parts of a child's microsystem work together to support the child. (4)

metacognition. Engaging children in thinking about why they think what they think. (9)

microsystem. The level of the ecological systems theory which includes the groups a child interacts with on a regular basis, such as family, school, sports teams, and religious organizations. (4)

modifications. Changes to what a child is taught or expected to learn. (5)

Montessori curriculum. Designed using unique learning materials in a classroom environment that fosters children's natural desire to learn. (3)

morphology. The study of where words come from. (9)

Multiple Intelligence (MI) Theory. Gardner's theory which suggests that no one set of teaching strategies works best for all children at all times. (7)

muscular endurance. The ability to maintain posture. (9)

N

NAEYC Code of Ethics. Defines the core values of the field and provides guidance for what professionals should do when they encounter conflicting obligations or responsibilities in their work. (7)

nature play. Unstructured play time in nature. (2)

neural connections. The pathways in the brain that allow cells to connect to each other. (10)

nonfiction. Informational. (9)
nonverbal cues. An action used to signal children. (8)
norm-referenced assessment. A type of assessment that compares individual performance with the average performance of a group. (7)

O
one-on-one. A time in the early childhood classroom for a child to have the full attention of a teacher. (8)

P
pairing. A dynamic in which children with differing abilities can support each other and is an effective way to encourage peer learning. (5)
parentese. The animated voice parents use to get the baby's attention. (10)
participation chart. Artifacts that provide details around children's preferences and participation patterns. (7)
pedagogy. Teaching. (2)
pedagogy of play. Teaching of choice, wonder, and delight. (2)
performance indicator. Describe performance expectations of students and a common term used in grade schools. (12)
phoneme. Small sounds in a word that distinguish one word from another. (9)
phonemic awareness. The ability to hear and manipulate sounds in spoken words. (9)
phonograms. Common groups of letters that represent the same sounds. (9)
phonology. The speech sound a letter or series of letters makes. (9)
physical domain. Includes fine (small muscle) and gross (large muscle) development. (1, 10)
physical environment. The overall design and layout of an area, including its learning areas, materials, and furnishings. (5)
piggyback. Songs that are common tunes with new words added. (9)
plan-do-review process. A process in which children are allowed to make choices about what they will do during certain designated times of the day. They are then given the opportunity to reflect upon their activities and experiences with adults and their peers. (3)

play. Promotes happy learning experiences and promotes self-regulation, language, cognitive and social competencies, and knowledge. (2)
play plans. Plans that help children develop cognitive, self-regulation, and higher-level play skills. (3)
playworld. A dramatic experience initiated by teachers and shared by teachers and students. (9)
portfolio. An organized, purposeful compilation of assessments that documents a child's development and learning over time and can include both authentic as well as formal assessments. (7)
prepared environment. An environment that includes materials that are precise, simple, and inviting to support the children's learning and channel the information surrounding them. (3)
pretend play. Fantasy, make-believe, or dress-up. It provides opportunities to try out social skills, develop language, and role play, and is connected to self-directed and guided play. (2)
private speech. Self-regulatory speech used to tell ourselves what to do or what not to do. (3)
process portfolio. A portfolio that is a purposeful collection of a child's work that documents growth from novice to proficiency. (7)
process-focused art. An open-ended project that provides an opportunity for self-expression through art creation. (9)
product-focused art. Art that is structured around instructions and has a right or wrong result. (9)
Project Approach. A set of strategies that enables teachers to guide children through in-depth studies of real-world topics. (3)
props. Physical items used strategically throughout circle time to engage children during storytelling. (8)
prosody. Reading with expression. (5)

R
rare words. An early literacy strategy that integrates rich and sophisticated or unusual words when conversing with children, rather than common terms. (10)

rating scale. An assessment artifact used to evaluate a child's performance based on the specific characteristics under consideration and then ranking the child along a predetermined continuum of high to low frequency. (7)
readers' theater. A style of theater, without props, costumes, or scenery, in which the actors read directly from a script rather than memorizing lines. (9)
receptive language. The understanding of both words as well as facial expressions and gestures. (10)
reflection. The final section of the daily learning plan which shows the development that spanned the different standards, as well as domains of development. (8)
Reggio approach. Supports learning from the particular interests of children with topics derived from talking with children and their families, as well as from things that are known to be interesting to children. (3)
resources. The supplies needed in the learning areas. (8)
risky play. Unstructured, thrilling play that children engage in when they assess their physical limits. (2)
routines. Movements repeated daily including diapering, feeding, and sleeping. (10)
rubrics. An assessment artifact that uses a specific set of criteria to evaluate a performance. (7)

S
scaffolding. An instructional technique in which the teacher, peers, or materials provide support to children as they practice a skill within the child's zone of proximal development. (8) Teachers providing the support or assistance that allows the child to succeed at a task that is just beyond their current level of skill or understanding. (1)
screen time. Use of digital media. (2)
self-directed play. Free play that can included child-led and adult-led experiences, but the teacher's direct role is lessened. (2)
self-regulation. The ability to stop, think, and then make a choice before acting. (1, 3)

semantics. What a word means. (9)

sensory system. The primary means of gaining information about the world in the early stages of life. (10)

sensory-texture area. An area that combines the senses as children explore and connect to the materials while engaging with each other. (5)

sequential neurodevelopment. An infant's brain growth occurs in a sequence, from the brainstem, the most basic area, progressing to the more complicated areas. (2)

serve-and-return. Responsive interactions between children and the people who care for them. (10)

shared learning. A way to scaffold learning by working cooperatively with others. (3)

showcase portfolio. A portfolio that contains a child's best or favorite work and should be created with input from the child and family. (7)

skill. The ability to do something intentional. (9)

social-emotional domain. Focuses on feelings and impulses. (1, 10)

social environment. Grouping of children, including the interactions that occur between peers, teachers, and family members. (5)

social-emotional learning (SEL). The process through which children understand and manage emotions, set and achieve positive goals, feel and show empathy for others, establish and maintain positive relationships, and make responsible decisions. (12)

spatial awareness. The ability to explore surroundings. (9)

standardized assessment. A type of formal assessment which requires that the procedures for assessment be the same for every child. (7)

state standards. Standards that connect the state's own culture to the curriculum and developed by education experts and teachers in each state. (12)

STEM area. Science, technology, engineering, and math area is an integration of four subjects into one area with opportunities to develop and practice a range of core skills and attributes, including hypothesizing, investigating, analyzing, reasoning, and problem-solving. (5)

story problems. Scenarios that give children a starting direction and problem to solve when arriving at the dramatic play area. (8)

storyboards. A graphic organizer presented as a set of picture cards of sequential drawings that can tell a visual story. (6)

strategies. Reflect ways to support the individual in achieving benchmarks. (10)

superhero play. A form of pretend play in which a child pretends to be a superhero. (2)

supervision. Monitoring the children and their activities. (5)

syntax. How words are arranged in a sentence. (9)

T

teacher-initiated catalytic event. A moment in which a teacher centers a lesson around a certain topic and introduces an idea. (6)

teacher-led play. Involves a high level of adult decision-making about the play experience. (2)

teacher-led play. Dramatic play in which the teacher can be viewed as an improvisational collaborator. (9)

technology. Any human-made devices that is used to solve a problem or fulfill a desire. (2)

temperament. Children's individual way of responding to the world around them. (10)

temporal environment. The daily learning experiences, schedules, timing, length of routines, and child-to-teacher ratios. (5)

thematic curriculum. A curriculum that follows a specific theme that can be child- or teacher-led. (3)

Tools of the Mind curriculum. ToM stems from Vygotsky's belief that people can use mental tools to extend mental abilities. (3)

topic of interest. The main idea that results from the catalytic event and from which many smaller learning opportunities arise. (6)

transitions. Intentional, well-thought-out activities that signal an upcoming change that involves stopping what you are doing and starting something else. (8)

trauma informed care (TIC). A treatment framework that requires understanding, recognizing, and responding to the effects of all types of trauma. (1)

U

uniform. Referring to the Common Core, the learning criteria expectations of what is taught is the same in every state that has adopted them. (12)

Universal Design for Learning (UDL). A way of teaching that creates flexible and diverse ways to engage learners by incorporating the foundational principles of UDL: engagement, representation, action, and expression. (6)

V

VARK. Learning styles that include visual, auditory, read/write, and kinesthetic learning. (7)

Venn diagram. A graphic organizer that shows relationships between a set of items using circles that overlap. (6)

verbal cues. Spoken words used to signal children. (8)

visual arts. Product- or process-focused art that are a valuable component of the creative arts discipline used for practice, observation, and learning. (9)

W

Waldorf curriculum. Based on the beliefs of Rudolph Steiner that humans have the intellectual capacity to understand the truths of the universe and the spiritual world. (3)

working memory. A skill that allows people to work with information and keep track of what they are doing. It involves communicating and making connections. (1)

written speech. Oral speech on paper that reflects capacities for high-level thinking. (3)

Z

zone of proximal development. What a child can do with maximum assistance and what the child can do alone. (3)

INDEX

504 plan, 159

A
academic disciplines, 195
accommodation, 158
ACE. *See* adverse childhood experience
active learning, 13–14
adaptations, 100
adverse childhood experience (ACE), 10
agency, 168
agility, 214
AI. *See* artificial intelligence
anchoring phenomena, 266
anecdotal notes, 147
annotated photographs, 146–47
antecedents, 75
anthroposophy, 56
apps. *See* digital applications
approaches, 46
artifacts, 145
artificial intelligence (AI), 287
arts
    curriculum resource, 260
    first grade, 280
    kindergarten, 277
    process-focused, 211
    product-focused, 210–11
    second grade, 280
    third grade, 285
assessment
    assessment bias, 143–44
    authentic assessment, 144–50
    criterion-referenced assessment, 152
    definition, 142
    dynamic assessment, 148
    formal assessment, 150–53
    norm-referenced assessment, 152
    standardized assessment, 151
assistive technology (AT), 158–59
AT. *See* assistive technology
atelierista, 65
authentic assessment, 144–50
authentic learning, 103
availability, 100–101

B
backward design, 128
balance, 214
baseline, 150
belonging, purpose, and agency, 14
benchmark, 224
bias, assessment, 143–44
bilingual, 196
bilingual language development, 197
block area, 103–7
Bloom's taxonomy, 126
brain activity, 28–29

C
CASEL. *See* Collaborative for Academic, Social, and Emotional Learning
catalytic events, 133–34
character education, 273
    first grade, 282
    kindergarten, 278
    second grade, 282
    third grade, 287
checklists, 145–46
child development
    knowledge and learning in context, 16–19
    principles, 9–16
child-initiated catalytic events, 134
children, engaging with, 75–77
chronosystem, 73
circle time, 173–78
CIRCLE, acronym, 174
    Come, 174
    Concept, 175
    Exit, 176
    Invite, 174–75
    Learn, 176
    Routine, 175
classism, 39
classroom, technology in, 201
cognitive brain development, 230–31
cognitive domain, 10, 230–31
cognitive flexibility, 11
collaborations, 82
Collaborative for Academic, Social, and Emotional Learning (CASEL), 275
colleagues, 82
common charts, 150

Common Core, 268
    English Language Arts, 269
    Math, 270
commonality, 7
communication
    engaging with children, 76–77
    forms of, 79
    other forms of, 81
community
    creating, 73–74
    engaging with, 82–83
concept diagrams, 130
concept webs, 130
concepts, 194–95
consequences, 75
constructivism, 133
context, 8
cooperative learning, 77
cooperative play, 34
coordination, 214
COR advantage, 53
creative arts
    discipline, 207–12
    drama, 209–10
    metacognition, 211–12
    movement, 209
    music, 208–9
    visual arts, 210–11
creative arts area, 113–14
criterion-referenced assessment, 152
critical thinking, 76
cross-cutting phenomena, 266
CSEFEL. *See* Social Emotional Foundations for Early Learning
cultural contexts, 12–13
culture, 38, 97–98
    in block area, 106
    in bonus areas, 118
    in creative arts area, 113–14
    in dramatic play area, 103
    in library area, 115
    in music-movement area, 112–13
    in outdoor area, 110
    in sensory-texture area, 107–8
    in STEM area, 117
    in writing area, 114
curriculum
    across domains and state lines, 224–43
    defined, 46
    environment as, 222–23
    HighScope curriculum, 50–53

infant-toddler integrated curriculum, 218–47
kindergarten-third grade curriculum, 264–90
Montessori curriculum, 54–55
preschool integrated curriculum, 248–63
Project Approach, 61–63
Reggio Emilia approach, 63–66
routine as, 223
term, 220
thematic curriculum, 59–61
Tools of the Mind curriculum, 46–50
Waldorf curriculum, 56–59

D

daily learning plans
    catalytic events, 133–34
    components of, 180–86
    definition, 132
    elements of, 132–33
    strategies of, 180–86
DAP. *See* developmentally appropriate practices
developing brain, 28–29
development
    children, 9–16
    language-literacy-communication domain, 231–36
    physical domain, 236–43
    social-emotional domain, 226–30
development and learning, 9–10
developmentally appropriate practice (DAP), 6, 166
    core considerations, 6–8
    recommendations, 20–22
differentiation, 155
digital applications (apps), 79–81
digital media, 37–38
disciplines, 194–95
    creative arts, 207–12
    integration of, 195
    language discipline, 196–98
    literary discipline, 196–98
    physical education, 213–14
    social studies, 204–7
    STEM discipline, 198–204
displays, 95
disposition, 167
documentation portfolio, 154
documentation panels, 147
domains
    cognitive domain, 230–31
    curriculum across, 224–26
    language-literacy-communication domain, 231–36

physical domain, 236–43
social-emotional domain, 226–30
domains of development, 7, 10
domains, curriculum across, 224–26
    benchmark, 224
    indicators, 224
    strategies, 224
drama, 209–10
dramatic play area, 101–3
Dreaming Zebra® Foundation, 260
dual language learners, 235
dynamic assessment, 50, 148

E

Early Childhood Art Educators (ECAE), 260
Early Childhood Music and Movement Association (ECMMA), 260
early learning environment
    culture in, 97–98
    designing, 92–95
    labeling, 96–97
    learning areas, 101–18
    setting stage for, 98–101
early learning standard, 124
early literacy, 259
early math, 202–3
ECAE. *See* Early Childhood Art Educators
ECMMA. *See* Early Childhood Music and Movement Association
ecological systems theory, 72–73
educational standards, 267
emergent curriculum, 59
emergent literacy, 236
engagement strategies, 176–78
engineering, 116
engineering, STEM, 200–201
English Language Arts Common Core, 269
    first grade, 278–79
    kindergarten, 275–76
    second grade, 278–79
    third grade, 284
English language development, 196–97
environment as curriculum, 222–23
environmental print, 97
epistemology, 195
evaluation portfolio, 154
executive functions, 11, 31
exosystem, 72
experiences, 12–13
explicit bias, 143
expressive language, 231

F

facilitator, 102
factors, infant-toddler curriculum development, 221–24
families
    engaging with, 77–82
    family-initiated catalytic events, 134
    participation, 79
festivals, 57–59
fiction, 197
field trip, 211
fine motor skills, 214
first grade, integration strategies, 278–82
fish, daily learning plan, 180–81
    reflection, 184–86
    week 1, 181–83
    week 2, 181–83
    week 3, 183–84
focus topics, 134
force, 214
formal assessment, 150–53
foundations, 251
frequency charts, 148
funds of knowledge, 166

G

Grandparents' Day, 80
graphic organizers, 128–30
great Americans, topic of interest, 256–57
gross motor skills, 213–14
group dynamics, 100
group size, 173
guided play, 34
guidelines, 251

H

health
    curriculum resource, 261
    discipline, 213–14
HighScope curriculum, 50
    assessment, 53
    structure, 51–53

I

IDEA. *See* Individuals with Disabilities Education Act
IEP. *See* Individualized Education Plan
ILA. *See* International Literacy Association
imaginative play, 49–50
implementation phase, 167
    circle time, 173–78
    elements, 178–80
    instructional strategies, 170–73
    learner characteristics, 166–68
    schedules, 168–70

implicit bias, 143
indicators, 224
individual differences, 12–13
individual grouping, 100
individuality, 7
Individualized Education Plan (IEP), 159
individualized planning, 223
Individuals with Disabilities Education Act (IDEA), 159
infant-toddler integrated curriculum, 220
    biology, 222
    environment as curriculum, 222–23
    five factors, 221–22
    individual learning plans, 223–24
    resources, 244
    routine as curriculum, 223
infant-toddler learning, biology of, 222
inhibitory control, 12
instructional strategies, 48–49, 170–73
integrated curriculum
    academic disciplines, 192–217
    infant-toddler integrated curriculum, 218–47
    kindergarten-third grade curriculum, 264–90
    preschool integrated curriculum, 248–63
integration, 14–15
integration strategies
    first grade, 278–82
    kindergarten, 275–78
    second grade, 278–82
    third grade, 282–87
intentional teaching, 97–98
International Literacy Association (ILA), 259
International Play Association (IPA), 261
International Society for Technology in Education (ISTE), 260
interviews, 149–50
invented spelling, 114, 198
investigative play, 34
invitation tables, 95
IPA. *See* International Play Association
ISTE. *See* International Society for Technology in Education

K

KDI. *See* key developmental indicator
key developmental indicator (KDI), 51
kindergarten-third grade curriculum
    academic resources for teachers, 287–88
    anchoring phenomena, 266
    character education standards, 273–75
    crosscutting concepts, 266
    integration strategies, 275–87
    lesson plan, 266
    national standards, 270–73
    social-emotional learning standards, 273–75
    state standards, 267–70
kindergarten, integration strategies, 275–78
Know, Want, How, Learn (KWHL), 129–30
KWHL chart, 129
KWHL. *See* Know, Want, How, Learn

L

labeling, 96–97
language, 196–98
language development
    bilingual language development, 197
    English language development, 196–97
language-literacy-communication domain, 231–36
learner, characteristics of, 166–68
learning areas
    block area, 103–7
    bonus areas, 117–18
    changing, 99
    creative arts area, 113–14
    dramatic play area, 101–3
    library area, 115
    music-movement area, 112–13
    outdoor area, 109–12
    placement, 99
    science/technology/engineering/math (STEM) area, 115–17
    sensory-texture area, 107–9
    writing area, 114–15
learning formats, 173
learning outcomes
    creating, 124–26
    planning strategies, 127–32
learning plan
    component alignment, 255–58
    components of, 250–51
    putting together, 251–55
    reflection, 180
    term, 220
learning sequence, 135
learning, approaches to, 259
lesson plan, 266
library area, 115
Lindqvist, Gunilla, 210
linguistic domain, 10
literary discipline, 196–98
Lobman, Carrie, 210
looping, 57
loose parts, 107

M

macrosystem, 73
manipulatives, 61
materials, 180
math, 202–4
    Common Core, 270
    first grade, 279
    kindergarten, 276
    second grade, 279
    third grade, 284
math symbolism, 203–4
math talk, 202
mathematics. *See* math
mediators, 48
mesosystem, 73
metacognition, 211–12
meth, curriculum resource, 260–61
microsystem, 72
mobile devices, apps for, 79–81
modifications, 100, 158
Montessori curriculum, 54–55
morphology, 197
movement, 209
movement opportunities, planning, 215
MTI. *See* Multiple Intelligence Theory
Multiple Intelligence (MI) theory (MTI), 156–57
muscular endurance, 214
"Museums Around the World," topic of interest, 251–55
music, 208–9
music-movement area, 112–13

N

NAEYC. *See* National Association for the Education of Young Children
NAEYC Code of Ethics, 144
NASPE. *See* National Association for Sport and Physical Education
National Association for Sport and Physical Education (NASPE), 261
National Association for the Education of Young Children (NAEYC), 6, 259
    guidelines, 16–19
National Core Arts Standards (NCAS), 271–72
National Council for the Social Studies (NCSS), 260

National Council of Teachers of Mathematics (NCTM), 260–61
National Science Teachers Association (NSTA), 260
National Social Studies, standards, 271–73
national standards, 270–73
nature play, 33
NCAS. See National Core Arts Standards
NCSS. See National Council for the Social Studies
NCTM. See National Council of Teachers of Mathematics
neural connections, 222
Next Generation Science, standards, 270
nonfiction, 197
nonverbal cues, 172
norm-referenced assessment, 152
NSTA. See National Science Teachers Association
nutrition, 214

O

observation, 211
Ogden Museum of Southern Art, 212
one-on-one, 173
opening circle, 174
orthography, 198
outdoor area, 109–12
outdoor play, 33
outreach, 84

P

P.S. ARTS, 260
pairing, 100
Paley, Vivian, 210
parentese, 235
participation charts, 148
pedagogy, 29
performance indicators, 269
Peter's Chair (Keats), 212
phonemes, 197
phonemic awareness, 197
phonograms, 197
phonology, 197
physical activity, 213
physical domain, 10, 236–43
physical education
    curriculum resource, 261
    health discipline, 213–14
piggyback, 208
placement of furnishings
    in block area, 107
    in creative arts area, 114
    in library area, 115
    in music-movement area, 113
    outdoor area, 110–12
    in sensory-texture area, 108–9
    in STEAM area, 117
    in writing area, 114–15
plan-do-review process, 53
planning strategies, 127–32
    backward design, 128
    concept diagrams, 130
    graphic organizers, 128–30
    Venn diagrams, 131–32
planning tools, 128–30
play
    brain activity and, 28–29
    categories of, 31
    cooperative play, 34
    cultural differences, 38–40
    curriculum resource, 261
    definition, 28
    developing brain and, 28–29
    guided play, 34
    implementing, 35–36
    investigative play, 34
    nature play, 33
    outdoor play, 33
    pedagogy of, 29
    planning for, 35
    pretend play, 33
    as principle, 12
    risky play, 31–32
    self-directed, 31–34
    stages and categories, 30–31
    superhero play, 33
    teacher-led play, 34–36
    technology and, 36–38
playworlds, 210
portfolio, 153–55
    documentation portfolio, 154
    evaluation portfolio, 154
    process portfolio, 154
    showcase portfolio, 154
prepared environment, 54
preschool integrated curriculum
    component alignment, 255–58
    components, 250–51
    putting together learning plan, 251–55
    teacher resource evaluation, 259–61
preschool, engineering in, 201
pretend play, 33
principles, child development, 9–16
    active learning, 13–14
    belonging, purpose, and agency, 14
    cultural contexts, 12–13
    development and learning, 9–10
    domains of development, 10–12
    integration, 14–15
    play, 12
    scaffolding, 15
    technology, 15–16
private speech, 48
process portfolio, 154
process-focused art, 211
product-focused art, 210–11
Project Approach, 61–63
props, 177
protagonist, 63
provocateurs, 64

R

rare words, 235
rating scales, 148
readers' theater, 210
receptive language, 234
reflection, 184–86
Reggio Emilia approach, 63–66
resources
    credible academic subject resources, 287–88
    evaluating, 259–61
    implementation phase and, 180
    infant-toddler, 243
    for teachers, 287
    verifying, 259
responsive teaching, 209
risky play, 31–32
routine as curriculum, 222–23
rubrics, 148–49

S

scaffold writing, 49
scaffolding, 15, 172
scaffolds, 48
schedules, 168–70
science
    curriculum resource, 260
    first grade, 280
    kindergarten, 276–77
    second grade, 280
    STEM, 199–200
    third grade, 284–85
science/technology/engineering/math (STEM)
    engineering, 200–201
    mathematics, 202–4
    science, 199–200
    STEM area, 115–17
    STEM discipline, 199–204
    technology, 200–201
screen time, 37
second grade, integration strategies, 278–82

SEL. *See* social-emotional learning
self-directed play, 31–34
self-regulation, 11, 47
self-regulation skills, 275
semantics, 197
sensory elements, 93–95
sensory system, 231
sensory-texture area, 107–9
sequential neurodevelopment, 28
serve-and-return, 222
showcase portfolio, 14
skills, 194–95
social dynamics, 98
Social Emotional Foundations for Early Learning (CSEFEL), 74–75
social studies
    curriculum resource, 260
    discipline, 204–5
    early social studies development, 204–6
    first grade, 280–82
    kindergarten, 277–78
    second grade, 280–82
    teacher training, 206–7
    third grade, 286
social-emotional domain, 10, 226–30
social-emotional learning (SEL), 273–75
    first grade, 282
    kindergarten, 278
    second grade, 282
    third grade, 287
spatial awareness, 214
special events, 178
stages of play, 30
standardized assessment, 151
standards
    character education, 273–75
    national, 270–73
    National Social Studies, 271–73
    Next Generation Standards, 270
    state, 267–70
state standards, 267–70
STEM. *See* science/technology/engineering/math
story problems, 177

story theater, 210
storyboards, 132
strategies, 224
superhero play, 33
supervision, 100
synapses. *See* neural connections
synchronous interaction, 179
syntax, 197

T

talking rights, 177
teacher resources
    approaches to learning, 259
    early literacy, 259
    evaluation, 259–61
teacher-initiated catalytic event, 134
teacher-led dramatic play, 209
teacher-led play, 34–36
teachers
    academic resources for, 287–88
    block area role, 106
    bonus area roles, 118
    creative arts area role, 113
    dramatic play area role, 102–3
    library area role, 115
    music-movement area role, 112
    outdoor area role, 109–10
    sensory-texture area role, 107
    STEM area role, 116–17
    teacher-initiated catalytic event, 134
    teacher-led dramatic play, 209
    teacher-led play, 34–36
    training in social studies, 206–7
    writing area role, 114
teaching pyramid model, 74
technology, 15–16
assistive technology, 158–59
    curriculum resource, 260
    play and, 36–38
    STEM, 200–201
temperament, 226
theater of the mind, 210
thematic curriculum, 59–61
    structure, 60–61
    theme selection, 59

thinking domain. *See* cognitive domain
third grade, integration strategies, 282–87
TIC. *See* trauma-informed care
ToM. *See* Tools of the Mind
Tools of the Mind (ToM)
    dynamic assessment, 50
    imaginative play, 49–50
    instructional strategies, 48–49
    structure, 46–48
topics of interest, 134
    great Americans, 256–57
    museums, 251–55
    weather, 256
transitions, 171
trauma-informed care (TIC), 10

U

UDL. *See* Universal Design for Learning
uniform, 268
Universal Design for Learning (UDL), 128

V

VARK Learning Approach, 157–58
Venn diagrams, 131–32
verbal cues, 171
Veterans Day Celebration, 80
video, 147
visual arts, 210–11

W

Waldorf curriculum, 56–59
    festivals, 57–59
    structure, 56–57
weather, topic of interest, 256
working memory, 11
writing area, 114–15
written speech, 48

Z

zone of proximal development (ZPD), 46
ZPD. *See* zone of proximal development

REFERENCE LIST

Chapter 1

Adair, J. K., Tobin, J., & Arzubiaga, A. E. (2012). The dilemma of cultural responsiveness and professionalization: Listening closer to immigrant teachers who teach children of recent immigrants. *Teachers College Record, 114*(4), 1–37.

American Academy of Pediatrics Council on Communications and Media. (2019). Media and young minds. *Pediatrics.*

Center on the Developing Child. (2010). *The foundations of lifelong health are built in early childhood.* https://developingchild.harvard.edu/wp-content/uploads/2010/05/Foundations-of-Lifelong-Health.pdf

Centers for Disease Control and Prevention. (2022). *Early brain development and health.* https://www.cdc.gov/ncbddd/childdevelopment/early-brain-development.html

Council on School Health. (2013). American academy of pediatrics policy statement: The crucial role of recess in school. *Pediatrics.* aappublications.org/content/pediatrics/131/1/183.full.pdf

Diamond, A., & Ling, D. (2016). Conclusions about interventions, programs, and approaches for improving executive functions that appear justified and those that, despite much hype, do not. *National Library of Medicine. 18,* 34–48.

Donohue, C. & Schomburg, R. (2017). Technology and interactive media in early childhood programs: What we've learned from five years of research, policy, and practice. *Young Children, 72*(4), 72–78.

Hirsh-Pasek, K. & Hadani, H. (2020, October). A new path to education reform: Playful learning promotes 21st-century skills in schools and beyond. *Brookings Institute.* https://www.brookings.edu/wp-content/uploads/2020/10/Big-Ideas_Hirsh-Pasek_Playful-Learning.pdf

Immordino-Yang, M. H., Darling-Hammond, L., & Krone, C. (2018). *The brain basis for integrated social, emotional, and academic development: How emotions and social relationships drive learning.* Aspen Institute.

Ladson-Billings, G. (2022). *The dreamkeepers: Successful teachers of african american children.* John Wiley & Sons.

National Association for the Education of Young Children (2012). *Technology and interactive media as tools in early childhood programs serving children from birth through age 8.* https://www.naeyc.org/sites/default/files/globally-shared/downloads/PDFs/resources/position-statements/ps_technology.pdf

National Association for the Education of Young Children. (2020). Developmentally appropriate practice.

National Association for the Education of Young Children (2020). Professional standards and competencies. *Professional Standards and Competencies for Early Childhood Educators Copyright © 2020 by the National Association for the Education of Young Children.*

NAEYC & Fred Rogers Center for Early Learning and Children's Media. (2012). Technology and interactive media as tools in early childhood programs serving children from birth through age 8. Joint position statement. Fred Rogers Center at St. Vincent College.

National Academies of Science, Engineering, and Medicine. (2015). *Transforming the workforce for children birth through age 8: A unifying foundation.* https://doi.org/10.17226/19401

National Academies of Science, Engineering, and Medicine. (2017). *Promoting the educational success of children and youth learning english: Promising futures.*

National Scientific Council on the Developing Child. (2004). *Young children develop in an environment of relationships.* Center for the Developing Child, Harvard University. https://46y5eh11fhgw3ve3yt-pwxt9r-wpengine.netdna-ssl.com/wp-content/uploads/2004/04/Young-Children-Develop-in-an-Environment-of-Relationships.pdf

National Scientific Council on the Developing Child. (2018). *Understanding motivation: Building the brain architecture that supports learning, health, and community participation.* www.developingchild.harvard.edu

Nebraska Department of Education (2017). *Integrated curriculum in the primary program.* https://www.education.ne.gov/wp-content/uploads/2017/07/IC.pdf

Power to the Profession. (2020). *Unifying framework for the early childhood education profession.* http://powertotheprofession.org/unifying-framework/

Rogoff, B., Paradise, R., Arauz, R. M., Correa-Chávez, M., & Angelillo, C. (2003). Firsthand learning through intent participation. *Annual Review of Psychology. 54,* 175–203.

Skinner, A. L. & Meltzoff, A.N. (2019). Childhood experiences and intergroup biases among children. *Social Issues and Policy Review. 13*(1), 211–240.

Tominey, S. (2016, February 24). *How to help your child develop executive function and self-regulation skills.* https://www.noodle.com/articles/how-to-help-your-child-develop-executive-function-and-self-regulation-skills

Yow, Q. & Markman, E. (2015). Bilingualism: Language and cognition. *18*(3), 391–399. https://doi.org/10.1017/S1366728914000133

Chapter 2

Bales, D. W., Falen, K., Butler, T., Marshall, L. E., Searle, L., & Semple, P. (2018). *Better brains for babies trainer's guide,* (2nd ed.).

Barker, J. E., Semenov A. D., Michaelson, L., Provan, L. S., Snyder, H. R., & Munakata, Y. (2014). Less-structured time in children's daily lives predicts self-directed executive functioning. *Frontiers in Psychology, 5,* 593.

Barros, R. M., Silver, E. J., & Stein, R.E.K. (2009). School Recess and Group Classroom Behavior. *Pediatrics, 123*(2).

Bodrova, E., & Leong, D. J. (2019). Making play smarter, stronger, and kinder: Lessons from tools of the mind. *American Journal of Play, 12*(1), 37–53.

Canadian Paediatric Society. (2018). Screen time and young children: Promoting health and development in a digital world. *Paediatrics & Child Health, 23*(1), 83.

Cooper, P. (2014). From the editor: Challenges to guiding the teacher of guided play. *Journal of Early Childhood Teacher Education, 35*(4), 293–296.

Donohue, C. & Schomburg, R. (2017). Technology and interactive media in early childhood programs: What we've learned from five years of research, policy, and practice. *Young Children, 72*(4), 72–78.

Edwards, J. O., & Derman-Sparks, L. (2010). *Anti-bias education for young children and ourselves.* United States: National Association for the Education of Young Children.

Epstein, A. S. (2014). *The intentional teacher: Choosing the best strategies for young children's learning* (2nd edition). Washington, DC: National Association for the Education of Young Children.

Gongala, S. (2023). *16 positive and negative effects of superheroes on children*. https://www.momjunction.com/articles/positive-negative-impact-of-superheroes-on-children_00692531/

Gosso, Y. & Carvalho, A. M. (2013). Play and cultural context. *Encyclopedia on Early Childhood Development*. http://www.child-encyclopedia.com/play/according-experts/play-and-cultural-context

Heroman, C. (2017). *Making and tinkering with stem: Solving design challenges with young children*. National Association for the Education of Young Children.

Jelleyman, C., McPhee, J., Brussoni, M., Bundy, A., & Duncan, S. (2019). A cross-sectional description of parental perceptions and practices related to risky play and independent mobility in children: The new zealand state of play survey. *International Journal of Environmental Research and Public Health, 16*(2), 262.

Lavrysen, A., Bertrands, E., Leyssen, L., Smets, L., Vanderspikken, A., & De Graef, P. (2015). Risky-play at school: Facilitating risk perception and competence in young children. *European Early Childhood Education Research Journal, 1* (11).

McCoy, D. C., Yoshikawa, H., Ziol-Guest, K. M., Duncan, G. J., Schindler, H. S., Magnuson, K., Yang, R., Koepp, A., & Shonkoff, J. P. (2017). Impacts of early childhood education on medium- and long-term educational outcomes. *Educational Researcher, 46*(8), 474–487

NAEYC & Fred Rogers Center for Early Learning and Children's Media. (2012). *Technology and interactive media as tools in early childhood programs serving children from birth through age 8*. Joint position statement. Fred Rogers Center at St. Vincent College.

National Academies of Sciences, Engineering, and Medicine. (2017). *Promoting the educational success of children and youth learning english: Promising futures*. Washington, DC: The National Academies Press.

National Association for the Education of Young Children. (2020). *Developmentally appropriate practices*. National Association for the Education of Young Children.

Nell, M. L., Drew, W. F., & Bush, D. E. (2013). *From play to practice: Connecting teachers' play to children's learning*. The National Association for the Education of Young Children.

Pyle, A., & Danniels, E. (2017). A continuum of play-based learning: The role of the teacher in play-based pedagogy and the fear of hijacking play. *Early Education and Development, 28*(3), 274–289.

Roopnarine, J. L. & Davidson, K. L. (2015), Parent-child play across cultures: Advancing play research. *American Journal of Play, 7*(2).

Reid, J. L., Kagan, S. L., & Scott-Little, C. (2017). New understandings of cultural diversity and the implications for early childhood policy, pedagogy, and practice. *Early Child Development and Care, 189*(6), 976–989.

Rice, M. (2017). *Teachers' role in supporting play in early childhood classroom*. https://playandlearn.com/children-2/teachers-role-supporting-play-early-childhood-classrooms

Riley-Ayers, S. & Figueras-Daniel, A. (2019). *Engaging and enriching play is rigorous learning. In serious fun: How guided play extends children's learning*. Washington, DC: National Association for the Education of Young Children.

Sandseter, E.B.H., & Kleppe, R. (2019). *Outdoor risky play*. Encyclopedia on Early Childhood Development.

Schulz, L. E., & Bonawitz, E. B. (2007). Serious fun: Preschoolers engage in more exploratory play when evidence is confounded. *Dev Psychol 43*(4), 1045–1050.

Sosik, J. J., & Jung D. I. (2002). Work-group characteristics and performance in collectivistic and individualistic cultures. *The Journal of Social Psychology, 142*(1), 5–23.

Spiegal, B., Gill, T. R., Harbottle, H., & Ball, D. J. (2014). Children's play space and safety management: Rethinking the role of play equipment standards. *SAGE 4*, 1–11.

Vygotsky, L. S. (1967). Play and its role in the mental development of the child. *Soviet Psychology, 5*, 6–18.

Weisberg, D. S., Hirsh-Pasek, K., & Golinkoff, R. M. (2013). Guided play: Where curricular goals meet a playful pedagogy. *Mind, Brain and Education, 7*(2), 104–112.

Yogman, M., Garner, A., Hutchinson, J., Hirsh-Pasek, K., & Golinkoff, R. M. (2018). The power of play: A pediatric role in enhancing development in young children. *Pediatrics, 142*(3).

Zosh, J., Hopkins, M., Jensen, E. J., Liu, H., Neale, C., Hirsh-Pasek, K., Solis, S. L., & Whitebread, D. (2017). *Learning through play: A review of the evidence*. Billund, DK: The LEGO Foundation.

Chapter 3

American Montessori Society. (n.d.). *History of montessori*. https://amshq.org/About-Montessori/History-of-Montessori

Bodrova, E. & Leong, D. (2018). Tools of the mind: The vygotskian-based early childhood program. *Journal of Cognitive Education and Psychology 17*(3).

Bonnay, S. (2022). *History of eanrly childhood education: Then and now*. www.himama.com/blog/early-childhood-education-then-and-now?cat1=Leadership&cat2=Leadership

Cadwell, L. B. (1997). *Bringing reggio emilia home: An innovative approach to early childhood education*. United Kingdom: Teachers College Press.

Chard, S. C. (1998). *The project approach: Developing the basic framework. Practical guide*. New York: Scholastic.

Edwards, C. P. (1993). *The hundred languages of children: The reggio emilia approach to early childhood education*. Norwood, N.J.: Ablex Pub. Corp.

Epstein, A. S., & Hohmann, M. (2012). *HighScope's curriculum content areas and the KDIs*. https://highscope.org/wp-content/uploads/2018/08/152.pdf

Fiore, A. (2013). *The reggio emilia approach to early childhood*. La Scuola d'Italia: New York.

Gandini, L. (1993). Fundamentals of the reggio emilia approach to early childhood education. *Young Children, 49*, 4–8, 1993.

Harbor Waldorf School (n.d.). https://harborwaldorfschool.org/

Helm, J. H., & Katz, L. G. (2016). *Young investigators: the project approach in the early years*. 3rd ed. Teachers College Press.

HighScope. (n.d.). *Preschool curriculum*. https://highscope.org/our-practice/preschool-curriculum/

Katz, L. (2017) *Lively minds at work*. https://www.exchangepress.com/eed/view/4442/

Katz, L. G. (1994). The project approach. *ERIC Digest*, 368–509.

Katz, L. G. (2007). What to look for when visiting early childhood classes. *Gifted Child Today, 30*(3).

Koetzsch, R, & Riegel, A. (2020). *Letting the children be children*. https://www.waldorfearlychildhood.org/uploads-new/articles_3_1770873492.pdf

Leong, D. (n.d.) *What makes tools unique?* https://ncchildcare.ncdhhs.gov/Portals/0/documents/pdf/T/tools_prek.pdf

Montessori.org (n.d.). *What is montessori education? A historical perspective*. https://www.montessori.org/montessori-brief-biography/

Montessori, M. (1995). *The absorbent mind: A classic in education and child development for educators and parents*. New York: Holt.

Project Approach (n.d.) Explicit Instruction. https://www.projectapproach.org/systematic-instruction

Rawson, M. (2020). *Waldorf education today: a critical introduction*. Abingdon: Routledge.

Research Institute for Waldorf Education. (n.d.). *Teacher looping literature search*. https://www.waldorfresearchinstitute.org/research-on-looping/#:~:text=Looping%20The%20idea%20of%20a,two%20or%20three%20consecutive%20years

Rinaldi, C. (1991). *The reggio emilia approach*. https://eric.ed.gov/?id=ED355034

Scholastic Parents Staff. (n.d.). *Social skills and challenges in kindergarten*. Scholastic. https://www.scholastic.com/parents/school-success/school-life/grade-by-grade/social-skills-and-challenges-kindergarten.html

Schuler, D. (2000). The project approach: Meeting state standards. *Early childhood research & practice, 2*(1).

Tools of the Mind. (n.d.). *Transforming teaching and learning*. https://toolsofthemind.org/

Tucson Waldorf School. (n.d.). *Festivals & annual events*. https://tucsonwaldorf.org/festivals-annual-events/

Vygotsky, L. S. (1986). *Thought and language*. (Trans.) Cambridge: MIT Press.

Vygotsky, L. S. (1987). *The collected works of L.S. Vygotsky, Volume 1: Problems of general psychology*. New York: Plenum Press.

Waldorf.com (n.d.) https://www.waldorfeducation.org/

Waldorf world list: Directory of Steiner-Waldorf schools, kindergartens and teacher education centers worldwide. (2022). Freunde der Erziehungskunst Rudolph Steiner. https://www.freunde-waldorf.de/fileadmin/user_upload/images/Waldorf_World_List/Waldorf_World_List.pdf

Wiggins, G. (2015). My reply to Willingham, part 2. *Granted, and…* https://grantwiggins.files.wordpress.com

Chapter 4

Beecher, C., & Buzhardt, J. (2016). Mobile technology to increase parent engagement. *Interaction Design and Architecture Journal, 28*, 49–68. https://www.researchgate.net/publication/305816552_Mobile_technology_to_increase_parent_engagement

Bredekamp, S. (2014). *Effective practices in early childhood education: Building a foundation*, 2nd ed. Upper Saddle River, N.J.: Pearson.

Bronfenbrenner, U. (2009). *The ecology of human development: Experiments by nature and design*. Cambridge: Harvard University Press.

Center on the Social and Emotional Foundations for Early Learning. (n.d.) http://csefel.vanderbilt.edu/

Division for Early Childhood. (2014). *DEC recommended practices in early intervention/early childhood special education 2014*. http://www.dec-sped.org/recommendedpractices

Evangelou, M., & Sylva, K. (2003). *The effects of the peers early educational partnership (PEEP) on children's developmental progress*. http://www.dfes.gov.uk/research/data/uploadfiles/RR489.pdf

Fox, L., Dunlap, G., Hemmeter, M. L., Joseph, G. E., & Strain, P. S. (2003). The teaching pyramid: A model for supporting social competence and preventing challenging behavior in young children. *Young Children, 58*(4), 48–52.

Gauvreau, A. N., & Sandall, S. (2017). Using mobile technologies to communicate with parents and caregivers. *Young Exceptional Child*. https://doi.org/10.1177/1096250617726530

Ho, L. H., Hung, C. L., & Chen, H. C. (2013). Using theoretical models to examine the acceptance behavior of mobile phone messaging to enhance parent–teacher interactions. *Computers & Education, 61*, 105–114. https://doi.org/10.1016/j.compedu.2012.09.009

Howell, J. & Reinhard, K. (2015). Rituals and traditions: Fostering a sense of community in preschool. Washington, D. C.: *National Association for the Education of Young Children*.

National Association for the Education of Young Children (2020). Developmentally appropriate practices.

National Association for the Education of Young Children (2020). Professional standards and competencies. *Professional Standards and Competencies for Early Childhood Educators*.

Sewell, T. (2012). Are we adequately preparing teachers to partner with families? *Early Childhood Education Journal, 40*, 259–263.

Texas Child Care. (2016). Creating a caring community of learners. *Texas Child Care Quarterly*. https://www.childcarequarterly.com/pdf/fall16_community.pdf

Chapter 5

Association for Psychological Science. (2014). *Heavily decorated classrooms disrupt attention and learning in children*. https://www.psychologicalscience.org/news/releases/heavily-decorated-classrooms-disrupt-attention-and-learning-in-young-children.html/comment-page-1

Boaler, J., & Zoido, P. (2016). Why math education in the us doesn't add up. *Scientific American. 27*(6), 18–19. https://doi.org/doi:10.1038/scientificamericanmind1116-18.

Colker, L. (2015) Supporting one and all in the dramatic play center. *Teaching Young Children, 9*(1) 16–17. https://www.naeyc.org/resources/pubs/tyc/oct2015

Department of Education and Training. (2022). Three-year-old kindergarten teaching toolkit. *Victoria State Government*. https://www.education.vic.gov.au/childhood/professionals/learning/Pages/Environments-for-Learning.aspx

Gentry, R. (2017). Landmark study finds better path to reading success. *Psychology Today*. https://www.psychologytoday.com/us/blog/raising-readers-writers-and-spellers/201703/landmark-study-finds-better-path-reading-success

National Association for the Education of Young Children (NAEYC). (2019). *Professional standards and competencies for early childhood educators*. https://www.naeyc.org/resources/position-statements/professional-standards-competencies

National Association for Music Education. (2019). *Early childhood music education: A position statement from the national association for music education*. https://nafme.org/about/position-statements/early-childhood-music-education/

National PE Standards-Highly Effective Physical Education. (n.d.). https://www.shapeamerica.org/MemberPortal/standards/pe/default.aspx.

National Science Teachers Association. (n.d.). *NSTA position statement: Early childhood science education. National Association for the Education of Young Children*.

Nicholson, S. (1971). How not to cheat children: The theory of loose parts. *Landscape Architecture*, 30–34.

Paley, V. G. (1990). *The boy who would be a helicopter: The uses of storytelling in the classroom*. Cambridge: Harvard University Press.

Pattison, S., Ramos-Montañez, S., & Svarovsky, G. (2020). *Early childhood engineering: Supporting engineering design practices with young children and their families*. https://www.researchgate.net/publication/340234317_Early_Childhood_Engineering_Supporting_Engineering_Design_Practices_with_Young_Children_and_Their_Families

Reid, J. L., Kagan, S. L., & Scott-Little, C. (2017). New understandings of cultural diversity and the implications for early childhood policy, pedagogy, and practice. *Early Child Development and Care 189*(6), 976–989.

Rosenow, N., & Jaffe, K. (2015). It takes all of us: Thinking together about effective and inspiring spaces for children. *Child Care Exchange, 37*(4), 8–13. https://www.childcareexchange.com/

Skinner, A. L. & Meltzoff, A. N. (2019). Childhood experiences and intergroup biases among children. *Social Issues and Policy Review 13*(1): 211–240. https://doi.org/10.1111/sipr.12054

Wilkins, A. (2019). Fluorescent lighting in school could be harming your child's health and ability to read. *The Conversation*. https://theconversation.com/fluorescent-lighting-in-school-could-be-harming-your-childs-health-and-ability-to-read-124330

Wolfgang, C. H., Stannard, L. L., & Jones, I. (2009). Block play performance among preschoolers as a predictor of later school achievement in mathematics. *Journal of Research in Childhood Education, 15*(2), 173–180.

Chapter 6

Arizona Department of Education. (2018). *Arizona early learning standards, 4th edition*. https://www.azed.gov/sites/default/files/2018/04/ELS%202018%20DRAFT%20FOR%20COMMENT.pdf?id=5acd475b3217e1183c539fa5

Asasher. (2021). Taking advantage of teachable moments: Capitalizing on teachable moments with children. *CCEI a Straighter Line Company*. https://www.cceionline.com/february-2021-newsletter-taking-advantage-of-teachable-moments-capitalizing-on-teachable-moments-with-children/

Bowen, R. S. (2017). Understanding by design. *Vanderbilt University Center for Teaching*. https://cft.vanderbilt.edu/understanding-by-design/

Brillante, P., & Nemeth, K. (2018). *Universal design for learning in the early childhood classroom*. New York, NY: Routledge

Center for Applied Special Technology (CAST). (2018). *The UDL guidelines*. http://udlguidelines.cast.org

Center on Enhancing Early Learning Outcomes. (n.d.). *State by state*. http://ceelo.org/state-map/2021

Cooper, P. A. (1993). Paradigm shifts in designed instruction: from behaviorism to cognitivism to constructivism. *Educational Technology, 33*(5), 12-19.

Dexter, D. D., Park, Y. J., & Hughes, C. A. (2011). A meta-analytic review of graphic organizers and science instruction for adolescents with learning disabilities: Implications for the intermediate and secondary science classroom. *Learning Disabilities Research & Practice, 26*(4), 204–213.

Indiana Department of Education. (2015). *Indiana's early learning development framework: The foundations*. https://www.in.gov/doe/students/indiana-academic-standards/early-learning/

National Association for the Education of Young Children (NAEYC). (2019). *Early learning program accreditation standards and assessment items*. https://www.naeyc.org/sites/default/files/globally-shared/downloads/PDFs/accreditation/early-learning/standards_assessment_2019.pdf

National Association for the Education of Young Children (NAEYC) (2020). *Professional standards and competencies for early childhood educators*. https://www.naeyc.org/search/professional%20standards%20and%20competencies

National Association for the Education of Young Children (NAEYC). (2010). *Side-by-side of the 2010 NAEYC professional preparation standards and the professional standards and competencies for early childhood educators*. https://www.naeyc.org/sites/default/files/globally-shared/downloads/PDFs/resources/position-statements/side_by_side_standards_comparison.pdf

National Association for the Education of Young Children (NAEYC) and the National Association of Early Childhood Specialists in State Departments of Education (NAECS/SDE). (2002). *Creating the conditions for success*. https://www.naeyc.org/sites/default/files/globally-shared/downloads/PDFs/resources/position-statements/position_statement.pdf

Chapter 7

Arizona Department of Education. (2018). *Arizona early learning standards*. https://www.azed.gov/sites/default/files/2018/04/ELS%202018%20DRAFT%20FOR%20COMMENT.pdf?id=5acd-475b3217e1183c539fa5

Armstrong, T. (2009). *Multiple intelligences in the classroom*. Alexandria, VA: ASCD.

Cherry, K. (2019, November 27). *Overview of vark learning styles*. https://www.verywellmind.com/vark-learning-styles-2795156

Division for Early Childhood of the Council for Exceptional Children. (2014). *DEC recommended practices*. https://divisionearlychildhood.egnyte.com/dl/7urLPWCt5U/?#content

Dixon-Roman, Ezekiel & Everson, Howard & Mcardle, J. (2013). Race, poverty and SAT scores: Modeling the influences of family income on black and white high school students' SAT performance. *Teachers College Record, 115*(4). doi:10.1177/016146811311500406.

Edelman, L. (2014). *Using digital video in early care and education and early intervention*. https://inclusioninstitute.fpg.unc.edu/sites/inclusioninstitute.fpg.unc.edu/files/handouts/Edelman%20-%20Using%20Video%20in%20EI-ECE%20%285-4-14%29.pdf

Gardner, H. (1997). Multiple intelligences as a partner in school reform. *Educational Leadership, 55*(1), 20–21. https://eric.ed.gov/?id=EJ550526

WrightsLaw. (n.d.). *Guidance on IDEA 2004*. https://www.wrightslaw.com/idea/osep.statute.htm

Hansel, L., ed. (2019). Intentional and supportive: Appropriate uses of early assessment. *Young Children, 74*(3). National Association for the Education of Young Children. https://www.naeyc.org/resources/pubs/yc/jul2019/appropriate-uses-early-assessments

Jung, L. A. (2017). *Is it an accommodation or a modification?* ASCD Student Growth Center. https://www.leadinclusion.org/post/2017/05/22/is-it-an-accommodation-or-a-modification

Katz, L. (n.d.). Peabody College, Iris Center. Vanderbilt University. https://iris.peabody.vanderbilt.edu/module/di/cresource/q1/p01/[BP1]

McAfee, O., Leong, D., & Bodrova, E. (2016). *Assessing and guiding young children's development and learning*. New York, NY: Pearson.

National Academies of Science, Engineering, and Medicine (NASEM). (2017). *Promoting the educational success of children and youth learning English: Promising futures*. https://nap.nationalacademies.org/catalog/24677/promoting-the-educational-success-of-children-and-youth-learning-english

National Association for the Education of Young Children. (2019). *Advancing equity in early childhood education: a position statement of the national association for the education of young children*. https://www.naeyc.org/sites/default/files/globally-shared/downloads/PDFs/resources/position-statements/advancingequitypositionstatement.pdf

National Association for the Education of Young Children (2020). *Developmentally Appropriate Practices*. https://www.naeyc.org/sites/default/files/globally-shared/downloads/PDFs/resources/position-statements/dap-statement_0.pdf

National Association for the Education of Young Children. (2019). *Early learning program accreditation standards and assessment items*. https://www.naeyc.org/sites/default/files/globally-shared/downloads/PDFs/accreditation/early-learning/standards_and_assessment_2019.pdf

National Association for the Education of Young Children. (2011). *NAEYC code of ethical conduct and statement of commitment*. https://www.naeyc.org/sites/default/files/globally-shared/downloads/PDFs/resources/position-statements/Ethics%20Position%20Statement2011_09202013update.pdf

National Association for the Education of Young Children. (2019). *Professional standards and competencies for early childhood educators.* https://www.naeyc.org/resources/position-statements/professional-standards-competencies

Prashing, B. (2005). Learning styles vs. multiple intelligences (mi): Two concepts for enhancing learning and teaching. *Teaching Expertise,* (9). https://www.rcsdk12.org/cms/lib/NY01001156/Centricity/Domain/9842/ls%20vs%20mi%20tex9_p8_9.pdf

Tomlinson, C. (2022). *What is differentiated instruction?* IRIS Center, Vanderbilt Peabody College. https://iris.peabody.vanderbilt.edu/module/di/cresource/q1/p01/#content

Valencia, S. W., Place, N. A., Martin, S.D., & Grossman, P. L. (2006). Curriculum materials for elementary reading: Shackles and scaffolds for beginning teachers. *Elementary School Journal, 107*(1), 93–120.

Chapter 8

Alanís, I., Salinas-Gonzalez, I., & Arreguín-Anderson, M.G. (2015). Kindergarten through grade 3: Developing biliteracy with intentional support: Using interactive word walls and paired learning. *Young Children, 70*(4), 46–5. https://www.jstor.org/stable/ycyoungchildren.70.4.46

Arizona Department of Education. (2018). *Arizona early learning standards.* https://www.azed.gov/sites/default/files/2018/04/ELS%202018%20DRAFT%20FOR%20COMMENT.pdf?id=5acd-475b3217e1183c539fa5

Bodrova, E. Leong, D. (2018). Tools of the Mind: The Vygotskian-based early childhood program. *Journal of Cognitive Education and Psychology, 17*(3). https://eric.ed.gov/?id=EJ1225726

Hatch, J. A. (2002). Accountability shove down: Resisting the standards movement in early childhood education. *Phi Delta Kappan, 83*(6), 457–62. https://eric.ed.gov/?id=EJ640866

Katz, L. (2007, July). What to look for when visiting ECE classrooms. *The Gifted Child Today, 30*(3), 34–37. https://doi.org/10.4219/gct-2007-41

Katz, L. G. (1993). *Dispositions: Definitions and implications for early childhood practices. Perspectives from ERIC/EECE: A monograph series, no. 4.* https://eric.ed.gov/?id=ED360104.m

Levin, D. (2016). *Time matters: The importance of sustained play in child development.* Child Care Exchange. http://www.truceteachers.org/uploads/1/5/5/7/15571834/timematters_inplay_7.16-levin.pdf

Martinelli, K. (2020). *How can we help kids with transitions?* Child Mind Institute. https://childmind.org/article/how-can-we-help-kids-with-transitions.

National Association for the Education of Young Children (2020). *Professional standards and competencies for early childhood educators.* https://www.naeyc.org/resources/position-statements/professional-standards-competencies

Perry, B. (2011). *Curiosity: The fuel of development.* Tarrant Cares. https://tarrant.tx.networkofcare.org/family/library/article.aspx?id=452

Rabinowitch, TC, & Knafo-Noam, A. (2015). Synchronous rhythmic interaction enhances children's perceived similarity and closeness towards each other. *PLoS One, 10*(4).

Self, E. (2018) *Dimensions of deep learning: Levels of engagement and learning.* https://www.ascd.org/blogs/dimensions-of-deep-learning-levels-of-engagement-and-learning

Tardos, A. (2013). Facilitating the play of children at Loczy. In D. Greenwald & J. Weaver (Eds.), *The RIE manual for parents and professionals* (168–176). Los Angeles, CA: Educaring: Resources for Infant Educarers (RIE).

Chapter 9

Zero to Three. (2009). *Activity level.* https://www.zerotothree.org/resources/350-activity-level

Alegria, M. (2017, June 7). *Music as a teaching tool.* https://www.edutopia.org/blog/music-teaching-tool-maria-alegria

Bach, D. (2017). *Bilingual babies: Study shows how exposure to a foreign language ignites learning.* UW News. University of Washington. https://www.washington.edu/news/2017/07/17/bilingual-babies-study-shows-how-exposure-to-a-foreign-language-ignites-infants-learning

Becker, D. R., McClelland, M. M., Loprinzi, P., & Trost, S. G. (2014). Physical activity, self-regulation, and early academic achievement in preschool children. *Early Education and Development, 25*(1), 56–70.

Blank, J. (2018). The design process: Engineering practices in preschool. *Young Children, 73*(4).

Block, D. (2015). *Letter names can cause confusion and other things to know about letter–sound relationships.* NAEYC. https://www.naeyc.org/resources/pubs/yc/mar2015/letter-sound-relationships

Brillante, P., & Mankiw, S. (2015). *Preschool through grade 3: A sense of place: human geography in the early childhood classroom. Young Children, 70*(3), 16–23. http://www.jstor.org/stable/ycyoungchildren.70.3.16

Carpenter, T. P., Franke, M. L., Johnson, N. C., Turrou, A. C. & Wager, A. A. (2016). *Young children's mathematics: Cognitively guided instruction in early childhood education.* Portsmouth, NH: Heinemann.

Chen, W. & Adler, J. L. (2019). Assessment of screen exposure in young children, 1997 to 2014. *JAMA Pediatr, 173*(4), 391–393. doi:10.1001/jamapediatrics.2018.5546

Clements, D. & Sarama, J. (2023). Rethinking STEM in the elementary grades: Honoring the special role of math in cognitive development. *American Educator, 47*(1). 16–21.

Corbeil, M., Trehub, S., & Peretz, I. (2013). *Speech vs. singing: Infants choose happier sounds.* Frontiers in Psychology. 4. 372. 10.3389/fpsyg.2013.00372

Cresswell, T. (2013). *Geographic thought: A critical introduction.* West Sussex, UK: Wiley- Blackwell.

De Houwer, A. (2007). Parental language input patterns and children's bilingual use. *Applied Psycholinguistics, 28*(03). doi: 10.1017/S0142716407070221

Educational Playcare. (2018, August 16). *Product art vs. process art.* https://www.educationalplaycare.com/blog/product-art-vs-process-art/

Epstein, A. S. (2009). *Me, you, us: Social-emotional learning in preschool.* Ypsilanti, MI: HighScope.

Foxwell, B. (2022) *Why you should use music in the classroom.* https://blog.savvas.com/why-you-should-use-music-in-the-classroom/

Gersema, E. (2016). *Children's brains develop faster with music training.* USC News. https://news.usc.edu/102681/childrens-brains-develop-faster-with-music-training/

Ginsburg, H., Lee, J., & Boyd, J. (2008). Mathematics Education for Young Children: What it is and How to Promote it. Society for Research in Child Development, *Social Policy Report, 22*(1), 3–22.

Grossman, S. (2012). *The worksheet dilemma: Benefits of play-based curricula.* Early Childhood News. www.earlychildhoodnews.com/earlychildhood/article_view.aspx?ArticleID=134.

Helmenstein, A. (2019, June 27). *Why mathematics is a language.* https://www.thoughtco.com/why-mathematics-is-a-language-4158142

Hillman C. H., Erickson K. I., Kramer A. F. (2008). Be smart, exercise your heart: Exercise effects on brain and cognition. *Nature Reviews Neuroscience, 9*(1), 58–65.

Jensen, E. (2009). *Teaching with poverty in mind: What being poor does to kids' brains and what schools can do about it*. Alexandria, VA: Association for Supervision and Curriculum Development.

Kabali, H. K., Irigoyen, M. M., Nunez-Davis, R., Budacki, J.G., Mohanty, S. H., Leister, K. P., & Bonner, R. L. (2015). Exposure and use of mobile media devices by young children. *Pediatrics, 136*(6). https://doi.org/10.1542/peds.2015-2151

Kirk, E. W. & Clark, P. (2005). Beginning with Names: Using Children's Names to Facilitate Early Literacy Learning. *Childhood Education, 81*(3), 139–44.

Kisida, B. & Bowen, D. H. (2019, February 12). *New evidence of the benefits of arts education*. Brookings. https://www.brookings.edu/blog/brown-center-chalkboard/2019/02/12/new-evidence-of-the-benefits-of-arts-education/

Klibanoff, R. S., Levine, S. C., Huttenlocher, J., Vasilyeva, M., & Hedges, L. V. (2006). Preschool children's mathematical knowledge: The effect of teacher "math talk." *Developmental Psychology, 42*(1), 59–69.

Kovács, Á. (2012). Early bilingualism and theory of mind: Bilinguals' advantage in dealing with conflicting mental representations. *Access to Language and Cognitive Development*. Oxford, United Kingdom: Oxford University Press. https://doi.org/10.1093/acprof:oso/9780199592722.003.0011

Kris, D. F. (2019). *How movement and exercise help kids learn*. KQED. https://www.kqed.org/mindshift/53681/how-movement-and-exercise-help-kids-learn

Larm, B. & Jaros, A. (2017, January 20). *The art of scientific thinking: Why science is important for early childhood development*. MSU Extension. https://www.canr.msu.edu/news/art_of_scientific_thinking_in_early_childhood_development

Leeuwen, B. (2018). *Explainer: what's the difference between STEM and STEAM?* The Conversation. https://theconversation.com/explainer-whats-the-difference-between-stem-and-steam-95713#:~:text=STEM%20represents%20science%2C%20technology%2C%20engineering,arts%2C%20design%20and%20new%20media.&text=The%20main%20difference%20between%20STEM,explicitly%20focuses%20on%20scientific%20concepts.

Leonhardt, M. (2021). *Parents spend an average of $8,355 per child to secure year-round child care*. CNBC. https://www.cnbc.com/2021/05/19/what-parents-spend-annually-on-child-care-costs-in-2021.html

Lindqvist, G. (1995). *The aesthetics of play: A didactic study of play and culture in preschools*. PhD dissertation, Uppsala University, Sweden.

Lindsay S. (2020). Exploring skills gained through a robotics program for youth with disabilities. *OTJR: Occupational Therapy Journal of Research, 40*(1), 57–63. https://doi.org/10.1177/1539449219868276

Lobman, C. L., Clark, K., & Ryan, S. (2015, May). Preschool through primary grades: From the dress-up corner to the stage: dramatic activities for early childhood classrooms. *Young Children, 70*(2), 92–99. http://www.jstor.org/stable/ycyoungchildren.70.2.92

Maine Department of Education. (2015). *Maine's early learning development standards*. Maine Department of Health and Human Services. https://www.maine.gov/doe/sites/maine.gov.doe/files/inline-files/Maine-ELDS_0.pdf

Mardell, B. (2011). *Learning is a team sport: Kindergartners study the Boston marathon* (video). Project Zero, Harvard University Graduate School of Education. www.pz.harvard.edu/resources/learning-is-a-team-sport-kindergartners-study-the-boston-marathon

Marjanovic-Shane, A., Ferholt, B., Miyazaki, K., Nilsson, M., Rainio, A.P., Hakkarainen, P., Pešić, M. & Beljanski-Ristić, L. (2011). Playworlds: An art of development. *Play and Performance: Play and Culture Studies, 11*, 3–32. Lanham, MD: University Press of America.

McClure, E. (2017). More than a foundation: Young children are capable STEM learners. *Young Children, 72*(5), 83–89. https://www.jstor.org/stable/90015862

McElroy, M. (2013, January 2). *While in womb, babies begin learning language from their mothers*. University of Washington. https://www.washington.edu/news/2013/01/02/while-in-womb-babies-begin-learning-language-from-their-mothers/

McNair, J. C. (2007, September). *Say my name, say my name! Using children's names to enhance early literacy development*. YC Young Children, 62(5), 84–89. https://eric.ed.gov/?id=EJ776613

Moran, K.J.K. (2006, May 26). Nurturing Emergent Readers Through Readers Theater. *Early Childhood Education Journal, 33*(5), 317–23. https://link.springer.com/article/10.1007/s10643-006-0089-8

NAEYC. (2012). *Selected examples of effective classroom practice involving technology tools and interactive media*. https://www.naeyc.org/sites/default/files/globally-shared/downloads/PDFs/resources/topics/PS_technology_Examples.pdf

National Council for the Social Studies. (2019). *Early childhood in the social studies context*. https://www.socialstudies.org/position-statements/early-childhood-social-studies-context

National Geographic Education. (n.d.) *What is geography?* Education, Topic Collections. www.education.nationalgeographic.com/education/what-is-geography/?ar_a=1.

National Research Council (NRC). (2012). *A framework for K–12 science education: Practices, crosscutting concepts, and core ideas*. Washington, DC: National Academies Press.

National Science Teaching Association. (2014). *Early childhood science education*. https://www.nsta.org/nstas-official-positions/early-childhood-science-education

Next Generation Science Standards (NGSS). (n.d.). *Three dimensional learning*. https://www.nextgenscience.org/three-dimensional-learning

Ouellette, G., & Sénéchal, M. (2017). Invented spelling in kindergarten as a predictor of reading and spelling in grade 1: A new pathway to literacy, or just the same road, less known? *Developmental Psychology, 53*(1), 77–88.

Paley, V. G. (1993). The boy who would be a helicopter: The uses of storytelling in the classroom. *Drama/Theatre Teacher, 5*(2), 16–19.

Pearson, B. Z. (2008). *Raising a bilingual child*. New York, NY: Random House.

Pica, R. (2008). *Why motor skills matter*. Beyond the Journal, NAEYC. https://www.naeyc.org/sites/default/files/globally-shared/downloads/PDFs/resources/pubs/btjlearningleapsbounds.pdf

Sarrazin, N. (n.d.) *Music and the child*. MLINE Library. https://milnepublishing.geneseo.edu/music-and-the-child/chapter/chapter-12/

Shaffer, S. (2011, November). Opening the doors: Engaging young children in the art museum. *Art Education, 64*(6), 40–46. http://www.jstor.org/stable/41480628

Stevens-Smith, D. A. (2016). Active bodies/active brains: The relationship between physical engagement and children's development. *The Physical Educator, 73*(4), 719–732.

The Annie E. Casey Foundation. (2021, June 21). *2021 kids count data book*. https://www.aecf.org/resources/2021-kids-count-data-book

USDA. (n.d.). *Farm to preschool: Local food and learning in early child care and education settings*. Farm to Preschool: Local Food and Learning in Early Child Care and Education Settings | Food and Nutrition Service (usda.gov)

Chapter 10

Alaska Early Learning Guidelines. (2020, January) *Birth to 9 months*. https://www.alaskaelg.org/wp-content/uploads/2020/01/Alaska-ELG_0-9-months.pdf

Arkansas Head Start. (2016). *Arkansas child development and early learning standards: Birth through 60 months*. https://www.arheadstart.org/Ark_Early_Learning_Standards%20(19)%20(1).pdf

Bialystok, E., Barac, R., Blaye, A., & Poulin-Dubois, D. (2010). Word mapping and executive functioning in young monolingual and bilingual children. *Journal of Cognition and Development, 11*(4), 485–508. https://doi.org/10.1080/15248372.2010.516420

California Department of Education. (2009, February). *Infant/toddler learning & development foundations*. http://www.cde.ca.gov/sp/cd/re/itfoundations.asp

CAST. (2011). Universal Design for Learning Guidelines, version 2.0. Wakefield, MA: Author. http://www.udlcenter.org/aboutudl/udl-guidelines

Center for Early Care and Education Research – Dual Language Learners (CECER-DLL). University of North Carolina, Chapel Hill. https://cecerdll.fpg.unc.edu/sites/cecerdll.fpg.unc.edu/files/imce/documents/%233016_Working-Paper%232.pdf

Center for the Developing Child. (n.d.). *A guide to serve and return: How your interaction with children can build brains*. https://developingchild.harvard.edu/guide/a-guide-to-serve-and-return-how-your-interaction-with-children-can-build-brains

Center for the Developing Child. (n.d.). *Neglect*. Harvard University. https://developingchild.harvard.edu/science/deep-dives/neglect/

ChildCare.gov. (n.d.). *Oregon: Child development and learning*. https://childcare.gov/state-resources?state=42&type=204

Connecticut Official State Website. (n.d) *Guidelines for the development of infants and toddler early learning birth-3* http://www.ct.gov/dss/lib/dss/dss_early_learning_guidelines.pdf

Department of Social Services Couth Carolina. (2017). *South Carolina early learning standards*. https://www.scchildcare.org/media/57847/South-Carolina-Early-Learning-Standards-2017_Accessible-Version.pdf

Institute of Medicine and National Research Council (2015). *Transforming the workforce for children birth through age 8: A unifying foundation*. National Academies of Science, Engineering, and Medicine (NASEM)

Lally, R. (2000). Infants have their own curriculum: A responsive approach to curriculum planning for infants and toddlers. *Curriculum in Head Start Bulletin, 67*.

Mass.gov. (2022). *Massachusetts early learning guidelines for infants and toddlers*. https://www.mass.gov/service-details/massachusetts-early-learning-guidelines-for-infants-and-toddlers

Minnesota Department of Human Services (2017). *Early childhood indicators of progress: Minnesota's early learning standards: Birth to kindergarten*. https://edocs.dhs.state.mn.us/lfserver/Public/DHS-7596A-ENG

National Association for the Education of Young Children (2020). *Developmentally appropriate practices*.

National Association for the Education of Young Children.

National Scientific Council on the Developing Child (NSCDC). (2018). *Understanding motivation: building the brain architecture that supports learning, health, and community participation: Working Paper No. 14*. www.developingchild.harvard.edu

North Dakota Department of Public Instruction. (2018). *North Dakota early leaning standards: Birth to kindergarten*. https://www.nd.gov/dpi/sites/www/files/documents/Academic%20Support/EL2018.pdf

Office of Public Instruction. (2014). *Montana early learning standards*. https://opi.mt.gov/Portals/182/Page%20Files/Early%20Childhood/Docs/14EarlyLearningStandards.pdf

Ohio Department of Job and Family Services. (2006). *Ohio's infant & toddler guidelines*. https://jfs.ohio.gov/cdc/InfantToddler.pdf

Pan Qianqian, Trang Kim T., Love Hailey R., Templin, J. (2019). School Readiness Profiles and Growth in Academic Achievement. *Frontiers in Education, 4*.

Utah.gov. (n.d.) Utah's early learning guidelines: Birth to age three. https://jobs.utah.gov/occ/provider/early_childhood.pdf

Zero to Three. (2015). https://www.zerotothree.org/resources/74-infant-and-toddler-curriculum-and-individualization

Zero to Three. (2014, November 16). *Early Cognitive Development*. https://www.zerotothree.org/resources/710-vol-35-no-2-early-cognitive-development

Chapter 11

2020 Colorado Academic Standards Online. https://www.cde.state.co.us/apps/standards/9,1,34

Department of Children, Youth, and Families. (2021). *Washington state early learning and development guidelines: Birth through 3rd. grade*. https://www.dcyf.wa.gov/sites/default/files/pubs/EL_0015.pdf

Department of Education. (n.d.). *Early childhood education*. https://www.nj.gov/education/earlychildhood/

Department of Education. (n.d.). *Louisiana's birth to five: Early learning & development standards (ELDS)*. https://www.louisianabelieves.com/docs/default-source/academic-standards/early-childhood-birth-to-five-standards.pdf

Department of Education. (2014). *Pennsylvania learning standards for early childhood: Pre-kindergarten*. https://www.education.pa.gov/Documents/Early%20Learning/Early%20Learning%20Standards/Early%20Learning%20Standards%20-%20Prekindergarten%202014.pdf

Division of Early Learning. (2017). *Florida early learning developmental standards and professional competencies*. http://flbt5.floridaearlylearning.com/standards.html#d=IV,VI,VII,VIII&a=three_year_olds

Georgia Dept of Early Care and Learning. (2022). *Georgia early learning and development standards (GELDS)*. https://www.decal.ga.gov/Prek/GELDS.aspx

Hawai'i early learning and developmental standards: Framework and continuum from birth to end of kindergarten. (n.d.). Hawaii.gov. https://earlylearning.hawaii.gov/wp-content/uploads/2014/02/HELDS-continuum-2014.04.01.pdf

Illinois State Board of Education. (2013). *Illinois early learning and development standards*. https://www.isbe.net/documents/early_learning_standards.pdf

Mississippi Department of Education. (2017). *Mississippi college and career readiness arts learning standards for music*. https://districtaccess.mde.k12.ms.us/curriculumandInstruction/MississippiCurriculumFrameworks/Visual%20and%20Performing%20Arts/MS%20CCR%20Arts%20Learning%20Standards%20for%20Music%202017%20FINAL.pdf

Mississippi Department of Education. (2020). *Mississippi early learning standards for classrooms serving infants through four-year-old children*. https://www.mdek12.org/sites/default/files/final_infants_through_four-year-old_early_learning_standards_2020.08.21_jg.pdf

National Association for the Education of Young Children (2020). *Professional standards and competencies for early childhood educators*. https://www.naeyc.org/resources/position-statements/professional-standards-competencies

Nebraska Department of Education. (2017). *Integrated curriculum in the primary program*. https://www.education.ne.gov/wp-content/uploads/2017/07/IC.pdf

Nesin, G., & Lounsbury, J. (2019). Curriculum Integration: Twenty Questions- With Answers. *Becoming: Journal of the Georgia Middle School Association, 30*(1). https://doi.org/10.20429/becoming.2019.300103

North Carolina Foundations Task Force. (2013). *North Carolina foundations for early learning and development*. https://ncchildcare.ncdhhs.gov/Portals/0/documents/pdf/N/NC_Foundations.pdf?ver=2017-05-16-105950-953

State of Vermont Agency of Education. (2016). *Vermont early learning standards*. https://education.vermont.gov/sites/aoe/files/documents/edu-early-education-early-learning-standards.pdf

Texas Education Agency. (2015). *Texas prekindergarten guidelines*. https://tea.texas.gov/academics/early-childhood-education/texas-prekindergarten-guidelines

West Virginia Department of Education. (2019). *West Virginia pre-k standards (ages 3-5): Resource booklet for universal pre-k*. https://wvde.us/wp-content/uploads/2019/05/PKStandardsBookletUPDATE-Final-May-2019.pdf

Williams, B. (2017). *How to help kids become technology creators, not just consumers*. https://www.primotoys.com/creating-with-tech/

VanTassel-Baska, J. (2003). Content-based curriculum for high-ability learners: An introduction. In J. VanTassel-Baska & C. A. Little (Eds.), *Content-based curriculum for high-ability learners*, 1-23). Waco, TX: Prufrock Press.

Chapter 12

Common Core State Standards Initiative. *Key points in english language arts*. http://www.corestandards.org/other-resources/key-shifts-in-english-language-arts/

Gabriel, A. (2019). State laws promoting social, emotional, and academic development leave room for improvement. *Child Trends*. https://www.childtrends.org/blog/state-laws-promoting-social-emotional-and-academic-development-leave-room-for-improvement

Jones, E. (2014). How cursive can help students with dyslexia connect the dots. *PBS*. https://www.pbs.org/newshour/education/connecting-dots-role-cursive-dyslexia-therapy

Lackaff, J., & Mindes, G. (2013). Social studies background and criteria. *Social Studies Research Summary for The Work Sampling System*. https://iagepg.pearsonclinical.com/images/Assets/WSS_5/Research_Summary_Social_Studies_FNL.pdf

Loveless, B. (2015). Learning to read, reading to learn: Why third-grade is a pivotal year for mastering literacy. *NSBA*. https://www.nsba.org/-/media/NSBA/File/cpe-learning-to-read-reading-to-learn-white-paper-2015.pdf?la=en&hash=8E0E470C3E263C66E4491EC035224DC9018C6D5F

Mindes, G. (2015). Preschool through grade 3: Pushing up the social studies from early childhood education to the world. *Young Children, 70*(3), 10–15.

Ucus, S. (2018). Exploring creativity in social studies education for elementary grades: Teachers' opinions and interpretations. *Journal of Education and Learning, 7*(2).

Wells, B. (2017, December 7). Strategies for teaching kids self-regulation. *PBS for Parents*. https://www.pbs.org/parents/thrive/strategies-for-teaching-kids-self-regulation

Specific State Social Studies, Arts, SEL Resources used in 12.2

Delaware

www.deartsstandards.org

The Delaware State Board of Education adopted new arts education standards in March 2016, including Dance, Media Arts, Music, Theatre and Visual Arts.

Kentucky

https://kystandards.org/home/ky-acad-standards/

New York

https://www.p12.nysed.gov/earlylearning/standards/documents/KindergartenLearningStandards2019-20.pdf

South Dakota

Art

https://artssouthdakota.org/education/

Social Studies

https://doe.sd.gov/contentstandards/

Wisconsin

Art

https://dpi.wi.gov/sites/default/files/imce/standards/New%20pdfs/ArtDesign2019.pdf

Social Studies

https://dpi.wi.gov/sites/default/files/imce/standards/New%20pdfs/2018_WI_Social_Studies_Standards.pdf

SEL

https://dpi.wi.gov/sspw/mental-health/social-emotional-learning

Kansas

Art

https://www.ksde.org/Agency/Division-of-Learning-Services/Career-Standards-and-Assessment-Services/Content-Area-F-L/Fine-Arts-Dance-Media-Arts-Music-Theatre-Visual-Arts/Visual-Arts/Visual-Arts-Standards

Social Studies

https://www.ksde.org/LinkClick.aspx?fileticket=4TJXZgAyaIs%3d&tabid=472&portalid=0&mid=4744

SEL

https://www.ksde.org/LinkClick.aspx?fileticket=-co2In4YF-kU%3d&tabid=1042&portalid=0&mid=3102

Maryland

https://earlychildhood.marylandpublicschools.org/system/files/filedepot/4/msde-pedagogy-report-_appendix_2016.pdf

Missouri

Social Studies

https://dese.mo.gov/media/file/curr-mls-standards-teacher-view-ss-k-5-2016

Nevada

Arts

https://doe.nv.gov/Nevada_Academic_Standards/Fine_Arts/

Social Studies

https://doe.nv.gov/Nevada_Academic_Standards/Social_Studies/

SEL

https://doe.nv.gov/uploadedFiles/ndedoenvgov/content/Boards_Commissions_Councils/State_Board_of_Education/2017/November/nvstatesocialcompetencies.pdf

Wyoming

Social Studies

https://edu.wyoming.gov/wp-content/uploads/2018/12/Social-Studies-Standards-20142018-additions_FINAL.pdf

Arts

https://edu.wyoming.gov/wp-content/uploads/2019/03/2013_Fine_and_Performing_Arts_Standards.pdf

Iowa

https://iowacore.gov/standards/iowa-core-standards

Arts

https://www.nationalartsstandards.org/sites/default/files/Visual%20Arts%20at%20a%20Glance%20-%20new%20copyright%20info.pdf

Michigan

https://www.michigan.gov/mde/services/academic-standards

Arts

https://www.michigan.gov/mde/-/media/Project/Websites/mde/Year/2014/06/06/Complete_VPAA_Expectations_June_2011_356110_7.pdf?rev=8eada332459f4890b-8148858cd62890b

Nebraska

https://www.education.ne.gov/oec/standards-and-guidelines/

Arts

https://www.education.ne.gov/wp-content/uploads/2017/07/Final_FAS_Visual_Arts.pdf

Oklahoma

https://sde.ok.gov/oklahoma-academic-standards

Arts

https://sde.ok.gov/sites/default/files/Elementary%20Art%20Standards_3.pdf

Oregon

https://www.oregon.gov/ode/educator-resources/standards/pages/default.aspx

Arts

https://www.oregon.gov/ode/educator-resources/standards/arts/Documents/visual-arts-standards-pk-3.pdf